THE KINGDOM OF MAN

CATHOLIC IDEAS FOR A SECULAR WORLD
O. Carter Snead, *series editor*

The purpose of this interdisciplinary series is to feature authors from around the world who will expand the influence of Catholic thought on the most important conversations in academia and the public square. The series is "Catholic" in the sense that the books will emphasize and engage the enduring themes of human dignity and flourishing, the common good, truth, beauty, justice, and freedom in ways that reflect and deepen principles affirmed by the Catholic Church for millennia. It is not limited to Catholic authors or even works that explicitly take Catholic principles as a point of departure. Its books are intended to demonstrate the diversity and enhance the relevance of these enduring themes and principles in numerous subjects, ranging from the arts and humanities to the sciences.

THE KINGDOM OF MAN

Genesis and Failure of the Modern Project

RÉMI BRAGUE

Translated by Paul Seaton

University of Notre Dame Press
Notre Dame, Indiana

University of Notre Dame Press
Notre Dame, Indiana 46556
undpress.nd.edu

Copyright © 2018 by the University of Notre Dame

All Rights Reserved

Published in the United States of America

Paperback edition published in 2021

Originally published as *Le Règne de l'Homme: Genèse et échec du projet moderne.*
© Editions GALLIMARD, Paris 2015.

Library of Congress Cataloging-in-Publication Data

Names: Brague, Rémi, 1947- author.
Title: The kingdom of man : genesis and failure of the modern project / Rémi Brague ; translated by Paul Seaton.
Other titles: Règne de l'homme. English
Description: Notre Dame : University of Notre Dame Press, 2018. | Series: Catholic ideas for a secular world | Includes bibliographical references and index. |
Identifiers: LCCN 2018021922 (print) | LCCN 2018032921 (ebook) | ISBN 9780268104276 (pdf) | ISBN 9780268104283 (epub) | ISBN 9780268104252 (cloth) | ISBN 0268104255 (cloth) | ISBN 9780268104269 (paper) | ISBN 0268104263 (paper)
Subjects: LCSH: Philosophical anthropology. | Philosophy, Modern. | Catholic Church—Doctrines.
Classification: LCC BD450 (ebook) | LCC BD450 .B642413 2018 (print) | DDC 128—dc23
LC record available at https://lccn.loc.gov/2018021922

Contents

Translator's Foreword		vii
Preface		xiii
Introduction		1

PART 1   PREPARATION

1	The Best of the Living Things	9
2	Domination	17
3	Three Incomplete Prefigurations	26
4	Metaphorical Dominations	35
5	The New Lord of Creation	42
6	Attempts and Temptations	51

PART 2   DEPLOYMENT

7	The Formation of the Modern Project	63
8	The Beginnings of the Realization	73
9	The Master Is There	84
10	Moral Dominion	95
11	The Duty to Reign	101
12	The Iron Rod	113
13	The New Meaning of Humanism	121
14	The Sole Lord	128

PART 3 FAILURE

15	Kingdom or Wasteland?	141
16	Man, Humiliated	153
17	The Subjugated Subject	160
18	Man Remade	169
19	Man Surpassed and . . . Replaced	181
20	Checkmate?	191
21	Lights Out	201
	Conclusion	212
	Notes	217
	Bibliography	268
	Index	317

Translator's Foreword

Rémi Brague is a scholar and a philosopher. As a philosopher, he thinks about the Big Three: God, the world, and the human. As a scholar, he reads an enormous amount, in multiple languages, ancient and modern, in order to think well about them. He thinks and reads so much that he tends to conceive of his projects in terms of trilogies. *The Kingdom of Man* is the culmination of one such trilogy.

The previous two works focused on antiquity and the Middle Ages, respectively, but did so in a distinctive way. The first focused on the discovery of "the world" as such, the *kosmos*, by the Greeks; the second on the biblical God, who called the ultimacy of the world in question, but who created it and saw it to be very good.[1] In both cases, human beings were measured by a superior instance, cosmos or Creator. But they also possessed great dignity as microcosm and as image and likeness of the Creator. To be human was a *task* and a great adventure, especially if one took seriously both vocations, as many did in the Middle Ages.

Now we come to modern times and to our world. Thanks to major thinkers, starting with Bacon and Descartes, the God/world/human relationship has been inverted. Modern humanity has long embarked upon the project of the conquest of nature by means of technological science, and God has become a private matter for those who have the inclination or need to believe, while publically he is more and more a persona non grata. And humanity's dignity resides elsewhere than before: squarely in human beings themselves. "Rights," "autonomy," and "creativity" encapsulate a history of articulations of human dignity *sans Dieu et contre le monde*.

The foregoing is fairly well known. What does Brague add to it? A great deal. To begin with, a genealogical method or archaeology of concepts, requiring considerable erudition. "I employ the same method as in the first two works of the trilogy (admittedly implausible in its pretension): a history of ideas over the long run, which in principle encompasses the entirety of the course of history." Ambitious, indeed! What one has here is a vast *histoire raisonnée* of a conceptual structure, what Brague entitles "the modern project."

Because it is the focus of the investigation, he sketches its contours early on in the introduction. The sketch certainly catches the reader's eye and whets his appetite for the argument to follow. It portrays a figure of human being who, on one hand, is totally cut off—who was designed to be cut off—from all authorities outside of himself, or his self. Cut off from any divine, to be sure, but from a normative nature as well. Time itself is cut in two: into a past that is simply repudiated and a present pregnant with a radiant future ("Progress"). On the other hand, the emancipation is the precondition for a great empowerment of human beings. As the Baconian title of the work indicates, the modern project is the technologically armed pursuit of the dominion of human beings over all things, including, paradoxically, their very humanity. Even more paradoxically, the technological dominance is the necessary means for the realization of their humanity. Assuredly, there is matter for reflection (and concern) in all this, and Brague does not fail to reflect on it, discreetly along the way and explicitly toward the end.

He does so in part by way of a dialogue with a twentieth-century Jesuit thinker, Henri de Lubac (1896–1991), who coined the phrase "atheistic humanism" in a book devoted to its analysis, *The Drama of Atheistic Humanism* (1944). In part prompted by de Lubac, in this work Brague discusses the full meaning and internal logic of this distinctive understanding of the human, which he calls "exclusive humanism." According to Brague, the drama has played itself out to a point where one can see its necessary consequences. He does not mince words: among them is "the self-destruction of man," the unwillingness to continue the human adventure and the inability to give reasons to do so. The contemporary European scene is exhibit A. In a little work he calls a "satellite" to this one, *The Legitimacy of the Human*, he provides "greater developments" of the argument, but even here the testimony of decidedly modern thinkers who are mute (and worse) before the existential questions—Is it good for human beings to exist? Is it legitimate? Should the human adventure continue, now that everything is subject to human choice?—powerfully supports the chilling conclusion.[2]

In executing this ambitious archaeological project, Brague works at several levels. At the top, he attends to major thinkers, especially Bacon and Descartes and the German idealists, Kant and Fichte, but others such as Locke as well. Between and among them, the project of mastering nature and thereby fulfilling human nature was clearly conceptualized. Along the way, nature was reconceptualized (Brague focuses upon its ontological and moral "devaluation"), as was humanity itself. In fact, my use of "human nature" above was misleading. Quite what humanity is when divorced from teleological nature and a providentially ordered creation is a great question, one that Brague addresses head on. (Hint: humanity itself becomes "a project" and a "self-creation," with the consequences alluded to above.)

Of course, none of the major thinkers worked in an intellectual vacuum. To begin with, Descartes read and developed Bacon, and Fichte, Kant. But their intellectual contexts were not only occupied by major thinkers; they were the recipients and transformers of the aggregate labors of lesser lights. And their ideas were refracted and transmitted by any number of other writers, including novelists and poets. All this is a second level of Brague's ideational scholarship, where quite striking erudition is on display. "What *hasn't* Brague read?" the reader will often ask.

In this group there are thinkers one may know—say, Auguste Comte or B. F. Skinner—and others one may not, such as the papal physician Giovanni Maria Lancisi, who in 1693 endorsed the experimental sciences in the domain of medicine, thus striking a blow for the new science against Aristotelianism. The mixture will vary for each reader. But all should be prepared for a tour de force of enormously wide-ranging, but still quite focused, scholarship, as Brague retraces the appearance of the intellectual materials that were forged into the conceptual components of the modern project. Once forged, the ideas were transmitted, refracted, and further developed, and Brague is a sure detective following this further trail. The mad ideas of Russian Soviet thinkers concerning human perfectability and mastery are but some of the many highlights—or revealing low-lights—of the subsequent investigation.

However, although it began and continued in the domain of ideas, the modern project emphatically aimed at transforming concrete reality. Hence, there are two broad dimensions to Brague's analyses. To use the French phrases he does: he considers what occurs *dans les idées et dans les faits*, in the realm of ideas and in the realm of facts. In the latter domain, the analysis is less continuous, more high points than narrative, but still pertinent to the story, especially as the project becomes reality.

Three passages can indicate a triangle of factors that need to be knitted together as the reader proceeds. First, the modern state and science:

> The great discoveries [of the New World] . . . already presuppose the conjunction of science and the other "great discovery" of modernity: the sovereign nation-state. Maritime astronomy, which made possible the circumnavigation of Africa, then that of the world, seems to have been born in Portugal around 1480–1490, in the context of a scientific policy inaugurated by the king, John II: "Here, . . . probably for the first time in history, was a coherent effort to put science at the service of a great national enterprise."[3]

As Pierre Manent has reminded us, the modern project essentially involved the theory and construction of the modern state, as well as its concomitant political form, the nation.[4] While he does not make them a major theme, Brague is quite aware of these "facts."

Then capitalism and its concomitants:

> The modern birth of the capitalist economy was accompanied by a rationalization of life. Virtues were promoted that Antiquity and the Middle Ages barely knew: order, work ethic, thrift. Other virtues existing in religious form were reinterpreted and secularized; thus sloth, which despaired of salvation and caused one to neglect it, became laziness in work. Bells structured the rhythm of monastic hours; the clock which precisely measures time allows for the punctuality of trains, even the clocking-in of factory workers. But beyond these changes in mentalities, which have been discovered and studied by historians, the very nature of virtue changed.

The new economy coexists between, and unifies, ever-new technologies and a new moral order. A moment's reflection indicates, however, and hindsight confirms, that the package is far from stable, or satisfactory to all. The debate over *doux commerce* in the eighteenth century will give way to "the social question" in the nineteenth, and so on until our day. Such moral and economic discontents are endemic to the modern capitalist project.[5]

And, finally, a significant passage on the importance of, of all things, electricity:

> At the end of the nineteenth century, technology became capable of producing and transporting electricity, a source of energy that did not exist in that form in our ordinary perception of nature. It permitted the communication

of energies from different sources, which it rendered commensurable, as money does for goods. It also allowed for the transport of energy without too much loss. Moreover, it created technological objects that took on their meaning, and did so *exclusively*, in the context of a complete system. Other mechanisms depended upon the human activity that could activate them, if need be: until a recent date, one could still turn a gramophone or start a car by hand; but an electrical appliance cut off from its source is nothing at all. In this way, it is only with electrification that technology can create a world at once capable of, and condemned to, self-sufficiency, thus realizing a model of integral autonomy. [italics original]

With electricity, a thoroughly artificial world, a technological cocoon, laid its real foundation. Heidegger thought that encompassing technology was the fate of modern man. Brague more convincingly argues that it was a matter of quite deliberate intention.

Heidegger also famously declared that "only a god can save us." Here, too, Brague does him one better. He reminds Heidegger, and his fellow Europeans, that they already knew a God who saved them. Perhaps it is time to (re)turn and listen to what he has to say. If they do, when they do, Brague says they will find a surprisingly contemporary message: It is good that you exist! Please continue! As for your fears concerning me, despite what many say, I am not your Master, but your Father and your Friend.[6]

Paul Seaton
St. Mary's Seminary & University
Feast of Saints Peter and Paul

Preface

This book is the third part of a trilogy whose common theme is the knowledge of man, also called "anthropology" in the etymological sense: discourse (*logos*) about the human (*anthrōpos*). Man is not immediately everything he is: he is what he does and what he *makes himself* while doing what he does. Anthropology therefore culminates in an ethics.

In two previous works, I studied the context of anthropology, its cosmological bases, then its theological frame.[1] The ensemble of norms that govern and define the human first appeared as prefigured, illustrated, or at least guaranteed, by the structure of the physical universe; then as set by divine commandments revealed in history or inscribed in the conscience. My two narratives had in common that they ended with modern times, where the knowledge of man freed itself from nature and from the divine. It remains for me to study directly what results from such a dismantling: the refusal for humanity to have any context, to derive its existence and legitimacy from any place other than itself. This program was formulated with a vengeance in modern times. The idea of a "kingdom of man," my title, is its mantra, whether avowed or implied. Beyond the deliberate parallel with the titles of the two previous works, their two inquiries lead to this idea.

I therefore had to take a global view of the modern project. And to acknowledge something that made me tremble: to wit, that this project is bound to fail, or even that it has already failed in principle. To deprive the human of any context leads to its destruction. I show this less by explicitly criticizing the modern project than by showing how the internal logic of its development leads to a self-destructive dialectic. It will be enough to point this out.

The trajectories described by my two previous works found a different summit for each, the time in history when the central problematic was engaged: for the *Wisdom of the World*, that summit was antiquity; for the *Law of God* it was the Middle Ages. Modern times were relegated to the periphery. With the present work, however, I install myself squarely in modernity, and especially in the period between the seventeenth and nineteenth centuries. This choice made me leave the Mediterranean basin in order to concentrate on Europe, where the passage to modernity began and produced its most radical effects, before extending to the rest of the world in a process that is far from having ended, if it ever will. This retrenchment is compensated by an initial enlargement in the direction of regions that came later to the European concert, Russia for example. A second enlargement belongs to the nature of the subject. Since I am studying a project rather than a realization, I had to take into account literary genres, which are more apt to express desires or dreams than philosophical sobriety can. Hence the presence of poems or novels, some of which do not belong especially to "great literature."

The present work has two smaller "satellites": *The Anchors in the Heavens* and *The Legitimacy of the Human*. And there is a parallel in the third part of my "little" trilogy, *Moderately Modern*. There one will find many references and thoughts previously formulated. There too I develop lines of thought presented here in abbreviated or transversal form. To them I refer the reader, whom I ask to forgive inevitable repetitions and cross-references.

Here I employ the same method as in the first two works of the trilogy (admittedly implausible in its pretension): a history of ideas over the long run, which in principle encompasses the entirety of the course of history. Because I am quite conscious of what my ambition possesses of immoderation, I chose to multiply references and citations. In so doing, I risked being suspected of pedantry, but I wanted to provide the reader with the means of verifying that I had not extrapolated too far beyond what one could confirm for oneself, as well as the assurance that he could steal from me with impunity.

Several of my advanced seminars at the Sorbonne and my courses at the University of Munich allowed me to present a first version of my research. Dr. Janine Ziegler, my *Hilfskraft* at Munich, spared me precious time by procuring difficult-to-find texts. Once again, Irene Fernandez read a penultimate draft and helped me with her comments; and my wife, Françoise, confirmed her remarkable dexterity in the employment of a red pen. A stay at Boston College (September–October 2011) allowed me to exploit the resources of the O'Neill Library. The wealth of American libraries helped me understand something: I previously believed that I only succeeded in reading a tenth of what was necessary; now I know that it is a hundredth. But I had to finish if I wanted the book to appear before my death.

THE KINGDOM OF MAN

Introduction

Before examining the consequences, disastrous in my view, of the abandonment of all *context* for knowledge of man, it is good to clarify the word. In what way were cosmology and theology contexts for the anthropology and ethics that crowned them? By themselves, they did not allow one to understand what the human was, nor did they aid in doing so: the description of the human remains possible even if one abstracts from them and is conducted in a neutral manner vis-à-vis them. On the other hand, these two contexts provide a supplementary dimension to the description. Here I will study the intention to do without any context, which constitutes the modern project. Now I must clarify this formulation. I will begin with the adjective.

Historians designate by the phrase "*modern* times" not one, but two periods. The point of departure is always located at the fall of Constantinople (1453) or the discovery of the New World (1492) or perhaps the Reformation (1517). On the other hand, the point of arrival remains open. Either one stops at the French Revolution, in which case one speaks of the sixteenth to the eighteenth century as the modern period, which is followed by the contemporary period, or one includes in modern times everything that follows the Middle Ages, up until our day. It is in this second sense that I use the term here, without losing sight of the ruptures or "waves" that articulate modernity.[1]

"Modern" is originally a relative concept, because it is mobile, a sort of cursor: every period is more modern than the one that preceded and less modern that the one that will follow. The birth of modernity as a historical period is due to the decision to stop the cursor and to consider what preceded as not yet being modern and what follows as definitively being modern. As a consequence, he is modern who wills to be modern and defines himself as such.[2] One sees the paradox: the halting of the cursor makes movement possible. This paradox is only apparent, though, because it is only fixing a point of departure that allows one to measure the progress made. Consciousness of progress requires that one fix the past, which then becomes "history."

What I mean by "modern project" should not be confused with the content of the modern period, nor even with its specific contributions. Everything that happened in this period, and even everything that happened that was novel, whether good or bad, does not necessarily belong to the modern project. On the other hand, everything that one claims to sever from what preceded, from which one separates by expelling it, does belong. The project entails a rejection. It puts what it expels into the category of "the Middle Ages,"[3] understood as empty and willed as such, a universal trash can as it were, always open to new contents which, even if they appear during modernity, are denounced as marking a step back vis-à-vis the project and thus as "medieval remnants."

The phrase the "project of modernity" comes from Jürgen Habermas, in a lecture on modernity as an unfinished project. The idea that its contents ("Enlightenment") have never been fully realized is also found in the history of ideas.[4] But if the expression is recent, one can observe much earlier, precisely at the period called "modern," an increased prevalence of words that designate "essay," "attempt," "experience" in the sense of "experiment." It is sufficient to mention Montaigne and his *Essays*, whose title was taken up by Bacon and many others after him, or Galileo with his *Assayer*. The accent placed on experimentation is even more remarkable as the intent came before the effect: Bacon's "experiments" were fantasies, and even real scientists have not talked so much about experimentation as at the moment when the facts they invoked were pure "thought experiments."[5] The rise to prominence of "project" is connected with a displacement of emphasis from reason to imagination in the definition of man, henceforth understood as the living thing capable of conceiving possibilities.[6]

For a long time, modernity was not merely lived, but also conceived, as a project. Descartes wanted to entitle the *Discourse on Method*: "The project of a universal science that can raise our nature to its highest degree of perfection."[7] Nietzsche characterized his time as "the age of attempts."[8] Two centuries earlier, in one of his first works (1697), Daniel Defoe indicated that the fashion was all for projects, to the extent that one could call the time "the age of projects." Above all he had in mind the speculations of transatlantic commerce, such as the one that had just ruined him, since commerce was "in its principle, all project, machination and invention."[9] In 1726, Jonathan Swift satirized the members of the Royal Society under the features of the distracted passengers of the flying island of Lagado, whom he ridiculed with the name of *projectors*, in that way also performing a self-critique because he confessed to having been "a sort of projector" in his youth. The embodiment of this type, after the Spanish *arbitristas* of the seventeenth century, was the Abbé de Saint-Pierre and his "Project for rendering peace perpetual in Europe." However, in itself the word *projector* had nothing pejorative or ironic. One could claim it for oneself, as was the case with Mary Shelley's Frankenstein.[10] According to a more serious anthropology, man is a being who is not merely unrealized, but one who is "projected." Thus Fichte: "All the animals are fully developed and complete, man is but a sketch and a project." Heidegger defined the life of *Dasein* as a "project," then deepened the idea by making the project no longer a human initiative, but a fundamental trait of Being. Sartre took from it the definition of man, who "is nothing other than his project"; and contemporary ethicists conceive of the history of the individual as a "life-project."[11]

The word "project" is not without its teachings. Its Latin form does not correspond to a word in the Roman lexicon. The Romans knew the adjective *projectus*, with the meaning of "preeminent," often with a pejorative nuance, "excessive." But the substantive is not found in antiquity. A pro-ject is above all what its etymology declares: a *-ject* (from *jacere*, "to throw or toss"), a movement in which the thing in motion (the "projectile") loses contact with what set it in motion and pursues its trajectory. Ancient physics did not find a place for the phenomenon in its explanatory schemes, except by means of very implausible theories. Oddly enough, modern times, the age of pro-jects, are also the time when, in physics, one began to make *-ject* as such conceivable.[12] Napoleon, the very type of modern man—that is, "Faustian"—sensed this, he who compared himself to "a bit of stone thrown into space."[13] Three ideas fundamental to modernity can be derived from this master-image of -ject. A project implies (1) vis-à-vis the past, the idea of a new beginning which causes the forgetting of everything that preceded; (2) vis-à-vis the present, the idea of the autonomy of the acting subject; and (3) for the future, the idea of a supportive milieu that prolongs the action and ensures its successful completion (progress).

The modern project bears two faces turned in opposite directions, one toward below, to what is inferior to man, the other above, to what is superior to him.

It is first of all the project of the mastery of nature. It reverses the taking into account by anthropology of the cosmological context. Instead of the cosmos that gives man his measure, it is man who must create a dwelling to his measure. The meaning of the idea of *order* thus changes radically, as well as the place where it is to attest its reality. For the premodern age, order is above all, if not almost exclusively, that of the celestial realities that are inaccessible to man, which justify calling the world a *cosmos*, with the ordered character of the sublunary world being rather dubious. In contrast, with the modern project, what encompasses man is in itself a chaos; there is no order except where it is created by human effort. By that same token, it becomes idle to seek order elsewhere than in what is accessible to man, a domain, however, that is not determined from the get-go, but can expand indefinitely.

In the second place, the modern project appears as an emancipation vis-à-vis everything that presents itself above man, as his inaccessible origin: a creator and/or legislator god, or a nature whose active character renders it divine. It reverses the taking into account by anthropology of the theological context. Instead of the claim that it is man who ought to receive his norm from an external authority, it is he who determines what can claim authority over him. The relationship between man and the divine takes on the form of "it's either him or me." Humanism must then tend to become an atheism.

It is well known that the stock of images and slogans that undergird modernity has a biblical origin, whether this observation serves to legitimate modernity or, to the contrary, to denigrate the Bible by making it bear the responsibility for modern errors. The first aspect, subjecting nature, is present as early as the Old Testament; the second aspect, emancipation, is more visible in the New.

From the first book of the Old Testament, one hears the command addressed to every human being to have dominion over the plants and animals, what will later be called "nature" (Gen. 1:26b, 28b). More profoundly, the domain given over to the activity of humanity is already the object of a devaluation: the natural is demoted as a power and an authority, in favor of history, the province of humanity (Deut. 4:19).

In the New Testament, Paul formulates the idea of autonomy (Rom. 2:14).[14] He employs the image of "emancipation" to express a new relationship to what transcends the human: the adult status granted humanity, become adult vis-à-vis the "elemental spirits of the world" that until then had been "disciplinarians" (Gal. 3:25; 4:2–3). On the other hand, the divine is presented in a form that, if taken seriously, should deprive atheism of its objection: the one who possesses the divine nature having taken on the form of a slave (Phil. 2:7), any idea of a possible rivalry between humanity and God loses its meaning. In John's Gospel, it is not a question of making oneself independent of the divine; on the contrary, it is God himself who grants man to live his relationship with him in a way other than dependence, making man pass from the condition of a slave to that of a friend (John 15:15).

I therefore can now ask: if the program of modernity is thus already sketched at the end of the ancient world and in the texts that founded the medieval word, in what sense does the modern project merit the adjective "modern"? The answer is found in the fuller phrase: it is modern to the extent that it is, precisely, a project. For it is not at all necessary that the human enterprise should conceive itself as a project. The genus "enterprise" in fact contains, alongside of project, another species that one could call *task*. And task is opposed point for point to the three characteristics of the project that I laid out above. Each in fact changes its sign: with a task, (a) I receive the mission to do something from an origin I cannot control, but must discover; (b) I also must ask myself if I am up to my task, agreeing even to divest myself of what has otherwise been irrevocably entrusted to me; and finally, (c) I alone am responsible for what I am asked to accomplish, without being able to outsource it to an instance that would guarantee its success.

Now, with this idea of task, we are able to distinguish the Bible from modernity. All the biblical images invoked above, including the idea of "straining forward [*epekteinomai*] toward what lies ahead" (Phil. 3:13 NRSV), need to be understood in the light of task, not that of project. The passage to modernity therefore can find its symbol, if not its symptom, in the evolution of literary genres from the epic, where the hero is invested with a mission he must accomplish, to the novel, in which he departs seeking adventures, and hence following his fancy.

The relationship of humanity to nature can know many models. It is not necessary that it be a conquest, nor that this conquest be connected with the idea of a "kingdom of man," nor, finally, that it take on the aspect of a domination realized by technology.[15]

The idea of a domination of nature in general is logically and chronologically prior to its particular application to the technological domination of nature. The idea of a *moral* domination preceded it. What was necessary in order for the object that philosophical or religious asceticism proposed to master to come to bear the name of "nature"? When did this appear?

In order to understand this, and to situate the idea within a system of possibilities, one can reconstruct a genealogy beginning from the basic idea of anthropology in general. At the very least, the latter presupposes that its object distinguishes itself from other realities. The difference then can be interpreted as a superiority of humanity. This idea did not await modernity; quite the contrary, it is of ancient date, even from the beginning of history. Thus, why did the affirmation of the superiority of humanity take on the aspect of a conquest of nature? This question divides into three subordinated investigations. One will ask when and why this superiority came to be understood according to three characteristics:

(a) No longer as a condition that is already acquired and peacefully possessed, but as a situation not yet realized, and still **pending**. The idea of a kingdom of man yet to come appears in the Bible with messianism. It supposes a promise made to man, but whose advent "depends ... on God who shows mercy" (Rom. 9:16 NRSV).

(b) No longer as having to await an external divine factor, prior and superior to man, natural or divine, but as a work proper to man and to be realized by him. It is not only the realization of this enterprise that depends upon man, but, already, its origin. He must not receive a command like the biblical command (Gen. 1:28), but give the order to himself, that is, determine himself as the virtual lord of being.

(c) No longer as consisting in an asceticism, in an internal work of man on himself to realize the human potentials, but as concretized in a domination of external nature, perceived as an object to conquer.

This implies, on one hand, that nature is considered as still imperfect but perfectible. One therefore must ask where this view of insufficiency came from, which was brought to bear upon something that for a very long time was viewed as perfect. This equally implies that humanity is held to be incapable of realizing its destiny without the intermediary of external nature. In this way, humanity is constrained to take control of it. One must therefore also ask about this sentiment of inferiority or illegitimacy, which this conquest seeks to compensate for.

I therefore will begin by considering the three possibilities of messianism, divinization, and asceticism. They constitute the alternatives to the project of the conquest of nature put in place by modern times, which suppressed those alternatives. I will attempt to unearth the reasons that prevented stopping at just one of them. I then will examine how the idea of the kingdom of man guaranteed by the conquest of nature itself became sovereign and conquering, but also how it turns on itself.

PART I

PREPARATION

1

The Best of the Living Things

It does not go without saying that man distinguishes himself from the rest of what populates the earth, even less that he can claim to be better than the other living things. What had become something obvious to us and remained so until recently was the result of a process that I need to sketch.

A Unique Living Thing

I will lay out three logically distinct stages: man is singular among the other beings; he is superior to them; he dominates them.[1] In this nested ensemble, the previous stage does not necessarily entail the one that follows, which therefore must come from elsewhere.

For Kant, "what is man?" is the fourth fundamental question of philosophy. The *Critique of Pure Reason* had earlier posed three, concerning knowledge, action, and hope, each with a distinctive modality (is able to, ought to, is allowed to . . .). In the fourth and last question, formulated later, the three concerns converge, and the three adjunct modalities are combined in the simple verb "to be."[2] Now, the question of knowing what man is was not raised in antiquity except rarely, and Colotes, friend of Epicurus, mocked a question that presupposed such an ignorance of oneself.[3] The oldest occurrence is found, perhaps, in Psalm 8:5 (RSV): "What is man that thou art mindful of him?" The question, rhetorical, does not lead to a search for what constitutes man, but continues with a reflection on the place that God has accorded him. The psalm had begun by evoking the celestial bodies, in the light of which man is implicitly measured, and clearly to his disadvantage. On the other hand, man is situated just below the "gods" (doubtless, angels), and in any case above the terrestrial and aquatic animals. Seneca asks twice "what is man?" But he does so to affirm not a definition but human fragility.[4]

When antiquity sought to determine what the situation of man has that is unique, it put to work an entire series of notions and metaphors. All agreed in conferring on man an exceptional situation, but not always the place of honor. Thus, man is the most fragile of beings. Or again: while nature or the gods have given animals what they need to defend themselves, man is abandoned by stepmotherly nature; he is naked, like someone shipwrecked and tossed on the shore, obliged to fend for himself alone.[5]

Most of the time, however, what man has that is unique is seen as positive. He alone has commerce with the highest of the beings. Wisdom texts from ancient Egypt affirm that the world was made for man, whom God created in his image. Thus the *Teaching for King Merikare* (ca. 2060 BCE): human beings "are his copies, who have come from his body." The *Teaching of Ani* (ca. 1300) specifies that the resemblance with the god does not hold only for the wise: "As for men, they are the doubles of god. . . . It is not only the wise who is his double." The Egyptian word used designates a fixed representation of a god—in contrast to a mobile statue carried in procession—a word used when one says that the king is the image of a specific god.[6] The idea of man created in the image of God is also found in the two sources the West has never forgotten: in the Bible (Gen. 1:27), but also in the pagan poetry of Ovid, who spoke, though, of *gods*.[7]

As a consequence, man is the best of the living things.[8] The reason given for such an advantage varies. That man is what is best under the heaven is an idea found equally in Xunzi (Hsün Tzu), a Chinese philosopher of the third century BCE, who explains this superiority by the fact that man possesses the sentiment of duty.[9] Most often, it is attributed to his capacity to receive excellence. This is a possibility that remains ambiguous, though, because it can turn on him and make him the worst of the beasts.[10] It can also be the case that he is the best of all the sublunary beings, but not the best of all beings, because the celestial bodies are greater than he. For an ancient such as Chrysippus, the greatest arrogance for man is to imagine that there is nothing above him. But this claim is cited in a dialogue of Cicero by the skeptic Cotta, who responds that man at least has the advantage over the heavenly constellations of being conscious and intelligent; Pascal recalled this when he wrote: "The advantage that the universe has over him, the universe knows nothing of it."[11]

However, to be superior does not always mean to exercise a real, concrete domination. One can see in it merely a metaphor, as when one says: "He towers over the others." To be superior would then be to possess a series of advantages that one can list (not without satisfaction), which seem to make man the gods' favorite, and which even allow him to be seen as a kind of god vis-à-vis the other beings.[12] The possession of these advantages is peaceful and uncontested.

After the invention of writing, literary works formulated the superiority of man in admiring evocations of his prowess at the hunt and in fishing, connected to the superiority of human astuteness over the intelligence of animals with lesser or more dense minds.[13] His adventurous endeavors, such as navigation or the exploitation of mines, are also frequently evoked, from the book of Job to the Greek tragedies, and in China, where the idea is at least implicit in Mozi (Mo Tzu), in the fifth century BCE.[14] These activities, are they the cause or the consequence of human superiority? It would seem that they merely express the adroitness of man, of him who is the most "formidable" of the living beings. In Sophocles, one cannot derive the idea of self-creation from the chorus that sings man's capacity to "teach himself." To be an "autodidact," far from excluding inspiration from the gods, implies it.[15] It is in this context that it is best to understand the enigmatic declaration of Protagoras: "Man is the measure of all things."[16] It caused many individuals to reflect, including Nicolas of Cusa.[17] To begin with, the text of the fragment is not fully guaranteed. Plato, perhaps our sole source, interprets it as an argument for the relativism of sensations. In any case, the "things" in question are the "things" that one needs and makes use of. That man would be, for the things that are, the measure of what they are, that is still understandable. But that he would be for those that are not, the measure that they are not, that is more problematic. These "things" are perhaps only sensations, for example, those of hot and cold, of light and heavy, of which each individual is de facto the measure. In his last dialogue, Plato responds that it is not man, but God, who is of all things the most precise measure.[18]

Valorization

One can distinguish three stages in the valorization of man: the dignity of the human species, the nobility of an elite, the perfection of an individual. But the qualities that attach to these three moments (the universal, the class, the individual) indicate everything of which the human is capable, even if each person is not always at the height of such a valuation.

The idea of dignity most often implies a protest against a condition where it is denied. Historically speaking, after a prefiguration in Stoicism,[19] the idea of an intrinsic and inalienable human dignity clearly appeared only in Christianity, which placed the accent on the liberty of the person.[20] Its pertaining to the modality of "ought-to be" received a historical transposition in Christianity: dignity had been lost by the sin of Adam, then recovered by the sacrifice of Jesus. Thus it is the result of divine grace and the economy of salvation, which works itself out in history. It is because Christ gave his life to redeem him that man can recover his dignity wounded by sin. The fathers of the church invited Christians, who knew themselves to be situated in the economy of salvation, to be aware of their dignity. The term was still connected to its original meaning of social role, but went beyond it when one specified that this dignity is even prior to the coming into being of the one who bears it.[21] These reminders were especially given at Christmas, for example in the sermons of St. Leo and St. Bernard: for human nature, the incarnation of the Word was the cause of an undreamed-of promotion.[22]

Thomas Aquinas recapitulates and powerfully synthesizes the ideas of human dignity when he asks, Why was it fitting that the Word became man? Citing Augustine and other Latin fathers, he shows that the incarnation was a particularly well-adapted way to enable man to progress in the good, even to divinization, by the practice of the three theological virtues, faith, hope, and charity, and to heal him of evil, by freeing him from preferring the devil to himself and keeping him from tarnishing the dignity of human nature with sin.[23] The dignity of man comes from his nature as an intermediary and a microcosm who contains a bit of everything in the world. In this way, he realizes in himself the union of all the universe, material and spiritual. This idea has a venerable antiquity. But in Christianity it received a new dimension, historical. The microcosmic nature of man prefigures the union of God with his creation, realized by the union of his Word with man.[24] Thus Maximus the Confessor compares man to a workshop, because of the syntheses that he effects in himself, at all the levels of being. This workshop is already at work in him by his mere existence and not by his action, which is why it is wrong to make of the Byzantine theologian a precursor of the "theology of work."[25]

The idea of nobility was initially social. Its ancient definition invoked the antiquity of the family and the exploits of the ancestors who made one "well born."[26] The Middle Ages added the possibility of arriving at nobility by the excellence of services rendered, to be thus "son of something" (in Spanish: *hidalgo*). In the fourteenth century, Dante and Meister Eckhart constructed a theory of the noble man.[27] Averroës (Ibn Rushd), or rather his translators, by means of the idea of "nobility" had expressed the status of things as ideas of the divine intellect, before their realization by the creative act.[28] Eckhart was inspired by this to identify the noble man, as the image of God, with the interior man, which he conceived as man insofar as he was in God before his creation.

The idea of the nobility of man thus transposed into the metaphysical order the structure which had been presented historically in the idea of dignity. With this important change: nobility lost its connection to heredity and became accessible to whoever would aspire to it by appropriate conduct. In any case, this understanding of nobility, far from entailing a claim of independence vis-à-vis God, to the contrary expresses the idea of a perfect submission to his will, or a perfect expression of the order of ideas according to which nature had been created.[29] It was the same with the ancient idea of a "divine man," which designated not a figure arrogating superhuman powers to himself, a thaumaturge or soothsayer, but the authorized transmitter of truths of divine origin that merely pass through him.[30]

The human perfection of Jesus Christ, model of virtue, was little discussed by Christianity, which sees in him a "true man and true God." St. Paul distinguishes the "spiritual man" from the "natural man," declaring that "the spiritual man judges all things, but is himself to be judged by no one" (1 Cor. 2:14–15 RSV). He thus furnishes the first formulation of the idea of sovereignty, and the text was often cited by defenders of the power of popes. The epistles of the captivity speak of Christians as having to become perfect human beings (Eph. 4:13; Col. 1:28).

The idea of the perfect human being was not clearly developed in the lands of Christianity. The formula "perfect in humanity" is found in the definition of the Council of Chalcedon (451), but it signifies that Christ is "perfectly human" and not "perfect man."[31] However, one encounters it in the *Anticlaudianus* of Alain de Lille (1184), an allegorical poem on the creation of a perfect man by the reunion of the personified virtues, who send one of them, prudence, to heaven. Indeed, if the body of man is the work of nature, his soul must be sought with God. This perfect man ends by allying with the virtues to combat the vices and triumph over them. The idea reemerges with somewhat marginal figures such as Jacob Boehme.[32] Not to speak of its dubious incarnations among the disciples of Stefan George or in totalitarian "cults of personality."[33]

Islam, in contrast, considers that the perfection of humanity was realized in the Prophet. His biographies therefore distance themselves more and more from the narration of facts and veer towards hagiography, at the same time as a cult of the Prophet develops and feasts celebrating his birth appear.[34] Here too, in any case, the perfect man is not a rival of God. On the contrary, he is the most faithful expression, the most complete manifestation, of him in this lower world.

The Primordial Man

It was not only the value of the empirical man, his qualities and his achievements, that antiquity considered. One also encounters conceptions that placed, well above concrete humanity, a Man who transcends our experience, since he constitutes its Archetype. We find this in gnosticism, in the Hermetic writings, and in the idea of the perfect man in Islam.

Indian mythology knew Puruṣa, the original man from whom came the castes and all the animals. A similar representation is found in Iran with Gayomart; with Plato, in a philosophical transposition that renders the procession of the living beings from man, by way of a fall of the latter; and even in the Talmud with the idea of the "initial man" (*adam qadmon*).[35] One finds in authors called "gnostics" a representation of the genesis of the world that perhaps comes, in part, from Iranian myths. This idea links that genesis to a transcendent figure, of a human nature. Several versions are known. According to one, the supreme Being is already the original Man, model for the creation of the concrete man made in his image. Another version adds a stage: the original Man is himself a creation of the supreme God, who creates a celestial Man, sometimes called "Son of Man," who is similar to God and is the model of the concrete man.[36] A radical condemnation of idolatry follows. "Men fabricate the gods and adore their own creation. It is the gods who ought to adore man."[37] Ideas of this sort lasted for a long time, for example in Swedenborg, where the idea of a primordial man resurfaces, perhaps to counter the divinization of man by the Enlightenment.[38]

According to the Hermetic writings, man desires to arrive at the knowledge of God; but God himself desires to make himself known by the most glorious of his creatures. Animated by a divine spark, man is himself divine. However, only a few human beings are aware of their divinity. The highest task of the disciple of Hermes therefore consists in aiding man to know his true nature, to know God, and, by that means, to reclaim his own divinity.³⁹ According to the *Asclepius*, man is "a great marvel," which the writer develops according to customary themes: upright posture, the role of intermediary between superior and inferior realities, the rapidity of his thought, the possession of an intellect. Man touches the divine: he "passes in the nature of a god, as if he himself were god."⁴⁰ Other Hermetic writings nuance the picture. The intellect, father of all things, engendered a man similar to it and delivered to him all its works. The man also wanted to work, and the Father granted this to him. Man was created to know the divine works, to dominate all that exists beneath the heaven, and to discover the art of fabricating fine things. The Intellect of the Whole fabricates all things by using fire as an instrument; the fire of man only fabricates what is on earth. The "rays" of man are the arts and sciences; it is by them that he acts.⁴¹

Here retracing the genealogy of *European* cultural phenomena, I would not have any reason to treat the Islamic idea of "the perfect man" if others had not sought it behind its resurgence in Renaissance Europe, in Fracastoro, Cardano, Bovelles, Bruno, Gracián.⁴² It runs through all of Islamic thought, but it probably has more ancient sources.⁴³ In any case, it appears in Arabic in the translation of extracts from Plotinus called the *Theology of Aristotle*, but in a passage not found in the *Enneads*. Here it is a question of "the truly first man . . . the radiant light in which are found all the human states, except that in him they are of a more excellent sort, nobler and more powerful."⁴⁴ The idea then is often found, as in Christendom, among thinkers who are at the margins of orthodoxy. Thus, in the *Letter of the Animals* of the "Sincere Brethren," the lawsuit of the beasts against man, who exploits and eats them, is dismissed by a man who synthesizes in himself all the qualities possessed separately by the different human groups.⁴⁵

Finally, the idea culminates in the mystical monism of Ibn Arabi (1240). The perfect man is more than an individual, and even a species; he is less a creature than an archetype of a creation conceived as the manifestation of God himself: "A synthesizing being by which what He has that is hidden manifests itself to Him." "He [Muhammad] says apropos to the creation of Adam, complete model for the properties of the divine presence—essence, attributes and actions—that 'God created man according to his image'; this image is nothing other than the divine presence, and he caused to exist in the concentrated nobility of the Perfect Man the ensemble of divine names and truths which he emitted into the world in a dispersed manner." Playing on the word *insān*, which means both "man" and "pupil," Ibn Arabi writes that this man is to God what the pupil is to the eye; it is by him that God sees his creation and pardons it. He is the caliph of God. The world subsists by him and would disappear if he did. Like the signet ring, he reassembles the truths of the world and its separated realities. His superiority, however, does not belong to his essence, but to the position granted him by God.[46]

This teaching found its classical expression in the treatise of Abd el-Karīm al-Ǧīlī (a/k/a Jîlî; d. 1425) which bears the eponymous title. In it he synthesized the thought of Ibn Arabi, whom he nonetheless criticizes several times. The idea according to which man is a little world (microcosm) occupies a central place. To be sure, this perfect man is deemed to be the Prophet. But this no longer has anything to do with the Muhammad of the biographies. He constitutes the preexisting model of the entirety of the created. In this perfect man, God and man no longer are distinguished. It is the perfect self-expression of reality, like the Word according to Philo, a copy of God. It appears under different forms and under different names, including those of Sufi masters. Adam is the spirit of the world here-below, which will exist as long as humanity exists in it.[47]

In any case, it is not a question of endeavoring to conquer nature. Nature no longer needs to be conquered, but was already subject to an essential subordination. It is even less a matter of a rivalry between this man and God. The bond that unites them is too deep, even to the point of touching identity. All the images that express it (caliph, mirror, pole) exclude the possibility that one can play the Creator and creature off against each other.

Perhaps, though, one could establish some connections between the supremacy of the primordial Man and earthly activity, as the *Asclepius* already invited one to do. The doctrines of the perfect man that we have just considered leave it understood that this man can exercise an authority or power over all things.[48] A Hebrew poem of Ibn Naghrela (d. 1056) can provide an example. The poet is out walking in the marketplace among butchers and fishermen, and he asks why the animals allow themselves to be killed. That would not be possible if God had not given them to man as food; if he had not refused to give them a spirit, the beasts would have turned against their tormenters. The lesson that the poet addresses to "the pure and to princes" is that "if they understand the profound meaning of the world, they will know it is *the whole [tout]* man." Does this last formulation allude to the idea of the "total man," a model of all creation which contains all its ideas? One finds a century later, in Abraham Ibn Ezra, instances of the same adjective where it is easy to identify an idea similar to the archetype of the created.[49]

2

Domination

We just saw that even where the distinctive character of man is conceived as a superiority, this does not necessarily translate into the search for domination over what is not man. Let us now study this other idea.

The Ancient East

It does not seem that the ancient civilizations conceived of a control of nature by human activity. The accent rather was on the supple way that this activity ought to adapt itself to the exigencies of things, for example, by adapting to the rhythm of the seasons. The idea itself of a "nature" confronting man was not clear. Rather, man was experienced as a part of a whole that also embraced plants, animals, and the stars. In this connection, Joseph Needham has proposed the hypothesis according to which in Europe it was the idea of a personal and creative divinity that entailed the idea of a law that this divinity introduced, which must be deciphered by observation and reasoning. The absence of this idea in China would have prevented this development.[1]

The exceptions, however, are always more interesting than the rule; let us cite one. A poem found in the work of Xunzi (Hsün Tzu) has led some to think that certain minds in the China of the "Warring Kingdoms" might have entertained the project of a domination of nature.[2] They have written in this vein: "Nowhere else in the history of Chinese thought is the idea of the control of nature so clear and strong. It is sad that that did not lead to the development of the science of nature."[3] But the actual text is very ambiguous, and the most recent translator does not see in it any prefiguration of the

Western project of conquest.[4] A century later, the prince Liu An (179–22) set the technological successes of man in opposition to nature left to itself and indifferent to the well-being of man.[5]

Closer to us by geography, but as early as 5000 BCE, and therefore before writing, the art of the ancient Middle East teemed with scenes where a figure is represented as fighting and defeating animals being hunted, unless it was some hero—for example, Gilgamesh, who carried around a lion as one would a pet.[6] In Greece, in contrast, the pictorial theme of an anthropomorphic divinity among savage beasts or between two horses held by a bridle is perhaps only an image of the Earth-Mother, which does not imply any relationship of domination or control.

However, images in which animals are represented, no doubt as an amusement, as performing human activities are found just about everywhere in the ancient East and have survived in caricature until our day.[7]

The invention of writing and the invention of the state, which is connected to it, seem to have marked a decisive turn in several domains, which also influenced the way that man understood himself. In Egypt, one observes a remarkable evolution in representation: before 3000 BCE, powerful beings were presented as species of animals; then, they took on human features. I will limit myself to citing Erik Hornung: "In the tremendous exertion of his intellectual and bodily forces which the construction of the first civilization entailed, man attained a new way of understanding himself. He put in order the world in a creative way, he bent it under the dominion of his spirit which foresees and interprets, and he ceased to see himself as the plaything of incomprehensible forces. This perhaps is connected with the fact that the powers that he honors as divinities increasingly show a more human face, that their form, initially that of an animal or a thing, humanizes."[8] In any case, toward the twenty-second century BCE, the *Teaching for King Merikare* presents the realities of the earth as having been created for human beings, "for their intention."[9]

Greece

Greek culture distinguishes itself from those that preceded it, in particular from Egypt, by the progressive transition to anthropomorphism in its representation of the gods. Those of Egypt are at least in part zoomorphic. Porphyry already accounted for it by the Egyptian concern to mix beasts and men.[10] The gods of Mesopotamia and of Canaan are removed from common humanity by the presence of a tail, horns, an enormous erect penis, or several breasts. In contrast, the gods of Greece are represented like human beings, idealized to be sure, but still normal. The human form is suitable for those whom the Greeks called "the powerful" par excellence.[11]

According to Leo Strauss, the Greeks conceived the possibility of man controlling nature, but rejected it.[12] Their actual practice, however, witnesses to a belief that the natural beings reworked by human activity—for example, trees—are thereby improved and found in a state better than their natural one.[13] And the idea of a domination of nature by man is not totally absent from classical literature. At the beginning of a treatise on simple machines attributed to Aristotle, one reads the formulation of the sophist Antiphon, according to which, "By art, we overcome what overcomes us by nature."[14] Later authors reprised the idea—for example, Pappus, speaking of the pulley that allows one, against nature, to raise a heavy weight with slight force, or later, at the dawn of the Middle Ages, Cassiodorus, who describes a mechanical clock.[15] Alchemists prided themselves on manufacturing pearls better than natural ones.[16]

The idea of man's domination over animals is found in Ovid: "Still lacking was an animal more sacred than those [i.e., the other animals], one that more than they received a mind capable of depth and who can dominate the others [*quod dominari in cetera posset*]." Cicero has the Stoic Balbus say that man, by the munificence of the gods, was made capable of creating a second nature, as it were, in the midst of the first by means of his hands.[17] In the *Secret of Creation*, the Arab Pseudo-Apollonius interprets the superiority of man as a dominion over the other living things.[18] The idea is perhaps found in a Greek source of the work that we have lost.

The Biblical Traditions

Would the Bible be the ultimate source of the modern idea of the domination of nature? The hypothesis has been proposed, in the context of an ecological protest. For example, by Lynn White Jr., a historian of medieval technology. His 1957 article is itself rather nuanced, but it provided arguments to those who are much less so.[19] For a long time, the Bible and the Christianity that issued from it had been accused of having delayed the progress of the sciences and technology. With this new way of viewing things, however, they found themselves responsible for the exact opposite: for having exaggeratedly privileged man and allowing the excesses committed in the exploitation of a nature deprived of any divine aura.

As the foregoing suggests, a distant premise of the domination of man over the earth is the "disenchantment" of nature. Hegel saw a first figure of this in Abraham: it was the universal doubt of nature, a consequence of the flood, that made nature an enemy and constrained man, if he wanted to survive, to the project of dominating it.[20] On the other hand, if one remains with history, this disenchantment was effected by the prophets of Israel, with their rejection of the rustic deities of trees and brooks, and was continued by the fathers of the church in their critique of the pagan gods. Thus, Firmicus Maternus polemicized against those who saw in natural beings more than they are. The only worship to render the earth is to work, while respecting its temporal rhythms. He has the sun say that it is nothing more than it appears to be.[21]

At the dawn of the Middle Ages, Augustine enumerated the technological and artistic successes of man, whom he nonetheless considered to be fallen. All these marvels, however, were nothing beside what Adam would have been able to achieve if he had not sinned. The ingenuity of human beings is not considered an attempt to rebel against the natural order instituted by God, nor is it the peak of human possibilities. The admiration remains sober and does not degenerate into exaltation. In an implicit wordplay employing the verb *colere*, "to worship" and "to cultivate," Augustine explains that the Earth is not something that should be adored, but rather ploughed. But there is no violence in this, no project of coercing or even of subjugating: agriculture is conceived as a *dialogue* with nature: man, the rational creature, discovers a reason already present in the nature he develops, and he brings to birth what it contains in germ.[22]

Genesis contains a passage in which man receives the mission of subjecting the earth. Adam and Eve are to dominate the plants and animals (Gen. 1:26b, 28b).[23] The verb "trample under foot" traditionally expresses the superiority of a Middle Eastern king over his enemies, which now is extended to all human beings. The idea of a dominion of the king, the "Great Man" (in Sumerian, LU-GAL), over the beasts is present in the ancient Middle East, and even in the Bible (Jer. 27:6; 28:14). It could be the case that Psalm 8 represents a "democratization" of privileges that initially were reserved to the king. Thus, in Egypt, the quality of being an image of God above all concerned the king.[24] Its extension to man as a species, rather marginal in Egypt, in the Bible becomes exclusive. As a result, the object to dominate changes. The Egyptian king was the image of God insofar as he reigned over his subjects. Biblical man is the image of God, but his domination, no longer being able to bear upon another man, henceforth is exercised over nature.

However, the superiority of man cannot in any case lead to exploiting the animals; in so doing man would derogate and lose his royal dignity. Even less does it entail a right to kill and eat, because at this primitive period, according to Genesis, the only food was vegetarian. The parallel with Egypt suggests that man ought to intervene only when the order instituted by God is threatened and that his role is limited to holding in check the powers of chaos.[25] Moreover, other biblical passages recall that "the just takes care of the life of beasts," in contrast to the cruelty of the wicked (Prov. 12:10), or they authorize hoping for a rediscovered harmony between man and the animals (Hosea 2:18).

The idea of a submission of the earth is found in the Qur'an, but with an interesting nuance: in the Qur'an, it is God who from the beginning subjects creatures to man; in the Bible, it is man who receives subjecting creation as his *task*.[26]

Among the fathers of the church, the passage where the Bible affirms the dominion of man over the animals did not elicit an interest comparable to the narrative of original sin or the wealth of ingenuity displayed in understanding man's creation "in the image and likeness of God." The attention of commentators focused almost exclusively on the injunction to reproduce. Jews asked about its juridical or legal status: was it a command or simply a blessing? The Christians wanted to connect it with the advantage granted to continence. In any case, no one in antiquity or the Middle Ages ever saw in the verse a permission to involve oneself in nature's affairs in order to exploit it in a selfish manner or to threaten its integrity.[27]

Certain thinkers, such as Theophilus of Antioch, did not say a word about dominion. Some texts that speak about it have been collected in a useful anthology.[28] Here are a few more (without aiming to be exhaustive): Irenaeus of Lyon, who constantly cited the idea of man's creation in God's image, does not mention the dominion of man over the other creatures except in an eschatological context: it is after the resurrection that the animals will be subject to him.[29] Origen moves quickly over the literal sense and provides an allegorical interpretation.[30] Gregory of Nyssa uses it to attack slavery, which is not only an inevitable, although terrible, consequence of sin, but an assault on the dignity of man created in God's image. While man does receive the mission to have mastery over the other animals, it is a grave perversion to dominate other men.[31] Augustine understands the verse as speaking of the intellectual superiority of man, and does not comment on the power of man over the animals as such. The earth that one must dominate is the flesh; the soul does so by acquiring virtue.³² For John Philoponus, the true master of the world is the creator God. In his goodness, he granted man to imitate him by dominating the animals with the power of his reason. This domination is realized and illustrated in the scene when man gives them their names.³³ Only Basil of Caesarea gives dominion a very concrete content: he explains that the elephant, despite its size and strength, allows himself to be mounted, even beaten, by man, because man is the image of the Creator.³⁴

The Jewish exegesis of the beginning of the Middles Ages did not accord any special importance to the verse. Ibn Ezra says nothing about it. Rashi only explains a grammatical point. Maimonides only mentions it once in the *Guide for the Perplexed* and seeks to minimize the idea according to which man would be the final end of creation. The theme of mastery appeared in the thirteenth century, in Christian lands. Should one see here an echo of the intellectual atmosphere at the time, one of technological progress? In any case, one reads in Nachmanides: "He gave them power and dominion over the earth to do according to their will with the beasts, reptiles, and everything 'that slithers in the dust' [Deut. 32:24], in order to build, 'to uproot what is planted' [Eccles. 3:21], 'hills out of which you can dig copper' [Deut. 8:9]." For his part, Gersonides (d. 1344) explains that the animals were created to serve man. He is the final cause of their creation, because he is the highest of the forms that prime matter contains in potential. If God blesses the animals, it is so that they can put their superior strength at the service of man.³⁵

For all these thinkers, man is not the owner of creation. In antiquity, some thinkers saw in man the steward of God on earth; the idea constantly reappeared. Since he is such, his dominion is itself subject to a condition—namely, obedience to the Creator. For a Christian like Augustine, man is not lord of creation except to the extent that he is son of God.³⁶

Be that as it may, the realization of the superiority of man entails a command to fulfill; it results from an order received from without, not from an enterprise freely assumed. It is a task, not a project.

Limits of Mastery

Human dominion, whether realized or simply wished for, is relativized by the fact that the plane on which it is deployed is sandwiched between a "below" and an "above," and also because the status of man is far from being obvious, located as it is between the beast and the angel.

On one hand, the superiority of man over the animal did not at all remain uncontested. It was denied, even in the Bible: "The advantage of man over the animal is nothing" (Eccles. 3:19). Both are subject to contingency and death, have the same vital breath, and, having come from the earth, return to it. Some authors of the kabbalah give a positive meaning to the verse cited above: the superiority of man over the animal is nothing, in the sense that negation is a privilege of man.[37] The idea according to which man and the animal are not radically distinguished is not unusual in Greece. It even happens that the standard classification is overturned and the animal gains the advantage over man. Thus in Diogenes the Cynic, and in the comedic lines of Philemon and Menander, or in Philo, Diodorus, Ovid, Seneca, Pliny, or Plutarch. The companions of Odysseus, changed into swine by Circe, weep when they return to being human. Plutarch has one of them (well named Gryllos [from grunting]) give an argument in favor of the superiority of beasts that Machiavelli will recall. At the dawn of modern times, Montaigne powerfully marshaled all the arguments in favor of the animal and transmitted them to European authors. Similarly, the critique of the mastery of man over the animals, sometimes placed in the mouth of animals who were miraculously capable of speaking, occurs from time to time (in La Fontaine, for example).[38]

One work merits special mention: the *Letter on the Animals*, the longest of the fifty-one letters that form the Encyclopedia of the "Sincere Brethren" of Basra, probably composed around AD 960. This one, as well as the others, did not enter the West before the nineteenth century. But it had been translated into Hebrew as early as 1316. Moreover, it is one of the sources of the *Dispute of the Ass* of the renegade Anselm Turmeda (written ca. 1417). Although printed, the Catalan original of *Letter on the Animals* was lost, and we only have a French translation of 1544.[39] A trial opposes man to the animals concerning his dominance: man domesticates beasts, submits them to the yoke, even captures and eats them. Chosen for his neutrality, the judge is the king of the Jinn. The "Sincere Brethren" are not precursors of "deep ecology." Rather, the proceeding ends with a change of perspective: the static, "natural," dominance of man is placed in the historical context of a theory of cycles. The animals "will participate for a cycle." The domination of man as a species over the other living things is considered like that of the perfect man over the vulgar in the human species. The perfect man participates in the world of the Secret and the Royalty.[40] His dominance is a participation in the sovereignty of God himself. Whatever may have been the original meaning of the narrative, whose sources are perhaps in India, the "Sincere Brethren" made it a parable for the superiority of the (Ismaili) elite over the vulgar. Thus one sees, perhaps for the first time, a dialectic that we will encounter later: the domination of man over nature (here represented by the animals) will turn into a domination of the superior man over other men.[41]

As for Turmeda, he lets the ass refute all the arguments of man in his favor, before delivering his decisive argument: the Word of God became incarnate as a man and not as an animal.[42] The argument is surprising, however, when one considers that its author had abjured Christianity for Islam. Still, it is the case with the Majorcan as with the Ismaili that man possesses not so much an intrinsic superiority as one he receives from God.

On the other hand, the relation of man to the angel provides a model of superiority that can never be a domination. St. Paul recalls the dignity of human beings to the Corinthians: not only will they judge the world, but "do you not know that you will judge the angels?" (1 Cor. 6:3)—basing his argument on texts that speak of a reign of the just at the end of times.[43] "To judge" in Hebrew had a political meaning: the judge is a military and/or political leader, like the judges in the Bible or the Carthaginian suffetes, or in Christ's promise to his disciples that they would "judge the twelve tribes of Israel" (Matt. 19:28; Luke 22:30). Paul gives it its contemporary meaning and encourages his listeners not to bring the internal differences of the community before the pagan tribunals. He reasons a fortiori: Christ is superior to the angels; therefore, even more so to the fallen angels. How could his disciples submit themselves to other human beings, much less to those who worship these demons?

The superiority of man over the angel is defended by several authors.[44] It already implies that one grants an advantage to the creature who has a history, who even produces one, over a static being, one with a superior status, to be sure, but stable and incapable of progressing, fixed in the eternal act of his freedom. The idea therefore already leads to the concrete realization of human superiority in history. The angel is only the term of comparison vis-à-vis which man declares himself superior. In no way is the angel the *object* of human domination: man is above the angel, but does not subject him. Even where it is a question of subjecting the rebellious angels, it is not man but God who submits them to his Messiah (1 Cor. 15:28).

Moreover, one can conceive that the kingdom of man succeeds that of the angels, but the kingdom over which he is to reign is nothing other than the earth. The idea of a translation of the powers of the angel to man is very ancient. It is probably at the root of the formula of the Qur'an—often misinterpreted—according to which man has been established as the "successor" (caliph) not of God—heaven forbid!—but of the angels, which explains their objections at the moment of Adam's creation.[45] It is still found at the beginning of the nineteenth century with the "unknown philosopher," Louis Claude de Saint-Martin, who has the added interest of using the expression that serves as my title: "The angels await the kingdom of man like men await the kingdom of God."[46]

The Middle Ages raised the question as to why man had been created. The question is distinct from the older question, whether it was good that he exists, which the more recent question supposes is answered in the affirmative. A possible response, the first proposed, consists in seeing in him a replacement for the fallen angels in the heavenly chorus.[47] By doing that, however, one risked lowering man to the rank of substitute.

A development begins to appear in St. Anselm, and more clearly in the twelfth century, when man is increasingly considered to be willed for his own sake. Later authors, who preserve the idea of a replacement of fallen angels by man, see in the creation of man not a means in view of another goal, but an end in itself.[48] In the ancient perspective, the ultimate reason for the creation of man was the perfection of the whole of the cosmos, to which nothing should be lacking. With the new way of seeing, one passes from a cosmocentric to an anthropocentric perspective. This revolution ended by affecting the ontological model itself. With Thomas Aquinas, the meaning of being is no longer conceived by taking the cosmos as one's guiding thread, but rather human subjectivity. He thus would have carried the Christian revolution into the heart of ontology.[49]

3

Three Incomplete Prefigurations

For a long time, the superiority of man had been a fact to note in a static fashion: man is located higher on the scale of beings than the other creatures. One also encounters, however, dynamic ways of conceiving this superiority. For them, this superiority must not only be *realized* by way of application, but *acquired* at the end of a process. These are the ones I will now examine.

Messianism

The ultimate source of the expression "the kingdom of man" is biblical, found in the prophet Daniel. Thus, Bacon cites an obscure passage from the book of Daniel about the end of times: "Many will rush to and fro and science will increase" (12:4).[1] The modern technology that Bacon desired has messianic traits. The *partus masculus* in the title of one of Bacon's first works, would he be the "male infant" who is to rule the nations with an iron rod, that is to say, the Messiah (Rev. 12:5)?[2]

The book of Daniel dates from the revolt of the Maccabees. Its author projects the resistance to the Hellenistic dynasty of the Seleucids and their policy of "normalization" of the Jewish people backward to the period of the Babylonian captivity. Presented as a Hellenization in the book of Maccabees, this policy was most likely a reduction to the religious vulgate of the peoples of the Semitic Northwest.[3] Daniel presents a vision of history as the succession of great empires, each represented by an animal: the winged lion of Babylon, the Median bear, the Persian panther with four heads and four wings, and finally the serpent with ten horns which is the empire of the Diadochi. The final reign is to be that of "man," the original meaning of the expression "son of man" (Dan. 7:13), subsequently enriched with many resonances, including its employment by Jesus. In Daniel this man represents the Jewish people, and what is said of him is immediately applied to the "people of saints" (7:18, 21–22, 25, 27). The man who will receive superiority over the animals is the one who respects the Jewish law.

Here it is interesting to see that humanity is already constituted as a single subject across the divisions among nations. But this is because one people considers itself coincident with humanity in its entirety, the others being more or less bestial. Judaism sometimes imagines that the humanity of pagans is doubtful: they do not know the Torah, whose commands have for their purpose distinguishing man from the animal as much as possible.[4] Be that as it may, the reign that is promised is situated in history, in a process that is oriented toward a messianic future. It is only from this moment that one can consider the victory of man not as given from the beginning with the natural superiority of the species but as acquired.

Nonetheless, the kingdom of man will be a deliverance effected by divine intervention, not by human activity, even less by the activism of human beings. The "son of man" does nothing, but receives what God, the "Ancient of Days," gives him. Even more, this kingdom of "the son of man" is not a domination over nature, but over other peoples. This dominance is not technological, but moral or political. It is barely a domination, however; it is rather a liberation. A sage of the Talmud, Rabbi Samuel, will later say that the only difference between the messianic time and the present is that the slavery of the people will have ended.[5]

St. Paul provides another version of the kingdom of the Messiah. The idea of a victory of Christ over the angelic powers of the cosmos appears in the epistles of the captivity: God raised Christ and "seated him at his right in the heavens, higher than any principality, authority, power and lordship" (Eph. 1:20–21). "After having disarmed the principalities and authorities, he made a public spectacle of them, triumphing over them in the cross" (Col. 2:15).[6] Christians are associated with this triumph and are seated in the heavens with Christ (Eph. 2:6).

This victory, however, is different from a project of dominating nature in that, on one hand, it is the work of Christ and is not granted to human beings until the victory is won, and, on the other, it consists in removing human beings from the empire of the powers of the world, rather than controlling those powers or taking control of what they themselves controlled until then; finally, this victory is situated in an eschatological time, not in human history. Thus, the project of mastering nature is not found in the New Testament. It is found, however, in gnosticism. This is what Valentine would have told his disciples: "When you dissolve the world and you are not dissolved, you are the lords of creation and of all corruption."[7] Still, here too, this is a way for the gnostic to escape from the control of the created, rather than a way to take control of it.

Divinization

The idea of a divine intervention in history, with its culmination in the incarnation of the Word in Jesus Christ, turns the idea of divinization upside-down. Previously, in a pagan context it designated the program of the highest enterprise a human being could engage in. For Christianity, it is the result of the grace of God.

The formulation "like a god" is ancient. But it can simply express a situation that is already acquired, as when Xenophon's Socrates explains that vis-à-vis the other animals, human beings lead a life of gods, an idea that Aristotle took up: despite all that his life contains of suffering and harshness, with respect to the other beings man seems to be a god.[8]

The resemblance to a god, however, does not take on all its meaning except where it appears as still to be attained. In Egypt, it is found in connection with the deceased who arrives without stain in the other world.[9] Divinization is connected with the transformation wrought by death. The defunct becomes Osiris and henceforth bears, in addition to his own name, that of the god. On the other hand, one encounters (at least once) the idea according to which "the heart of man is itself his god," where "heart" could designate what we would call the conscience. But the formulation shows up on a sarcophagus of the Ptolemaic period, and I suspect the influence of the famous *ēthos anthrōpō daimōn* of Heraclitus.[10] From the time of the Peloponnesian War, certain Greek cities rendered a cult to living people. The first was Lysander at Samos; then the phenomenon was generalized during the Hellenistic period. The Greeks did not distinguish clearly between worship and homage. The Roman rite of the apotheosis of the deceased emperors sanctioned the passage of the prince of this lower world into the company of the gods. While it was solemnly celebrated, was it taken seriously? Seneca's *Apocolocyntosis of the Emperor Claudius* and the last words of Vespasian ("Behold! I become a god!") cause one to doubt. And if the cult of the emperors was official, it does not seem to have given rise to a personal piety: we possess no votive offering dedicated to a divinized emperor. It was in this context that the term "superhuman" appeared, in Lucian; but barely has he recalled the more-than-human splendor of the tyrant when Lucian describes him in his misery in Hades.[11] According to Hippocrates, the philosophical doctor is "similar to the gods." According to Epicurus, the sage, sheltered from the fear of death, lives like a god among men, and for Epictetus, virtue divinizes.[12]

What distinguishes the different versions of the idea of divinization is the character of the divine in which man participates. In a doubtful Platonic dialogue, a character invokes the dream of all human beings: to exercise a universal tyranny, to even become a god, a wish that Nietzsche hoped would return. In another dialogue, this one authentic, Plato speaks of an "assimilation to God" by the practice of the virtues. But other dialogues portray that this is achieved by knowledge and the contemplation of the truth.[13] The notion of the divinity this assimilation implies remains rather fluid. It was in this vague sense that Boethius wrote: "Whoever attains beatitude is a god." Divinization can be realized by the intellect. Once the Aristotelian God was conceived as Intellect, the conjunction of the intellect of a human being with the Agent Intellect can pass for divinization. It is in this sense that Averroës cites Themistius: thanks to intellectual knowledge, man becomes similar to God. Albert the Great has analogous formulations, which in large part he draws from the Arabs, above all Averroës.[14] The word "divinization," however, is not encountered until the extreme end of pagan philosophy, in Damascius. It remained suspect for Islam, which knows the word *ta'alluh*, but, while many words designating God can be uttered of creatures, Islam reserves the name "Allah" to God alone.[15]

God seeks to assimilate to himself the one among his creatures who is capable of divinization. Consequently, the human being who seeks to become divinized displays an entirely legitimate ambition. It is not a matter of interpreting the "you shall become as gods" of the Serpent (Gen. 3:5) as the mark of an excessive hubris and arguing to the contrary for a wise moderation, a point that is often made.[16] What is in question is not the goal, but the means of arriving. And more profoundly, it is the model of the divine that one aims to attain. The temptation consists in making a perverse model and conducting oneself in accordance with it. One constructs it by separating omnipotence from the paternity of God, omnipotence being but a modality of the latter, in order to retain omnipotence as an object of imitation; here one recognizes the fantasy of the child who, though entirely dependent, believes his parents are at his service.

Augustine found the essence of sin not in the imitation of God as such, which is the noblest of ends, but in "perverse imitation." Assimilation to God transpires by love and represents a particular case, though still quite remarkable, of the law according to which one becomes what one loves: "You love the earth? You will be earth. You love God? . . . You will be God."[17]

It is in this context that the patristic idea of "divinization" can be understood. It derives its meaning from the new model of the divine put in circulation by the incarnation. The imitation of a crucified God does not produce the same effects as the imitation of a mythological Zeus or a god of the philosophers. According to the central formulation expressing it: "God became man, so that man could become god." Man was already divinized by grace in the hypostatic union achieved in Christ: according to the dogma of Chalcedon, human nature is brought together with the divine nature in the unity of a single person. If the idea of divinization is present as early as Athanasius, the technical term that expressed it did not appear until the beginning of the sixth century with Dionysius the Areopagite, who defines it in Platonic and Plotinian terms: "Assimilation to God and union with him, to the extent possible."[18] Maximus the Confessor (d. 661) posed the principal concepts: "According to nature, nothing of what has come to be is a factor of divinization. . . . By nature, to gratify the existents, each according to their rank, with divinization, is the sole prerogative of divine grace which enlightens nature by means of a light that surpasses nature and which, according to the transcendence of the glory, is placed above the limits proper [to the existents]." Only the power of God can divinize: "Divinization is not among those things whose nature is to occur among us, because it does not depend upon us. . . . As a consequence, divinization is not an action of a power that is in us; it is something for which we do not naturally possess the capacity. It comes solely from the divine power. It is not a reward for just works given to the saints, but a demonstration of the generosity of the Creator. He gives to those in love with beautiful things, to be by convention what He is by nature." Divinization takes place by charity: "Nothing is more deiform, more similar to the mystery, more capable of raising men to divinization. . . . It makes us, who were men, gods. . . . God made us so that we could become participants of the divine nature, participants of his eternity, and we will show ourselves similar to him according to divinization by grace."[19] For the theology of the still-undivided church, divinization is a legitimate goal, one willed by God. It is the object of a commandment of God; it is not man who requires it, but God who orders it. Thus St. Basil has this magnificent phrase: "I cannot prostrate myself before a creature, I who find myself to be a creature of God, and *who received the order to be God.*"[20]

Divinization causes one to leave the sphere of the human. To express it, Dante invented the astonishing verb *transumanar*.[21] But far from being something Promethean, it is a process whereby, by obedience to God, one must be lifted to him who began by making himself obedient to the point of descending lower than all (Phil. 2:8). Alain de Lille called "divine man" the man that God had ornamented with the virtues, and Jean Tauler sees in humility the divinizing force.[22] Still in the sixteenth century, Giulio Camillo (Delminio) writes a little treatise on divinization for his daughter, larded with Scripture references, but also with references to Hermes Trismegistus and even more to the Zohar, making sure to explain why he departs from modern theology, as well as from the Aristotelian philosophy upon which it is based, for the sake of a simple faith in the words of the prophets. He specifies: "divinize" means "render divine," or "united to God." He presents a process in five stages: humility, abstinence, separation from the world, separation from oneself or mortification, and finally the ascent of oneself to the divine image that is in us.[23] It is in an entirely different perspective that Luther unmasks in man a natural incapacity to want God to be God and a desire to want to be God.[24] Russian theological and philosophical thought inherited this notion, borrowed perhaps from the Greek fathers, beginning with Gregory Skovoroda (d. 1794). Thinkers such as Vladimir Soloviev put it at the center of their vision of the world, not without balancing it with a meditation on the union of the divine and human natures ("theandrism") realized in Jesus Christ.[25]

Working on Oneself

Why want to dominate nature, rather than rise on the scale of beings, and perhaps arrive at God, by a self-mastery that is purely internal? The latter is what the sages of antiquity did, Stoic as well as Epicurean, each in his particular manner. Why then can the mastery of self no longer realize itself independently of the mastery of external nature? For the ancients, the latter was not what opposes man, who then must confront it. The program of the ancient philosophers could be formulated in a purely immanent manner. For the Epicureans, nature is totally foreign to man in what he has that is specifically human; but at the same time man is totally natural, made of the same atoms as the other things. For the Stoics, nature is divine and beneficent. At the head of its benefits is the existence of man.

But the idea of domination does not necessarily operate on an external object. It can very well apply first of all to the human subject himself. And in a double sense: the object of mastery can be the soul, in which case there is a perfect reflexivity. It can also be the body, as an intermediate zone, neither totally interior nor totally external. This is why the mastery of the body can be the proof of the soul's mastery over itself or the first beginnings of a domination extended to the entirely of the external.

For Plato in any case, the man whose rule is to be assured is above all "the little man" who represents the intellect. Lodged within the empirical man who is compared to a hybrid monster, he must be the strongest of three and dominate the lion (*thymos*) and the polymorphous beast (desires) with which he cohabits.[26] This would be impossible if the subject did not possess a certain spontaneity or freedom. The Greek sources provide a model. Plato had defined the soul as movement moving itself. Knowledge is a sort of dominion over that which one knows. Aristotle interprets the expression of Anaxagoras, "the intellect rules," as signifying that it knows. It can do so because it doesn't mix with any of the objects of its knowledge. For Marcus Aurelius, the "directive faculty" is capable of making all things appear as it wishes, and, according to Plotinus, the One has the capacity to make itself whatever it wishes.[27]

A father of the church like St. Gregory of Nyssa, with a smattering of Platonism, combines these models of spontaneity in a bold image: man is his own father (we would say: "child of his own deeds"). He is such because his moral conduct causes him to rise or fall on the scale of beings, to become an angel or a beast.[28] But everything takes place in the inner stage, and it is out of the question to leave that stage for the sake of some dream of mastery without. A fragment of Hermes Trismegistus cited by an alchemist expressed this by way of a critique of magic: "It is unnecessary for the spiritual man, he who has learned to know himself, to correct anything by magic, even if that appears to be good, nor that he do violence to Necessity, but that he let it act according to its nature and decree; let him make progress solely by the search for himself . . . and let him allow fatality to treat the clay that belongs to him as it will, that is to say, his body."[29]

The mastery of the body is a point of departure for the mastery of nature. From forever, the first technology is the body, the anthropological subject analyzed by Marcel Mauss in a famous lecture. The body, received from nature and continuing to attest its presence in us, is itself formed by what Mauss calls "techniques." From them it receives symbolic gestures, whose meaning varies from culture to culture. Thus the gesture of indicating heaven by raising one's finger, which is religious in Russia (above sits a Judge who sees all), is secularized in Germany (beware of the cudgel!).[30] Now, our body, which "belongs to us," still largely escapes our control. St. Augustine attributed this mutiny to the consequences of the sin by which Adam disobeyed God. Only a few exceptional individuals have a perfect mastery of their body. Augustine cites some, and one is not surprised to find among this elite one of Joseph Pujol's ancestors, who, circa 1900, was well known on music hall stages.[31]

Asceticism, pagan and Christian, can push the disdain of the body to the extreme. Its Christian version raises the mastery of self to the ideal. But self-mastery is not the ultimate goal. Rather, it aims at allowing the integral gift of self in charity. The work on external nature in monastic life does not have the mastery of nature as its goal. Labor itself is an ascetic exercise. The nature to be dominated is, by this detour, the will of the monk.[32]

As the baseline of this, Buddhism is perhaps the best example of the attitude that renounces modifying the external world. The Romantic critique of Europe to the advantage of the "Orient" developed the theme. A tale by Gobineau constitutes one of the first examples: a dervish proves to the narrator that he perfectly controls his body by stopping his pulse, then by placing his finger in a brazer without being burned; he then displays his mastery of matter by changing lead to gold. The narrator concludes: "This poor devil who had nothing . . . possessed the world." But it is not the conquest of the external world that interests him.[33]

The Model of Mastery

The ancient human ideal is that of self-mastery. In the first place, this is a reflection of the social circumstance, which admitted slavery as self-evident and characterized the free person as a master. Domination is first of all that of a master (*dominus*) of the household (*domus*) over the animals which, as the saying goes, he "domesticates," then over his slaves, his "servants" or, again, his "domestics."[34] This situation produced its own image. What has come down to us from the ancient world is what it left to us, either by writing or in plastic form, of free persons. The actual slaves are mute, and those that comedy presents are caricatures.

However, mastery is above all self-mastery.[35] For the slave is deemed to be the one who is not capable of mastering himself, and who therefore must suffer an external mastery, who even needs one. This is how Aristotle understood it, and much later, in an entirely different context, Locke, then Hegel.[36] Ancient self-mastery, however, in this different from the modern version, does not imply domination over external nature. Even more, it renders it otiose. On the economic plane, the abundance of cheap servile labor dispenses the free person from the obligation of seeking the assistance of mechanical slaves. This perhaps explains why antiquity never saw in natural forces like steam anything other than an amusement and never sought to mechanize production.[37] On the other hand, the one who masters himself as he ought to no longer needs anything external. The disappearance of slavery is the condition that permitted the birth of mechanization. It is also what rendered conceivable a dominion exercising itself over something other than humans. Freed from its link to the human, domination can henceforth bear upon "nature" in general.

Ancient mastery does not prefigure the modern project. Why? Because far from positing himself on his own, the ancient subject of self-mastery begins by receiving himself from elsewhere. Questioned about the origin of man and his humanity, the anthropology of the classical philosophers responds with the idea of nature, of which man is the product. It does not oppose itself, however, to artifice or to the work of self-formation. Thus Aristotle observes, as self-evident, that politics does not manufacture human beings, but receives them from nature. The Stoics were more nuanced: man is sketched by nature, and he then is to be perfected by his work on himself. But this work is not at all disconnected from the instincts that are already provided by nature.[38] Concerning this work on oneself, Plotinus provided a splendid image—one, however, that has been often misunderstood: to sculpt one's own statute.[39] It has nothing to do with an idiosyncratic design. The statue very much does belong "to us," in that the task of sculpting it falls upon us alone; but it is not us that it ought to represent, but rather the gods, to whom we ought to liken ourselves. In this last example, therefore, neither the origin nor the goal of mastery is in man's power.

This model was continued until the dawn of modern times, even to the period when the modern project was put in place. There is a beautiful example in the first work whose title expresses the idea of a kingdom of man, *The Monarchie of Man*, by Sir John Eliot (1590–1632). It locates itself in the traditional conception of self-control that, according to Aristotle, exercises a royal authority and not a despotic one. This monarchy is that of man over himself, by which he imitates the monarchy of God over the universe. It is realized when the inferior parts of man are submitted to the intellect.[40]

4

Metaphorical Dominations

I just evoked the cases in which a single element of the modern project was put in place, but disconnected from the others, in such a way that the system could not "take." In the phenomena I now will examine, all the elements are brought together, and the project of domination is freed from the mere static affirmation of superiority. But it remains at a metaphorical level and does not imply a real intervention in material nature.

Construction

Even before the project of a concrete domination of nature, the idea of an intellectual domination appeared with the idea of construction, which is going to become the dominant paradigm of modern knowledge.[1] From its geometric origins, it will extend to all the products of the imagination.

The ancients knew the procedures of demonstrating by the construction of figures. But in them they only saw the means of putting into evidence properties that preexisted in the nature of mathematical objects, by moving them from potency to act.[2] It was in his treatise on potency and act that Aristotle wrote that it is "by making"—in this context, by tracing lines that go beyond the figure whose properties one wants to demonstrate—that geometers "know."[3] The passage, however, did not particularly attract Averroës, Thomas Aquinas, Michael of Ephesus (Pseudo-Alexander), or Agostino Nifo.[4] At the end of the sixteenth century, the Jesuit Pedro Fonseca generalized and included in the rule posed by Aristotle the construction of concrete objects, such as a house, and noted that it remains true even if the architect had begun by constructing it in his imagination. On the other hand, he did not consider what mathematics has that is distinctive.[5]

The idea of creative construction appeared with the modern age. Thus with Hobbes, for whom those arts alone are demonstrable whose construction remains in the power of the artist himself, who in that way only deduces the consequences of his own operation.[6] Kant underlines the privilege of mathematics, by which man "becomes as it were master of nature." He wishes to distinguish what mathematics can do and what philosophy can only dream of: construct its concepts. Several times Kant explains that we only truly understand what we are capable of making.[7] This capacity renders us like to God. This is what Jerome Cardan and, later, Salomon Maimon, inspired by Kant, will say, who see in mathematical activity an analogue to divine creation.[8]

In the next century, Richard Dedekind will note, again apropos to numbers: "We are of a divine race and doubtless possess the power to create not only in the material domain (railroads, telegraphs), but especially in intellectual matters."[9] This is an extreme formulation of a much older idea according to which, in certain domains, our knowledge is distinguished from God's only by quantity. All the thinkers of the classical age from Galileo to Spinoza, with the notable exception of Descartes, thought so. Kepler foresaw the risk of excess and parried it by means of a distinction: "Only fools fear that we will make a god of man; because the designs of God are impenetrable, but not his material works."[10]

The imagination is the faculty of fabricating what does not exist in external reality. The idea that everything is subject to this faculty develops gradually. Proclus is perhaps the first "modern" in that he considers the imagination as capable of forming, even creating, forms. But that the human mind is the "generator of artificial forms" is found for the first time in John Scotus Eriugena (810–ca. 877), then reappears in the twelfth century with an anonymous figure of the School of Chartres.[11] Nicholas of Cusa cites Hermes Trismegistus affirming that man is a second god, and proves it by showing that man is the creator of beings of reason (*entia rationis*) and artificial forms; the human intellect is the likeness of the divine intellect. Paracelsus gives to the "imagination" an etymology worthy of the *Cratylus*: the magical production of an image. God himself creates by imagining, and, for Jerome Cardan, "the science of the mind that makes things is almost the thing itself."[12]

Vico expresses his central intuition by affirming that we only know what we make: "The true and the made are convertible," and "we demonstrate geometric [truths] because we make them; if we could demonstrate physical [truths], we would make them." The formulation is repeated by Paul Valéry: "Perhaps one only understands well what one has invented."[13] Marx makes of imaginary construction the foundation of an anthropology. For him, the capacity to construct the object in one's head before constructing it in concrete reality is what ensures the superiority of the worst of architects to the best of bees.[14]

Fictions

Thanks to the faculty of imagination, reality sees itself constrained to enlarge its boundaries to admit entities that are not in nature, but which will prepare concrete action on it. These are found in the domain of law, then of art.

The legal fiction represents the first example of a creation of entities that are fictive but which are susceptible of exercising their influence on very real things.[15] It is thus that law transforms groups into subjects capable of acting, groups that thereby become "corporations."

The sovereignty of the jurist gives him a power to make and unmake that is similar to the power of God, who creates something from nothing, especially when the jurist is at the service of the pope, and a fortiori when he is the pope himself. It is in this context that for the first time one encounters extreme formulations of the unlimited power that the "*sovereign pontiff*" (which is a completely nonobvious translation of the Latin *summus pontifex*) would have to create or annihilate whatever he wants, formulations later taken up by kings on their own account.[16] Even if claims that are so extreme should be understood as arguments in a negotiation with the civil power or as thought-experiments of pure theory, they enlarged the field of the thinkable and the sayable. In that way, law furnished more than a metaphor. The modern project of a domination of nature presupposes a certain representation of nature and the place that one occupies in it, but also a specific model of what it is to dominate in general. This model had to be elaborated within the human domain, in the relations between human beings, before being applied externally, to the relations between man and what is not-man. In other words, the rule of man over nature presupposes a theory of the monarchy, the theory that permitted the absolute monarchy of the classical age. It could not be conceived as a "sovereignty" except after a previous juridical mutation which culminated in the general concept of sovereignty, such as was formulated for the first time by Jean Bodin in 1576.[17]

The idea of fiction did not take on an aesthetic value except in a second phase. It redeems what the fiction of artists has of the deceptive. Dante sees in allegory a "beautiful lie." In the nineteenth century, Leopardi spoke of lie in a positive sense, seeing in it the essence of his work as a poet.[18] The passage of the idea of fiction from the domain of law to that of art comes from the reflection of Renaissance writers. The concepts that allowed the artists of the period to theorize about their practice came from law. Thus, the Aristotelian formula "to imitate nature" was first a rule proposed to the jurist who was bound not to enact dispositions contrary to nature. For example, the child being necessarily younger than his parents, it would be absurd to adopt persons older than oneself. The idea of sovereignty passed from the legislator to the poet, then to the artist in general. The idea of inspiration, which implies a direct access to the divine, was first of all invoked by the legislator, who thus exempted himself from all superior jurisdiction. It then fell to the artist, who pled his "genius" in order to escape from moral judgment and, already, from the courts.[19] The case of Benvenuto Cellini, a repeat murderer, is particularly interesting, both in itself and because it provided the historiography of the nineteenth century with a typical example of "the big cat of the Italian Renaissance." Diderot noted the proximity of the artist and the criminal: both defy rules, love power and glory, and refuse the tranquil life of the civilized man.[20] The nephew of Rameau that he depicts is a failed example of this attitude and is the ancestor of the "bohemian" of the following century. The idea that the "creator" is above "morality," itself reduced to the epithet "bourgeois," is abundantly represented from the nineteenth century on. It is given a social dimension in the antagonism between the "bohemian" and the "philistine." It found its titles of nobility among authors like Oscar Wilde, and its concrete realization in the fine painter and dubious man Picasso. In any case, it is striking to recall that this maxim of transgression was formed in the very milieu of those whose function was to defend the law.

Invention

Mathematics and law thus provide us with the model of the sovereign subject. But in these cases the objects produced are only beings of reason. One therefore must move to the examination of the artistic domain, in which the idea of man as the creator of sensible realities appeared for the first time.

The idea of a human spontaneity revealed in the practice of the arts had been preceded by a previous step. The dominant model of artistic activity had been the imitation of nature.[21] However, an element of mastery already had announced itself, with the idea that human art can represent natural realities with perfect exactitude and, therefore, could equal creative nature or the divine Demiurge. Realism in the arts of representation, even the care to adhere perfectly to the real by way of trompe l'oeil, is an ancient ideal. Several anecdotes illustrate it, such as the one, often repeated since Pliny, of the birds coming to peck at the grapes painted by Zeuxis.[22] The return of this ideal at the Renaissance had several dimensions: it witnesses to a will to totally control the visible; it provided to sovereigns dreaming of absolute dominion a convincing metaphor; it prepares the scientific project of giving an account of the entirety of reality.[23] It is the same with the exhaustive enumerations (or desired to be such) by which the real is inserted in the meshes of a classificatory scheme deemed to have nothing escape it. Or again, with maps presented as the mirror of the world. Or, finally, the cabinets of curiosities where one no longer finds mere representations, but rather a series of objects that one is to contemplate. The program of such cabinets was formulated in 1594 in the "discourse of the second counselor, recommending the study of philosophy," attributed to Francis Bacon. One should establish a library, a botanical garden, a cabinet of curiosities, a laboratory of alchemy, with each containing collections as complete as possible.[24]

To characterize an artist, even a fashion designer or a stylist, as a "creator," which today is such a banality that no one recognizes its implausible pretentiousness, had already become hackneyed in the nineteenth century, for example in Baudelaire: "The artist . . . dominates the model like the creator, creation."[25] Such an assimilation, however, did not go without saying, so yawning did the chasm seem between divine and human art. In antiquity, Dion of Prusa had said that no mortal artist can compare to Zeus, responding to comparisons ventured by Democritus or Macrobius. The father of the church Theodorus of Mopsuestia had recalled that to create from nothing is proper to God and cannot be the work of man. In the Middle Ages, Thomas Aquinas and Dante had reiterated the observation, and they had followers up until the century that invented aesthetics.[26] Even in the nineteenth century, it was the critics who spoke of "creation"; the real artists were more circumspect. Thus, Delacroix was very conscious of the metaphorical character of the expression: what is called creation "is only a particular way for each to view, coordinate, and render nature." A little while earlier, Alessandro Manzoni rejected the "disastrous word, create." The idea is not the object of an impossible creation, but of a rediscovery. Mallarmé found the right phrase: "Nature occurred, no one will add to it."[27]

The invention of creativity, unknown in antiquity and the Middle Ages, is one of the great conquests of the Renaissance, which completed its concrete artistic achievements with a theoretical reflection. It broke with the model of divine creation described in the *Timaeus*, according to which the Demiurge copies the ideas.[28] The valorization of the status of art also served to legitimate the place of the artist in society, by liberating him from the servile status of artisan, to introduce him into the arts that are worthy of being exercised by free persons and that are therefore called "the liberal arts."

To exalt art, one first of all had to get rid of its servile status as imitation, as Plato had defined it at the end of the *Republic*. Plotinus had responded to him by going back from the nature brought into being to the nature that brings into being: the artist does not copy things, but goes back to the "reasons" according to which they have been produced. His response was widely accepted and disseminated, especially since these "reasons" could be assimilated to the "ideas" that, according to an interpretation going back to Albinus, are found in the divine understanding. The artist thus attained the status of an imitator of God (although not at all as his rival in the sense of nineteenth-century Prometheanism). Imitation did not oppose itself to creation; on the contrary, in Petrarch, then Ficino and Pico della Mirandola, creative imitation was located in the movement of divine kenosis and manifestation. Far from being a gesture of rebellion, it fulfilled a task entrusted by the Creator.[29]

The first to have applied the term "create" to art was Cristoforo Landino, inspired by his friend Marsilio Ficino (1461): the *poiein* of the poet is intermediary between *create*, which is unique to God, and *make*, involving matter and a form; the fiction of the poet does not create, because he cannot make it from nothing, but "he escapes from mere making and comes close to creating."[30] The artists of the sixteenth century widely echoed him. Thus Leonardo da Vinci: "The divine character of the painter's knowledge makes it that his spirit is transformed into a likeness of the divine spirit, because with a sovereign power he proceeds to the creation of various essences." It is interesting that Leonardo considers the ability to represent as a species of mastery. This is even clearer in a passage where he compares painting and poetry, to the advantage of the former: "If the painter wants to see the beauties with which he is enamored, he is lord and can engender them; if he wants to see monstrous things in order to be frightened, or that are buffoonish and ridiculous, or truly worthy of pity, he is their lord and god." According to Dürer, the artist has the power because he "creates a new creature in his heart," an affirmation, however, that follows recalling the impotence of human power vis-à-vis divine creation.[31] The idea was taken up in the Anglo-Saxon world by Shaftesbury, who compared the authentic poet to Prometheus.[32] Curiously, if the passage had little influence in England, it was very much read in Germany by the young writers of *Sturm und Drang*, beginning with Goethe. Romanticism represented the apogee of this tendency. On one hand, it valorized the creative will of the artist; on the other, it denied that reality presents a preexisting structure, or sought to destroy it by its own practice.[33]

The activities that we now call "the arts" only distinguished themselves gradually from crafts. Craft, as the production of artifacts, was only introduced rather late into the domain of that by which man conducts himself as God. Thus, with Vico: as God is the artisan of nature, man is the god of artifacts.[34] The idea of the "creative" character of art had many long-term consequences. First, the rejection of the notion of a model, with so-called "abstract" art, not that the visible is uninteresting, or because art had exhausted its expressive possibilities, but because the presence of an external model limits the creative capacities of the subject. A second consequence is the insistence on the "originality" of the artist, a word that itself saw an inflation. Each artist must distinguish himself as much as possible from his predecessors and claim a prickly independence from every influence. Each artist must be the founder of a school or a tendency. Finally, the idea of creation leads to the abandonment of the very notion of a work, for the sake of the "creativity" of the artist, even his personal display: "The work of art is the occasion for the artist to present himself as artist. . . . The author *retains* the work at the same time that he produces it." The creative deed, even the "artistic temperament," becomes the essential. The genius is no longer he who creates, but he who could create. At the extreme, the artist is less the one who produces work than the one who leads "the life of an artist," thus realizing the ideal of "the artist without a work."[35]

5

The New Lord of Creation

The singularity of man allows itself to be conceived, we just saw, in two ways. On the one hand, it can be viewed statically, as a superiority possessed from the beginning, because tied to his very nature (paganism) or because restored by the divine work of salvation (Christianity); it therefore cannot be the object of a conquest, because, quite simply, it has no need, or no longer needs, to be conquered. Or the singularity of man can be dynamic, understood as a historical process by which man takes control of what is not him. The first way is premodern, the second way characterizes modernity.

The New Concept of Human Dignity

The idea of the domination of nature appeared several centuries before the concrete conditions of its realization, which will not appear until the first industrial revolution. One therefore can ask what allowed for the passage from the first to the second of these two ways of conceiving human singularity. They do have a point in common: they belong to the order of being. On the other hand, the passage from one to the other pertains to ought-to be. It is ensured by the idea of the *dignity* of man, which represents a middle term between being and ought-to be. Dignity cannot be acquired, but on the contrary is presupposed to be present in an inalienable way; it has no meaning other than the requirement of respecting what too often in fact is violated. A dignity immune from all assault would no longer be a dignity, but a *majesty*. Dignity thus implies a tendency to a realization that cashes out, for the one who is aware of it, in a *duty*. As a consequence, it is radically distinct from the different ways of conceiving human superiority known to pagan antiquity.

The Italian historian Eugenio Garin has shown how Renaissance humanism displaced the idea of human dignity from contemplation to action, envisaged as production, "replacing the relationship between theory and practice by that between theory and poetics." Dignity is henceforth located less in the possibility of contemplation than in the liberty to produce.[1] Thus the Renaissance, and more precisely the fifteenth century, effects an interesting change in the idea of human dignity: it is connected with the mastery of external nature, which is simultaneously its expression and its condition. Two traditional ideas are combined into a new idea. The first is the mutability of man, a Proteus capable of deciding for himself what he will be. It is at least as old as the concluding myth of the *Republic* concerning the choice of lives, and it persisted among ecclesiastical writers: for Gregory of Nyssa, man can raise himself to the rank of angels or fall to that of demons. In the exordium of his discourse that will later be entitled *On the Dignity of Man* (1486), Pico della Mirandola reprised this commonplace.[2] The second idea is the technical inventiveness of man, of which we have seen several examples.

The two ideas, however, remained separated. The human capacity of transformation only obtained on the vertical axis where rational creatures were ranged in tiers, and man's relation to nature was left to the side. On the other hand, the human capacity to change nature merely translated into concrete reality a superiority already possessed and which had no need of proving itself. It rested on the creation of man by God. To be sure, created by God in his image, which man cannot lose entirely, man certainly had to restore the lost resemblance. But he did so more by cooperating with grace than by working on nature. The combination of the two ideas was prefigured at the beginning of the twelfth century with Theophilus Presbyter and Rupert of Deutz, for whom the resemblance of man to his Creator is displayed in his technical ability. The combination was fully realized in the Renaissance and produced the idea according to which the self-determination of man should be verified by means of technical creativity.[3] It is by the transformation of nature that man takes full possession of his capacity to transform himself.

This observation obliges us to reformulate the question of who is responsible for the project of the conquest of nature. Too often, one is content to see here the consequences of human immoderation, a modern version of Greek *hubris*.[4] Hence come sermons from different sources and in different styles, but all in favor of the virtue of moderation, presupposing that the conquest of nature, the result of a free choice of man, could be imputed to him. Now, however, we see that the constellation put in place in the fifteenth century makes this conquest inevitable, once one has defined an anthropology that necessarily presupposes this conquest.

The Sources

This setting of the stage at the time of the Renaissance was the consequence of two principles posed much earlier, which then slowly entered the public mind, or were rediscovered after a long period of being forgotten: a rehabilitation of work and a new representation of the divine.

Christianity had rehabilitated work in the face of the aristocratic ideal of leisure. Paul took pride in working with his hands in order not to be a burden to anyone (1 Thess. 2:9). The fathers of the church insisted on the necessity of not being a burden to others, hence earning one's livelihood. For example, Augustine did so in his little treatise on the activity of monks. Work, however, is not valorized as a transformation of nature, but rather as a labor on oneself: the one who works finds the means of controlling his passions. The *ora* (pray) and *labora* (work) that summarizes the Holy Rule of St. Benedict is in fact *audi* (listen), *ora et labora*, in which hearkening to the God, who speaks in nature and in his book, takes precedence over the two responses that hearkening determines, prayer and work. Work, and with it the entire task of transforming the earth, are placed on the foundation of a "Christian *entente* with the visible" which is profoundly rooted in the biblical vision of the world.[5]

An analogous valorization is found in Islam. The "Sincere Brethren" of Basra see in human work an imitation of the divine Worker: "Excellence in every art is the imitation of the Wise Artisan who is the Creator." Human work is placed in a series of activities: of the Creator, the universal Soul, Nature, and finally man. In the final analysis, human work reproduces the activity of the universal Soul. The context of these declarations is interesting. First of all, it perhaps was social, if the "Sincere Brethren" were Ismailians. They recruited primarily among artisans, whose activity thus received a new dignity. Moreover, for the first time the exaltation of human work was connected with an enterprise of an innovative, even "revolutionary," character, as will be the case a millennium later in the *Encyclopedia*. Finally, the very idea of an encyclopedia having for its purpose propaganda, which some think is unique to Bayle or Diderot, was also prefigured.[6]

Hermes Trismegistus was rediscovered in Florentine Neoplatonism, after the translation of the first fourteen treatises by Marsilio Ficino (1472).

Then a "hermetic window" opened for Europe, between the Latin translation of the Corpus and the demonstration by Isaac Casaubon of its inauthenticity (1614), which nonetheless did not put a complete stop to its influence. The *Asclepius*, on the other hand, already translated in the fourth century—different, in this, from the other texts of the Corpus, which were not translated into Latin until the fifteenth century—was known in the patristic period, for example by Lactantius and St. Augustine, and in the Middle Ages from the twelfth century; it is cited by Nicholas of Cusa in 1458.[7] While we only have fragments, its Greek original no doubt dates from the third century. The way in which "Hermes" conceives of the dignity of man has nothing original to it. But it adds an interesting nuance concerning his relationship to inferior realities. God created man, "who ought to imitate both his reason and the care that he takes of things." Man disdains the earth to the extent that it is one of his parts—that is, his body; but "he takes care of the earth" as exterior to him. He must not only "admire and adore the heavenly things" but also "take care of terrestrial things and govern them." The passage specifies, in an unusual way, that this should be accomplished by the arts and crafts: "This terrestrial part of the world is maintained by the knowledge and practice of the arts and sciences that God has willed the world cannot do without in order to be perfect."[8]

An important consequence follows: one must not read the double nature of man, and the presence of a body along with the soul, in a purely negative light. The corporeal nature of man is also what allows him to be attuned to the care of the inferior elements. In this way his mortal nature, far from constituting a privation, represents a gain. According to a striking phrase, man is "augmented with mortality." In this way he is the governor of the world. It is by the care that man takes of it that he becomes the ornament of the world, the second image of God after the world. Man can preserve, and even enhance, the beauty of the world. This is a task received, and man must fulfill it by imitating the action of the superior God who entrusted him with it. The care that man takes of the world is not at all a transgression; on the contrary, it represents a way for him to be in accord with the divine will.[9]

The idea of divinization then changes meaning. Everything depends on the type of divinity one aims to imitate. The Renaissance is also the period when one recommenced representing the pagan gods, who had never been totally forgotten, but who became favorite themes of poets and artists. The Enlightenment has also been understood, at least in part, as a return to paganism.[10] This revival made possible a change in the model of the divine. A crucified God lends himself less easily to becoming the support of omnipotence than a Jupiter capable of moving everything by raising his eyebrow or a Mercury whose winged sandals allowed him to arrive in an instant. On Olympus, the fantasies of omnipotence found abundant material on which to nourish themselves. In a parallel way, one sees a tendency to put man and his interests at the center, even when God is present. Thus Ramon Sibiuda, the Raymond Sebond of Montaigne, in a work finished in 1436, articulated a natural theology that proposed "to found everything on man."[11] The guiding question then becomes whether an article of faith is good for man, in which case it should be admitted.

The Renaissance Interpretation of Dignity as a Reign

In the Italian Renaissance from the fifteenth century on, human dignity was the subject of numerous treatises. It began to include the idea of domination. What was new was not the idea of the dignity of man, which, as we have seen, was ancient, patristic, and also quite medieval.[12] If Lothar of Segni had collected into a treatise all the commonplaces on the misery of the human condition, it was in order to announce a second volume on the grandeur of man; however, having become Pope Innocent III, he did not have the leisure to compose it.[13] On the other hand, what *was* new was the rapprochement between the idea of the nobility of man and the capacity to transform nature by work. For antiquity, work was the contrary of social nobility, the sad privilege of slaves; at the Renaissance, however, it became the sign of the ontological nobility of man.

The most important of the treatises on the dignity of man is doubtless that of Gianozzo Manetti, composed in 1452–53 at the request of King Alphonse of Aragon. It was a response to a short text by Bartolomeo Facio, which was written toward 1447 at the suggestion of the Benedictine Antonio de Barga and was the first of these treatises, at least by date.[14] Facio's was not a particularly well-composed literary work: it very quickly passed over the announced theme in order to move on to the evocation of the ultimate destiny of man and the joys of paradise, described with great prolixity.

Manetti proceeds more systematically. His three initial books praise, successively, the qualities of the human body, the human soul, and the composite of the two; then a fourth and last book refutes the arguments of the denigrators of man, among whom it notably cites Innocent III. Manetti's description of the marvels of the body is based on Cicero and

Lactantius, whom he cites extensively. The privileged place of man is that of a king and emperor, titles that are symbolized by his upright posture.[15] The perspective is theological. It is God who established man this way, according to Genesis 1:28, by making him his image. It is God who created the world for man, then man at the end so that the animals could serve him. Man was created "master and possessor" of all that had been created before him. By his will, he can command all creation. The world is subject to him, not to the angels, who are at his service.[16] The dignity of man, however, ought not to lead to an excessive anthropocentrism: man is also the most sensual of animals, and Manetti also recalls that the awareness of his dignity leads to sins of pride.

Strictly speaking, dignity coincides with the concept of "original justice," which Manetti acknowledges comes from the theologians.[17] The perfect man is Adam come from the hands of the Creator, not the one we experience daily, degraded by the fall; it is from the fall, not from human nature, that human weaknesses come. Nothing better manifests the dignity of man than the incarnation of the Word of God in Jesus Christ, which, according to an idea taken from Duns Scotus, would have taken place even if Adam had not sinned.[18] Wisdom is the privilege of man, but it is nothing other than the knowledge of God. If the weaknesses of man are to be put to the account of the fall, his ultimate perfection on the other hand, which administers the coup de grace to all the lamentations concerning the miseries of the human condition, is reserved for the domain of eschatology: this perfection will be the resurrection of the body and the vision of God in paradise, a point on which Manetti is in full accord with Facio. In this life, what ensures happiness to the master of creation and his assimilation to God is not technology, but the practice of virtue.[19]

In his praise of the qualities that pertain to man, Manetti places all the products of human art: buildings, the works of painting and sculpture, the productions of language, and, finally, machines. As examples, he mentions developments in navigation and those in the plastic arts, naming Brunelleschi, Giotto, and Lorenzo Ghiberti. Taking up an idea of Lactantius, he recalls that while animals only make use of three of the elements, man has acquired the mastery of the fourth, fire.[20] But not that of the furnace, that of Vulcan or Prometheus, but rather the fifth celestial element, the "quintessence" of ancient cosmology. Not what transforms here-below, but what raises to heaven.

Not long after, Manetti's treatise elicited a response from Poggio Bracciolini (1455), which again took up the negative attitude of Innocent III, as well as his title. After that, the theme degenerated into a school exercise:

every self-respecting humanist had to write on human dignity, or if a treatise just appeared in its favor, against it. The controversy continued throughout the Italian fifteenth century.[21] The tradition of treatises on the dignity of man was not limited to Italy and to Latin, but crossed borders and passed into vulgar languages: in Spain with Fernán Pérez de Oliva (d. 1531), who combined the two theses by having them maintained by the protagonists of a dialogue, one supporting the common view of pagans, the other "what God had done for human beings"; then in France with Pierre Boaistuau (1558).[22] The literary form seems to have been lost during the classical age, even if, or perhaps because, the idea was found almost everywhere, although diffused.

In 1474, Marsilio Ficino composed a vast *Platonic Theology of the Immortality of Souls*. In addition to a series of supposedly demonstrative proofs, it also provided dialectical arguments destined to make this immortality at least plausible, as Avicenna had done. Among these, a number of signs indicate the grandeur of man and the superiority of his soul over the other principles that animate living things. In our context, Ficino explains that the dominion of the soul over the body, a trace of its immortality, is proven by technologies; the desire of man to become a god has for sign that the soul wants to do all things and to master them.[23] All the effort of our soul is to become god, a desire as natural to man as that of birds to fly. Man does not tolerate a superior, nor even an equal. The status of sovereignty without equal is God's alone. Man therefore aspires to a divine status.

Works of art manifest the genius of the artist. Reflection and wisdom shine in painting and architecture. In them, the spirit expresses and represents itself. In the areas where matter does not contain any productive principle, the artist is called "lord and teacher (instructor) of matter"; in those where matter contains this principle (e.g., in agriculture), he is "the one who awakens nature and serves it."[24]

The power of man is almost similar to the divine nature, because he directs himself. The arts are the proof. Their works are an amplification of his fecundity and a proof of his excellence. Man fulfills the role of God by inhabiting and cultivating all the elements. By the providence that he exercises over all the beings, animate and inanimate, he is like a god for them. Being capable of knowing the order of the heavens, their measures, the effects they produce, he could also fabricate heavens, like their Author did, granted that the relevant instruments and celestial matter had been put at his disposal. He manifests this capacity by making models of these movements.[25] In France, Charles of Bovelles, in his *Liber de sapiente* (1510), took up the fundamental intuitions of Ficino. Nature contains in a dispersed way all the powers of man, who must therefore seek throughout it what is his.[26]

A short time after, the global project of mastery appeared in full light, first of all in practical philosophy. Leone Battista Alberti (d. 1472) minimized the role of chance in the success or failure of a family, to the advantage of "industry."[27] Machiavelli characterized human action as a mode of mastery, of "subjecting" *fortuna*. He compared it to an impetuous river that one could contain by dikes.[28] The *fortuna* of the Italians is not the "chance" of Epicurus, the cause of the collection of atoms, nor the quasi-divinized Fate of Polybius, which directs history in an unforeseeable fashion. It designates the look the world assumes insofar as it escapes, definitively or—who knows?—provisionally, from the control of man, who ought to accommodate himself to it in order to draw the greatest profit from it. The idea of *fortuna* is perhaps the first representation of the *object* of mastery, even before it was called "nature." It is the intention of mastery that causes its proper object to appear in a distinctive light—that is, as what requires, but also admits, being mastered. *Fortuna* is the way things appear once they are seen in the optic of mastery.

Giordano Bruno, in one of his dialogues of 1584, has Jupiter say that the gods have given man intelligence and hands and have made him similar to them by granting him a power by which he triumphs over the other animals, that of "not only being able to operate according to nature and in an ordinary manner but also beyond and outside the laws of the former, so that he succeeds in maintaining himself as the god of the earth." This capacity makes him capable of "forming other natures." He thus expresses a liberty without which the resemblance of man to the gods would not exist. It is work that confers nobility upon man. If he remained in the idleness of the Golden Age, he would be no more virtuous than the animals, and perhaps less intelligent than they. It is the various occupations that distance man from animality and cause him to approach the divine being.[29]

This text reprises earlier ideas, ancient and Christian, philosophic and proverbial, but gives them a new inflection. The capacity to form other natures is found in Cicero. To place the divine image in human liberty is an idea found in St. Bernard and, before him, St. Gregory of Nyssa. To see in man a god of the earth comes from the *Asclepius*. However, the idea of a human action that *transgresses* the laws of nature is without doubt original. John Scotus Eriugena, then Nicholas of Cusa, had already associated man's nature as a second god with his capacity to form concepts.[30] But here, it is a matter of fabricating concrete realities. Campanella, in *On the Sense of Things and on Natural Magic* (1604), bases the eminence of man on the idea according to which art can profoundly change nature, thanks to the use of fire.[31]

The extension of the domain controllable by man beyond the limits of nature is not only encountered in the practical realm but also at the level of theory. The telescope extends the domain observable by man beyond the limits of his senses; it is the sign of an increase in power. Kepler sees in this invention, which he compares to a scepter, the proof that man is constituted king and lord of the works of God.[32]

6

Attempts and Temptations

The traditional models of human activity saw in it an extension of the activity of nature or of God. According to Aristotle, art was to add to nature and lead to its perfection. Nature, however, each time retained the upper hand, art being nothing but its servant.[1] Shakespeare's Polyxenes put it magnificently:

> Yet nature is made better by no mean
> But nature makes that mean. So over that art
> Which you say adds to nature is an art
> That nature makes.[2]

With modernity, to the contrary, other models of technical activity aim to substitute for nature, even to rival the Creator.

Thaumaturgic Man

Domination over nature can be demonstrated by the capacity to do miracles. However, to interpret them as a sign of *power* does not go without saying. Christianity sees in them a sign of salvation. The canonical Gospels therefore privilege the acts that symbolize salvation, such as healings, while the Apocryphal Gospels abundantly recount the terrifying deeds of the all-powerful brat of Nazareth. Islam too retains among the miracles of Jesus those that the canonical Gospels ignore, but which are spectacular and marvelous, such as the creation of clay birds by the child, which he animates and which then take flight.[3]

In Islam, authoritative teaching distinguishes the "miracles" which only prophets can do and "prodigies" which the "saints" have the ability to perform. The philosophers reflected on these prodigies. Avicenna provided a theory which, however, only made it into the Latin world in part, because of the lack of translations. He gives prodigies a psychological explanation based on a specific concept of the imagination. He cites as examples interventions in the external elements: to cause the earth to tremble or lightning to flash, to pray for rain and to be heard. That the imagination is capable of producing physiological effects is well known. But what the common run of men can do with their own bodies only, the prophet can do with external bodies.

> It happens that we imagine things and that we thus become the cause of natural things. . . . We can also imagine and produce without the mediation of any movement something that is generally realized by means of it. . . . We can sometimes imagine something and our body changes in accord with our humors and the imaginations of our soul. It is possible that the soul influences something other than its own body, in the same way it influences the latter. The soul can also influence another soul, as is recounted about Indian illusionists, if what is said is true.

This presupposes that there is no unbridgeable difference between the human body and the rest of nature. Avicenna takes up the traditional idea according to which "supremacy belongs to the nature of man. . . . He was made regent of the entirety of things found on the earth, their governor and their embellishment, while the other species of creatures were put at his disposal," as if there were "certain souls whose mastery surpasses the limits of their bodies and which, by their power, are a certain soul for the world."[4]

In Christian lands, Roger Bacon recalls the power of the word and all the miracles that it produces. He refers to Avicenna and his treatises on the animals, whose teaching he summarizes: "Nature obeys the thoughts of the soul . . . , of the sensitive soul, certainly, but even more so those of the intellective soul."[5] Albert the Great derives his theory of miracles from the *Asclepius*: man possesses in himself a divine intellect such that even matter models itself on its conceptions. We see that excellently endowed men can proceed to the transmutation of bodies. In that way, "in the part by which he is connected to the world, man is not subject to it, but appointed to be its governor." Like light, intelligence is everywhere. It is in this way that the souls of human beings of an elite encompass more than their bodies. External things obey them like the forms of the world, and such persons are said to work miracles.[6]

The theory of miracles is found in great detail in Marsilio Ficino, who devotes an entire chapter to it.[7] According to Agrippa of Nettesheim (d. 1535), it is the three theological virtues—faith, hope, and love—that allow man to transcend his nature towards the divine. Only the person thus transformed can know the causes of natural phenomena, foresee the future, and transform things. Closely following the humanist Reuchlin, Agrippa writes: "From this it comes that we who are in nature dominate nature, to the point where we command the elements, give rise to clouds, winds and rain, heal the sick and raise the dead."[8]

However, all these changes, as spectacular as they are, are not placed in a program of taking control of nature by man. The instance that orders them—that sponsors them, as it were—is less man than the agent intellect, insofar as it communicates itself to man. In that way, the true lord of nature is not man but the intellect in which he participates and which transmits to him the orders of God, or the forms according to which God creates things. It is not a matter of the conquest of nature; nature is subjected to man from the beginning by God, even more so if it relates to some superior human being. The advantage of the latter is displayed precisely by the fact that he has no need of constraining nature to obey him.

Magic as Domination over Nature

Miracles remain exceptional; God bestows them in singular cases and for reasons that escape us. Magic represents an effort to transform miracle-working into a permanent ability of man. To be sure, the origin of extraordinary phenomena remains outside and above man; but magic claims to be able to capture this source and put it at his service.

The modern enterprise of a conquest of nature has the same project as magic. As for history, it reconnects with late antiquity by bypassing the Christian Middle Ages. The latter was little tempted by magic, which the Bible forbids. Bishops and emperors, pagan then Christian, adopted the interdiction, the church and the state reserving the monopoly of the marvelous for themselves, the first also tolerating pagan magic in its less shocking, less terrifying, practices.[9] The chief argument of medieval theologians against magic was that it arrogates to itself powers that God has reserved to himself. While the Creator entrusted the earth and its inhabitants to man, he reserved for himself the control of winds, hail, and rain.

This is what Agobard of Lyon (d. 840) recalled in a small text against those who said they could cause it to rain . . . and for that purpose leveled a special tax. Outside of the saints whose prayer can obtain rain, the rule remains: God alone is the master of atmospheric phenomena; it is he who retains the keys to the treasures of the hail.[10]

Medieval magic hardly exceeds popular practices and was not considered an abominable crime. Thomas Aquinas reports one of the superstitions: a bowl of milk left on the window sill to feed *janae* (perhaps butterflies, believed to be disguised sorcerers); he simply shrugs and says nothing.[11] On the other hand, among the late Platonists, the presence of magic was massive. Plotinus accepted it in principle but was very reserved about its actual practice. For him the human soul has not entirely descended here-below; a part remains above, which allows it to save itself by the exercise of dialectic. For his successors, in contrast, the soul has completely fallen and cannot rise except with external assistance. Magic allows one to obtain such assistance and therefore becomes a legitimate and honorable activity. Iamblichus prefers magic to philosophy, because it is more efficacious. The emperor Julian declared himself a "fan" of Iamblichus in philosophy and of his homonym Julian the Chaldean in magic. Proclus opened wide the doors of philosophy to magic under the name of theurgy. Olympiodorus classifies philosophers according to their predilection for philosophy or for "the sacred art." Porphyry and Plotinus were among those with the former inclination; later thinkers like Iamblichus, Syrianus, and Proclus among the latter.[12] The goal of theurgy, however, was not to act horizontally to change nature, but rather to establish a vertical link, by causing a superior being to descend into a statue or by elevating man. Thus, according to the Latin version of *Picatrix* (the idea is absent in the original Arabic), Hermes had found the means of rendering human beings virtuous by suitable talismans.[13]

Contrary to what is often said, magic has nothing medieval about it. To the contrary, in this area the Middles Ages represented a step back. Its revival is one of the traits of modernity. It was tied to the rediscovery by the Florentine Renaissance of pagan Neoplatonism, which gave it philosophical dignity; magic ceased being a relic reserved to uncouth country-folk and became a practice of distinguished city-dwellers. In a general way, the Renaissance was not an age of the progress of rationality; rather, it was accompanied by a rebirth of credulity. "The Renaissance was occultist, that is why the University classifies it among the eras of progress." The century of Enlightenment was also that of charlatans, of Cagliostro, Mesmer, the Rose-Croix or Masonic sects. Without speaking of the complicity between socialism and occultism throughout the nineteenth century.[14]

The overall movement of modernity is a passage from magic to technology, which took over for the discredited magic.[15] Among the scholastics, Albert the Great and Roger Bacon interested themselves in technologies. The latter proposed applications to medicine.[16] The practical orientation of science found in him at least a precursor, who, like Francis Bacon later, took alchemy as a model of a knowledge of nature that was as experimental as it was effective. Nonetheless, if the sciences are judged according to their utility, what they serve remains eternal salvation, not the control of natural operations.[17] William of Auvergne distinguishes two etymologies of the word "magic," each corresponding to an appreciation: *magna agentes* (those who do grand things) or *male agentes* (those who do evil).[18] The word "mechanical" is sometimes connected with *moechas*, "adulterer." The mechanical arts are adulterine, because they are copies of copies.[19] For Paracelsus, the doctor ought not to seek to dominate nature, but to aid it. However, the idea of a domination of the earth appears, but it requires superhuman assistance: "We would not be able to cultivate the earth and dominate it as it ought to be dominated if we did not have a supernatural light to teach us."[20] As for concrete realizations, the classical age is the age of machines of all sort, possible or not, which an entire literary genre describes and portrays with great care.[21]

According to the philosophers, ancient magic encompassed all the nonmechanical effects and proceeded by "sympathy." They considered nature as the central paradigm and guarantor of the effectiveness of magical operations.[22] "Natural magic," such as it was defined by Cornelius Agrippa in 1530, was thought to depend on a knowledge of nature that allowed it to act, by producing surprising, but not in any way miraculous, effects.[23] The modern conception reverses the perspective and considers magic as paradigmatic for artifice, so much so that every sort of artifice constitutes a form of magic. This can also be the case with philosophy in general, as the physician Thomas Browne notes in 1635: "A good part of philosophy was initially sorcery"; or it can be true more particularly for legislation, according to Campanella: "The greatest magical action of man is to give laws to people."[24] Since forever it was recognized that the ultimate origin of laws was mysterious; but it is notable that this enigma was expressed by the image of magic. Francis Bacon rehabilitated magic, beginning with the word itself, unjustly discredited according to him. He effected a decisive transition by leaving the moral terrain for that of technology: magic was traditionally rejected as bad; Bacon rejects it because it is not effective. For theologians it was too effective, because it succeeded in establishing contact with evil spirits. The technology one dreamed about occupied the place of magic and thus reconnected with its probable origins, but henceforth it was a magic that yielded a return.[25] At the same period, a work of Gabriel Naudé, *Apology for All the Great Personages Who Were Accused of Magic* (1625), represents the expulsion of magic from the domain of knowledge at the dawn of the classical age. Naudé classifies the different sorts of magic in order to wipe away the suspicion cast on the great men of the past.[26] However, the exclusion of magic could not occur except after it was reinterpreted as technology. Excretion was made possible by a previous digestion.

Alchemy as Modification of Nature

Among the magical practices, alchemy occupies a central place. It is designated for the first time, although without the word, toward the middle of the fifth century in a text of Proclus. From the beginning, it did not cease receiving critical assaults.[27] However, whatever may have been its concrete results, it effected a major theoretical revolution. People have seen in it both "the final stage of a very old program . . . to change nature by human work" and the prefiguration of the modern project. It would be the "millennial dream" taken up, by secularizing it, of "the ideology of the new epoch, crystallizing around the myth of infinite progress, accredited by the experimental sciences and by industrialization."[28] Alchemy represents the first attempt to *modify* nature and not merely to use it for human purposes while accommodating to it. Ancient technology wanted to make things produce the maximum return, but in the strict framework of their respective natures: a blade of barley was to provide the greatest amount of grain, but in no case become wheat; this dream of a universal cereal, according to Meister Eckhart, was to remain unfulfilled.[29] The idea of transmutation, however, according to which the appropriate work could ennoble a base metal, presupposes a transgression of the limits that separate natural realities from each other. In so doing, it breaks with the fixity of natures, even anticipates the characterization of being as "becoming" and as "dialectical."[30]

The decisive step was hazarded by the Arabs, beyond what the ancients had dared. Greek alchemy considered manual labor as not sufficient on its own; one must add the activity of nature, which is above man. In contrast, the author of the corpus transmitted under the name of Jâbir (Geber) "had enough audacity to think that he had wrested from nature its last secret. It is the characteristic of his science not to recognize any limit to human thought." To be sure, he starts with the ancient idea of an imitation of nature. But he combines it with the definition of philosophy as assimilation to God and "applies it to natural science: the human artisan imitates the Demiurge, creator of the universe, by also exercising a creative power." The alchemist then becomes capable of changing things into what he wishes. The idea will persist in Christian milieux as well as Jewish.[31]

And this changing of things into whatever one wishes is exactly what alchemy's opponents will accuse it of. Thus Avicenna, in a passage of his encyclopedia whose Latin translation exercised great influence, had declared transmutation impossible. As a good Aristotelian, he saw each species as contained in its borders and refused to grant the artificial the ability to rival with the natural. Averroës distinguished natural and artificial causes; different causes cannot produce the same effects—in this case, the same metals. Alchemy, therefore, can only produce what resembles reality, not reality itself.[32] Against Avicenna, alchemists defended the theory according to which the capacities of man to transform the natural world are virtually unlimited. They submitted that man can create substances that do not exist in nature, such as "glass, whose manufacture saw a spectacular increase in the twelfth and thirteenth centuries." Jean de Meung notes that one can make glass from ashes of ferns, which have nothing in common with it.[33] "In obscure treatises of the thirteenth century, one finds that a literature of propaganda in favor of technological development emerges." In the second half of the thirteenth century, Paul of Taranto put forth his ideas in his *Theorica et Pratica*. The preface, influenced by the *Liber de causis*, identifies the intellect according to Plotinus with the human intellect. The latter receives from the supreme Intellect the capacity to dominate nature. Art permits nature to become the instrument of the intellect.[34]

The idea of a rivalry with God then comes to light. Not with the alchemists, who remained prudent and preferred to orient their practice toward the moral transformation of the adept,[35] but among their opponents, who reproached them with immoderate ambition: not content with imitating or ameliorating what is already there, but wanting to create out of whole cloth something new. The critique is found everywhere in the Middle Ages and the Renaissance. It is found among the Arabs in the *Secretum secretorum*, then in Ibn Khaldun: "It is impossible to produce gold or silver; because it is not possible to equal God in the works that are uniquely his."[36]

The suspicion against those who seek to modify what God has created entered canon law at the beginning of the tenth century with the *Canon episcopi*, probably due to Reginald of Prüm. A tradition adverse to the practice persists among the jurists, but, once the possibility of transmutation is acknowledged, that tradition bears above all on the means employed, which cannot appeal to magic, and on the risk of fraud in the exchange of gold and the falsification of money. This is the case of the decretal of 1317 in which John XXII condemned alchemy.[37] Bernard Palissy recalls that "gold and silver are a divine work, and it is to work rashly against God's glory to want to usurp what belongs to his state alone."[38] The foolish ambition of a rivalry with God belongs to Satan, at least as his fault is often interpreted. Nothing was easier than to suspect the alchemists of complicity with the devil.

Man the Magician

Before the control of nature became actual, even before its conditions of possibility were assembled, a human type appeared, that of the man exercising this control and being defined by it. This is the figure of the magician, which allowed a psychological reorientation of the will towards action.[39] Literature gave him the name of Dr. Faustus, which appeared in a popular German work in 1587. His literary figure was established in the tragedy of Christopher Marlowe, around 1589. His torturous itinerary in European literature is well known, especially in Goethe, and later Valéry, Thomas Mann, then Lawrence Durrell, while passing through Lenau, without counting Oswald Spengler, who added the Faustian to the Apollonian and Dionysian of Nietzsche, as characteristic of modern times, and even to sober economic historians who in this way name the human type that permitted the Industrial Revolution.[40] Marlowe's hero enumerates the different sciences of which he has become the master and finds in each one some defect. Arriving at magic, he cries out, this time enthusiastically:

> O what a world of profit and delight,
> Of power, of honour, of omnipotence,
> Is promis'd to the studious artizan!
> All things that move between the quiet poles
> Shall be at my command: Emperors and Kings
> Are but obey'd i' their sev'ral provinces,
> Nor can they raise the wind or rend the clouds;
> But his dominion that exceeds in this,

> Stretcheth as far as doth the mind of man;
> A sound magician is a mighty god.
> Here, Faustus, tire thy brains to gain a Deity.

The evil angel that, immediately afterward, encourages him in his aim suggests: "Be thou on earth as Jove is in the sky, / Lord and Commander of these elements."[41]

In imagining the human type that was going to become the symbol of modern times, Marlowe perhaps thought of concrete individuals such as Paracelsus, or rather the legend that attached to him. He wrote a few years after the Italian writings of Giordano Bruno, which he had written in England. An influence, at least indirect, is not excluded.

Whatever be the case concerning the coherence of these dreams, one fact remains of first importance: the intention to dominate nature preceded the birth of the technology that allowed its realization. This intention expresses a deeper aspiration than the results allowed by the sober confrontation with reality.

PART 2

DEPLOYMENT

7

The Formation of the Modern Project

The modern project results from the conjunction of several factors, each of which existed long before it. For if modernity defines itself as what put an end to the Middle Ages, in the actual facts the relation is more complex: what is rejected is also that on which one relies. It is fitting, therefore, to recall what in the Middle Ages made modern times possible.

Medieval Incubation

In the West, the Middle Ages represented not just a period of latency vis-à-vis modern times, but just as importantly a time of preparation and maturation, by bringing forth innovations in technology, as well as in ideas.

First of all, this was a time of important technological breakthroughs. It developed, or imported and generalized, inventions that allowed for demographic and economic takeoff in Europe. In agriculture, it applied crop rotation, the harness, the heavy plow, the watermill, and the windmill. In architecture, it introduced the ogival crossing, the condition for the diaphanous structure of Gothic art. In navigation, it utilized the compass and invented the rudder blade, at the origin of the great discoveries at the end of the fifteenth century. In this connection, some have spoken of an "industrial revolution."[1]

In any case, these advances preceded the awareness of their novelty and, a fortiori, their thematization as systematically willed and sought-for projects. They were noted, of course, sometimes with wonder—including in Europe itself, where Dante mentioned the windmill and the clock.² But also outside Europe: between 1443 and 1446, the emperor of Byzantium sent the future Cardinal Bessarion on a study trip through Europe. The cardinal then recommended to his master that he take to heart the technological advances of the Latins: automatic sawmills, bellows, everything that allows one to produce an iron of better quality.³ In the second half of the thirteenth century, Roger Bacon mentions several ingenious procedures deemed to allow the construction of boats steered by one man, wagons moving at incredible speed, instruments capable of flying or lifting great weights without any problem, submarines, and even binoculars. These marvels had existed in antiquity, since Alexander the Great had used one to explore the depths of the sea. Roger Bacon acknowledges that he has never seen a flying machine, but says he knows a sage who claimed to be able to make one.⁴ His goal is to show that none of these (purported) marvels requires magic. In that way, he gives technology a sober cast, brought back to the profane realm.

As for the awareness, the idea of a transformation of nature is suggested perhaps by a notable change that occurred around CE 830 in the illustration of calendars: until then, the months were represented by the constellations that are observable in them; now they are represented by the human works, above all, agricultural, connected with them.⁵ The awareness of innovating, as I said, lags behind the concrete innovation. It appeared during the first half of the thirteenth century in the treatise on falconry by Frederick II of the Holy Roman Empire. In it, the emperor observes that Aristotle departed from the truth on a subject, birds, about which he had only secondhand knowledge, and Frederick corrects Aristotle on the basis of his personal experience; he maintains that he wants to "bring to the status of an art certain subjects [about which] at present no one has the science or art."⁶

In the Latin West, the aptitude to innovate first manifested itself concretely in an unexpected domain, music. Guy of Arezzo, around 1020–30, formulated for the first time the idea of a progress: "This art gradually grew by developing itself until this day, because the Master himself always illumines human darkness and His supreme Wisdom lasts through all the centuries." It was in music that the idea—already present in Pythagoras and which will be continued in Galileo's physics—of a relation between sensible reality and mathematics began to be accredited. The application of the latter to practical tasks was first of all what we could term a retrospective dream, manifested in a reinterpretation of the figure of Archimedes, whose talents as a military engineer are now highlighted. The Englishman John Dee, in 1570, is perhaps the first to insist on the practical interest of geometry: knowledge of Euclid will permit people of modest conditions "to invent and conceive new works, engines, and curious instruments serving different ends in the republic or their private pleasure, and better assuring their fortune."[7] However, the awareness of innovating only slowly freed itself from the idea that discoveries are only *re*discoveries of a forgotten ancient knowledge. With Raymond Lull, however, innovation no longer hides itself but, to the contrary, parades itself: the adjective "new" figures in nine of his treatises. The notion of a "new science," born in Islam with Ibn Khaldun, appeared in Europe with Niccolò Tartaglia, who thus entitled his work on ballistics (1537), then spread with Galileo, not to mention Vico.[8]

The project of a technology conceived as the application of scientific knowledge to the pursuit of the practical ends of man can be seen in the Latin adaptation by Domenico Gundisalvo, shortly after 1150, of al-Farabi's *Enumeration of the Sciences*. Among others, he treats of the "science of ruses"—that is, mechanics, the science of "simple machines." The Latin translation defines it as the art of finding "how natural bodies can be adapted by some artifice to some use that we would like to come from them." Significantly, the phrase does not appear in the Arabic original that we possess, and it seems that the translator added it.[9] Another translator of the same period, James of Venice, the first to have translated Aristotle's *Metaphysics*, commits a revealing error on a passage of the text. There where the philosopher recalled, following the Delphic Apollo, that "the nature of man is enslaved," he, to the contrary, writes that "nature is the slave of man."[10]

Some have seen a sign of the emergence of a desire to capture natural energies for the sake of human purposes in the enthusiasm with which the thirteenth century adopted the idea of perpetual motion, of Indian origin. From it one would have come to conceive the world as a vast reservoir of energy to be placed at the service of human intentions.[11] At this period, technology sought its legitimacy less in the dream of dominating nature than in the more modest concern to compensate for human weakness.[12] Technology can also show human strength, however. Thus, automata fascinated the entire Middle Ages, in Byzantium, Islam, and Europe. In 1475, Marsilio Ficino marveled at a box made by a German artisan in which the movement of a single ball moved animals and musical instruments. However, these machines did not serve to dominate nature, but conferred a particular aura on a mastery of another sort, this one purely human, that of sovereigns over their subjects. What was symbolic, however, knew a very concrete translation in the dreams of military engineers such as the *Bellifortis* of Konrad Kyeser (1366–1405), which describes machines of war aiming either to kill the enemy or to sap his morale by causing terrifying visions to appear.[13]

The New

Modern times understood themselves, almost from the beginning, as representing a rupture vis-à-vis what preceded them, even what we could anachronistically call a revolution—in any case, *res novae*. The real discovery of a new world was accompanied by the project of also remaking the old and of rethinking the human being who inhabited it.

The sixteenth century is the century of great geographic discoveries made possible by medieval inventions, and of the intoxication they created. Discreet in the fifteenth century, enthusiasm grew in the sixteenth century. Invoking the triad of the printing press, gunpowder, and the compass became almost ritualistic, even if some pitted the "divine inspiration" that gave the printing press against the "diabolical suggestion" that gave rise to the discovery of gunpowder.[14] Others had less scruples. Thus, while the ancients believed that thunder was inimitable, Francis Bacon spoke with satisfaction of an *imitabile fulmen*.[15] And the same thinker compared technological discoveries with political, religious, or astronomical revolutions to the advantage of the former, which would have exercised a greater influence over human affairs. However, technological and ideological innovations were not without connections. The great geographical discoveries, beyond their multiple consequences, already presupposed the conjunction between science and the other "great discovery" of modernity: the sovereign nation-state. Nautical astronomy, which made the circumnavigation of Africa possible, then that of the world, seems to have been born in Portugal around 1480–90, in the context of a scientific policy launched by King John II: "Here, doubtless for the first time in history, was a concerted effort to put science at the service of a grand national enterprise."[16] If this is the case, we see before us the first instance of an alliance between technology and the modern state, which since then has grown prodigiously.

The project of "remaking the world" was also favored by a new intellectual climate. Let us mention three possible influences, in the chronological order of their appearance.

First, the idea of a nature to be remade could have gnostic sources. It is only if the world is imperfect that it is morally imperative to modify it. The *Corpus Hermeticum* sometimes considers the world as botched, as badly made.[17] Would the rediscovery of these texts in the fifteenth century have allowed a new perspective on the world, a pessimism concerning what already is, leading to the intention to put it back in order? Next, the Reformation itself could be indirectly connected with the project of conquering nature. The connection of Calvinism and capitalism on the moral plan is a commonplace since Max Weber and the criticisms that have nuanced the thesis. But is the new vision of fallen human nature somehow related to the enterprise of a technological correction of physical nature? Certainly, the relationship between nature and grace was rethought. The Middle Ages started from the axiom of Thomas Aquinas: grace does not suppress nature, but ennobles it. The Reformation conceives the action of grace in a more aggressive fashion, as correcting nature. Would what was true for human nature have been transposed and applied to external nature? Finally, with Bacon, Hobbes, Spinoza, and Gassendi one sees a return of Epicureanism, made possible by the rediscovery of a manuscript of Lucretius's *De rerum natura* in 1417 by Poggio Bracciolini, then an edition of Diogenes Laertius (which included the three "letters" of Epicurus) by Ambrogio Traversari in 1472. According to Lucretius, with nature being incomprehensible, art cannot seek to imitate it; one must replace it with a human-made order.[18]

With modern times, the question of man's place among the creatures is posed anew. First of all, as we have seen, because the traditional characteristics of man were emphasized anew, with his specific difference, rationality, being interpreted as production rather than action. Also, and perhaps above all, because the creatures vis-à-vis which man had been customarily measured dimmed, even disappeared, from the horizon of Western consciousness. Man had been located in second place after the celestial bodies by the Greek philosophers and after the angels by the Bible.[19] He was distinguished from the animals by reason and from the angels, pure spirits, by his corporeal nature. Now, with modern times began a movement of great amplitude that would lead to the expulsion of both celestial bodies and angels from the vision of the world. Their existence would not be denied, but both would be neutralized, as it were. Elsewhere I have laid out how the elements of the physical world lost their relevance to the self-understanding of man.[20] For the angels, who are only manifest by their actions, the denial of action is equivalent to a disappearance, whose history needs to be written. Here I will limit myself to indicating that great minds such as Kant, Schopenhauer, or Tocqueville realized this: "We no longer have angels."[21] For their part, the heavenly bodies, if they lost none of their splendor, lost a good deal of their charm. Astrology became one of the principal victims of modernity, which made it slink away to the very bottom of the social ladder, from a "distinguished" activity to the crudest superstition, from Kepler to tabloids at the checkout counter.

With the effacement of his most direct rivals, man saw himself constrained, as it were, to assume the first place on the scale of creatures. In his attack against the founders of modernity, Jacques Maritain saw in Descartes's thought an attempt to refashion human thought on the model of angelic thought. He observes that the famous phrase concerning man as "master and possessor of nature" is perfectly applicable to the angels as conceived by scholasticism.[22] But this first place—man cannot content himself with enjoying it in peace; rather, he must constantly develop it. Auguste Comte seems to have grasped the logical connection of these ideas. For him, the conception of the "true general situation of man, as spontaneous head of the real economy . . . , at the head of the living hierarchy," ought to give rise to the sentiment of the preeminence of man over the other living beings. From it will come a "just pride . . . above all . . . succeeding the *so often declared inferiority of man vis-à-vis the angels*." But this pride "ought not . . . to justify any dangerous apathy." This is not the indolent haughtiness of the aristocrat, but the feverish activity of the emancipated. Indeed, the principle that founds the superiority of man constitutes "a *type* of real perfection" that one can approach only asymptotically. "From it will result only a noble audacity to develop the grandeur of man in all directions."[23]

Francis Bacon

Francis Bacon was the first, it seems, to have put forth the idea of a domination of man over nature, not without having been influenced by alchemy and "natural magic," as he sometimes acknowledges.[24] He begins with a reorientation of the entirety of philosophy, until then based upon an error concerning the ends of knowledge. Knowledge ought not to be sought for pleasure, but for the results. It is because of their sterility as "consecrated virgins" that final causes are disqualified. In this way Bacon breaks with the ancient idea according to which the goal of knowledge is contemplation. The true goal is henceforth power, unless knowledge and power are simply identical. Bacon poses their equivalence as early as 1597, but the holder of the two is then not man, but God.[25]

The primacy of contemplation was previously justified inasmuch as man was to attain his perfection by it. Bacon thus makes, with the greatest discretion, a weighty decision which revolutionizes anthropology: man can no longer derive his humanity from contemplation. Bacon, however, does not devalue contemplation for the sake of its traditional rival, practice understood as political activity. What he plants in front of contemplation is productive activity, what Aristotle called *poiēsis* and distinguished from *praxis*. The long-term result of Bacon's operation was a change in the meaning of the word *praxis*, now a hybrid union of production and action. Far from arguing for politics (which he himself practiced professionally), Bacon attempts to show that, at best, politics can benefit the city, but not humanity in general, as does the inventor of new technologies. Bacon's argument takes up the argument of Marlowe's Faust: sovereigns only dominate their people, not nature itself.[26]

This domination will therefore not be that of a prince over his country, but rather "the kingdom of man." The phrase appears in a privileged place, in the title of a part of the *Novum Organon*. Later, in the first occurrence of the expression outside the title, Bacon specifies that "the entrance into the *Kingdom of man*, founded upon the sciences, [is] not much other than the entrance into the Kingdom of Heaven, where-into none may enter except as a little child." There is a very interesting parallel, with the same allusion in bad taste to Matthew 18:3, in which it is a matter of entering, not the kingdom of man, but that of nature.[27]

The project is to repair the fall. Bacon understands the fall as having entailed the loss not only of innocence (which he seems not to be concerned with at all) but above all of dominion over creatures. The true end of knowledge is "to restore man and reinvest him (to a great extent) with the sovereignty and power that he had in the primitive state in which he had been created." Perhaps this program is understandable on the basis of the millenarianism that already agitated England and later would cause the "new science" of Newton to be seen as the prelude of a "restoration of all things."[28] To be sure, one already finds among the fathers of the church and in the Middle Ages the idea that technology ought to attenuate the effects of the curse that struck Adam and Eve and the earth itself.[29] Thus Hugh of Saint-Victor (1130) explains that the goal of human action is "to repair the integrity of human nature or to attenuate the inevitable defects of our present life," and he places the mechanical arts among the means of repairing, in this way granting them a dignity that was often denied them.[30] But Bacon's emphasis on human power is new. The final goal must be to augment it. The highest ambition is "that which attempts to establish and augment the power and empire of the human race over the ensemble of things."[31] Thus, in the utopian Bensalem of *The New Atlantis*, the head of the college of scientists declares: "The end of our foundation is the knowledge of causes and secret motions of things, and the enlarging of the bounds of human empire, to the effecting of all things possible." The goal ultimately to be achieved is the maximal satisfaction of the unlimited desires of man, who has become purely a consumer.[32]

Experimentation represents a first aspect of domination, provisional because it only leads to knowledge, but still necessary. The action that reveals nature precedes that which will transform it. Nature presents itself as having to be forced to confess. It must be unmasked, its veil must be ripped off, "not to gently reorient it, but to defeat it, subject it and overturn it to its ultimate foundations," and even to dissect it, according to a formulation in which Dilthey saw the deepest of Bacon's ideas.[33] This idea is not new. Thus, Hippocrates praised medicine for having found the means of constraining nature to yield the symptoms of the illnesses that affect it, and the alchemist Zosimus explains that one cannot succeed without submitting nature to torture and forcing it to allow itself to be examined; but here it is a matter of constraining it in order to pass to a superior level of *spiritual* existence.[34] Bacon makes the submission of nature to the will of man an end in itself.

That is why he distinguishes three states of nature—free, perverted, and constrained—according to which nature resides in the appearance of things, in monsters, and in artifacts. In the last, nature suffers the yoke of man. A new face of things appears, like another universe or another scene.[35] The idea is based on a reinterpretation of the relationship between nature and artifice: artifice is now part of nature; without this idea, one would only see in artifice an addition to nature, destined to perfect or correct it, while it is really a matter of radically changing it.[36] Curiously, this seems to imply that it is nature that changes itself, from the inside. The ancient ideal of a life conformed to nature, which presupposes that one submit to it, but from a certain distance taken from it, is abandoned, or reversed. The question then becomes to know where to seek the model on which one must model nature. Here one sees a difficulty that will resurface, for example, in Marx: how to direct a process of change that one claims is spontaneous?

Descartes

Descartes knew Bacon's work and could draw from it. The presence of a "practical" philosophy in the Baconian sense is attested as early as Descartes's famous encounter with Bérulle in 1628. Descartes would have divulged to the Cardinal: "He [Bacon] let him [Descartes] see the consequences that his thoughts could have, if they had been well directed, and the utility that the public would derive, if his way of philosophizing was applied to medicine and mechanics, one of which would produce the restoration and preservation of health, the other the lessening and relief of men's labors."[37]

In the last part of the *Discourse on Method* (1637), Descartes formulates his project:

> They [some general notions touching on physics] let me see that it is possible to arrive at knowledge that would be very useful to life, and that instead of the speculative philosophy that is taught in the schools, one could find a practical one, by which knowing the force and actions of fire, water, air, the stars and the heavens, and all the other bodies that surround us, as distinctly as we know the different crafts of our artisans, we could employ them in the same way to all the usages for which they are suitable [*propre*], and thus make ourselves as it were masters and possessors of nature.[38]

The passage, isolated in the work of the philosopher, seems more Baconian than Cartesian. The term of comparison that is chosen is more artisanal than mechanical (in the sense of the use of machines).[39] Ever since Aristotle, "practical philosophy" was a technical phrase that designated a branch of knowledge also taught "in the schools"; here it takes on a new sense, in which action and production are brought together. The decisive phrase, "masters and possessors," is not new; we saw it in Manetti.[40] *Dominium* and *possessio* are technical terms in law, which Descartes had studied. Medieval law had laboriously distinguished political sovereignty from economic property: the lord is suzerain of his vassals, but not the owner of their goods; he is both in the case of the serf. With Descartes, nature is the object on which the two notions converge. Therefore it is a matter, literally, of *enslaving* it. The use of the adjective "suitable" (*propre*) also indicates an important move. It no longer designates the characteristic a thing intrinsically possesses and which should be allowed to operate, but rather the best possible exploitation of the thing to ends that are not its own. Curiously, this program figures in the very work that set as the third maxim of a provisional maxim, "to always attempt to conquer myself than fortune, and to change my desires rather than the order of the world."[41] It pertains, therefore, to a morality that, this time, is definitive.

Descartes distinguishes speculative knowledge and practical knowledge, "useful to life and contemplation of the truth." The sovereign good is "the knowledge of truth by its first causes—that is, wisdom." The joy of knowledge is almost the only pure joy. But it is better to be less cheerful and have more knowledge. The goal is "assurance," which includes the certainty of knowledge and the certainty of practice. It allows one just as much "to be assured of the acquisition of all the knowledge of which [one] will be capable" as "to walk with assurance in this life."[42]

The idea of mastery and the deepest meaning of the idea of industry, first employed in connection with method, return apropos to morality: "If there is something in our *power*, it is our thoughts, that is, those that come from will and free choice.... I do not observe in us but one thing that can give us just cause to esteem ourselves, to wit: the use of our free will and the *empire* that we have over our wills. For ... it makes us in a certain way similar to God, by making us *masters* of ourselves."[43] To locate the resemblance to God in the sovereignty over ourselves is an old Stoic idea: the sage has nothing to envy the gods.[44] The will must use "industry" toward the passions: "to acquire an absolute empire over all the passions, if one employed enough industry to arrange and conduct them." The mastery of the passions receives the name of "generosity," and those who exhibit it are "entirely masters of their passions."[45]

Thus, in the Cartesian revolution, the source of the project of mastery is deeper than its application to nature, and this project bears upon a much vaster domain. Descartes begins by "determining the possession of his own nature on the model of mastery. The taking up of distance from oneself has for its goal, on one hand, the stabilization of the subject of mastery, as self-certainty, and, on the other, the domination of nature.... It is as slave of his practical philosophy that man becomes the lord of nature."[46]

8

The Beginnings of the Realization

What was only a dream with the great innovators at the beginning of the seventeenth century became a *concrete* program that, as the century progressed, gradually gave itself the means of realization. "Experimental philosophy" gradually replaced Aristotelianism in medicine, the domain that was eminently practical and bore directly upon the human. In this way, the mastery of nature began by what was of nature in man. The discourse pronounced in 1693 by Giovanni Maria Lancisi, the papal doctor, marked a turning point in favor of the application of sciences to the treatment of diseases. Like Galileo, whose "nature speaks in the language of mathematics" he quotes, Lancisi went back to Plato and made the novelty palatable by covering it in a flurry of ancient quotations.[1] For the technological bases, though, it was necessary to await the nineteenth century and the first industrial revolution.

Bacon's Posterity

Today Bacon is still considered a precursor by certain proponents of "transhumanism," who would like to make 1620, the date of the publication of the *New Organon*, the ground zero year of a new calendar.[2] But his reputation, although in part unfounded, is almost as old as he, in England as well as the continent.

A generation after Bacon, a tradition inspired by him was established in England, which attained a peak in the 1660s. Thus, Hobbes coined the motto "Knowledge is for the sake of power" (*scientia propter potentiam*), and Robert Boyle saw in Bacon "one of the first and greatest of the experimental philosophers."[3] Unlike Bacon, however,

Boyle was a true scientist and made several important discoveries in chemistry. According to a text published in 1661, science could be pursued for either of two objectives: to know nature or to command it. Certain people only desire to discover the cause of phenomena; others desire to produce new phenomena and "to lead nature to put itself at the service of their individual ends, be they health, wealth, or sensual pleasure." He developed these ideas in a treatise on the utility of experimental physics. He who truly devotes himself to it knows a thousand things that others do not, but he can also do many things that the others cannot. In fact, his competence allows him not only to understand the marvels of nature but to imitate some and increase others in quantity and quality. To be sure, the Creator does not allow the "naturalists" to produce even a single atom of matter, but he allows them to create forms that are nobler than matter. The modifications that he realizes in nature are such as Adam, come back to life, would admire: "what new world, so to speak, or what group of things has been added to the initial creatures by the industry of his posterity." To be sure, man is only the minister of nature. But his artfulness makes him capable of doing marvels. Moreover, the empire of man pertains to a type of power and sovereignty much more satisfying than any other: the domination it ensures is a power that suits man as such; it brings more satisfaction in that it testifies to his knowledge; and it cannot do so without proving his strength or enriching his pantry.[4]

The same year, 1661, Abraham Cowley, in a short work, proposed the foundation of a university college joined to a school, and he sketched their organization. The tone of the whole is "modern": Cowley denies that everything has already been discovered by the ancients, who could not even imagine certain discoveries such as the Americas. The projected institution would have as its task to study everything contained in the catalogue given by Bacon as an annex to his *New Organon*. On the other hand, it would not be guided by the model of "Solomon's House" imagined in the *New Atlantis*, which is a "project of experiments that cannot be conducted."[5] In this way, Baconianism begins to surpass Bacon himself. Locke notes in his diary in 1677: "Behold a vast field of knowledge suitable to the use and advantage of men in this life: i.e., to invent new and rapid machines which shorten or facilitate our work, to combine the wise application of several workers or materials that assure us new and beneficial products we can use, and thus to increase the sum of our wealth, i.e., things useful to the commodiousness of our existence."[6]

The concern for utility is not absent on the Continent, in particular in France, a country that many "philosophers," as early as the eighteenth century, too quickly opposed to England, experimental and pragmatic, as being merely devoted to verbal speculation. To begin with Voltaire: he spoke of the century of Louis XIV as also "the century of the English."[7] And in fact, the search for the practical application of knowledge was conducted by several institutions, sometimes supported with public funds.[8] As for theory, Fontenelle defended the utility of the sciences, and that of the scientific society of which he was the secretary: mathematical advances which at first were only jeux d'esprit had shown themselves fruitful; however, the practical applications of scientific knowledge represent only a part of their utility.[9]

In Holland, Spinoza presented his work as an undertaking for liberation, which was to be accomplished by means of mastery. This mastery, however, does not bear upon external nature, which in fact is not truly external to man, but on man himself. "The human inability to master and control the affects, I call Servitude; the man who is subject to affects is under the authority, not of himself, but of fortune." One recognizes the use of the Machiavellian term. It is only human beings whose mind can give us contentment. All the rest can be preserved, destroyed, or adapted to our use according to the rule of utility. In particular, animals can be utilized in the way that suits us the best: the rule that forbids killing them only rests on vain superstition or effeminate compassion. The perfection of human nature requires a sufficient natural knowledge, as well as moral philosophy with pedagogy, medicine, and mechanics. In a passage that recalls the description of bourgeois happiness in the sonnet of Christopher Plantin or, closer, the Dutch painting of the period, Spinoza describes the envisaged human ideal: what he later will call "comfort."[10]

In Germany, Leibniz insisted on the utility of an academy of sciences. It should not content itself with theory and examine only curiosities, but add to the commodious character of human life and the supply of objects. The dominion of minds over matter produces "marvelous ordinances" and makes men "little gods who imitate the great architect of the universe."[11] One ought not, however, to ignore the dose of propaganda found in these declarations, destined to "sell" science to sponsors.[12]

The ideal of a purely disinterested knowledge remained alive for a long time. In 1808, Cuvier still says that he sees in the immediate utility for society of the sciences "the least of the aspects" one should consider. More important are the discovery of the truth, the education of the people, victory over prejudices and passions, and the sovereign place accorded to reason. The mathematician Jacobi still wrote to Legendre in 1830 that "the sole goal of science is the honor of the human spirit."[13] It is perhaps only since the Second World War that the aim of knowledge has become truly subordinate to the elaboration of know-how.

The eighteenth century covered Bacon with praise and saw in him the herald of a new era of knowledge. Voltaire saluted him as "the father of experimental philosophy"; Rousseau clearly indicated him, even though he did not name him, as "the greatest, perhaps, of the philosophers"; d'Alembert and Condorcet renewed the importance that England granted him less and less since Newton had eclipsed him. In 1755, the French hack-writer Alexandre Deleyre (1726–96) composed a synthesis of Bacon's thought. This vogue lasted far into the nineteenth century. Thus in his schemas of the history of thought, Auguste Comte regularly associated him with Descartes, called him "the great Bacon," as well as "this eminent philosopher," and even recognized in him a certain superiority over the Frenchman.[14]

The first to have broken with this concert of praise was, no doubt, Joseph de Maistre, in his *Examen de la philosophie de Bacon* (1815). It was above all as the inspirer of the Enlightenment, and, indirectly, of the French Revolution, that Bacon attracted the thunder of their most determined enemy. In criticizing the English thinker, de Maistre above all sought to show that the movement of ideas that led to the Revolution was not intellectually respectable. It is the case that he hit his mark in revealing the chancellor's naïveté, even his dishonesty. Two generations later, in 1863, a true scientist, the German chemist Justus von Liebig, delivered a devastating attack on Bacon. He reproached him for having drawn the facts that he said that he had himself observed from books that he pillaged, without even mentioning the authors; his purported experiments are pure inventions; he neither knew nor understood the science of his time, neither Gilbert, nor Copernicus, nor Harvey, and especially not Galileo; his empirical and inductive method is the contrary of the true method of science; and finally, his project of putting knowledge at the service of human utility is the very negation of the scientific ideal. Two years later, Claude Bernard, while more brief, was not more gentle, and referred to de Maistre's critique.[15]

Technological Dreams

According to Bacon, the application of science to the improvement of human life ought to bring spectacular advances. For two centuries, they remained rather feeble, even rather fantastic. The real advances took place in the domain of the theoretical sciences. This, however, did not prevent the Baconian project from being given full rein in the domain of dreams.

The eighteenth century did see some particularly spectacular scientific triumphs, two of which were especially symbolic: the discovery of electricity and the means of producing it at will; above all, the almost simultaneous (1752) invention of the lightning rod by the Moravian premonstrant Václav Prokop Diviš and by Benjamin Franklin, the latter remaining in the annals of Enlightenment historiography. Thunder, until then the privilege of the Greek Zeus or the Canaanite Baal and even the biblical YHWH (Ps. 29:3–9), thus found itself domesticated, even captured. The machine that allowed one to reproduce its bolts on a small scale in the form of sparks remained for a long time a curiosity. But the new science left the confined space of the laboratory to acquire a social, even a global, dimension.[16]

The decomposition of air (1777) and of water (1783) by Lavoisier gave the coup de grâce to the traditional notion of the four elements. Hot-air balloons (1783) allowed one to gain a new perspective on the earth, until then the province of the painters who had introduced it, such as Leonardo da Vinci or Altdorfer. But actually attaining it was impossible and remained a dream, despite numerous attempts. Balloons led to an emancipation of sight, parallel to that of the citizen, and led to the replacement of the theocentric vision of the world by another, this one anthropocentric. One century later, aviation represented a remarkable advance by permitting the flight of objects heavier than air; this stirred the enthusiasm of contemporaries. Thus Proust saw in the aviator a modern demigod.[17] But if the airplane represented a gain in speed, it did not bring a change of perspective.

At its origin, the literary genre of the utopia had nothing to do with progress, either observed or hoped for, in the technological transformation of nature. The knowledge that the Socrates of the *Republic* wished to put in authority was not technological, and the contribution it made to the city was that it brought the rulers closer to the truth, not that it increased their power. An increase in power would have doubtless seemed dangerous to the Greeks, who were distrustful of all immoderation. The book by Thomas More, who coined the term "utopia" (1516), was not the first evocation of an ideal city, and the literary genre of a voyage to a far-off island whose inhabitants, thanks to a perfect political system, live in happiness also goes back to Greek antiquity.[18] But neither More nor his predecessors thought that the regime described could be *led* by progress in human knowledge and the interventions in nature it made possible. The Utopians "search the secrets of nature," but this is in order to admire the order of the world and to make themselves agreeable to God. One does not see any trace of the unlimited appetite for power that Bacon will later endorse.[19]

Scientific utopias appeared with modern times. The first to have imagined one is perhaps the anonymous author of the manifestos of Rose-Croix: in 1614, *Fama fraternitatis rosae crucis*, then in 1615, *Confessio*.[20] In 1619, the Swabian Lutheran pastor Johann Valentin Andreae, himself also the author of the *Noces chimiques de Christian Rosenkreuz* (1616), described the ideal city, Christianopolis. In it there are what we would call research centers.[21] But science there remains separate from every technological application. The ideal city is certainly favorable to science, but the presence of science in it does not modify it in any way. In contrast, with the *New Atlantis*, written around 1624 and published in 1627, a year after his death by his secretary Rawley, Bacon inaugurated a literary genre, scientific utopia, where science is systematically placed at the service of the improvement of the human condition.

With the project of the submission of nature somewhat crazy dreams arose. The strongest, no doubt, is the immemorial one: immortality. Roger Bacon had suggested that art, by means of a perfect equilibrium of the four elements, could prolong life almost indefinitely.[22] Four centuries later, his compatriot and homonym Francis Bacon let slip the idea that one could ensure immortality by technological means, which would represent the height of the sovereignty that he wished to restore to man; but he adds quickly: "if it were possible."[23] Descartes dreams of perfecting medicine to the point of finding the means of lengthening life to a hundred (letting immortality be glimpsed on the horizon). This was the goal of his *Treatise on Man*.[24] The philosopher ends, however, by being content with not fearing death, because he has come to understand that it is inevitable.[25] At the end of the century, however, Miss de Saint-Quentin published a study on the subject with a positive tone.[26] The successful flight of the first balloon provoked an uncontained enthusiasm.[27] In his discourse in memory of Carnot, Arago says that he heard the old Marshal de Villeroi bitterly exclaim: "Yes, it is decided, now it is certain; THEY will find the secret of no longer dying, *and it will be when I am dead!*"[28]

For Christianity, original sin entails a loss of man's control over his own body: before the fall, Adam and Eve were so much masters of themselves that their soul controlled all the movements of their organs; sexual pleasure was therefore more intense.[29] Bacon already dreamed of reversing the effects of the fall, and with the French Revolution, the dream grew larger. Thus, in his *Enquiry concerning Political Justice* of 1793, William Godwin cites, following Price, a sentence of Benjamin Franklin: "Mind one day will become all-powerful over matter." Men will then no longer need so-called justice, or government. And there is more: a perfect control over our own body can one day make us immortal. Of these last two projects, Godwin adds that "it is not impossible that some of the present race of men can live to see these things realized."[30]

The necessary consequence of immortality will be the abandonment of sexual reproduction, henceforth useless. It remained the standard of the absolute utopia. Dostoyevsky has Kirillov say: "I believe that man ought to cease reproducing." And one could see in this attitude the logical consequence of contemporary "transhumanism": once they are immortal, human beings, no longer having any need to reproduce, will all be adults, and childless.[31] The conceit of a humanity finally emerged from childhood and its prejudices and fully installed in adulthood, until then a dream or a metaphor, will thus be realized. Auguste Comte named "ideal resurrection" the way in which the heart commemorates the deceased, and Renan entrusted it to a future God.[32] A half century later, the Russian librarian Nicolai Fedorov (1903) dreamed of a much more concrete resurrection of past generations, which would be obtained by technological means. The articles in which he puts forth the necessity of this task, brought together after his death, filled two thick volumes. It is difficult to overestimate their influence on all the currents of Russian, then Soviet, thought. "Fiodorovism is one of the ties that connects the periods across the rupture of 1917."[33] Like Godwin a half century earlier, Fedorov foresaw the abolition of death, and with it, the end of the necessity of reproducing. The global task of human beings will be reoriented from the future to the past. Humanity henceforth will not reproduce, but will bring its ancestors back to life: "engendering children" will be replaced by "producing fathers."[34] Roman Jakobson recalls a conversation with Mayakovski in 1920 in which the latter said that he was "totally convinced that death would cease to exist and that the dead were going to be resurrected." The technological resurrection of animals will be part of Soviet utopias, while people await something better—the "better" being perhaps nothing other than the reanimation of Lenin's corpse. In any case, the architect of his mausoleum, Constantin S. Melnikov, compared the crystal sarcophagus that he foresaw to that of Sleeping Beauty.[35]

The Idea of Progress

All this hope is undergirded by a certain conception of our relationship to time, which the technological successes, in turn, constantly corroborate, and which thus easily allows itself to be generalized into a positive vision of the future: progress.

This idea was rarely found in antiquity, except when real advances were made that were verifiable, above all by the learned, but not without being counterbalanced by fears of decadence. One finds it in Seneca, Tacitus, and Macrobius. Some will at least admit that their time produces virtues at the same level as before. Augustine distinguishes material progress from spiritual progress and denies that the former is always a sign of the latter.[36] Orthodox Islam is hostile to the idea of progress and circulates statements of Muhammad declaring mistrust of innovation. On the other hand, the idea is found among the alchemists and in Razi.[37] Medieval Europe knew the very equitable comparison of the modern dwarf found on the shoulders of ancient giants. This comparison illustrates the quite real fact, recognized among the Christians as well as the Jews, that the learned of a later period can add to earlier knowledge a "surplus of meaning." The Franciscan Guibert of Tournai (d. 1285) refused to limit possible knowledge to what was already known.[38] The theoretical possibility of progress was formulated by Nicholas of Cusa, who affirmed the superiority of an image of the true that was less accurate than another, but susceptible of being perfected, over a better image that was fixed.[39]

With modern times appeared the idea of a connection between scientific-technological advances and the amelioration of the human situation. It seems that it was due as much to a renaissance of the millenarianism of *The Book of Revelations* in seventeenth-century England as to the successes of the new science. Scholasticism had kept millenarianism in wraps; the Reformation gave it a boost, in order to legitimate its own arrival. Progress is understood as a manifestation of providence.[40] Nature and human history, spiritual improvement and the successes of science, are considered as parallel manifestations of the divine design. The long-term tendency was to reduce the place of the catastrophic aspects of the idea of the millennium and to relocate it in a profane history moved solely according to immanent laws.

However, it was in the eighteenth century that the idea of progress appeared in all its clarity, now shorn of ideas that still qualified, even contradicted, it.[41] Its appearance presupposed that happiness was redefined, no longer as obtaining an ultimate end, but in a dynamic fashion as movement toward what is desired. This is the revolution wrought by Hobbes.[42] A vision of history as animated by a quasi-spontaneous movement toward the better was put in place from the middle of the century. Not without some hesitations, though. Voltaire, whose *Essai sur les moeurs* (1756) innovated with its global historiographical method, which did not limit itself to political facts, sees in history a series of luminous isles emerging from an ocean of absurdities, but sharing in reason.[43]

Since then, the public opinion of Western societies has made adhesion to progress the criterion of the good, and the suspicion of rejecting or opposing it capable of discrediting the accused, without appeal or recourse. The appearance of the adjective "progressive," with its positive connotation, witnesses to this. Attested in English as early as 1848,[44] since then it has spread to the various European lefts, where it never ceases to triumph over constantly renewed enemies ("conservative," "reactionary," "integrist," "fundamentalist"). However, as much as the growth in knowledge and technology is incontestable, so too is it difficult to affirm that the human race has progressed in civilization. Even more contestable is the connection of cause and effect between the growth in knowledge and power over things, on the one hand, and the moral consequences they are deemed to produce, on the other. Progress therefore becomes the object of a belief, as with Auguste Comte, who made progress "the truly fundamental *dogma* of human wisdom, whether practical or theoretical."[45] Others believed it ineluctable. Thus Herbert Spencer: "Progress is not an accident but a necessity."[46]

With Darwinism, progress received a scientific basis. "The attraction of Darwinism was that it gave to a pre-existing myth the scientific guarantees it required."[47] Progress is not only a fact of human history; it prolongs a universal tendency of nature. For Ernst Haeckel, who popularized Darwinism in Germany, progress through the struggle for life governs plants and animals, but also languages and peoples: "This progress is a natural law," and thus irresistible, a force tyrants and priests cannot stop. Marx, who admired Darwin and would have dedicated *Capital* to him, from the beginning of his reflections, that is, fifteen years before the *Origin of Species*, considered the passage to communism as the result of a natural movement.[48] By rooting progress in the spontaneous evolution of nature, however, one engaged in an ambiguous dialectic. On one hand, one gains in certainty: there is no need to hope; it suffices to wait, even if it is better to help evolution give birth to what it is pregnant with by pushing in the right direction, even clearing the path of obstacles that encumber it. But on the other, the results can no longer be credited to man, dragged along as he is by a current that surpasses him and of which he is not the master. At this point it is not certain that the river, which comes from well before him, one day might not leave him on the banks, an empty shell.

The thought of progress turns spontaneously toward the past in order to measure complacently the distance already crossed and to draw reasons to expect an even better future. Hence the birth of a "progressive" historiography whose first representative was perhaps Joseph Glanvill in 1668. The famous quarrel of the ancients and the moderns, conducted at the end of the 1680s, represented the culmination of a tendency older by more than sixty years that began with Francis Bacon. Alessandro Tassoni, in 1620, spoke of it as a contemporary topic.[49] However, it was the eighteenth century that was to dedicate an entire literary genre to expressing its self-satisfaction. And the satisfaction was great, as Melchior Grimm candidly acknowledged: "The eighteenth century has surpassed all the others in the praise it has lavished on itself." This genre was born with the historical fresco of Turgot, *Tableau philosophique des progrès successifs de l'esprit humain* (1750). It gave birth to a new discipline, the history of science, with Antoine Yves Goguet and Alexander Savérien. "Progress" became the title of journals, for the first time in 1780 with *I progressi dello spirito umano* of Antonio Graziosi.[50] The progressive vision culminated in the treatise that Condorcet could only sketch. Put into the minority in a conflict among revolutionary factions, the mathematician and philosopher hid and, when captured, committed suicide. His *Esquisse d'un tableau historique des progrès de l'esprit humain* (1794) remains the best illustration of a naïve faith that concluded from progress in knowledge to that of manners and political regimes. Since then, the genre has disappeared; but perhaps only because it no longer was needed, as progress became the invisible atmosphere shaping the historical vision of Western societies.

The English were not to be outdone. Joseph Priestley envisaged unlimited progress: "Whatever was the beginning of this world, the end will be glorious and paradisiacal, beyond what our imaginations can now conceive"; Richard Price sees in the progress of Newtonian science (and in the suppression of the Jesuits) the signs of an approaching millennium. He combines the faith in providence of a Presbyterian minister with the historical vision of Condorcet, whose *Vie de Turgot* he cites.[51] The central content of progress is power, as Buffon says clearly: "Man only knew late the extent of his power, and . . . even now he does not adequately know it; it entirely depends upon the exercise of his intelligence; thus, the more he observes, the more he cultivates, nature, the more he will have the means of subjecting it and faculties for drawing new riches from its bosom, without diminishing the treasures of its inexhaustible fecundity. And what would he be able to do with himself (I mean: on his own species), if will was united to intelligence? Who knows to what extent man could perfect his nature, be it his moral nature or his physical nature?"[52]

The retrospective look at the past was completed by a prophetic vision of the future. Hence the emergence of the novel of anticipation. The Irishman Samuel Madden, with his *Memoirs of the Twentieth Century* (1733), is the first to have penned one, but he limits his fictional history to political and military events, and barely evokes science and technology.[53] The genre's first French representative was the polymath Louis Sebastien Mercier (d. 1814). In his *Year 2440, or Dream, If Ever There Were One* (1771), he describes a king's cabinet, an institution analogous to Bacon's "Solomon's House," in a passage directly inspired by the *New Atlantis*. He enumerates the marvelous collections and instruments the scientists of the future possess. He summarizes their program in a formulation that is also borrowed from Bacon: "We only walk in the light of the torch of experience. Our goal is to know the secret movements of things and to extend the dominion of man by giving him the means of executing all the works that can enhance his being." One must therefore bring it about "that our works respond to the fortunate liberality of nature, who only awaits the hand of the master to whom the creator has, in a manner of speaking, subjected her."

However, the point of the work is not found there. Knowledge is not appreciated because of its possibilities of technological application, to the point that the most important and useful science is none other than astronomy, which causes the existence and wisdom of God to be known. To be sure, henceforth hospitals are salubrious, and inoculation a current practice.[54] Bad books have been burned, radically reducing the library of the king and permitting the "rebuilding of the human sciences."[55] One no longer teaches useless or vain knowledge such as ancient languages, history, or theology. But no spectacular technological achievement is described either, which would allow the marvels to be accomplished that later will fill the novels of anticipation. And the Prometheus who is praised in connection with Aeschylus's play is less the inventor than the rebel.[56] The clearest part of the narrative is concerned with a critique of the manners of the century, in a rather declamatory style. The literary genre then had a development that is impossible even to survey here. I will have to list just a few examples.[57]

The future is not only the object of literary dreams. There is a sociological translation and there are, as it were, advance "deposits" in the existence of certain individuals said to be "ahead of their time," the collection of whom constitutes a sort of "avant-garde" vis-à-vis the rest of the pack and the laggards. This metaphor, already attested in the sixteenth century, in the nineteenth knew a remarkable success.[58]

9

The Master Is There

The eighteenth century did not loudly play the theme of the domination of nature by man handed down by the previous century. The theme did emerge from time to time, for example in Buffon, who dreamed of employing the heat of volcanoes against the cooling of the planet, in such a way that man could "master nature."[1] But it did not take on the character of an ideal capable of defining and orienting every human action except with German idealism. On the other hand, the eighteenth century contributed something even more essential to the modern project: it provided its very subject, by defining man in such a way that he could assume the task that awaited him.

The Science of Man

Anthropology only appeared with modernity. Before, the question of man concerned less his essence than the paradox of his condition. Two points of view formed a subtle counterpoint. On one hand, the superiority of man vis-à-vis the other beings was perceived with such calm evidentness that it did not invite one to ask, what exactly is man? On the other hand, this superiority did press one to ask why everything in man was not up to what it ought to be. And first of all, in connection with his nature. If man is fundamentally his soul or his intellect, what ensures the unity of a being that is not simply reducible to them? Plato identified man with his soul, even with the reasoning faculty (*logistikon*); he also depicted souls descending into the body, thereby producing the concrete human being. The question of the unity of such a composite was raised at least from Plotinus, who devoted a little treatise to it. The title asks, "What is man?"

and employs the word as a synonym for "living" and for "composite." The answer is a graduated "I," whose authenticity varies according as it turns above or below.² The question returned in the Middle Ages with the discussions around the Aristotelian doctrine of the active intellect carried on by Greek and Arab commentators. Elsewhere, the question also appeared in the context of history: consequent to what fall of Adam, who was created perfect, did he find himself in the situation of moral decline and, consequently, physical decline that belongs to man today? In this sense, man has forever been the object of direct or indirect study. However, the first treatise that studied him as a specific object was the *Summa de homine*, the first work of Albert the Great. The *Torat ha-Adam* (doctrine of man) of his contemporary Nachmanides does not treat anthropology, but the laws relative to man as mortal: concerning mourning, but also the rewards and sanctions in the beyond.³

The project of a knowledge of man was thematized by Montaigne: "The study that I undertake, whose subject is man . . ."; then with Pierre Charron: "The true science and true study of man is man." But the project of a science that would take man as its object, thus an anthropology *avant la lettre*, was born at the beginning of the seventeenth century. Thus Francis Bacon in 1605: "I do take the consideration in general and at large of Human Nature to be fit to be emancipate and made a knowledge by itself." It is interesting that Bacon wants to distinguish his project from the discourses on the dignity, or misery, of man, in order to have the inquiry bear upon the relations of connivance and mutual influence between the soul and the body. He thus situates himself in a continuation of ancient and medieval reflections. Toward the same period, the Iberian scholastics moved the treatise on the soul from metaphysics to physics. Some have "recognized in this the first concern for an anthropology distinct from metaphysics and the initial sketch of a 'physical discourse on man.'"⁴

It is at the same period that the word "anthropology" took on its current meaning.⁵ "Science of man" is attested for the first time in Guillaume Colletet and in Chevalier de Méré. Hume made it the fundamental science. "The science of man is the only solid foundation for the other sciences." For Auguste Comte, after Saint-Simon, anthropology becomes the all-encompassing science, and one "must no longer conceive, all things considered, but one science, the human science, or more exactly: the social science, for which our existence is at once the principle and goal." One can then "envisage our different actual knowledges as composing a single science, that of humanity, of which our other positive speculations are at once the preamble and the development."⁶

As a consequence, the idea of dignity is displaced. It no longer qualifies man as the object of knowledge, but the science itself that studies him. Spinoza expressed it negatively: "It is much more preferable, and more *worthy* of our knowledge, to examine the actions of men than those of animals." At almost the same moment, Malebranche said it in a positive vein: "Of all the human sciences, the science of man is the most worthy [*digne*] of man." In 1733, Alexander Pope reprised the idea in a famous verse, cited everywhere: "The proper study of mankind is man."[7] The tone is Apollonian: the science of man is within our reach, while that of God surpasses us. That man is worthy goes without saying. That he is good, also evident. The century of Enlightenment, however, relegated to the shadows the two enigmas of human decline over which classical understanding had stumbled. In his typical fashion, Voltaire expressed the received wisdom of his time in response to the anxieties of Pascal: "Without any mystery, I understand very well what man is. . . . Man is not an enigma. . . . Man appears to be at his right place in nature."[8] It only remains to praise him.

"Human" as Laudatory Adjective

In antiquity, the adjective "human," where it was not purely descriptive, often referred to a weakness. With modernity, it became a quality. Modern times continued a long-term movement toward the rationalization of legal procedures and the softening of penal practices. This process began several centuries before them. If one does not want to go all the way back to the reservations Augustine expressed about torture, one can locate an important juncture at the moment when the church, in 1215, delegitimated the ordeal, improperly called "God's judgment."[9] The institution of the Inquisition (1231) represented a progress over the civil procedures of the time, without mentioning popular lynchings, its rules providing the accused with guarantees that were absent from civil instances.[10] The witch trials saw a peak in the seventeenth century throughout the entire West, and especially in Protestant countries with the Great Witch Hunt in early modern Europe, as well as in France. The existence of witches was admitted by the most "modernist" of minds, such as Jean Bodin, the theoretician of the sovereignty of the state, who devoted a lengthy treatise to the necessity of punishing them, followed by the refutation of Jan Wier, who had argued against such proceedings in 1563.[11] The legitimacy of the use of torture in witch trials was called into doubt for the first time by the Jesuits Adam Tanner (1572–1632) and Friedrich Spee von Langenfeld (1591–1635), the latter better known than the former, but as the author of hymns.[12]

The propagandists of the Enlightenment had the adroitness to claim for themselves the monopoly on a movement they had not initiated. Thanks to their rhetorical effectiveness, they managed to install in European consciousness the idea of a connection between themselves and the movement of humanization. In particular, they reserved to themselves the credit for having fought for the abolition of torture, in France with Montesquieu and Helvétius, and in Italy with Cesare Beccaria, who borrowed the most important of his ideas from them. Pietro Verri merits a particular mention, since he took as his example the charge leveled against the unfortunate (purportedly) *untori*, deemed to have been responsible for the plague in Milan in 1630. Manzoni, the grandson of Beccaria, was to recount the epidemic and reopen the dossier of the trial.[13] Pertaining to the same movement were the early stages of the battle against the deportation of blacks and against slavery in general, the softening of the treatment of the mentally disturbed, and the fact that children were increasingly considered as children, not simply as objects to be trained.

It is characteristic that people thought to assemble all of these undeniable improvements under the name of "humanize." The word itself was still thought to be a neologism by Bakunin in 1868. But it is interesting that the adjective "human" passes from descriptive to normative: the human no longer designates what man is, but what he ought to be. It is no longer to utter a tautology to declaim as Rousseau did to educators: "Men, be human." A generation later, Schiller extols the greatest gift of Demeter: to have caused "that man became man."[14] Roman antiquity knew the virtue of humanity, but assigned it a subordinate rank, as a subcategory of justice, and the word still seems weak to Bacon vis-à-vis "goodness." For Voltaire, in contrast: "Without humanity, *the virtue that includes all the virtues*, one would not merit the name of philosopher." With Beccaria, the word "humanity" signifies more the human race than the quality associated with "beneficence" and assumed to distinguish it. Laws should be inexorable, and judges do not have the right to interpret them. But the legislator ought to be "gentle, indulgent and *humane*." Pietro Verri shaped the Italian term *umano*, and in the sense that has become our own sense of the word "humane," by associating it with "reason" and by qualifying the life of Jesus as "patient, beneficent, *humane [umano]* and compassionate."[15] Negatively, "inhuman" and its cognates in other languages became the cesspool of all the vices, as with Schikaneder: Tamino, believing the calumnies against Sarastro leveled by the Queen of the Night, cried out, "He's an inhuman type [*Unmensch*], a tyrant!"[16] The vogue for the word struck Rousseau, who spoke of the "beautiful word of humanity, hackneyed to the point of insipidness, even ridiculousness, by the most inhuman people in the world." But he could not foresee the declarations of the revolutionary Barère ("Humanity consists in exterminating one's enemies") and Carrier ("It is by the principle of humanity that I purge the earth of the liberty of these monsters")—formulations that were to find an echo, no doubt unconscious, in the Auschwitz doctor, Fritz Klein, who said he acted "out of respect for human life."[17]

Innocence Rediscovered

This evolution would not have been possible without the removal of a hypothesis that until then compromised the idea of humanity: the Christian doctrine of original sin. Paul had drawn it from the second biblical narrative concerning the origins; Augustine had furnished the Roman church with its classical form; Pascal had made it the key to anthropology, and it will be against the Enlightenment that Vico or Baudelaire will return its luster to it.[18] The doctrine did not at all deny human dignity; quite the contrary, it liberated it by showing that its corruption, having had a beginning, could have an end. But by placing sin in a history, the doctrine prevented human dignity from prevailing as an absolute. The only human dignity was that which had been lost, possessed *in nuce*, and recovered. And this dignity did not have the status of a natural quality except in a prehistory or, if one wishes, a meta-prehistory, which was inaccessible to experience.

The Enlightenment will therefore give itself, explicitly or implicitly, the goal of rehabilitating human nature. The "philosophes" refrained from denying the obvious, that man does evil, but they denied the dogma of original sin, and even more so the necessity of grace to eliminate its consequences. It will no longer be a matter of saving man, which is what Christianity proposed by means of an economy of redemption, but rather of showing that man is already fundamentally good and, as a consequence, has no need of salvation. At most, the philosophers could talk about "salvation" in a purely metaphorical sense, as with Spinoza.[19] Rousseau is far from being the only one who affirmed the original goodness of man; but he did so with an exceptionally powerful rhetoric: "The first movements of nature are always right; there is no original perversity in the human heart." This candor was to cause scandal with the archbishop of Paris, who condemned the book in which it appeared, but also with a pious Anglican like Samuel Johnson, who wanted to send Rousseau to prison.[20]

Thus, to speak of humanity as bearing a dignity aims at a polemical goal, that of doing away with the Christian idea of original sin. Here again Voltaire indicates quite clearly what the invocation of dignity aims at. For him, instead of calling man to again acknowledge his fallen condition, "one ought to say to each individual: remember your dignity as a man." This last phrase, we have seen, was already powerfully asserted by the fathers of the church, and Voltaire here does not invent anything new.[21] However, for Christianity the idea of a fall only takes on meaning in connection with the idea of salvation, and is nothing but that *from which* man is to be saved. For apologetic purposes, Pascal had isolated the first moment, "the misery of man," from what should be seen in a dialectical context. Voltaire remained at this first moment but directly opposed to it a dignity that no longer is located in the history of a loss and a recuperation, but in the affirmation and defense of a good already possessed. Original sin, therefore, if it took place, must be a gain rather than a loss, because it opened man's eyes. The Enlightenment thinkers who reflected upon the biblical narrative interpreted it in this positive sense, and Kant follows in the wake of a formulation of Rousseau: "Instead of degrading his nature, it seems . . . that the sin of Adam ennobled him by developing his mind and making him capable of reason."[22]

Another operation occurred, symmetrical to the first. Man was no longer considered as being called to a transcendent destiny, to assimilate to God. The patristic doctrine of "divinization," still present among the Platonizing theologians of Cambridge or the German spiritualists such as Caspar Schwenkfeld, was then lost to sight.[23] Unless it was found in another register. Thus, from 1700, Claude Gilbert, a lawyer from Dijon, connected the use of reason and divinization: "It [divinization] is just to take this happy guide [reason] which always leads us to the good, and the good is found wherever it leads. In following it, we only depend upon ourselves and we thereby become, in a certain way, gods." The following page, however, nuances the claim: "To complain that we do not have the fullness of science, to complain that we are not infallible, is to complain that we are men, it is to complain that we are not gods."[24] The praise of reason here has nothing original to it. One also encounters elsewhere the connection between its use and the divine faculty of creating, especially in mathematics. In contrast, the emphasis placed on reason's practical role and on the possibility that it offers for absolute self-sufficiency and self-determination is more rare.

In vindicating the goodness of man at the same time as affirming the independence of man from every superior instance, modern thought made him responsible for everything, including evil. In a representative way, Rousseau declared: "Man, no longer seek the author of evil, this author is you."[25] Christianity, especially in its Pauline version, certainly made man that by which evil had entered the world. But, on one hand, it allowed a certain space between the first Adam and me as a singular subject, and, on the other, it suggested that the fall was the work of the evil one, the devil. Modernity did away with him—with his terrors, to be sure, but also with the possibility he offered of assuming a part of the responsibility. Once original sin was rejected, a task of vast extent announced itself to modern thought. It had to tack between two reefs: maintain the sovereignty of man while also unloading from him the crushing burden it implied.[26]

One of the easiest ways will consist in isolating a corrupting agent and charging him with all the evils: a substitute devil. As a result, past history will change into a history of perdition. Involuntary candidates for the role of scapegoat will not be lacking, and their plots will always have to be unmasked. Thus, the Freemasons became responsible for all evils according to the reactionaries, in Germany even before the French Revolution, beginning with von Göchhausen, in revolutionary France from Abbé Barruel on.[27] Their recent appearance, however, made them a rather implausible object of condemnation. The search for a guilty party imposed its own exigencies. The object of condemnation must be not so much guilty as *accusable*. And for that, on one hand, it must be from the perceived beginning of history, so that one can lay to its charge all crimes; on the other hand, it must be able to receive avenging blows, and hence still be around; that will be the case if it claims an uninterrupted continuity with the most remote past. Only two social groups present these characteristics: the Jewish people and the Catholic Church. The accusers of the first go back to pagan antiquity, which above all reproached the Jews for not agreeing to join the other nations. Christianity then added a religious accusation: infidelity to the covenant. With the Enlightenment, the accusations took on a new cast. Israel appeared to be retrograde, attached to antiquated beliefs, posing an obstacle to the progress of civilization. In this connection, recall that belief in progress goes beyond the so-called progressive regimes. According to Hitler, the elimination of the Jews sought by the Nazi state was conceived as eliminating an obstacle to progress, conceived not in social terms but in racial ones.[28] Judaism was also reproached for having given birth to the second available target, Christianity. "Enlightened" anti-Semitism therefore coexisted with attacks on the Catholic Church, which became the "infamous thing" to crush (Voltaire), or the "Queen of the

Night" (Schikaneder). At the beginning of the nineteenth century, the Jesuits were the object of a collective paranoia which almost drove Edgar Quinet crazy. Moreover, the accusation can construct a composite object for itself. Each group accuses the others of mutual complicity, even a subterranean identity, while modeling itself on the image that it creates of that omnipresent Other: between the Jesuits, the Carbonari, the Masons, the Jews, the Templars, and the Assassins, the roles constantly change, in an unchanging circle.[29]

The Cult of Humanity

Having become "good" again, as long as he was not corrupted by "evil" external agents, man became the object of sentiments that were even more intense because they redounded upon the one who experienced them. And beyond this sentimentalism, the human gained a new status with Fichte, who made man an object of faith. With the moral law, God is also clearly given, and becomes an object of knowledge in that there is no longer any need to "believe"; on the other hand, to affirm that man is capable of doing his duty despite the countless crimes to which history witnesses demands nothing less than an act of faith. The idea was in the air: the same idea is found, just a year before Fichte, in Wordsworth. At its origin is perhaps Rousseau, who reduced "goodness" to consciousness of the good, while the capacity of doing good was abstracted from the actual doing of it; he thus considered himself to be the best of men who had ever lived.[30]

The idea of a religion of humanity appeared in certain cults of the revolutionary period such as theophilanthropy. During the Romantic period one saw such formulations as "the apotheosis of humanity" (Quinet) or the apostrophe by Béranger, "Reign, Humanity!" From 1846, Auguste Comte took it up again, while giving it a systematic cast. His project has certain rather ridiculous aspects which are easily mocked and which turned away from him certain admirers such as Mill or Littré. The maniacal concern to regulate everything, including the calendar, can make one smile; and anecdotal explanations, recalling the decisive encounter with Clotilde de Vaux, are not lacking. Nonetheless, the Comtean phenomenon remains an interesting symptom: the legitimacy of man can no longer rest on itself; there must be a "religious" support. Durkheim will draw from these reflections the necessity of returning to the idea according to which religion is indispensable to ensure the cohesion of society;

Maurras, a disciple of Comte, will come to the same conclusion concerning the nation.[31]

Progress must ensure the realization of the good in a future that is more or less distant. But it provides harbingers in the figure of the great man. It doubles down on the idea of human excellence in its different variants, from Greek *aretē* to Christian sanctity, which it secularizes. Certain human beings are thus more human than others. The king of the ancient Middle East, the "great man," was sometimes considered to be the sole true man. In a similar way, Michelet unselfconsciously remarks: "The people, in its highest idea, is found with difficulty in the people.... It isn't in its truth, in its highest power, except in the man of genius; in him resides the great soul." Misanthropy most often addresses itself to the human race in the abstract and makes as many exceptions as there are concrete persons, as Swift explained to Pope: "I hate this animal called man." With Michelet, one has the parallel attitude, which Dostoyevsky made fun of by having one of his most ridiculous characters say: "The more that I love humanity, the less I love human beings."[32]

On the other hand, the real people will authenticate the genius to the extent that it shows itself incapable of understanding him, and even persecutes him. Hence the Romantic legend of the artist who is always misunderstood by the "philistines" and therefore is unhappy. The idea of the catastrophes that strike great writers was already the subject of a treatise by Piero Valeriano (d. 1558), *De infelicitate literatorum*, published in 1620. But Valeriano did not make the misunderstanding of the public responsible for the sad fate of the genius. In contrast, with great talent Rousseau made his persecution very vivid, whether real or imagined. But it was Zola who, apropos to the Salon of 1879, raised this incomprehension to "an absolute rule that admits no exception."[33]

Humanity seeks to provide itself with models. These exceptional personalities merit being put forth as examples. The cult of great men was prefigured at the beginning of the eighteenth century with the Englishman Anthony Collins, who provided a list of individuals who were most distinguished by their intelligence and virtue and who had been "freethinkers."[34] The rest of the century began by making the praise of the great men of the nation an obligatory literary genre, before passing on to busts, statues, and mausolea. The notion of "genius" began its career and found its rigorous formulation in Kant. It passed from the domain of art to that of science and became the saw that Goethe complained about, before sinking to the level of the "genius horse" depicted by Musil.[35] The ancient idea of heroism was recycled. In the novelist Jean Paul, a petty king makes for himself a calendar of "moral heroes." Carlyle theorized about "hero-worship" and illustrated it with several historical personages.[36] The French Revolution produced real heroes, or invented them as needed. Byron, seeking one for his poem, noted with irony that "each year, each month, a new one is sent forth," before citing a string of members of the National Assembly or of generals. Napoleon himself became the object of a cult. Tatters of his undergarments were gathered as relics, and even (at least it was thought) their contents.[37] Later revolutions—the Bolshevik, then the Nazi, then the Maoist—did not fail to canonize the victims of their opponents, from Horst Wessel to little Pavel Morozov. There too, the historical existence of the people to venerate was only one option. That Lei Feng or comrade Ogilvy really existed or not was less important than their ability to inspire the sacrifices of others.[38]

Auguste Comte wanted to reorganize the entire calendar and replace the names of Christian saints, even the names of months, by those of the great men he wished to honor.[39] During the entirety of the nineteenth century, national movements produced heroes or exhumed persons from the past who ought to have been heroes; the nations in the process of giving themselves a state built temples to house the ashes or statues of their great men: thus the Pantheon in France, or Walhalla in Bavaria.[40] Later, the Bolsheviks will dream of more concrete museums, destined to house the cadavers of "heroes," and especially their brains, in order to display the physiological origin of their genius, or in the hope of a reanimation that the future progress of science would make possible. This is the way that Bogdanov conceived his "Pantheon." On the other hand, the project of resuscitating Lenin does not seem to have been officially that of the commission charged with his mausoleum, even if its architect Melnikov personally was interested in victory over death.[41]

Alongside the "good guys" to celebrate, some proceeded to a choice of officially hated "bad guys." Thus Comte completed the list of progressive heroes with a list of the "three principal retrogrades," to whom was devoted a "feast of the reprobates." In this way, the positivistic "beyond," if it contains a paradise, also includes a damnation more severe than the Christian hell. The latter is a threat that solely addresses . . . me, and which I do not have the right to think that anyone else can merit more than I. Comte himself decreed, with aplomb, that Julian the Apostate, Philip II, and Bonaparte must be condemned to the odium of all times.[42] However, in practice the paradox of Erostratus made it that that which was forbidden to remember was only better retained, and it encouraged another behavior: consigning individuals to oblivion pure and simple by eliminating them from the official history, from celebrations and monuments to school books, even cut-out pictures. This technique, perhaps invented by the painter Jacques-Louis David, who eliminated from his *Tennis Court Oath* deputies who had been guillotined since then,[43] found its apogee in the retouches done to photographic documents of the beginnings of the Soviet regime.

10

Moral Dominion

At the Renaissance, the notion of the dignity of man had changed from static to dynamic.[1] Domination over nature has a rebound effect on the human being who has claimed and assumed this role. Dignity no longer is a natural consequence of the superiority of man, who is better equipped, physically and intellectually, than the other living things. On the contrary, the superiority of man is a result of the way in which he dominates nature: domination constitutes the practical realization of the anthropology. The question of the origin of the initial capacity by which man distinguishes himself from the other animals—those who do not know work—is, however, bypassed in various ways.

Neutralization of Nature

The domain over which the action of man is exercised, and which he is to transform to his advantage, is "nature." In order to become an object malleable to his will, it must appear in a certain light. This occurred in the facts as well as ideas.

From the early modern period, nature was presented as something radically other than man and purely passive before his activity. The polarity masculine-feminine furnished an ever-recurring metaphor for their opposition. Some have drawn parallels between the project of the submission of nature and the contemporary submission, itself quite real, of women: it was above all women who were targeted during the great witch hunts.[2] The distance taken from nature included social dimensions. The reduction of matter to pure passivity was parallel to the submission of the lower classes. Human types emerged such as the city dweller and, especially, the courtier who, by not working, had no direct contact with nature; moreover, in the hunt, ballet, and military training, one finds the first examples of a dominion exercised over interior nature—that is, the body.[3]

This distance became concrete in certain innovations. Thus, the so-called French garden (in fact, inspired by the Dutch countryside) provided a small-scale image of nature mastered. At the same period, artists began depicting landscapes that until then only served as a setting for historical paintings, even as proof of sovereignty over a region, as in the oldest known representation of a particular rural scene, *The Miraculous Draught of Fishes* by Konrad Witz (1444). Henceforth, rural scenes are envisaged for themselves, for the first time in Dürer's watercolors. As a consequence, the spectator is placed at the center of the view, in the place corresponding to his position as master.[4] Even more so as painting itself is an artificial activity, which causes nature to appear in a specific light, precisely as "picturesque."[5]

In the Middle Ages, certain thinkers, interpreting the *Timaeus*, dared to make nature, to be sure, a creature, but also the workman of the designs of the Creator, and even a vice-God.[6] Modern times broke with this vision. On the plane of ideas, the neutralization of nature was accompanied by a rediscovery of Stoicism, ubiquitous at the dawn of the modern era. In the seventeenth century, in particular with Justus Lipsius, it acquired a philological foundation. The Stoics explained the universe by means of two principles, one active, the other passive; in the sixteenth century, Bernardino Telesio substituted them for the Aristotelian theory of the four elements.[7] Whether the rediscovery of Stoicism is a cause or a consequence, dawning modernity reduced nature to the status of an inert reality. Thus Descartes refused to make nature "some goddess or some other sort of imaginary power"; by "nature," he only meant matter.[8] A particular aspect of this neutralization of nature consisted of seeing animals as pure machines, an idea advanced as early as 1554 by the Spanish doctor Gómez Pereira, and given wide circulation by Descartes.[9]

A generation later, Robert Boyle devoted an entire treatise to expelling from nature any residue of spontaneity or freedom. He attacked all the formulations which granted it an active role, especially the *horror vacui* and its ability to heal diseases, which he critiques at length. His goal was to replace these so-called explanations with mechanisms. Nature is not a distinct agent, but a system of rules of action. Boyle also had a theological intention. He recalls that the notion of nature is unknown to the Old Testament, in order to eliminate a possible lieutenant of God, which could give rise to idolatry, even to a rival of the Creator, in any event capable of lessening the stark contrast between a wise Creator and the chance of Epicureans. Boyle's goal was also, more discretely, to get rid of the inhibitions limiting the conquest of nature, as suggested in a revealing passage: "The veneration wherewith men are imbued for what they call nature has been a discouraging impediment to the empire of man over the inferior creatures of God. For many have not only looked upon it as an impossible thing to compass, but as something impious to attempt: the removing of those boundaries which nature seems to have placed and established among her productions."[10]

Nature also ceased to be an authority in the moral domain. At the very end of the seventeenth century, Edmund Spenser presented nature as veiled, and opinions were divided over what this veil covered: a terrifying lion or a radiant sun. The theme of the indifference of nature to good and evil was born and saw a rich development in all of the European literature of the eighteenth century.[11] Henceforth it was no longer a matter of being guided by her, but rebuffing it. Nature was reconceived as pure passivity, offered to the action of the creative principle, which invests it with the properties it wishes to impart. But the place of the agent remains open. Initially reserved for God, it will increasingly tend to welcome man, who in this way implicitly guarantees the function of the active principle, one he will come to monopolize. Everything is in place to think about work.

Work

People did not wait for modern times to work, nor to grant work a dignity refused it by antiquity. But it was not until the seventeenth century that one began to see in work the specific difference of the human.[12] The first to do so was, probably, John Locke. His point of departure was political: to establish what will later be called liberalism. But his theory of knowledge is also a theory of the work by which the mind transforms the givens of sensation. Most deeply, Locke conceives of work as the self-creation of man. He emphasizes a verse that the church fathers had neglected to interpret literally enough: God gave man the entire earth and commanded him to master it. We appropriate what we work on, because work introduces something of us into the object. In truth, the products of the earth are almost without value, and it is only human labor and industry that confers it. Property, itself founded upon work, in turn founds political society, which only exists to safeguard it.[13] The political existence of man is thus the indirect consequence of a first process of humanization. It is not the city that humanizes; the subject who engages himself in the social bond is already a man, made human by work. In the process of humanization, the decisive factor is therefore the encounter with nature, not with another human being. Before being a political animal, man is the animal who works.

For the moderns, everything occurs as if it were man himself who created man. More precisely (because, taken literally, the formulation would be a flagrant absurdity): as if man created his own humanity. This strange idea, rarely consciously entertained, nonetheless is a presupposition of contemporary consciousness, which only the greatest thinkers have brought to explicit awareness. Thus Vico defines history—different, in this, from nature, which is the work of God—as the kingdom of human creativity.[14] Rousseau was the first to explicitly treat the paradoxical thesis of man's self-creation, when he talked about the moment of the contract that founded the city. He expressed it in a phrase that, taken literally, is contradictory: "The passage from the state of nature to the civil state produces *in man* a very remarkable change, by substituting justice for instinct in his conduct and giving his actions the morality that was lacking to them previously." It was this contract that, "from a stupid and limited animal, made him an intelligent being *and a man*." In a passage of the first edition of the *Émile*, later cut out, Rousseau formulated the paradox: "The man of society is no longer the man of nature; one must make him act otherwise, and who will make him this new being if not man himself?"[15]

Kant divided anthropology into two rubrics. Knowledge of man is physiological or pragmatic, the latter being the only one he treated in a text of that title. Kant calls "physiological" whatever bears upon nature in general (from the Greek word, *physis*, for nature). The physiological knowledge of man seeks what nature made of man; pragmatic knowledge, what man as a free agent did, can do, or ought to do with himself.[16] Making the verb "to make" his common denominator, Kant then distinguishes two sorts of pragmatic anthropologies, one natural, the other human. Nature is not what makes man, but what does something with him, supposing him to already exist.

Valorization

The domain of work extends even further to a plane where it is not yet the production of objects, but of the very value that measures them. One can put in this context the rise of the idea of "value" in the eighteenth and nineteenth centuries. In the 1960s it entered into politics from the right, in the appeal to the "traditional values" one wished to defend. But this only brought to a higher level a sensibility dating from much further back.

The idea of value implies the entrance of the good into the orbit of subjectivity. The reduction of *bonum* to "values" has a long history, one that goes back before modernity. Things that are worthy are valuable in themselves. The Homeric gods have a greater perfection, a greater value (*timē*) and greater strength; and it is because of the divine mother of the sun, postulated by Pindar, that men es*tima*te that gold is holier than other things, and it is because of its value (*tima*) that competitors compete in the games.[17]

By translating the Greek Stoic phrase *axian echon* by the Latin *aestimabilis*, Cicero already took a first step in the direction of subjectivism.[18] But the Latin term implies that the object of our esteem *merits* it, that it contains what is necessary for the scales to tip in its favor. For Seneca, nothing is more important than to give things their just price, and Augustine wants man to be a just "appraiser" of what is, and in the seventeenth century, the Anglican priest and poet Thomas Traherne asked: "Can you be righteous, unless you be just in rendering to things their due esteem? All things were made to be yours and you were made to prize them according to their value."[19]

An important step toward the entrance of the idea of value into the orbit of subjectivity is already found in Montaigne: "That our opinion gives a price to things, this is seen by those things in great number which we do not look at for us to prize them, but to ourselves; and we do not consider their qualities or their usefulness, but only what they cost us to recover them: as if that were part of their substance; and we call 'value' in them not what they bring us, but what we bring to them."[20] Montaigne recognizes a fact: we measure things in accordance with what they cost us. But he also continues to consider what things are intrinsically worth beyond our calculations.

It was Descartes who took the decisive step: "The true office of reason is to examine the just value of all the goods whose acquisition seems to depend in some way on our conduct." A bit later he gives an even more radical formulation: "We must make use of experience and reason to distinguish good and evil and *to know their just value*, in order not to take one for the other."[21] That statement is staggering. It is no longer a matter of distinguishing true goods from illusory ones, or of classifying goods on a graded scale. The formulation marks a transition that makes an epoch: good and evil under the yoke of "value." Both, good as well as evil, have a common reference and are not as opposed as one would think: they have a "value." It is the latter's measure that alone allows us to distinguish them. The good no longer is directly worthwhile, as good, but rather as what has value. It no longer derives its goodness from itself, but from the value assigned to it.

The writers and philosophers of the Enlightenment generalized Locke's thesis according to which the sole origin of value is human work. Man arrogates to himself the privilege of valorization: he alone gives to things their meaning. Buffon puts in parallel wild nature and cultivated nature and shows that nature would be void (*vide*) without man's presence. For Rousseau's Savoyard curate, man is king of the earth. For Diderot, "if one banishes man or the thinking thing from the surface of the earth, this pathetic and sublime spectacle of nature is but a sad and mute scene. . . . It is the presence of man which renders the existence of beings interesting. . . . Abstracting from my existence and the happiness of my fellows, what does the rest of nature matter?" For Morelly, the desire to be happy is the effect of the concern for our preservation, itself dependent upon our sensibility: "This sensibility must first of all, without any deliberation or examination, make us report everything to ourselves and imagine that everything is made for us, and without us everything that exists would be useless."[22] The idea is found again in Romanticism, as in Coleridge: "In our life alone does Nature live."[23] Kant draws from such formulations when he notes "a judgment that no one, not even the most vulgar intelligence, can deny" that "without man, all of creation would be a mere desert, vain and without purpose." But unlike the French, he precisely determines what gives value to the existence of the things of the world. This value is "that which he alone can provide," to wit, "a good will."[24]

The notion of "value" finds itself inevitably drawn into a dialectic. If it is the subject who confers value on what he values, he can take it away. He, therefore, is worth more than all the values that it will please him to pose. Nietzsche's Zarathustra expresses this dialectic in an untranslatable wordplay: "Evaluation (*Schätzen*) itself is the treasure (*Schatz*) and the jewel of all things that have value." It is the subject and his power of valorization which then becomes the supreme value. The subjection of the idea of the good to that of value thus shows itself to be but one more expression of the sovereignty of the modern subject.[25]

11

The Duty to Reign

This sovereignty of the subject is not total unless he is only determined to act by himself, not by external movers. At the end of the eighteenth century, the project of controlling nature therefore took on a new aspect. The place of this change is the subject of the project himself and the motive that makes him initiate it. Until then, it was above all—we saw this in Bacon—the search for some material interest, which Kant would have qualified as "pathological." At the end of a process that culminates with German idealism, to dominate nature became a moral exigency. Earlier, commodious existence was desired, "comfort," a comfort that at bottom was based on a "hedonistic degradation."[1] Henceforth it will be a matter of fulfilling a duty. Technology thus enters into the domain of the *serious*.

Domination Enlarged

The moral impulse, before overflowing to the work to be done, begins by bearing upon the subject. He is first of all obliged to have made himself at least able to exercise dominion, by acquiring the necessary virtues. The Creator, explains Locke, gave the world to all human beings in common; but desiring that it be worked on, he especially gave it to the "industrious and rational."[2] The modern birth of the capitalist economy was accompanied by a rationalization of life. Virtues were promoted that antiquity and the Middle Ages barely knew: order, work ethic, thrift. Other virtues existing in religious form were reinterpreted and secularized; thus sloth (*acedia*), which despaired of salvation and caused one to neglect it, became laziness in work. Bells structured the rhythm of monastic hours; the clock which precisely measures time allows for the punctuality of trains, even the clocking-in of factory workers. But beyond these changes in mentalities, which have been discovered and studied by historians, the very nature of virtue changed.³

This began with an enlarging of the idea of dominion: its object until then, nature, remained external. Now dominion gained another dimension, but by going back to the source: what must be conquered is not an appendage, but rather the starting point. The nature to be controlled is, first, ours: the citadel to take is within. This presupposed a modification in the way of conceiving the relationship of man with himself. Virtue appeared less as the perfect development of nature, eventually with the aid of grace, than as constraint imposed on the former. In medieval vocabulary, one would say that the continent man, who had perverse desires but conquered them, took over from the virtuous man who only desired what was good.⁴

The idea of a mastery of oneself was already found in *The Imitation of Christ*: "The perfect victory consists in triumphing over oneself; for the one who holds himself in subjection [*semetipsum subjectum tenet*], such that sensibility obeys reason and reason, me [i.e., Jesus Christ], he truly is his own conqueror and *master of the world*."⁵ It is because he is his own subject that the one who from now on will be called "the subject" can attain to mastery. During the classical age, Corneille formulated the idea in his *Cinna* (1639), apropos to Augustus, in a way that has remained proverbial: "master of myself as I am the universe." In 1654, Milton praised a real person, Cromwell, for being "Commander first over himself, the conqueror of himself, it was over himself he had most learned to triumph."⁶ In Descartes, with "generosity" the first domain to master, the first object to which we apply "industry," is nothing other than the subject himself. Rousseau defines virtue as a victory over self: "Virtue not only consists in being just, but in being so by triumphing over one's passions, by *ruling over one's own heart*." And Hegel prolonged Descartes's formulation about mastery of nature by revealing its ultimate basis: "Man does not become master of nature before becoming master of himself."⁷

This last formulation indicates the chasm which separates the ancient moralities of self-control, such as ancient and renaissance Stoicism, from their modern versions. The former aimed at a self-mastery that was self-sufficient, which did not imply the conquest of the external world, and which even made it superfluous. Now self-mastery becomes the indispensable condition, but only preparatory, for the conquest that truly counts, that of nature, important because that conquest alone allows man to attain his authentic humanity. With positivism, the mastery of nature enters into what defines man's essence, as a being capable of morality. The anthropology implies technology and all its consequences as a feature that is not accidental, but constitutive.

German Idealism

The last step, by which the technological conquest of external nature became a moral duty, was taken by the German thinkers of the end of the eighteenth century. For them, man is bound to conquer nature because he must do so in order to be free, and he is "condemned to be free."[8] This way of looking at things appeared in Kant, then expanded with his disciple Fichte.

It was Kant who accomplished this revolution, which he formulated with the greatest depth. Within each person, nature is the "pathology" that must be repressed. At worst, nature is an enemy; at best, material to form. It is on this foundation that the concept of "culture" understood as opposed to "nature" is squarely placed. The third *Critique* (1791) gave it a philosophical foundation. Its second part examines teleological judgment.

> Insofar as he is the sole earthly being that possesses understanding, and thereby a faculty of posing objectives that he understands, man is truly the rightful sovereign of nature and, when one considers the latter as a teleological system, he is the final end of nature. But he is this on one condition, to wit: that he understands this and has the will to give to nature and to himself a teleological orientation of this sort, one that suffices unto itself, independently of nature, and thus can be a final end, but an end that he has no need of seeking in nature. . . . Thus, only culture can be the final goal that one is justified in ascribing to nature with respect to the human race.

This culture is neither the technical dexterity which develops the capacity of means to attain their end, nor the training that liberates from the instincts, because neither of the two can orient the will to a good end. Man receives the privilege of being the final end of creation, but only to the extent that he is "considered as noumenal . . . , a subject of morality, . . . a moral being."[9]

Kant concedes to Rousseau—whom he does not cite, but whose *First Discourse* he has in mind—that the refinements of taste and luxury can have deleterious consequences, by the multitude of needs they create and by nourishing self-love. On the other hand, refinement weans us from animality and frees the space for the development of humanity. In this way, "the fine arts and the sciences . . . prepare . . . man for a dominion in which only reason ought to have authority. . . . His existence contains in itself the supreme goal to which, to the extent he is able, he can subject all of nature, or at least against which he does not have the right to think himself subject to any of its influence."[10] Kant's modal wordplay is subtle: man has the physical possibility of subjecting the totality of nature to the supreme end he contains in himself; it is morally forbidden him to subject himself to an influence of nature which would contradict that end. Kant, however, does not explicitly draw the obvious conclusion of his affirmations—namely, that the subjection of nature is a moral duty. His contemporaries will take that step. Kant himself cites his student Willmans, for whom man is not passive towards nature, but creative.[11]

Schiller begins by reaffirming the neutral character of nature, its indifference to human activity, and hence the impossibility of taking it as a moral model; quite the contrary, it must be dominated. "Man, who was the slave of nature as long as he only felt it, becomes its legislator as soon as he conceives it. She who until then dominated him as a *power* is henceforth an object for his consideration as a judge. That which is an object for him has no power over him, because, to be an object, it must undergo his power."[12]

Fichte develops a Kantian intuition according to which the "I is the *proprietor* of the world."[13] The formulation deepens Descartes's (man as *possessor* of nature) by adding the idea of legitimacy. But right must become fact. Already the owner of the world, man has the vocation of becoming its possessor. Fichte conceives of "culture" as the exercise of all the faculties aiming at total liberty, at the "total independence from everything that isn't ourselves, our pure I." As a corollary to the deduction of intersubjectivity which allows Fichte to give concrete content to the concept of right, he sketches an anthropology. As he himself indicates, it brings together observations of earlier philosophers, several ancient commonplaces, some rather self-satisfied, others more somber. As for the commonplaces, there are observations on the upright posture of man, which allows for the liberation of the human hand; on the subtlety of man's sense of touch, which is its consequence; on the eye and face. As for the more somber side, there are observations on human nakedness and abandonment, with stepmother nature having abandoned man before giving him his final form.[14] However, all these properties of man are grouped around a central theme which itself is modern: the essential indeterminacy of man. Different from animals, man only exists as a project. The empirical existence of man "thrown" into the world is but the translation of the status of man as project. "Every animal *is* what it is; only man from the beginning is nothing at all. What he ought to be, he must become. And as he must be a self-determining being, it is by himself that he must become what he is to become." To become what he is does not mean an order coming from without, a divine command or a natural impulse. It must not be a task, but a project, an order that man gives himself: "We are nothing, let us be everything!"

The classical idea of human dignity is transformed: it was located in the clarity of his intellect; now it is rethought on the basis of the idea of mastery.[15] "Plasticity, as such, is the character of man." According to an etymological play on words that Fichte leaves implicit, the sole characteristic of the human is to possess no proper character and thus to be able to receive every mark. That by which man is human and appears as such, his face, in itself is nothing: "All that, all the expressive visage, as we leave the hands of nature is nothing . . . and it is precisely thanks to this lack of realization that man is capable of this plasticity." Fichte seems to say the same thing as Cicero: man is but the sketch of nature.[16] And one rediscovers an old theme, the only one for which Fichte names his source (Pliny the Elder), the abandonment by nature.[17] Moreover, one could attenuate the "nothing at all" by seeing in it only an extension to the entire human being of the status of the passive intellect in Aristotle.[18] What previously was only valid in the noetic realm, *nous* as nothing-in-itself, now defines an entire anthropology. The difference, however, depends on the answer to a question. This rough-hewn block, is it already a human being or no? Is it merely a person *in potentia*? Or a person who does not yet have the means of manifesting himself as one? Today's discussions concerning the status of the embryo repeat at the level of ontogenesis a dispute begun, at least implicitly, with modernity itself.

Fichte thus goes beyond Bacon, who proposed as his goal the greatest utility or comfort, taking a step already prefigured in Malebranche.[19] Mastery becomes the object of a moral exigency: "I wish to be the lord of nature, and it must be my servant; I want to have over it an influence commensurate with my strength, and it has no right to have any over me. . . . This is not just a pious wish for humanity, but is the vindication of its right, which it does not have the right to renounce, and of its destiny, that it live on the earth as lightly, as freely, as imperiously toward nature as the latter allows. Man has the duty to work."[20] Fichte thus became the inventor of the idea of the dignity of work. According to a late text by him, to have children is to draw from oneself new commanders over nature; it is "to give, beyond the limits of his earthly existence and for all eternity, lords to nature."[21]

Positivism and Pragmatism

Human action now attains a determinative role in the orientation to reality, to the point where it supersedes knowledge on its own terrain and reveals itself more capable of guiding us, even if this mastery has for its price the renunciation of truth. Prepared during the classical age, this idea moves to the center of Comte's thought, then Claude Bernard's, and finally to pragmatism.

The positivist attitude is not unique to modern times, but is encountered in antiquity, as the expression of the schizophrenia of the learned who were obliged to choose between the mathematical models that allowed one to predict astronomical phenomena and Aristotelian physics, which demonstrated the unreality of the epicycles and eccentrics postulated by these models. "Positivism is the child of the failure and renunciation" of astronomers before their "inability to penetrate the mystery of the true movements of the celestial bodies." The positivists of the nineteenth and twentieth centuries, added Koyré maliciously, "only replaced resignation with complacency."[22] I would add something that seems to me crucial: While the ancient astronomers were obviously unable to act on the phenomena that they could only describe, modern positivists compensate for their ignorance of causes with an emphatic intervention in the facts that they control. Domination does not even need to know that it has grasped the truth of reality; it suffices to have hold over it.

Bacon, the first to have assigned to science a technological orientation, is also perhaps the first to affirm that physics, once achieved, will render metaphysics superfluous. And why not forbid what is superfluous? In his utopia, Morelly places among the "laws governing studies which prevent the distraction of the human mind and every transcendent reverie . . . a sort of public code of all the sciences" confining metaphysics and morals within "limits prescribed by the laws," but giving free rein to the experimental sciences aiming at "the perfection of the arts useful to society."[23] The general formula of resignation, of renouncing knowledge of causes for the sake of knowledge of laws, can already be found in Locke and among the radicals of the Enlightenment, who, despite his intention, were inspired by him. Thus, d'Holbach: let man "submit himself in silence to those laws from which he cannot escape, let him agree not to know the causes that are covered with an impenetrable veil."²⁴ With these formulations, one remains on the plane of epistemology. But positivism, far beyond a modest maxim, presupposes a revolution in the very definition of man. In a straight line from German idealism (with which, however, it has no direct affiliation), it defines man's humanity on the basis of the domination of nature.

This anthropological revolution, probably not entirely self-conscious, is present in Auguste Comte as early as May 1822. The young graduate of the École Polytechnique proposed this definition: "Civilization consists . . . , on one hand, in the development of the human spirit, and in the development of the action of man on nature, which is its consequence." The equilibrium between the two aspects is merely apparent, for it is the action on nature that is to guarantee that the human mind develops in the right direction, without losing itself in vain speculations. This action even leads to the revision of the traditional definition of man as the political animal. In the same text, the founder of sociology writes: "Any system of society . . . has for its definitive object to direct the activity of all the particular forces to a general goal. For, there is no *society* but where a general cooperative action occurs." There is nothing but what is very traditional in the observation, and in the counterexample he provides of animals coexisting in the same flock or herd.²⁵ However, the identity of words hides a capital difference: "action" no longer means *praxis*, but production as the transformation of nature. Further on, one reads that in the "preparatory social system . . . action on nature was only the indirect goal of society." But in itself this action is first, and one ought not "to consider the social combinations but as means of attaining it." That is why "the government of things replaces that of human beings." This will be the case in "the regenerated society" that Comte expects. Then, "society . . . tends to organize itself in the same way [i.e., industrially], by giving itself as its goal the activity . . . of production." But this activity is not only the end of already established society; even more importantly it is the cause that produces it. In an amazing phrase, Comte characterizes his definitive society as "*constituting itself in order* to act on nature." The goal of society is therefore not the common life of human beings, still less the common good, but rather technology. The human is constituted as such via a detour through the nonhuman on which it works.[26] In this way, the domination of nature decides the very humanity of man as social.

This first version of the revolutionary positivist anthropology concerns man as political animal; the second, no less decisive, envisages man as the living thing endowed with reason. Until then man was defined by reason, not only as the faculty of social communication but as access to the truth. Henceforth he must reconceive reason in such a way that the model of truth that it allows passes under the rule of the industrial project. The price to pay is the abandonment of the search for causes. In searching for causes, reason, at bottom, was looking for itself in reality, by seeking what was profoundly called "the reason" of phenomena. Comte's positivism is based on just such a refusal, probably taken from the formulation of Jean Baptiste Joseph Fourier: "The primordial causes are not known to us; but they are subject to simple laws, which one can discover by observation, and whose study is the object of natural philosophy."[27] It is no longer a matter of submitting to laws, as d'Holbach proposed, but coming to know them. Comte can therefore take as his program, from one end of his oeuvre to the other, that one must not seek to know causes but content oneself with writing the laws.[28] "One ought to conceive the study of nature as intended to furnish the true rational basis of man's activity on nature, since the knowledge of the laws of phenomena, whose result is to allow us to foresee them, alone can lead us to modify them to our advantage in the active life." To be sure, Comte does not thereby neglect the "more direct and higher destination" of the sciences, "that of satisfying the fundamental need experienced by our intellect to know the laws of phenomena." It remains, however, that the principal criterion that allows one to measure the value of the different sciences is the action of man on the external world, without which the very genesis of man would have been stifled in the crib by a hostile nature. From this point of view, physics and chemistry, and to a lesser degree biology, are incomparably more important than astronomy.[29] In the same direction, two generations after Comte, Bertrand Russell could bid farewell to the very notion of cause, stained as it was (according to him) with an irreparable anthropomorphism.[30]

Already with Comte, a pragmatic tonality makes itself known. If he begins by affirming the necessity of basing himself on scientific knowledge, he is far from being scientistic. Rather, he proposes submitting theory to practice, reason to the heart. "Despite the scientific origin of the new philosophy, in it science will be reduced to its true office: to construct the objective basis of human wisdom, in order to provide an indispensable foundation to art and industry.... It will limit the study of the true to what is required by the development of the good and the beautiful." The rest is nothing but vain curiosity. Alone decisive is "the human point of view," which Comte explains by "social." "We must only seek to know the laws of phenomena capable of exercising some influence on humanity."[31]

A generation after Comte, the physiologist Claude Bernard reprised the project of a domination of nature made possible by the progress of the sciences: "With the assistance of these active experimental sciences, man became an inventor of phenomena, a veritable foreman of creation; and in this respect one cannot assign limits to the power that he can acquire over nature.... Man has already gained over mineral nature a power that shows itself splendidly in the applications of the modern sciences, even though this only appears to be its dawn." What science already allows us to do with the mineral kingdom, it ought to be able to do for the living. Claude Bernard puts it in Latin: *medicus naturae superator* (the physician is the conqueror of nature).[32] He rejected the Hippocratic attitude of observation and patient waiting, and in practice joined the rank of the empirical doctors, while substituting the rigor of the experimental method for their purported experience.

This method is founded on science. "Pure science has always been the source of all the riches that man has acquired and of all the real conquests that he has achieved over the phenomena of nature." In this difference from the Greeks, who emphasized the purely theoretical nature of science, and even going beyond Bacon, Claude Bernard affirms, in a phrase that would have probably seemed crazy to Aristotle, that *"true science acts and explains its action and its power."* Initially at least, the fecundity of science justifies the preference given to the experimental method, the sole effective means of getting results: "The intellectual conquest of man consists in diminishing or limiting indetermination, to the extent that with the assistance of the experimental method he gains ground towards determinism. This alone ought to satisfy his ambition, *because* it is by this that he extends, and will more and more extend, his power over nature."[33] The idea of mastery, however, does not limit itself to the domain of the applications of science; it is located in the heart of science itself and governs its very procedure. It is what defines the experimental method: the experimenter is distinguished from the mere observer "not [in] that he is active or passive in the production of phenomena, but [depending on] whether he acts or not on them in order *to make himself their master.*"[34] More essential to the action is the intention of mastery that guides it. Where the relation of mastery appears, not as the intervention of the technician transforming nature, but simply as the capacity of the experimenter to provoke or prevent a phenomenon, this is at first little more than a manner of speaking: "When the experimenter has arrived at knowing a phenomenon's conditions of existence, *in some sense* he is its master; he can predict its behavior and its manifestation, favor or inhibit it at will. At that, the goal of the experimenter is attained; he has, by means of science, extended his power over a natural phenomenon."[35] However, it could very well be the case that this innocent metaphor hides the true assertion of power, which is that of the method itself, which takes control of science earlier and more definitively than it takes control of nature. Nietzsche knew how to formulate the event: "It is not the victory of science that distinguishes our nineteenth century, but the victory of scientific method over science."[36] One glimpses a similar claim in a passage where Bernard opposes two types of relationship to knowledge. He calls the first, negatively, "scholastic," repeating the dark legend of a Middle Ages given over to the principle of authority. According to him, scholasticism believed itself in possession of absolute certainty, but its knowledge remained sterile. In contrast to that is "the experimenter, who always doubts and who does not believe he possesses absolute certainty in anything, but who arrives at mastering the phenomena that surround him and extending his power over nature." From this he derives a capital principle: "Man *can therefore do more than he knows*, and the true experimental science does not give him power except by showing him what he does not know."[37]

Here we see two strange reversals. First, the obvious one, a reversal of the well-known maxim of Bacon, that *science is power*. Then another, more discrete, of the Cartesian theory of error: Descartes explained error by the fact that the will has a larger scope than the intellect and precipitously judges before knowing.[38] With Claude Bernard, power does not presuppose knowledge. On the contrary, it is purchased at the price of renouncing absolute knowledge, a stance he qualifies as "modest." The biologist thus rejoins the reserve of Newton, who refused to present gravity other than under the species of "as if." Where it is a question of living things, modern science is even more explicit than the natural science of inanimate objects in its rejection of "the obscure notion of cause" that it proposes to replace by that of "relation or condition." This, to be sure, does not give an account of nature; on the other hand, it suffices "to render us its masters."[39] But by the same token, the adjective "absolute" is not totally abandoned; it passes from knowledge to power. It is power that in the rigorous sense of the phrase receives *absolute sovereignty*. During the Middle Ages, certain extreme theorists of papal authority did not hesitate to say that the pope could not know all that he could do.[40] The experimenter, become the pope of phenomena, agrees not to know the essence of things, but "by a marvelous compensation, to the extent that science humiliates . . . our pride, it augments our power."[41]

Claude Bernard announces a long-term tendency whose traces will be found long after him. Thus in 1929, the physicist J. D. Bernal, imagining the radiant future of science, acknowledges that "with time, the acceptance, the appreciation and *even the comprehension*, of nature will be less and less necessary. In their place will come the need to determine the desirable form of the universe controlled by man, which belongs totally to art."[42]

※

A close tie connects the positivist renunciation of the search for causes and the privilege that pragmatism accords to action. That tie pertains to the social legitimation of research. A science that renounces the idea of causality can no longer clarify the world for society; it therefore has no other way of verifying its relevance than by the power it confers.

One can call "pragmatism" the refusal to grant any importance to questions whose answers will change nothing in our behavior. This is an ancient attitude, already attested in India by the Buddha, who leaves open the questions that do not concern the "four fundamental truths," all of them practical, then later by Shankara, for whom the sage ought to disinterest himself from whatever does not concern his salvation. In Greece, Epictetus refused to lose time resolving problems that would not aid us in correcting our behavior. The fathers of the church and the Medievals criticized useless curiosity, which they distinguished from the *studiositas* by which we seek what truly serves us. Petrarch has this saying: "To will the good is worth more than to know the true."[43] One could also give Kant a pragmatic reading. In effect he begins from an implicit presupposition: we have the right to seek to know only what nourishes our practice. The rest, knowledge for its own sake, is useless, even culpable. With Kant, the action in the light of which knowledge ought to be measured is moral action. Fichte, who radicalized Kant's intuition, makes of knowledge the instrument of action, and in this way can be seen as a precursor of William James or Bergson.[44] Closer to us, the most famous of Brecht's "stories of Mr. Keuner," where the question said to be without relevance is none other than the question of God's existence, can be placed in a tradition of this sort.

With modernity, pragmatism took on a new cast, in that mastery became the ultimate goal and the criterion of truth. The primacy of practice was turned to the credit of work understood as fabrication. The English philosopher F. C. S. Schiller (d. 1937) named the "spirit" of pragmatism "humanism." Pragmatism is "a particular application of humanism to the theory of knowledge. But humanism will seem more universal. It will seem in possession of a method that is universally applicable . . . to everything about which man is concerned, as much as a theory of knowledge." In giving this meaning to the word "humanism," he only pushed to extremes the logic that had first led to giving it this meaning. In the United States, as early as 1904 William James approved the neologism of his colleague and accepted the word "humanism" as a synonym for "pragmatism" in the broad sense, according to which the truth of any proposition consists in its consequences. The narrow sense, according to which truths must have consequences, can be called "pragmatic method."[45] However, the word did not "take" in this sense. Another American, Richard Rorty (d. 2007), bid adieu to the effort to seek the "truth," for the sake of a practice that was, however, less technological than social. The renunciation of the truth is the price to pay to obtain "democracy." Mastery, however, remains the ultimate criterion, even if it is presented in the sweetened form of the self-mastery of a human group that, rejecting every external influence, only obeys its own exigencies.[46]

12

The Iron Rod

All these thoughts arose while the realization of the project of the domination of nature was merely beginning. With the first Industrial Revolution, the idea began to take on a new look. What until then had been pretty much a dream variously imagined by different individuals became a concrete reality that was methodically pursued.

The Historical Context

Bacon's program consisted in the systematic and exclusive application of scientific discoveries to the amelioration of the human condition. In the domain of facts, science and technology still remained separated for a good two centuries, and their representatives were hostile to one another. "The real contributions of science to technology remained insignificant for a long time."[1] They became noticeable in the nineteenth century and were accompanied by a theoretical justification. The first domain in which scientific research and industrial activity effected their union was in the chemistry of colorants.[2] I need to recall a few stages in a journey in which technology, whose history I cannot write, not only improved its performances but progressively annexed new domains of being.

At the end of the eighteenth century, the steam engine represented the first form of industrial motor, a separate source of energy applicable to any machine tool one wished. At the end of the nineteenth century, technology became capable of producing and transporting electricity, a source of energy that did not exist in that form in our ordinary perception of nature. It permitted the communication of energies from different sources, which it rendered commensurable, as money does for goods. It also allowed for the transport of energy without too much loss. Moreover, it created technological objects that took on their meaning, and did so *exclusively*, in the context of a complete system. Other mechanisms depended upon the human activity that could activate them, if need be. Until a recent date, one could still turn a gramophone or start a car by hand; but an electrical appliance cut off from its source is nothing at all.[3] In this way, it is only with electrification that technology can create a world at once capable of, and condemned to, self-sufficiency, thus realizing a model of integral autonomy. One thus understands that Lenin could define communism as socialism, plus the electrification of the entire country.

Another step was taken when technology fabricated new materials, whereas ancient technology merely imposed new forms on naturally pre-existing materials.[4] The first entirely synthetic material was produced in 1907 by the Belgian-American chemist Leo Hendrik Baekeland (d. 1944). He gave it its name, Bakelite, and in 1909 proposed the generic name of "plastic materials." Petrochemistry allowed for the generalization of their manufacture, and they became the new industrial materials: nylon replaced plant and animal fibers, polystyrene replaced wood or porcelain. Nuclear physics permits the exploitation of an energy that, even if it is easiest to derive from radioactive substances, in principle is found in every material. The fusion of the atom, if it is ever realized, will allow the perfect conversion of matter into energy, thus realizing an ancient dream.[5]

The industrial movement is in sync with a theoretical devaluation of nature, first of all under the purely technical aspect. Auguste Comte had a presentiment of this in a passage that contains one of the rare occurrences in his work of the expression "conquest of nature," the object of a poetry to come, liberated from the fascination that the purported wisdom of nature exercised over the ancients. "Real science has directly observed, under all the important aspects, the extreme *imperfection* of this so vaunted natural order. . . . Today, each feels that human works . . . are in general very superior, whether in arrangement or in simplicity, to whatever the natural economy can offer of the most perfect sort, and where, ordinarily, the size of the masses alone constituted the main cause of previous admiration." Nature can produce "large machines," but industry can trump her. The "real order" is "almost always inferior in wisdom to the artificial economy established by our feeble human intervention in its limited order."[6] This surprising, and questionable, judgment in any case stands in opposition to an ancient tradition that recalled the inferiority of human art before nature's. Thus Marsilio Ficino recalled: "The works of the earth are more beautiful than those of man."[7]

The devalorization of nature is also moral. The nineteenth century rediscovered the "black" vision of nature. Novalis saw in nature "the terrifying jaw of death," and in 1793–94, Tieck had one of his characters say: "The splendor of nature draws its matter from mould, and mould is nothing but putrefaction disguised."[8] Nature no longer can serve as a model. Nothing, therefore, opposes its transformation—what am I saying? Everything demands it! John Stuart Mill only conceives of nature as what must be corrected by human action. Schopenhauer, who in this perhaps had Romantic sources, sees nature as a mere field of battle for the will-to-live. It is also interesting to see that he approves of the machine as alleviating the pain of work.[9] In contrast, Vigny simultaneously harbors a dark vision of an indifferent nature and a rejection of mechanization.[10]

Industrial Intoxication

Technological innovations had already stirred the admiration of the sixteenth century. In the nineteenth, enthusiasm for the achievements of industry are found everywhere. Writers reflect it. Some do it in their own names, as with Heine, for whom the railroad (the modest Paris-Orléans line, a journey of four and a quarter hours) constitutes "a providential event." With it "begins a new period in the history of the world.... Even the elementary concepts of time and space have been shaken. Space was killed by the railroad, and only time remains to us."[11] There is the same enthusiasm in characters created by the writers, as, in Hawthorne, the character who is on fire about electricity and the telegraph it makes possible. Henry Adams opposed the modern dynamo and the Virgin Mary, who for him is the highest symbol of the Middle Ages. This is also true for the future: Goethe confided to Eckermann that he would agree to live another fifty years in order to see Suez and Panama cut across and see a canal join the Rhine to the Danube. Max Maria von Weber, son of the composer, a railroad engineer, connects the shortening of distances and the domination of the world in an equation: "The smaller the world, the greater is man."[12]

The temptation grew to measure human activity by the standard of industry and to seek in it a solution to all social problems. Thus, Henri de Saint-Simon and Auguste Comte dreamed of replacing the government of human beings with the administration of things. The nineteenth century is thus the time when industrial utopias proliferated in popular literature. It is also the time of the first warnings about the dangers of mechanization, in Jules Verne and later in H. G. Wells.

Jules Verne, the eulogist of technology, published his novels starting in 1863. According to one of his characters, everything seems possible: "They are ingenious men.... They exploit ... all the resources of art, science, and industry. With all that, one does what one wants"; according to the same character, an artilleryman to be sure, it is by technology, in this case the technology which created the cannonball, "that man came closest to the Creator."[13] The most revealing novel is probably *The Mysterious Island*, published in 1873–75. The context of the story is clearly inspired by the story of Robinson Crusoe. Five shipwrecked people find themselves on a deserted island, with no possessions, or almost none. The point of the story is conveyed in a very clear statement: they are "absolutely disarmed in the face of nature.... From nothing, they must arrive at everything." They succeed, however, in starting a fire, hunting, domesticating animals, and constructing furniture, a boat, even an elevator. And even in synthesizing sulfuric acid and nitroglycerin. This is because they were under the leadership of Cyrus Smith, an engineer, who "for them was a microcosm, a composite of all of science and human intelligence." The Baconian ideal is realized to the full, and science produces success: "They 'know,' and the man who 'knows' succeeds where others vegetate and inevitably perish." Hence the general lesson: "The need to do the work that lasts, that survives him, is the sign of man's superiority over all else that lives in this world. This is what founded his dominion, and what justifies it in the entire world."[14]

Nonetheless, the Robinsonesque industrial complex is not accompanied by an attempt to rival the Creator, or even to do without him. The colonists are pious, conscious of "their duty to be civilized and Christian." They address prayers of petition and of thanksgiving to God, respect the Sabbath, celebrate Easter and Pentecost. They count on their own energy and the assistance of heaven. Providence is often evoked, even invoked. "By transforming the products of nature, they had created everything by themselves, and thanks to their intelligence they had escaped from their difficulties. But did it not appear that Providence had wanted to reward them, by sending them ... several products of human industry?"[15] This particular providence, a crate of weapons and tools, will later reveal itself to be the discreet action of Captain Nemo. General providence, however, is first of all that of nature. Human ingenuity does not suffice for everything, as the discovery of a grain of wheat in the lining of his jacket by one of the marooned shows. This grain—"Cyrus Smith, with all his intelligence, all his ingenuity, would never have been able to produce it." Nature and human work complement and complete each other: "Everything succeeded, thanks to the activity of these courageous and intelligent men. Providence did much for them, no doubt; but, faithful to the great precept, they helped themselves first of all, and then heaven came to their aid.... If nature had constantly supplied them, their science had known how to derive profit from what it offered them."[16]

Jules Verne does not make industry the sufficient condition of happiness. In *The Begum's Fortune* (1879), written under the blow of the defeat of 1870, he opposes two uses of science, tied to the two nations: beneficent when applied by the French to peaceful ends, it becomes malevolent when a German employs it for war. Science's city, Stahlstadt, "the city of steel," is devoted to the perfecting of canons and their projectiles. The "bad guy," bent on the destruction of the rival city, expresses his convictions: "Law, and good and evil, are purely relative things and matters of convention. In truth, there are only the great natural laws. The law of competition for life has the same rank as the law of gravitation. To want to avoid it is foolish; to obey it and act accordingly is reasonable and wise."[17] The posthumous work of Flaubert (1881) illustrates the same duality: extracts of his plan sketch two contrasted visions of the future, rosy with Bouvard, dark with Pécuchet. The first develops the theme of the progress of technology; the second sees the world degenerate, but does not tie it directly to the influence of machines. It is rather "modern man himself who is diminished and has become a machine."[18]

H. G. Wells, in his *Men like Gods* (1923),[19] in a revealing way specifies in his subtitle that he writes a "positive utopia"; that was no longer a tautology, so much had the tone of novels of anticipation turned somber. A group of "Earthlings" finds itself in a parallel world, a Utopia three thousand years in the future. The negative aspect of the narrative comes from the presence of the Earthlings: they bring microbes against which the organisms of the Utopians have forgotten how to battle; the Earthlings, therefore, have to be put in quarantine. Worse, they attempt to import the habits of rivalry of our world, so they finally are sent away.

In the description of the marvels of Utopia, the accent is on the domination of nature, even if the technological means are only vaguely evoked. Science took control of human activities by means of physics and biology, but also psychology. It allowed for "the universal scientific state, the educational state." Man spontaneously put himself at the service of man, and the most perfect communism was realized. Science had led to "a great enlargement of practical human power. . . . Extraordinary possibilities of control over his own body and over his social life dawned upon the Utopian." The result is expressed in several ways that echo the first formulations of the modern project: an "empire over being . . . a world subdued, . . . mankind triumphant . . . the dominion of all things . . . the mastery of nature."[20] The world has become a "Promised Land," an "Earthly Paradise." Nature, scrubbed of noxious animals, is a vast garden. The theme of cleanliness is almost obsessive: a "great cleansing of the world" took place. It did not stop before man, but produced "a cleansed and perfected humanity."[21] A strict eugenics allowed for the halting of overcrowding, "the fundamental evil out of which arose all the others that afflicted the race." So that quantity might be limited for the improvement of quality, "the indolent and inferior do not procreate." A more handsome and healthy race has resulted, which one can call "supermen" or "demigods." The state of humanity is described in a formulation that, taken literally, is contradictory: "These Utopians were passing beyond man towards a nobler humanity."[22]

The attitude of the Utopians presupposes a specific vision of the world. It had occurred to the Earthlings that they could control their universe, but the idea was too terrible for them. They therefore imagined some Power, God or Evolution, which excused them from doing their duty. In contrast, "Utopia says: 'Do not leave things to themselves. Control them.'" Nature "is purposeless and blind. She is not an object of veneration, but of horror. She takes no heed to our values, nor to our standards of excellence. She made us by accident; all her children are bastards—undesired." This vision is that of Victorian neo-gnosticism, to which an Earthling alludes: "At times, the universe had seemed to him to be carelessly put together, but he had never believed that it was the work of a malignant imbecile. It impressed him as immensely careless, but not as, above all, cruel."[23] Despite everything—Wells does not explain how this could have happened—the irrational force of nature had created a being capable of reason: "With Man came Logos, the Word and the Will into our universe."[24] And these faculties allow him to take control of the nature that had thus produced him. One observes the same contradiction in the relationship of contemporary "transhumanists" to evolution: "They make it the source of everything, but at bottom they want to abolish it, in order to substitute for it human choices"; they complain about the inadequacies of

Mother Nature, but forget where the faculties that allow them to correct it come from.[25]

This rose-colored vision was prolonged until the middle of the twentieth century in the literature inspired or commanded by the Leninist ideological regime, whereas National Socialism, even if it knew how to utilize technology to its criminal ends, preferred to idealize an agrarian past. At the time when Wells wrote his utopia, in post-October Russia a technological Prometheanism was given free rein and grandiose projects abounded.[26] The "electrification of the entire country" dreamed of by Lenin and attempts to rationalize work in the manner of Henry Ford and F. W. Taylor were to be only a beginning.[27] In a discourse of 1920, Maxim Gorki announced a future (that he had the prudence to call "far-off") that would see the conquest of the universe and immortality. This goal was already found in an anonymous brochure of 1906, probably by Lunacharsky: "We cannot even imagine what will be the strength of the man of the future, to what point his power over the earth will be great. He will become the lord of the world, will extend his race through vast space, and will dominate the planetary system. Human beings will be immortal." Nikolai A. Rozkov did not hesitate to place the fabrication of planets among the projects that man will realize, even new solar systems, and Muravev saw the man of the future directing earths and suns, already not to be sneezed at.[28] Thanks to dreaming of these technological triumphs, people succumbed to the temptation of believing they were already realized. That is why the Soviet Union, poor in real inventions, armaments excepted, was the country of regimens of longevity, youth serums, even "resurrections" (anabiosis) of animals drained of their blood, accounts of which the western Marxist J. B. S. Haldane allowed himself to believe, but a writer like Mikhail Bulgakov knew to ridicule. The dream of the indefinite malleability of nature gave itself a pseudoscientific foundation in the neo-Lamarckian theory of the heritability of acquired characteristics exhumed by the self-proclaimed geneticist, the agronomist T. Lysenko.[29]

Thus the theme of the domination of nature resurfaced, and again as proving the superiority of man. However, it no longer has the same origin. Previously domination was granted by the Creator. Now it comes from nature itself, conceived as an evolutionary movement that produces man, who represents its crown. It was only at the beginning that Darwin's theory troubled; its propagandists emphasized that it promised unknown advances for man. It was in this context that the theme was reworked, this time in popularizations. Thus with Ludwig Büchner, in his *Force and Matter*, which was constantly reprinted until the end of the nineteenth century and beyond. "Where this progress will lead, I cannot tell you. But one thing seems certain to me, that for the man who makes full use of his reason and his forces, *nothing is impossible*, and that he is no doubt destined to a development of his capacities and, in particular, to a *domination of nature* which appears to surpass, by far, the limits currently assigned by it."[30]

13

The New Meaning of Humanism

The project of a domination of nature is the background against which the substantive "humanism" appeared for the first time in the first half of the nineteenth century, from there invading the entire field of thought. It came to designate pretty much everything and its contrary, to the point where it would be wise, perhaps, to do without it.[1] In any case, the unprecedented meaning that it took on at this period expresses a new self-understanding on the part of man.

Birth of the Word and the Concept

The adjective "humanist" was born in the schools of the end of the fifteenth century, to designate a professor of classical letters, the *litterae humaniores* of the Ciceronian tradition. The word was then applied to anyone who occupied himself with them, whether he taught or not. In contrast, the substantive "humanism" comes late. From its appearance in the nineteenth century it received different meanings: as a historical category, to designate the rediscovery of the ancient writers at the Renaissance, but also as an ethical and cultural program. In this second sense, it goes from the rehabilitation of the human, deemed to be previously devalued, to the exclusive concern for human realities.[2] The suffix "-ism" did not then indicate a mode of life, even less a job, but the valorization and choice of a privileged point of view from which everything is thought to receive meaning and value. The first type of humanism invites one to the effort of making oneself more human by frequenting the good authors; the second takes man as the point of departure and affirms his sovereignty vis-à-vis all that is not him, God or nature. Man must be the sole origin of man. This is the project implied in the second meaning of the term "humanism."

It was the young Hegelian Arnold Ruge who employed it for the first time in the sense of a claim of self-sufficiency, at the end of August 1840.[3] The word is found in 1843 in Feuerbach, who indicates that he employs it without defining it vis-à-vis a thousand other terms: all imply "the negation of theology, . . . essence of modern times." According to a casual note, "the distinctions between materialism, empiricism, realism, humanism are here, in this writing, naturally indifferent." In the same text one reads: "The new philosophy makes of man, *including nature* insofar as it is the basis of man, its sole, universal and supreme object. Anthropology, including physiology, becomes therefore the universal science."[4] Taken literally, the first sentence contains an absurdity that renders it something like an involuntary confession: "Man, including nature," makes nature a part of man, while one would expect the contrary. Only the parallel formulation, "including physiology," allows one to understand what Feuerbach wants to say. One must take man with what belongs to nature inside him—that is, the body. Still, anthropology cannot become the supreme science unless one slides, without saying so, from the nature in man to the nature around him, from the body to the world.

As early as 1835, Feuerbach had employed Hobbes's formulation reversing Plautus—*Homo homini deus*—in order to affirm that the other human being "constitutes for man a mediator between his nature and his conscience."[5] But after 1841, the formulation does not merely express one of the two poles between which social life oscillates—the other being the famous "man is a wolf to man" (*homo homini lupus*); now it designates a previous stage, a turning point, in the history of the world. In the same way that the human figure is what is highest in art, what is highest in philosophy is the human being: "For us at least, there is no higher being than man."[6] It is in this context that the word "superman," already present in theology, appeared for the first time in philosophy, in Moses Hess, another left Hegelian, with a negative connotation, however, to denounce those who believe they place themselves above human nature; above all, Bruno Bauer.[7]

If Feuerbach can call the negation of theology by any odd name, even that of humanism, it is because the denial constitutes the essential operation. And if one can declare every level above man to be empty, this is because what purports to fill it is itself borrowed from the human. The secret of theology is anthropology. The essence of theology is the transcendent essence of man, but placed outside of him. The fundamental thesis in connection with theology is that "God" is nothing other than the way in which the human individual represents the species to himself: "God as the peak of realities or perfections is nothing other than the summation and summary of the properties of the species for the use of the individual, properties that are distributed among human beings and which are realized during the course of history."[8] Feuerbach coins the term "anthropotheism" to designate "religion conscious of itself, the religion that understands itself."[9] The task of the modern period is the realization and humanization of God, the dissolution of theology into anthropology.[10]

In 1843 Marx expressed, very simply, an analogous idea: "The root for man is man himself." The absolute humanism thus decreed is the ultimate goal of history. Real humanism coincides with materialism, the logical basis of communism. For Marx, materialism and naturalism are the same. "This communism is, insofar as it is a completed naturalism = humanism, and insofar as a completed humanism = naturalism. Here one has the true solution to the conflict of man with nature and with man."[11] For Marx, "the history said to be universal is nothing other than the generation of man by *human* work," and for Engels "the worker creates everything.... The worker even creates *man*."[12] But where does the adjective "human" come from? How can work humanize the one who does it, if it is already "human"? This vicious circle, already seen in Rousseau, is found among the "socialists" of the same period.[13] "Spontaneous generation (*generatio aequivoca*)," writes Marx, "is the sole practical refutation of the doctrine of creation." The expression is curious; it presupposes that a being comes from another thing not belonging to its species. But here, taken in context, Marx's formulation supposes that man only comes from man. In effect he echoes Aristotle and even starts from the example that Aristotle gave of a *univocal* generation: "Man engenders man." Fifteen years later, the cyclical vision of species was to receive a blow from Darwin that Marx himself wanted to take as a model. Here, though, Marx observes that a human individual is engendered by another individual of the same species, which cannot render more plausible the idea according to which man as a species comes from a work of humanization which would itself already be assumed.[14]

The word "humanism" passed into French with Proudhon, who in 1846 asked himself about "atheism, otherwise put: humanism," and undertook its critique. It was a matter of "verifying if humanity ... fulfilled the plenitude of being, if it satisfied itself," thus "to find out if humanity, in keeping with ancient thought, tends toward God, or if, as the moderns say, it becomes God."[15] Renan chose the word in 1848 to name "the religion of the future . . . , the worship of all that belongs to man, all of life sanctified and elevated to a moral value." The same year Auguste Comte characterized as "humanistic" the "true point of view," the "priesthood" and the "cult" of his religion of Humanity.[16] In Russia, after his doctorate Chernyshevsky published a long essay on the "anthropological principle in philosophy" (1860). For him, Feuerbach (whom he does not name) is the father of modern philosophy, who "sees in man what medicine, physiology and chemistry see in him." Chernyshevsky, however, does not use the word "humanism." What he terms "anthropology," and does not define until the very end of his work, is a materialistic and scientistic monism.[17]

The Earth as the Kingdom of Man

With the return to a human being who is wholly satisfied with himself, his existential milieu acquires additional value. The immanent causes the transcendent to be forgotten; the earth eclipses heaven.

An image haunts the literature of the nineteenth century: the opposition between heaven and earth needs to be replaced by the rejection of heaven and the affirmation of the earth, the only field of action for man. Galileo had already sung the beauties of this lower world, which, for him, was not so low, because his cosmology ennobled the earth.[18] But in the nineteenth century, the earth became the object of a sort of worship. The doctor and psychologist Gustav Theodor Fechner (d. 1887) saw in it a living being, and perhaps influenced the *Lied von der Erde* of Mahler (1908). There is a more sober example, in 1856, in the tirade by a character of Karl Gutzkow. The earth merits respect: "It is such a remarkable product that I find it entirely honorable to belong to it." The reason given is its great antiquity, which geology, notably with Charles Lyell, had just brought to light. At the same period Auguste Comte completed his religion of Humanity (or the Great Being) with "a just adoration of the Earth, erected as a Great Fetish, the seat and station of the Great Being." One finds the same tones in Pierre Leroux.[19] In Germany, Heine schematizes the history of thought by means of an opposition between matter and spirit, body, and soul. He vindicates the rights of the first and wishes "to leave heaven to the angels and the sparrows." Marx invokes "the real, corporal man, standing upright on the solid and quite round earth, breathing in and breathing out all the natural forces." In Russia, Bakunin defined the task of man as consisting in "leading heaven back to the earth," or rather "elevating the earth to heaven." Nietzsche's Zarathustra preached "fidelity to the earth." And James Joyce opposed the indifferent dome of heaven to the earth, which carries man in its bosom.[20] The theme is found again in the Soviet regime of the 1920s in a text in prose of the "proletarian" poet Aleksei Kapitanovich Gastev (d. 1939): "We are not going to exhaust ourselves to attain the sad height called heaven. Heaven is the construction of the idle, the wallowers, the lazy and the cowardly. Let's cast ourselves below!" It was a matter literally, or perhaps merely as an image, of drilling wells and tunnels in the earth.[21]

Feuerbach put in place an entire system of images that found many followers, especially among writers. Among them were some with great talent who echoed his thought and caused it to pass beyond the borders of Germany, such as Wagner before his reading of Schopenhauer. In England, George Eliot translated *Das Wesen des Christentums* in 1854. In Switzerland, Gottfried Keller reported that if the reading of Feuerbach had estranged him from religion, far from stifling poetry and every elevated feeling, this break led to the contrary result. "For me the world became infinitely more beautiful and profound, life had more value and intensity, death is more serious and makes me reflect more; it is only now that it presses me with all its force to fulfill my task, and to purify and satisfy my conscience."[22] Feuerbach understood his task as recuperating for the sake of the earth what man has squandered by projecting it onto heaven. In Denmark, Jens Peter Jacobsen develops the theme in a page of his last novel, published in 1880: atheism ought to benefit the earth with the human love that, until then, had been squandered on God. Five years before, Dostoyevsky had lent the same idea to a character, Versilov, in his novel *The Adolescent*. The end of the belief in the "grand idea of immortality" ought to force human beings to an intense love of neighbor and nature. The novelist summarizes the socialist project, which he assimilates to atheism, in the image of a tower of Babel that had for its purpose not to attain heaven from earth but to lead heaven back to the earth.[23]

Another fundamental image is that of the body, an anthropological equivalent to the earth that is rather traditional. It is also a matter of reconciling it with the soul, supposed to be in conflict with it. This occurs among writers as well as a painter like Courbet, whose *Painter's Studio* (1855) realizes in its own way the equivalence between humanism and naturalism posed by Marx.[24]

The sun is the symbol of the domination of nature over man, when it is not the symbol of God himself, or simply God, as the uncle of Gérard de Nerval thought. The book of Revelation foresaw that at the end of times, with God being the light of the world, the two great luminaries would become useless (21:23; 22:5); illustrations showed angels in the process of removing them. The modern project dreams, if not of suppressing the sun, at least of making it less useful by replacing it by human light. Diderot counseled painters: "Illumine your objects with your sun, which is not that of nature." What remained a mere metaphor tended to become real. This could happen most concretely with artificial lights, which produce men who have never seen a star, without mentioning the "light pollution" which complicates the work of astronomers.[25] It can also, however, refer to the illumination, this time metaphoric, of the Enlightenment of a humanity become master of itself.[26]

Work as Concrete Humanism

The idea according to which the earth to work on can be the object of a mastery as perfect as the one that man has over his body, and thus that nature ought to be the external body of man, appears in the tenth century among the Ismailian propagandists, in an eschatological context. We have seen the view in Avicenna, in his theory of the thaumaturgy of the perfect man. It can be found in Lavater in a mystical context. It reemerges in Fichte, to culminate in Marx, who takes up Fichte's ideas on the basis of the Industrial Revolution.[27] In so doing, he provides the ultimate humanist goal with a foundation, a program that allows for its realization: work. Thanks to him, the world becomes the body of the perfect man. Work is that by which man "submits" nature "to himself" by appropriating it. Industry is made possible by the science of nature. Marx conceives the unity of man with nature, because man is a part of the latter. However, neither this unity nor the struggle of man against nature is a definitive formulation for him.[28] In the hymn to the bourgeoisie found in the *Communist Manifesto*, Marx places the "subjection of nature's forces to man" at the head of the list of the bourgeoisie's historical exploits. Later, he again takes up the thought: "Inasmuch as man conducts himself as an owner toward nature, the first source of all the means and objects of work, to that extent he treats nature as belonging to him, his work becomes the source of use values, thus of wealth." The capitalist mode of production "implies a domination of man over nature."[29]

The program of "Marxism" is formulated by Engels, the same year as Marx's death. The socialization of the means of production puts an end to the domination of the product over the producer; the conditions of life "enter under the dominion and control of human beings, who for the first time become the conscious and effective masters of nature. . . . The laws of their social action are . . . now in their control. The objective forces that dominated history . . . enter under humanity's control."[30] The nineteenth century abounds in evocations, even descriptions, of this kingdom of freedom. For Renan, it would be that of the spirit. It "will not begin except when the material world will be perfectly subject to man." It is necessary that "man begin by establishing himself as master in the world of bodies, in order to be able later to be free for the conquests of the spirit. . . . The ideal of human life will be a state where man will have so dominated nature that material need will no longer be a motive, where this need will be satisfied just as soon as it is felt . . . , in which all human activity . . . will turn toward the spirit, and where man only has to live the celestial life. This, then, will truly be the kingdom of the spirit."[31] One finds an echo of these ideas in the later Bergson, who sees mechanization and mysticism as complementary. The goal of the technological control of nature is to free man for his essential task, to place himself in the current of the vital élan.[32]

14

The Sole Lord

For a long time, the idea of a kingdom of man only concerned his relationship with what was beneath him and only constituted one of the ways of negotiating it, without implying any decision concerning relations with what was above him: the celestial world in its entirety, physically (stars) or metaphysically (pure spirits, angels), finally the divine, dispersed in a pantheon or concentrated in a single God.

Two centuries after the project of a domination of nature, the project of a rivalry with God appeared. Until then he was considered as the Creator of nature and of man himself. Even more, it was he who put at man's disposal the nature that from the beginning was inferior to him and which he was to subject by the ingenuity of his mind and the effort of his arms. The greatness of God and even his lordship did not appear as a dominion exercised for his own benefit. Then at a certain period lordship became the stakes in a struggle thought to oppose man not to nature, but to God. There could only be one Lord. Humanism became exclusive, and hence atheistic.

Atheism as Condition of Domination

The connection between exclusive humanism and the conquest of nature is not necessary.[1] The latter can be the execution of a *task* conferred by God. On the other side, atheism does not automatically entail the attempt to take control of anything other than oneself. It can be indifferent to everything that is external to the human subject. Epicureanism and Buddhism present examples of a style of life that exists apart from the gods and does not seek to "subtract" anything from them but the subject himself. If Buddhism came to the awareness of the West only rather late, for centuries Epicureanism represented a real possibility. For it, the gods are already remote, living in the interworlds, where they exercise no influence on human beings. Epicurus does not want to conquer nature, but to carve out a space where one can live without trouble, of which the *garden* is the symbol. On the other hand, the project of the conquest of nature was expressed by Christian philosophers. Physics was born in a Catholic milieu, and the social anchoring of technology was probably English Puritanism.[2] What connection, then, can one establish between the project of the conquest of nature and the rejection of God?

This connection which defines the modern project is not comprehensible except on two conditions: it supposes, first of all, the claim that the biblical God is the Creator of nature and intervenes in the history of humanity, and then the claim that God's presence has become intolerable. The second condition obviously is not required by the first. To explain it several hypotheses have been proposed. Leo Strauss explained that for modern man, nature is not only a stepmother—an idea found among many ancients, but an enemy that one can defeat. Man as the conqueror of nature is external to it. There is no preestablished harmony between the human mind and the world. Absolute doubt is required, because the world could be nothing but an illusion. One knows only what one makes. Dogmatism rests on the complete skepticism that Descartes brought to the fore. Man conquers nature because nature compels him to do so.[3]

Could the desire for domination possibly be of gnostic origin? This is the view of Eric Voegelin, who connects the project of a conquest of nature to gnosticism.[4] In this view, the Creator of the world is not the Father of all goodness, but a poor bungler against whom revolting would be a duty. For Hans Blumenberg, who responds to Voegelin, it was Christianity itself which made the hope of a harmony with nature impossible. The exit from the Middle Ages became necessary because of Christianity's inability to fully exorcise gnosticism. More specifically the project of conquering nature was born of despair in the face of the return of an analogous mentality, the tyrannical claims of nominalist theology. The nominalists' appeal to divine power without any connection with wisdom removes all privileges from reality, now reduced to the level of a mere contingent fact posed by the absolute arbitrariness of the divine will. Once the security guaranteed him by the world was lost, man was constrained to ensure his identity by, as it were, helping himself to nature.[5] The historian Johannes Fried presents a variation on Blumenberg's thesis, focused on a more certain historical domain, that of modern science. Modern science was the issue of a reaction against an apocalyptic worldview; the study of nature began by being a search for signs of the coming end.[6]

In any case, this project of domination supposes a certain representation of the divine, thus something like a theology. The key point is the question of the relation of God to the created, conceived now as domination. The "Lord" is understood as master. A secular tendency tended to separate among the attributes of God, whom the Credo confesses as "the Father almighty," paternity and omnipotence, while the latter is "entirely in his paternity."[7] Was nominalist theology the source of the unilateral emphasis on omnipotence? This has been affirmed since the Thomistic revival at the end of the nineteenth century, not without historical amplifications, beginning with the very idea of "nominalism."[8]

Once man understands himself as having to dominate, he must dispute the place of dominator with God. And he must do so for two contrary reasons: because it is supposed that God oppresses him, *and* because God has not been a sufficiently effective master. In keeping with this latter thought, Auguste Comte writes: "Industrial life is . . . contrary to all providential optimism, because it necessarily supposes that the natural order is imperfect enough to demand constant human intervention."[9] Comte connects the necessity of human action to the imperfection of the natural order.[10] But he also connects this order to the idea of providence. Comte sees providence as external to man (whom he did not conceive of as a part of nature, but as confronting it). As a consequence, human action is not the form of providence that God delegated to his creature, but instead opposes providence. At the same period, Proudhon supposed a simplistic teeter-totter between man and God, who are enemies. For him, human progress has as its goal to jettison God.[11]

The enterprise could not mobilize those one wanted to enlist without giving them stirring images. Since the model of the divine that it presupposes is pre-Christian, it was a recycled Greek mythology that became the source from which one drew. In it, one found the history of the revolt of the Titans against the Olympians. The Antichrist, whose figure had captivated the Middle Ages, had remained unnamed. The first proper name given to him, by Lope de Vega in a play of 1620, was "Titan." The surname was later applied to Fichte. Jean Paul made it the title of a novel of education. Eichendorff, a half-century later, still spoke of a "promethean youth" and a "race of Titans."[12]

A very particular Titan, Prometheus, came into new popularity, but at the price of a perversion in the original meaning of the myth, where, at the end of his trilogy, Aeschylus made him the "holy patron" of the guild of blacksmiths. Now he is nailed, both literally and figuratively, on the Caucasus, captured in his revolt, thus becoming the symbol of a program of emancipation. Not without difficulty. It was necessary to forget the

Christian reading that saw in him a figure of Christ, then to dismiss alternative readings and other competing characters. Charles de Bovelles seems to have been the first to see in him the tutelary figure of the individualism of the Renaissance. Bacon adds an interpretation of the relay races with torches that were instituted in his honor. They alluded to the collective character of the scientific enterprise.[13] Prometheus also had to supplant a rival, Hercules, whom Vico and Hegel still preferred. The difference between the two illustrates the difference between the two models of enterprise distinguished above. While Heracles received from Zeus the task of ridding the earth of its monsters, Prometheus gave himself the project of enlightening humanity.[14] It was with the radical Enlightenment that Prometheus arrived at the summit. According to Diderot, man is the "child of Prometheus." In his doctoral thesis, Marx makes Prometheus the "first saint of the philosophical calendar." And his figure still haunts the histories of the industrial revolutions.[15] Closer to us, however, the Scottish biologist J. B. S. Haldane, though a Marxist, finds Prometheus overrated and prefers the figure of Daedalus.[16]

The Project of an Empowering of the Human

Enlightenment combined two long-term movements of thought which, while fundamentally distinct, came together in the same reference to man. The first aimed at the humanization of morals and manners, for more "humanity" therefore, for example, in punishment, thus placing itself in a millennial process of civilization.[17] The second is the modern project of the empowerment of man vis-à-vis every external instance, whether it comes from the physical universe that encompasses him or from the divine that looks down upon him. For an ancient like Chrysippus, there was nothing more arrogant for man than to imagine that there was nothing above him.[18] One can therefore ask who was the first to risk such an idea. Bonaventure des Périers (d. toward 1543) describes the good man as

> similar to the rounded sphere
> of the universe, *gathered entirely in itself*
> and so nicely polished without
> that he cannot pick up even a hint of filth.

Some have seen in the italicized phrase the program of an exclusive humanism.[19] But one can ask if the adjective does not pertain first to the universe, such as the *Timaeus* describes it, and only indirectly to the good man who is to imitate it. In any case, the project is announced as soon as the change in the meaning of the word "autonomy," enlarged beyond its legal and political signification to designate the claim of human independence, perhaps for the first time in Feuerbach. The word thus began a career that will make it a constitutive claim of the human, to the point that Maldoror of Lautreamont can pose the alternatives: "Autonomy . . . or change me into a hippopotamus."[20]

The first exteriority from which modern man seeks to emancipate himself is chronological anteriority. Everything that was "before" needs to be relativized. A first stage, perhaps, was represented by St. Ignatius. His *Exercises* sought to grasp in the decisive instant of choice the entire previous life of the retreatant.[21] The idea of a radical recommencement is at the heart of Descartes's project, formed on Ignatian spirituality. It first bears upon the individual engaged in the solitary spiritual exercise of the critical reexamination of his knowledge in order to rebuild on a foundation wholly his own.[22] The model of a receptacle empty of every form, and thus capable of receiving any form at all, comes from the Aristotelian theory of the intellect.[23] Constitutive and hence inseparable, in Aristotle it was given from the beginning. With Descartes, it became a state to acquire at the price of an operation of the mind on itself. This asceticism had Neoplatonic sources in the "purgative way" received from Plotinus and Proclus by Dionysius the Areopagite.[24] Here it is no longer applied to the images that pose an obstacle to the pure grasp of the One, but to all the representations that precede the critical examination of their value.

Such representations needed a name. This became "prejudices." Descartes attributes error to "the prejudices of infancy." He does not claim to disencumber the mind of every prejudice, an impossible task, but to take away, at the moment of the critical examination of opinions, all the judgments that the mind has previously made.[25] The enterprise is not without a logical difficulty. In order for the "I" to be able to eliminate all its contents, it must first be able to grasp itself in a state of purity such that it can distinguish what it truly is from everything that was added to it. To be sure, an immediate grasp of the self by the self is assumed achieved in the "I think." But the *Cogito*, while it is thinkable as an act of the individual situated in the moment, cannot have a historical collectivity as its subject. The idea of prejudice, with its pejorative nuance, was reprised by Spinoza and Malebranche.[26] Beginning at the end of the seventeenth century and during the entirety of the eighteenth, the word provided "moderns" and "the Enlightenment" with one of their most piquant slogans. It is not surprising then that, conversely, their opponents defended the value of prejudices.[27] In our day, the struggle against "prejudices" takes on a more radical cast, forbidding even asking if certain judgments could be true.[28]

The philosophy of John Locke provided a model of this thought of recommencing. It would be difficult to overstate his influence in the eighteenth century; he is the master of Voltaire, Condillac, and Rousseau. His thought was expressed in the *Essay concerning Human Understanding*, published in 1690, then translated into French and Latin, which allowed for its diffusion on the Continent. In it, Locke defends a sensualist theory of knowledge: nothing preexists sensation, the intellect is a tabula rasa which receives everything from without and must elaborate everything. In an interesting way, the same idea is found in his practical philosophy: human freedom is also said to be absolute.[29]

Daniel Defoe's *Robinson Crusoe* appeared in 1719. The central intention of the work is theological. It is a treatise on the spiritual life revolving around the idea of providence. The hero attributes to its secret action all his history, and above all, his spiritual development. The description of the improvements that the sailor makes to his island remains marginal. This, however, was the only aspect that Marx wished to see, while he mocked the piety of the hero.[30] It is also what the versions of the story for children retain. The metaphor of shipwreck, classical illustration of the condition of man on earth, takes on a positive cast once it is placed in the plan of providence. In religion, Robinson starts from a state in which he has "no knowledge of God," "no sense of religion." His lot, however, leads him to reflect and to discover prayer. Like the Hayy ibn Yaqzan of Ibn Tufayl, from his reflections he deduces the existence of an all-powerful, just, and merciful Creator. His conscience is awakened, and he discovers himself a sinner and justly punished. He begins to read the Bible "seriously." He ends by catechizing Friday, the savage whom he saves from death.[31] In his economics and politics, Robinson considers himself "led back to a pure state of nature," and thus constrained to recover by his labors the advantages of civilization. This work makes him the king of the island.[32] The way in which he feels himself to be the owner of what he has made his by his work comes from the conception of property presented by Locke in his *Second Treatise of Civil Government* (1690).

The theme of a radical beginning marks the Enlightenment: "The entire century, haunted by the myth of the origin, dreamed about experiences of a second birth." But it was only the "Newton effect" that made concrete attempts at a global reworking of reality possible. One drew from successes achieved in the domination of nature, still rather unimpressive, the pretext to desire to extend them to the entirety of what is.[33] A preliminary condition deemed to make possible a new departure is the effacement of what preceded. Thus, the Marquis de Chastellux launched an attack against the past, especially Greek antiquity, and wrote that "in order to be happy, human beings have much more need of forgetting than learning."[34]

The project of a reconstruction of the human found its historical opportunity with the revolutions of the end of the eighteenth century, in America, then France. It is not insignificant that the idea of a self-constitution of man first imposed itself where it was a matter of defining the power that society exercises over itself via legislation. The idea of sovereignty was incarnate in a new subject, the "people." The most logical defenders of the French Revolution saw very well that institutions must be constructed. Now, the political is one of the properties of man, and as such, it provided a classical definition of humanity. By redefining politics, therefore, one prepared the redefinition of humanity in its entirety. The enterprise was unthinkable except on the basis of a sensualist anthropology, Locke's: it suffices to expose man to good influences (come from one-knows-not-where) in order to regenerate him.[35]

The American Revolution was conceived and conducted by disciples of Locke. It proves the possibility of a new beginning, of a *novus ordo seclorum*, the motto of the Great Seal of the United States reproduced on dollar bills.[36] The Englishman Thomas Paine wrote in 1776: "We have it in our power to begin the world over again. A situation, similar to the present, hath not happened since the days of Noah until now. The birthday of a new world is at hand." A few years later, this time considering the American example in the light of the French Revolution, he adds: "The case and circumstances of America present themselves as in the beginning of a new world.... We are brought at once to the point of seeing government begin, as if we had lived in the beginning of time."[37] The images employed by Paine are ancient,[38] but here they are put at the service of an active project. The new creation is no longer the description of a situation, but the summons to a work that only man can bring to a happy end.

※

The French Revolution realizes the explicit desire to break with the past that Rabaut Saint-Etienne expressed just before it: "Our history is not our code." Fichte theorized this intention and defended the right of a people to change its constitution, founding that right on the very nature of human freedom. For enthusiastic contemporaries, human nature seemed to be born anew, as Wordsworth recalls.[39] Among the revolutionaries themselves, the project is very self-conscious. Thus, for Marie-Joseph Chénier, one must "create and not compile, invent and not recall." Hence one heard a drunken immoderation in parliamentary rhetoric. For example, Boissy d'Anglas: "To set in order the destinies of the world, you have but to will. You are the creators of a new world, say 'let light be,' and light will be." Or Billaud-Varenne: "The establishment of democracy in a nation that has languished in chains for a long time can be compared to the effort of nature in the transition from nothing to existence, no doubt a much greater effort than the passage from life to annihilation."[40]

This enthusiasm ran into the reservations of the moderates, who recalled the impossibility of drawing anything living from nothing. Mirabeau evoked the biological necessities: "A skillful cultivator does not pretend to give birth himself to flowers and fruits"; Burke underscores that institutions are not manufactured, but grow like living things, and Joseph de Maistre says that he will never believe in the "fecundity of nothingness."[41]

To be sure, the French revolutionaries and their English or German defenders did not dream of a global redefinition of the human. For most of them, they retained the idea of nature, because it allowed them to delineate all the "usurpations" of the past and to appeal to betrayed "human nature." For their part, the British mentioned the Creator of Genesis, who had made man "in his image." This is still the case with Thomas Paine, originally a pastor, in his response to Burke. The same Paine had taken up in *Common Sense* (1776) the same arguments as the antimonarchical texts of the Bible.[42] However, with the remaking of institutions, the idea of a "new man," one who is "regenerated," sees the light. It constitutes (and this makes it logically untenable) at once the consequence and the preliminary condition of the political upheaval. One reads a strange sentence in Paine, a sort of involuntary confession. He becomes indignant before Burke's rejection of "the rights of man." Burke did not at all deny their existence, only that of an abstract man who would be their subject, and he recalls that it is concrete peoples who have acquired rights during the course of a history proper to each. Paine pretends not to understand, and he exclaims: Would Burke mean to deny rights to man? If yes, he must deny the very existence of all rights, beginning with his own, since, Paine asks (in a curious manner): "What is there in the world, if not man?"[43] To be sure, he wants to say: who besides man could be the subject of rights? But it is a significant lapse. There is much more in the world than man.

Man, the Supreme Being

The revolutionary claim aimed first at the reconquest of the horizontal sovereignty of the people against the "tyrants." For Robespierre, "the human race is sovereign of the earth."[44] On the other hand, human freedom tends to reject everything that is not itself.

Atheistic humanism manifested itself first by the refusal to place anything above man. Marx formulated it in his doctoral dissertation: "The Credo of Prometheus . . . is that of philosophy, its battle cry against all the celestial and terrestrial gods, which do not recognize human self-consciousness as the supreme divinity. There shalt not be any other beside it."[45] The blasphemous allusion to Exodus (20:2) suggests that man ought to replace the jealous God of Israel. This, however, naïvely assumes that between God and man there exists a relationship such that one party must lose if the other gains, that the level of one must rise if the other lowers.[46] In 1787, when Benjamin Franklin proposed to the American Congress to have prayers offered, Alexander Hamilton is said to have retorted: "I do not see the necessity of calling in foreign aid."[47] It is interesting that God would be perceived as a foreign power whose intervention would limit human liberty, not the inner master able to guide it toward the good.

Auguste Comte speaks of "henceforth dismissing every superhuman intermediary," an expression that contains one of the rare occurrences of the adjective "superhuman" in Comte and one of the first in French. Man's accession to the status of supreme being is tied by Comte to the passage to adulthood: "Humanity cannot be truly envisaged as having left the state of infancy as long as his principal rules of conduct . . . continue to rest essentially on foreign fictions." The old image of the succession of ages of life illustrates the idea of passage to autonomy by a human being now capable of doing without what is not him. In his encyclical on liberalism, Pope Leo XIII summarized the idea in order to condemn it. According to some, "There is nothing above sovereign human reason."[48]

The negative operation that refuses all instances superior to man culminates in the positive claim of his divinity. That God is within man is an idea with which Kant flirted; the presence of practical reason in us allows us to say with Ovid that "a god is in us." Schiller follows him on this point. But one can distort the idea, to the point of renouncing an external divine. Thus for the revolutionary Nicolas de Bonneville, "Man is God!"[49] Almost all the post-Kantians were accused of pretending to divinity. Fichte's philosophy was defamed as divinizing the subject, the I which he made the principle of his thought, and this, even when he did not equate it with the empirical individual.[50] The later philosophy of Hegel could be interpreted as an attempt to make man the sole true divinity. One of the greatest and most discussed of his interpreters, Alexandre Kojève, saw in the atheism that he attributed to Hegel the culmination of philosophy. That did not prevent him from playfully considering his disciples as an Olympus of which he would be the Zeus.[51] Heine, himself returned to the God of his ancestors, caricatured the "young Hegelians," including Marx and Feuerbach, by the oxymoron hard to translate: "atheists who are their own gods" (gottlose Selbstgötter). In his pantheistic period, he declared that he "fought, not for the human rights of the people, but for the divine rights of man." Charles Péguy rightly observed that modern man is less an atheist than, in a word of his coining, an "auto-theist."[52] Baudelaire interprets the states of consciousness of drug addicts as essays in divinization: the addict of hashish gives the impression of being a god. To take oneself as God is a rather rare phenomenon, but well attested in certain individuals. Dostoyevsky puts the character Kirillov on the stage, with his paradoxical strategy of divinization by means of suicide. He attracted the attention of Nietzsche, Kojève, and Camus.[53]

As we have seen, Comte took up the expression "Supreme Being"—first promoted in a Christian context, for example in Fénelon, then taken up by the Enlightenment and the revolution against the personal God of Christianity—in order to designate Humanity, the "new Great Being," "new Supreme Being." The religion of Humanity, named "humanitarianism" by its opponents, competes directly with God's.[54] "While Protestants and Deists have always attacked religion in the name of God, we must, on the contrary, finally get rid of God in the name of religion."[55] Comte thus represents a sort of Catholicism without Christianity. The formulation is found among his opponents, as well as his disciples Barrès and Maurras.[56] "The great conception of Humanity ... irrevocably eliminates that of God." Humanity ought to be "definitively substituted for God."[57] Comte does not hesitate to reverse the order. If the religion of Humanity succeeds the religion of God in time, this is because, in the logical order, it is humanity that preceded. He can therefore write that in the Middles Ages "God usurped the place of Humanity."[58] The terrain of this struggle and this substitution is that of domination: "the irrevocable exhaustion of the *reign* of God, which only the *ascendance* of Humanity can replace."[59]

PART 3

FAILURE

15

Kingdom or Wasteland?

The project of dominating nature entails effects, not all of which are beneficial. First of all, for nature, but also, indirectly, for man who goes about it. If Bacon's "knowledge is power" was still for Renan "the most beautiful word that has ever been said," Bertrand Russell, whom one would not accuse of disdaining scientific knowledge, speaks of science as "power-thought." A science thus conceived "increasingly tends to become sadistic," so that the technological power that it confers cannot be obtained except by way of an analogy with the worship of Satan—that is, the renunciation of love.[1]

The Victims: Slaves, Workers, Animals, Human Beings

The period which saw the rise to power of European rationalism, then the Enlightenment, is also one that saw a form of society reborn that was believed long gone and which not only included slaves but based its entire structure on the exploitation of their work, for example, in Brazil, the Caribbean Islands, and in the South of the United States. European expansion simultaneously produced among the colonists institutions of an extreme democratic character and among the workforce the extreme of slavery. At the same time as slavery disappeared from the European center (with the exception of Russian serfdom), it spread to the colonial periphery.[2] The question of its legitimacy had been discussed since antiquity, and Aristotle had given a nuanced answer. Few took up the question in connection with its American rebirth. Jean Bodin pronounced himself against slavery, but remained isolated.[3] The theorist of liberalism, John Locke, who, like his admirer Voltaire, possessed interests in the slave trade, is the only philosopher of the Enlightenment who argued in favor of slavery (although not without some ambiguity). He excluded slaves from the rationalized society, just as he excluded atheists and Catholics from the tolerance that he defended.[4]

The conquest of nature and its reorganization according to human needs benefits a specific human type: the engineer. He is keen to distinguish himself from the scholar and the businessman, and he constructs a very distinctive vision of the world for himself.[5] On the other hand, this vision is fatal to a traditional way of life, whose destruction is the price of industrialization. In his second *Faust*, Goethe illustrates this vision in the episode of Philemon and Baucis. The two old people live out of the way, in the harmony of an intact world. The great works that Faust directs demand their expropriation and deportation. Mephistopheles, pressed into Faust's service, applies the orders with a zeal that is so excessive that it leads to the death of the couple.[6] The poverty that industrialization caused among workers hardly need be recalled, so much has a rich literature taken upon itself to describe it, as early as the investigators of the 1830s, the physicians Ange Guépin, a Freemason, and Louis-René Villermé, a Catholic legitimist. Another Catholic, Alban de Villeneuve-Bargemont, author of a work on pauperism, was the first to argue that social reform was the responsibility of the government, and in 1841 he caused the first child labor law to be enacted. In England, the movement went from the description of the situation of the working class by Engels to the works of novelists and social reformers.[7] The description of the destructive effects of industrialization on individuals, even entire classes, was accompanied by different methods thought to address the social question, from all forms of corporatism and paternalism to the revolutions wrought in the name of the proletariat, passing through syndicalism.

❦

The awareness of wrongs done to animals is ancient. Vegetarianism has a long religious history, and ever since Porphyry it has had civic rights in the philosophic city. I have already reported the trial pitting the animals against man in the work of the "Sincere Brethren."[8] Several authors of the nineteenth century insisted on the kinship between man and the animals. As early as 1789, Jeremy Bentham recalled that the fate of animals is analogous to that reserved to slaves, and, in keeping with his ethics of the maximization of pleasure, he changed the perspective in which they were viewed: one must not ask if the animals can reason, but if they can suffer.[9]

In practice, vegetarianism returned to England in the eighteenth century with John F. Newton, based on a doubt concerning man's superiority. The Société Protectrice des Animaux was founded in Paris in 1846, a quarter century after similar organizations were formed in England, Holland, and Bavaria. The English endeavors received Schopenhauer's approbation.[10] That same year, 1846, Michelet discovered a guilty party: Christianity, which "keeps animal nature at an infinite distance from man and denigrates it." Schopenhauer had already reproached Judaism and the religions issued from it for the same thing, and opposed to them the Hindu teaching of the kinship of all living things.[11] Darwin gave this kinship a scientific foundation in his second masterwork, but he also recalled that man is distinguished from the animals by language and the use of fire.[12]

In the seventeenth century, vivisection had been justified on the basis of man's sovereignty by Robert Boyle but also attacked by others, including Henry More. A campaign to abolish it at the European-wide level began in the 1870s. In Germany, it found its argument in the book *The Torture Chambers of Science* (1879), by Ernst von Weber—to whom Wagner paid the honor of an open letter—and in the book's pictorial expression in Gabriel von Max's allegory, *Der Vivisektor* (1883). With the support of the queen . . . and of Lewis Carroll, the campaign against it passed the law of 1876 in England. The idea of the rights of animals appeared in 1892 with Henry Salt.[13] Our time sees the disappearance of animal species and ascribes a part of the responsibility to man. It emphasizes the continuity that connects man with the other living things, and even contests his privilege.

A new theme, vaster still, has appeared with the birth of the ecological movement, to wit: the dangers of technology for humanity, cutting across nations and classes. For a long time, natural catastrophes had been a subject for poets and philosophers, from the *Poem of Aetna* to the Lisbon earthquake (1755). In them, nature toyed with the works of man. Lisbon was thus metaphorically an earthquake for the optimism of the Enlightenment. It was in connection with that catastrophe that Rousseau, perhaps for the first time, made clear man's responsibility with a very simple question: Was it nature that built the buildings whose collapse buried so many victims?[14] With industrialization, the catastrophes due to technology became themselves the subject of poems—for example, a shipwreck in "The Wreck of the Deutschland," by Gerard Manley Hopkins

(1875), or the collapse of a bridge in *Die Brücke am Tay*, by Fontane (1879).[15] Railroad accidents provided matter to the disillusioned reflections of writers. For example, the accident that cost the life of the explorer Jules Dumont d'Urville and which inspired some nostalgic verses of Vigny.[16] Or again, the one that Charles Dickens survived, but which powerfully impressed him. Along with the catastrophes that struck those who trusted in machines, one must also include the suicides committed by their means. Thus the heroine of Tolstoy's *Anna Karenina* (1877), like her real-life model, threw herself beneath a locomotive, which is what the Hungarian poet Attila Jozsef (1937) will later do.

In a short story of 1843, Nathaniel Hawthorne suggested the dangers attached to the search for the absolute perfection of the human body. The wife of the chemist Aylmer was a perfect beauty—except for a small red birthmark in the form of a hand on her cheek. This is obviously a symbol, but of what exactly? Hawthorne leaves the reader without an answer. Obsessed by this single imperfection, and having communicated his obsession to his wife, the chemist seeks to eliminate it. The potion he administers to her does eliminate the spot, but by killing the wife.[17]

Some technological catastrophe could lead to the disappearance of all of humanity. Science leads to the production of weapons that are ever more effective. Many are the scientists who have refused to divulge their discoveries, for fear that they would serve military objectives, such as Leonardo da Vinci hiding the submarine that he had imagined, or Michael Faraday refusing to produce military gas for the Crimean War.[18] Others had less scruples, such as Fritz Haber, the father of chemical weapons. With nuclear weapons, the nightmare of the disappearance of humanity received greater plausibility. Ever since Hiroshima, the works that evoke it abound, from philosophical treatises by Karl Jaspers and Gunther Anders to comics and movies. But the idea of a deliberate explosion of Earth can be found twenty years earlier in Italo Svevo.[19]

Limited Time

Nature is not merely the indifferent scene where the drama of human action unfolds. It is also the object of human action, which believes that it can count on her, but soon enough runs up against limits.

The fear of the depletion of natural resources and, first of all, of arable land, is ancient. Plato establishes a connection between deforestation and soil erosion, and Theophrastus fears that the felling of trees might change the climate, as did prince Liu An in China in the second century CE. At the beginning of his treatise on agriculture, the Roman Columella, a century earlier, argued against Lucretius's idea that the earth would be exhausted for having already produced too much. Pliny the Elder and the anonymous author of the *Poem of Aetna* criticized mining, in particular the extraction of marble for purposes of luxury.[20]

Subsequently the theme remained dormant, and the Middle Ages, which cleared land with abandon, only took it up marginally.[21] It reemerged at the beginning of modern times with the deforestation of certain islands and the increased exploitation of the subsoil. Hence the protests against the devastation of the land by foresters and miners. Christopher Columbus, if one believes his son and biographer, would have feared that the Caribbean islanders would come to know the devastation he observed on the Canary Islands. The famous poem of Ronsard is well-known, where he asks the woodsmen of the forest of Gastine to stay their axes.[22] In 1713, Hans Carl von Carlowitz, the supervisor of the mines of the Metalliferous Hills, was the first to propose the rule of equilibrium: not to cut down more trees than one replanted.[23] At the end of the same century, the French engineer Jean Antoine Fabre established that the felling of trees on mountains is the principal cause of the formation of mountain floods.[24] He is one of the witnesses to a panic over deforestation that at the time of the Restoration will produce the first proposals for a more economical use of forest resources. We see this in France with François Antoine Rauch, who in 1818 took up the then-fashionable word "regeneration," and in Germany with Ernst Moritz Arndt, in 1820. The following year, Carl Maria von Weber made a forest keeper the hero of his *Freischütz*.[25]

As for mines, the first to worry himself about them was, perhaps, the humanist Paul Schneevogel (Niavis), with his *Judgment of Jupiter* (towards 1493). Written in the manner of Lucian, the little Latin work recounts an accusation leveled against man by the earth, which complains before Jupiter about the mining activity of man, who is accused of matricide. Attacked by Mercury, Bacchus, and Ceres, man is defended by the Penates. It is to accomplish Jupiter's will that man works and takes the globe under his protection; while the earth, which hides its treasures, is more of a stepmother than a mother. Jupiter leaves the judgment to Fortune, who recalls that it is man's destiny to pierce the mountains, cultivate the earth, to exchange—and so much the worse for the earth. The theme reappears in Edmund Spenser and Milton. For Calvin, the true danger would be that man's sin exhausts God's benediction.[26] Buffon exhibits the equilibrium of nature. All life presupposes the destruction of plant or animal life. But he uses the point to indicate that "man himself consumes and takes in more flesh than all the animals together do; he is therefore the greatest destroyer, and this is more by abuse than necessity."[27]

Ecological consciousness is ancient, as well as the wish that man be the lord, but not the tyrant, of nature.[28] In the United States, it was given a scientific foundation by George Perkins Marsh, who, in a book of geography that appeared in 1864, shows that man fashions his milieu, even intervenes decisively on the earth. Man perhaps is the product of the planet, but he is also the active subject of its transformation. Different from the other species, man, forgetful of what nature has given him in usufruct and not as property, is "essentially a destructive power," even if this power shows that he "belongs to a higher order of existence."[29] In 1868, the word "ecology" appeared in Germany with Ernst Haeckel, but not in its present meaning.[30] In a passage written between 1864 and 1875, Marx sketches the ideal of a man who would not consider himself the owner of the earth, but only someone who used it, bound to render it improved to future generations.[31] In the years 1870–80, Engels recalls that discoveries that originally were judged positive have had negative consequences; to avoid them, one needs to know the laws of nature, which alone allow man to conquer, while still feeling one with nature.[32]

Becoming aware of the finite character of natural resources is connected with becoming aware of geological time, one of the great intellectual revolutions of the nineteenth century, ever since the *Principles of Geology* of Charles Lyell (1830–33). Kant saw in the abundance of forests an effect of nature's provision, and Buffon still believed that coal resources were inexhaustible. From the 1860s, the thought of their depletion started to haunt minds. In *The Mysterious Island* (1864), Jules Verne has Cyrus Smith reflect on the conditions for the progress of civilization, which rests on coal. He predicts that once the coal deposits are exhausted, energy will come from the two gases that compose water. In 1872, Cournot observed that man spends rather abruptly the reserves that nature had taken centuries to accumulate. He is thinking of coal, since oil was then hardly known. He deduces from this that man has passed from the role of the king of creation to that of a mere "hired-hand on the planet. . . . He has an estate to work, a mine to exploit." As a consequence, "the future is limited, not only for individuals, but for nations, in another sense than was formerly thought."[33]

The Enlightenment began to understand that time is limited. The fear of the end of the world, which is ancient and gave rise to many philosophical and religious ideas, acquired a scientific dimension with Fontenelle, then Buffon, who was perhaps the first to think that the earth could grow cold and make human life impossible; Byron imagined this in a poem of 1816.[34] The physics of the nineteenth century endowed these phantasms with a scientific foundation, while also reducing them to immanence. The "heat death" of the universe was rigorously conceptualized by William Thomson (Lord Kelvin) in an article of 1852, summarized and popularized ten years later.[35] The idea of entropy, drawn from the thermodynamics of Carnot and Clausius, furnished a concrete basis to Schopenhauer's pessimism.[36] It then passed into the public domain, either as something ineluctable to which we must be resigned, or as something that obliges us to a thousand maneuvers of resistance or circumvention.[37]

How will this death occur? The answers varied. Saint-Simon evoked a drying up of the earth, as did J. H. Rosny Senior in a work of science fiction.[38] More seriously, in 1868 Father Angelo Secchi, S.J., discovered the "red giants" and saw in them the future of the Sun, condemned to collapse in on itself after a final explosion. The book in which this director of the Vatican Observatory popularized his discoveries was a great success.[39] And even if the *Internationale* sings that "the sun will shine forever," Engels took into account the predictions of astronomers and predicted the inevitable going-cold of the star.[40] In 1892, Camille Flammarion published *La Fin du monde* (*The End of the World*). Its first part was a novel of anticipation about the threat of a comet hitting the Earth in the twenty-fifth century; the second was situated ten million years in the future and presented, this time, a quite real end of our planet.[41]

The End of Man

The idea of an end of humanity was already in d'Holbach, who nonetheless was an untiring advocate of progress.[42] It was the object of a "secret fascination on the part of all the socialists," who introduced "the notion of the death of the human race in history."[43] Auguste Comte recalls that "the collective organism is necessarily subject, like the individual organism, to an inevitable spontaneous decline, even independently of the insurmountable changes in the general milieu."[44] The painter Paul Chenavard, in his rather hazy philosophy of history, fixed the end of history at 2800 and the end of humanity in 3500.[45] Gobineau, no less woolly, predicted the end not only of the Aryan race, by degeneration, but of all of humanity.[46]

The expression "last man" knew a strange vogue at the beginning of the nineteenth century. In France, it appeared in 1805 as the title of a novel by Cousin de Grainville, who committed suicide once his novel was finished. In it he recounts the story of the aptly named Omegarus, seeking the only woman who is still fecund in a decrepit world. He, however, renounces the task for fear of perpetuating a condemned race, and ends by killing himself. The work had the honor of being considered by Michelet as one of the two works typical of the sensibility of his time, the other being Malthus's essay.[47] The theme passed into England in a poem by Thomas Campbell (1823). The year 1826, which by a pleasant coincidence is also the year of the final edition of Malthus's book, saw a wave of titles with the "last man": a novel by Mary Shelley, where the end of humanity is due to an epidemic, a tableau by John Martin, and a parodic poem by Thomas Hood. Beyond the particular case of man, the period is obsessed by what is "last." Still in 1826, *The Last of the Mohicans* by James Fenimore Cooper appeared, and *Les Aventures du dernier Abencérage* of Chateaubriand. Between 1834 and 1848, Edward Bulwer-Lytton published no less than four historical novels whose title includes "the last," beginning with *The Last Days of Pompeii*, which made him famous.[48]

A year after the annus mirabilis of 1826, the Russian novelist Evgenii Boratynski, in "The last death," reports three successive visions of the future of humanity.[49] The first represents the triumph of reason and enlightenment: the earth is a garden, covered with towns; man has obliged the elements to recognize his law; he masters earth and sea. Abundance reigns: "The infertile years have disappeared; laborers at will call upon winds, rain, heat and cold" (lines 37–39). The third presents the horror of an earth devoid of men: "Nature in its majesty has reclothed itself in the purple of ancient times" (lines 87–88). The sun still illumines the earth; but only a vapor rises toward it, without any praise. The second vision explains the cause of this desolation. "Habituated to the abundance of the goods of this world" (line 56), human beings cast a blasé look on what their ancestors have achieved. "Forgetful of earthly desires, estranged from all crude inclination, the appeal of the things of the soul, sublime things, has replaced in them the other instincts. The imagination took hold of their being and possessed them completely. In them, corporeal nature ceded to spiritual nature. Living thought carried them on its wings toward the Empyreum and the chaos; but on earth they make their way painfully, and their marriages remain sterile" (lines 61–72).

In the work of H. G. Wells one reads a much more recent testimony, even more interesting as it comes from a eulogist of progress.[50] In his last brochure, he hammered home that the human spirit and even the human species were "burnt out." His impending death and the Second World War could have given a somber cast to the work. Radical and quite recent changes, to which Wells alludes without naming them (Hiroshima?), obliged him to repudiate his own forecasts. The sole hope is that man would be replaced by a better-adapted animal, unless "a small, highly adaptable minority of the species" survives.[51]

In the 1830s, an impertinent question appeared. Would the disappearance of man truly be an evil? Perhaps there are too many? The fear of overpopulation is itself also ancient, and in natural cataclysms one saw a means of avoiding it. We see this thought in the eleventh century with al-Biruni, in the twelfth with Averroës, and the fourteenth with Marsilius of Padua. In the fifteenth century, the cleric of the *Dream of the Orchard* defends the vow of chastity, by maintaining that "today, humankind has multiplied enough." Machiavelli and Vico see overpopulation as a danger that nature remedies with catastrophes or wars. At the end of the century of Enlightenment, which was rather natalist and blamed the chastity of monks, Malthus responded to Condorcet's enthusiasm with his *Essay on the Principle of Population* (1798). There he recalled that indefinite progress ran up against the limited character of natural resources. In the second edition (1803), he recommends the continence of the laboring classes. Galton objected to him that these measures would cause the most conscientious and scrupulous human beings to disappear, leaving the room open for the more intellectually and morally worse species.[52]

Perhaps even one human being is too many? The idea is conceived according to which man would be a danger for the earth, and with that idea the dream of a nature freed and returned to its native purity. The young Flaubert wrote in 1838: "The trees will grow, turn green, without a hand to strike and bruise them; rivers will flow in immaculate prairies, nature will be free, without man to coerce it, and this race will be extinguished, because it was cursed from its infancy."[53] We, however, are only a half-century after Diderot, for whom nature without man would only be a desert, and eighteen years before Auguste Comte, who had a similar formulation: "The future existence of our planet merits no attention if one supposes the Great Being who consecrates it [i.e., Humanity] extinct!"[54] The idea of a nature unencumbered by man regularly reappears, however, in 1899 with Wilfrid Scawen Blunt, in 1920 with D. H. Lawrence, and in 1924 with Alfred Döblin.[55]

The End of the Future

Even supposing that the days of humanity are limited, that is not a reason to hasten its disappearance, provided that one has an overall positive judgment on the human adventure. But still, should one desire to avoid that disappearance, and therefore to will the means? Is this will present? The question was posed as early as the beginning of the eighteenth century. In 1719, the Abbé Dubos noted:

> The philosophical spirit ... will soon do to a great part of Europe what the Goths and the Vandals did earlier. ... I see ... the most useful prejudices for the preservation of society abolished. ... We conduct ourselves without regard for experience ... and we have the imprudence to act as if we were the first generation that knew how to reason. The care for posterity is totally neglected. All the expenditures that our ancestors made in buildings and furnishings would be lost to us, and we would no longer find wood in the forests to build, nor even to warm ourselves, if they had been reasonable in the way in which we are. ... Individuals govern themselves as if their heirs were their enemies, and ... the present generation conducts itself as if it is to be the last shoot of the human race.[56]

Dubos doubtless was thinking of a depletion of natural resources. One will note the discreet rehabilitation of prejudice and the idea that we consume the goods accumulated by our ancestors without producing anything that we in our turn could bequeath to our descendants.

The first benefit we bestow on them is, of course, to give them life. Jean-Jacques Rousseau, ten years after the *Discourse on the Sciences and Arts* (1750), shows that that does not go without saying. He counterbalances the declamations of the period against "fanaticism" with a sober appreciation of its contrary.

> Irreligion, and in general the rational and philosophic spirit, attaches souls to life, renders them effeminate, and degrades them, concentrating all the passions in the baseness of individual interest, in the abjection of the human 'I,' and thus saps the true foundations of every society. ... If atheism does not cause men to be killed, this is less out of love for peace than indifference toward the good. ... Its principles do not have men killed, but they prevent them from being born, by destroying the morals that multiply them, by detaching them from their species, by reducing all their affections to a hidden egoism that is as injurious to the population as it is to virtue. Philosophical indifference resembles the tranquility of the State under despotism; it is the tranquility of death; it is more destructive than war itself."[57]

The disappearance of man, therefore, could just as well arrive by extinction, following lack of interest on his part for the future.[58] Before modern times, the concern for posterity was indirectly concern for the survival made possible by the glory attached to the illustrious deeds of great men.[59] It initially concerned noble families, desirous of assuring their offspring of the status received from their ancestors. Dante generalized the formulation, at the same time that he gave "nobility" a not-merely social meaning: the concern to convey to posterity what our predecessors have given us.[60] This attitude was nicely illustrated by the English theologian George Hakewill, who aimed to confront the fears of a near disappearance of the world: "Let not then the vain shadows of the world's fatal decay keep us either from looking backward to the imitation of our noble predecessors or forward in providing for posterity, but as our predecessors worthily provided for us, so let our posterity bless us in providing for them, it being still as uncertain to us what generations are still to ensue, as it was to our predecessors in their ages."[61]

With the rejection of a future life by the radical Enlightenment, posterity became the replacement for immortality and the recipient of the hopes of the "sage." Thus Diderot made concern for posterity the motive of the philosopher's action and his equivalent of what the future life is for the religious believer. Robespierre saw in such concern "the sweet and tender hope of humanity," and it was to "impartial posterity" that Mme. Roland appealed in her *Mémoires* composed in prison.[62]

John Stuart Mill used the word "posterity" in an interesting way in his book on Auguste Comte. The religion of Humanity would be the becoming-aware of the connection of each age of humanity with all the others, all generations thus forming a single image. This religion combines the power that the idea of posterity exercises over minds with our most positive sentiments toward the living world that surrounds us and toward the predecessors who made us what we are.[63] Significantly, however, the religion of Humanity says little about the future, accenting the past that culminates with us.

The lack of interest in posterity is one with the loss of a conscious relationship to the past. One must know oneself to have descended from ancestors to experience being called to become the progenitor of a posterity. This is what Burke expressed, arguing against the principles of the French Revolution. "People will not look forward to posterity, who never look back to their ancestors." Two generations later, Tocqueville, although a partisan of the new regime, repeats the idea and even the rhythm of the phrase: "Not only does democracy cause each man to forget his ancestors, but it also hides his descendants from him."[64] Our relationship to the past is such that we live off of cultural goods that we did not produce (that we even destroy), in the manner of parasites.

This image of parasite is at the heart of a paradox that became famous in its formulation by the German jurist Ernst-Wolfgang Böckenförde: "The liberal, secularized State lives off of presuppositions that it is incapable of itself guaranteeing."[65] The parasitical nature of modernity was not felt until rather late. Renan puts in parallel the depletion of "planetary capital" (coal) and moral resources; and Nietzsche notes: "We have ceased to accumulate, we spend the capital of our ancestors." A generation later, Charles Péguy unmasked and named parasitism as the essence of modernity, first at the end of 1907, then in 1914. "The only fidelity of the modern world, is the fidelity of the parasite. . . . The modern world is . . . essentially parasitic. It does not draw its strength, or its appearance of strength, except from regimes that it battles, from worlds that it sets about to undermine." A bit later, G. K. Chesterton reprised and developed the idea, without the word, in an essay in the 1920s.[66]

16

Man, Humiliated

At their beginnings in the seventeenth century, modern times based themselves on a certainty: they knew what man is, and there was no need to question themselves on the subject. Man enjoyed such an obvious superiority that there was no need to explicitly formulate it. One did not take the trouble, therefore, to continue the reflections of the Renaissance on human dignity. As a consequence, the project of elevating man to the place of master only exploited a capital that man had received from nature, or from God via nature. However, this evidence of the humanity of man and his privileged status was called into question, to the extent of arriving at a "mastery without a subject," a "kingdom without a king."[1]

Actually, emphasis on the dignity of man is only one of the themes of modern thought. As a counterpoint, an entire tradition is bent on belittling him. It has become customary to envisage the history of science as a series of wounds inflicted on "human narcissism" (Freud's phrase), although they are also seen as so much progress. This way of seeing things is false.[2] But if it only slightly illumines what really happened, it is an interesting symptom of a certain delight in humiliation.

The Upstart

The Renaissance humanists already sought to refute arguments aiming to show the manifold miseries of the human condition.[3] The theme of man's smallness is traditional, and the reasons given to diminish him of various sorts. Some were cosmological, involving man's location on the earth, at the lowest point of the universe;

some were biological, invoking the baseness of his original material, "an impure drop."[4] But the reminder of his humble status was compensated by the exaltation of the dignity he enjoys because of the presence of a spark of the creative fire in him, or the divine law granted him, or the intellect that can unite with the separate intelligences, or the liberty that makes him similar to God. With the modern undermining of these latter conceptions of man, nothing any longer parries the blows struck at his pride. The idea of the dignity of man was based upon a theological or philosophical anthropology. Once anthropology was reduced to a natural science, the idea of dignity had to suffer a mutation.

All the more so, as man now found himself attacked not only in his relationship with what he is not but at the interior of what makes him himself; and, first, in his way of seeing the world. The abandonment of geocentrism did not represent the "wound to narcissism" that Freud imagined, but it did show that man's perception of his situation was not adequate.[5] The critique of anthropomorphism began with Galileo, for whom the qualities that are called "secondary"—for example, colors—are not found in things, but only in human sense perception.[6] The sovereignty of consciousness was then contested by the notion of the unconscious, which, after a long preparation in the classical and romantic periods, imposed itself on the nineteenth century. For some, consciousness is only an epiphenomenon of physiological facts.[7] At the very least, it does not exercise an unqualified rule. The master of nature is himself the slave to nature in him. Freud does not tire of recalling that proud reason is not even the master of itself. He thus pushes to an extreme an observation already made before him.[8]

However, the project of the domination of nature does not disappear as a result. It can even become more exacerbated, but reduced to a pure relation of forces. Man no longer appears as the legitimate sovereign of creation, but as a sort of upstart parvenu. Perhaps he must affirm himself with greater insistence precisely because he senses himself ill founded in his claims. The recently ennobled distinguishes himself from the commoner with greater haughtiness than those who, belonging to an old, assured line, have an unquestionable superiority. The one who is "without nobility" (*sine nobilitate*, hence the abbreviation *s.nob*) will *snub* those whom he knows he is no better than.

Above all, he will snub the animals, whose proximity constitutes a threat that is increasingly perceived. Montaigne had taken up ancient examples of the astuteness of animals in order to challenge human pride.[9] The tradition thus renewed continued in a defense of the soul of animals against Cartesian mechanism, a defense illustrated by La Fontaine, which will last throughout the eighteenth century.[10] "Libertines" and materialists blurred the border between the human and the animal. The anonymous "Theophrastus Redivivus" reprised all the ancient arguments to this effect. Cyrano de Bergerac put on the same plane man and ... the cabbage.[11] Rorarius's book, written in 1544, was published one hundred years later, and his thesis on the superiority of animals in rationality entered the Republic of Letters with an encyclopedia article that Bayle devoted to it.[12] Spinoza criticized the idea that God has done everything for man, and the theologians of the period refused to believe that God would have created the world simply for man's advantage, and they extended God's benefits to all the living.[13]

In the seventeenth and eighteenth centuries, the development of the life sciences invited the learned to base a parallel between man and animals on comparative physiology. Above all, the effort bore on the animals that resemble human beings the most, such as the orangutan. Since forever the ape was perceived as a living caricature of man, and it retained this function through Hoffman, Hauff, and Kafka.[14] But modern times added kinship to likeness. In Scotland, James Burnett (Lord Monboddo) studied the great apes in this perspective. Before Charles Darwin, his grandfather Erasmus Darwin considered them to be the ancestors of man.[15] And Buffon recalled "a truth that is, perhaps, humiliating for man, which is that he must include himself in the class of animals, whom he resembles by everything he has that is material."[16] La Mettrie wrote: "All the animals—and man therefore, whom no wise man will ever advise to exempt himself from their category ..." The study of physiology has for its purpose to put man back in his place: "Without the animal operations ..., man, this proud animal, made of clay like the others, would believe himself a god on earth and would only have worshiped himself."[17] D'Holbach regards with disdain the illusions that man has constructed about his status. Sade follows him on this point, as well as on many others.[18] The idea even became banal, as those who criticized it pointed out.[19] Now, however, the target of the effort at undermining is not the superiority that is acquired, but the superiority that is *received*. The materialists do not deny the way in which man achieves a superiority by education. On the contrary, they glorify its conquests. Their true adversary is the teaching of the creation of man in the image of God.[20]

In the nineteenth century, Auguste Comte denied the classical definition of man as "rational animal," on the pretext that all the animals are.[21] With the theory of evolution, the parallel between man and the animal is completed with the idea of an unbroken passage from one to the other. The medieval authors, following Aristotle, insisted on the continuity of the ladder of the living, but they simply wanted to say that the observer did not observe any abrupt leap between the species, not that they would have really emerged from one another. With Lamarck, and more so with Charles Darwin, the idea of an ideal continuity between the species took on a concrete character. It then became tempting to transpose biological kinship into an identity and to topple man from his privileged position. In 1888, Maupassant exclaimed: "One must be blind and drunk with foolish pride to believe oneself anything other than a beast barely superior to the others!"[22] Here the reader will allow me a somewhat abrupt side comment. Those who disdain mankind in general are often those who in their private lives act as jerks toward other individual persons. (I provide illustrations in the note.)[23] The saints, who would have the right to look down on common humanity, only love their neighbor the more.

Still, one saw a valorization of the animal as free vitality reemerge, in contrast to the constraints that make man a domesticated animal. In this context, the way in which the image of the horse changes from negative to positive is interesting. For a long time it was the very type of the irrational, as its modern Greek name indicates, *alogo*, inherited from the Byzantine army, and it took the satiric genius of a Swift to imagine a world in which horses, alone rational, dominated uncouth men. With modernity it was precisely as irrational that the horse received a positive value, at least as a metaphor. Machiavelli had already exhorted the prince to enlist himself in the school of the centaur Chiron and, in case of necessity, to also employ Chiron's bestial nature. Finally, with the lyric poets and painters of German expressionism, the horse became the image of rebellious and indomitable vitality.[24]

Contempt for Man

The Enlightenment passes for having been humanistic. In fact, the authors who represent it often express a disdain that borders on misanthropy toward man. They reduce him to "a little mud, a drop of snot."[25] The book of Genesis recounts how Adam was drawn from the clay, then received the spirit that God inspired in him; the "Philosophers" reduced the difference of man to the "organization" of matter. Concerning this disdainful attitude, perhaps the most revealing utterance is that of a character in Sade: "Oh! What an enigma is man! . . . —Yes, . . . And behold what caused a man of wit to say that it was better to screw him than to understand him."[26] At the very end of the eighteenth century, he first sums up the wonderment that courses through Western thought since the Bible, the

Corpus Hermeticum, and the fathers of the church, not to mention the inflection that Pascal had given the idea: man "the chimera," "incomprehensible monster." (Sade borrows the term "enigma" from Voltaire's response to Pascal.[27]) But the employment of the term translated "screw" is even more darkly ironic as it is applied here in Sade to a particularly sickening perversion. The response is that one must give up understanding man and only "screw" him, really as well as figuratively (see the Russian slang verb *utilizirovat'*). The second sense of the word, even if it is quite crude and is deployed in a thousand variations in the rest of the work, is, although against Sade's intention, perhaps more anodyne than the literal sense. Be that as it may, the rejection of understanding in order to better dominate is prefigured by d'Holbach, from whom Sade drew all his "philosophy"; and, as we saw earlier, this rejection will be more clearly formulated by the positivists of the nineteenth century, Claude Bernard at their head.[28] Sade's formulation, however, is the logical consequence of the attempt to put forth a *science* of man and make it the basis of the edifice of knowledge. To the extent that man becomes an object of science, it is normal that one applies to him the rule that applies to every object of science understood in a Baconian way. One therefore will renounce the attempt to understand him in order to seek for laws that will better allow one to control him.

The 1840s, which saw the project of an atheistic humanism appear, are not, however, immune from a discreet disdain for man as he is, so little worthy of what humanism expects from him. Thus the young Marx says not to concern oneself with concrete man, corrupted as he is by the conditions of his actual life.[29] At the same time as Marx, Kierkegaard unmasks beneath the noisy self-satisfaction of his century a secret despair of man in himself. "In the midst of all this joy concerning our time and the nineteenth century, one perceives a secret disdain for the fact of being man; in the midst of the importance this generation ascribes to itself, one discerns a despair over the subject of the human condition."[30] A few years later, Flaubert, not particularly tender toward the human race, is even more radical in his suspicion: "The eighteenth century denied the soul, and the work of the nineteenth century perhaps will be to kill *man*?"[31] For the Dane as for the Frenchman, "man" designates above all the individual, even if they do not have the same idea of what makes for the individuality of man. Their observations, however, retain a general value. Dostoyevsky put forth a similar diagnosis in 1864, at the end of *Notes from the Underground*: "It is painful for us to even be human beings, made of body and blood; we are ashamed of this, we consider it shameful and we would wish to be some sort of universal men, who do not exist." Finally, Robert

Musil (1880–1942) summarized the spirit of his time: "Without knowing exactly why, it was good 'to humiliate' man."[32]

In our time, the disdain for man has not diminished. It remains in good taste to recall with amused condescension that man "isn't much." One employs the results of quite legitimate scientific research to this purpose, but using them ideologically. Thus, one underlines that man has almost the entirety of his DNA in common with the great apes, while, on the other hand, observing that many animals exhibit behavior that prefigures that of man: language, social life, even ethical behavior.

One also emphasizes not only the modesty of human nature but the baseness of human actions. Man is the universal predator, the living being most dangerous to his own species and the others. His industry represents a threat to the entirety of life on earth. Perhaps it would have been better if he had never existed. This idea is found in antiquity. Thus, the Latin poet Statius regrets that after the flood that cleansed the earth, it did not remain empty. This wish is also found in the French biologist Jean Rostand. According to Sade, it would even be desirable that humanity disappear. "The total extinction of the human race would only be a service rendered to nature." The idea became general and was radicalized in the movement of "deep ecology," and among those for whom an atomic war would only be a ruse of nature to do away with a species that has become too invasive.[33]

The reminder that the world is not obliged to submit to the demands of man is found just about everywhere. Sometimes it takes on an obsessive cast, as if a secret self-hatred was being expressed. The clever take pleasure in reducing whatever passes for elevated to what is base. One recognizes the attitude of moralists like La Rochefoucauld or the Nietzsche of the early 1880s, who enlisted in the school of the French. This reductive attitude takes over the public mind and is extended to the species. In this way, however, it changes meaning. Having started as a salutary counsel addressed to the individual, to distrust what appear to be his most praiseworthy impulses and to suspect possible ignoble motives, it arrives at the point of putting any reader of a journalistic account in a position of pronouncing a summary judgment on the rest of his fellow human beings, with the sole exception, to be sure, of himself.

Dialectics

All these attacks culminate in a well-known paradox, even two. Man *as a subject* is invested with supreme responsibility, without being able to offload his responsibilities, and this at the very moment when one works assiduously to see in him only the plaything of external or internal forces that he does not control.[34] On the other hand, man *as an object* becomes the sole cause to which it is worthwhile to devote oneself (as the program of "humanitarianism" expresses it), at the same time as he doubts that he possesses any value. In this way, man has "decreasingly found the wherewithal to ground his authority, at the very moment when he thought he was going to place himself at the center of authority in the universe; it even seems that there exists a dialectical process that withdraws from him his authority to the extent that he demonstrates that his independence gives him title to power." One thus arrives at an "anthropocentrism without man."[35]

This dialectic was already prefigured in the Renaissance by the conflict between the magician and the astrologer, one dreaming of a sovereignty of man, the other recalling him to order, by presenting him as subject to the stars. It continues with their contemporary descendants, the engineer bound upon the conquest of nature and the biologist defending a naturalistic determinism.[36] It was concretized in the eighteenth century in reflections on suicide. Thus Hume, in an essay that defended its legitimacy, simultaneously claims "to return men to their native liberty" and underscores that the life of a human being "has no more importance for the universe than that of an oyster."[37]

However, the first to have clearly expressed the problem was probably the young Vladimir Soloviev, in his *Lectures on Theandrism* of 1877–78. "Contemporary thought attributes divine rights to human personality, but it gives him neither divine strength nor divine content; quite the contrary, in his life as well as his knowledge, contemporary man only admits a limited and conditional reality, the reality of partial facts and phenomena, and in this perspective man himself is only one of these partial facts."[38] He thus put his finger on a difficulty that not only persists but has grown worse. We increasingly appeal to the "rights of man" in order to ground conduct that our ancestors conceived as obligatory, either because of moral virtues brought to light by philosophy or because of divine commands issued by revealed religions. The rhetoric extolling them today is increasingly hectoring, as more "rights" (as "entitlements") are proclaimed. But why should man have rights, why is *he* so made that he can have them? Why, even, is he the *only* living thing capable of having them? Having no answer to these questions is what caused Jeremy Bentham to say that the Declaration of 1789 was "nonsense upon stilts." And we haven't made any progress since then.[39]

17

The Subjugated Subject

The modern project wants man to be the master of himself as well as of the universe; its aim is that he take his destiny into his own hands. On this point the rhetoric of the Enlightenment was, and remains, inexhaustible. But this only states a necessary condition of the enterprise: mastery over himself precedes the domination of man over the earth. However, an ironic dialectic tends to cause this intention to eventuate in the domination of certain human beings over others, and even a domination of man by his own project.

Man, Controlled

Actually, the project of *self*-mastery poses two problems. The first is the nature of the self, which does not coincide with what allows itself to be observed. One therefore must lead man back to what is most authentic in him. This central core will be identified differently in different periods. One therefore will have to lead man in different ways to what is properly human. The second problem is the meaning of the relation. What does this mean: to act *on oneself*? This is an old problem, already posed for the individual in Greek philosophy.[1] In grammatical terms, it is the problem of the articulation between the reflective (self) and the reciprocal (each other). Can a reality truly have a relationship to itself? Or is what presents itself as this relationship not the relationship of one part to another? In the case of man, this action on the self will be that of some persons on other persons, with the former being the active subjects deemed to realize the idea of the "self" in its purest form.

The modern rationalization of life, however, has its reverse side. Whatever in man is a poor fit in the various rationalized settings is controlled, even repressed. Medicine (including psychiatry), law, and the police are the instruments. In antiquity, in his ideal agora Plato's Protagoras had indicated the place of the technically competent man. One listens to him when one wants to know how to build triremes, but his voice weighs no more than any other's when the discussion is strictly political.[2] With modernity, the technician discretely makes his reentry, but under a more disquieting figure. He is no longer simply the steward in charge of the distribution of goods; he intervenes in the production of the first of all goods, the producers themselves.

Charged with humanizing man, education changes meaning. Previously, its fundamental objective consisted in orienting desire toward its proper object, the sole object capable of satisfying it; rather than being rebuffed, desire was to be liberated. Now, however, it is channeled toward obtaining an object that it does not directly envisage. For "the optimism of the Enlightenment did not bear upon human nature, but rather on what one could make of it by progress in science, by education and government, and in general by the rational reconstruction of society. It had less confidence in the reasonable nature of man than in the power of reason to find the means of overcoming such a creature."[3]

From the dawn of modernity, education was conceived as the object of a distinct discipline, and pedagogy assumed its independence. It found its theoreticians in Alberti, then Montaigne and Comenius. It flourished in the eighteenth century, after Locke's *Some Thoughts concerning Education* (1693), with Rousseau's *Émile* (1762), Kant's *Lectures on Pedagogy* (published in 1803), then, also as practical, with J. H. Pestalozzi. Parallel to these, the "novel of education" became an independent literary genre, quite well represented ever since Fénelon's *Telemachus*. Enlightenment utopias were "pedagogical poems." Morelly has a very interesting formulation: man is to be "tamed by the mechanism of an education conformed to our principles."[4]

The pedagogical project took on a special amplitude with German idealism. Kant remarks that "man cannot become man except by education. He is nothing but what education makes of him." This "nothing" had already been thematized by Comenius. "Man is everything and nothing. Nothing of himself, when he is born. Everything comes from God's intention, in whose image he is formed, and from good education."[5] But it was Fichte who formulated the intention most radically. He insisted on the novelty of his project of a "national education" of Germany, one rendered necessary by the Napoleonic defeats. Until then, the goal of education was "at most, to form this-or-that in man; henceforth it is a matter of forming man himself." One must no longer content oneself with making man merely the one to whom morality is preached; one must "make man himself, make him such that he cannot will otherwise than you wish him to will." One must "introduce a human species totally different from the way men have been habituated until now, and make it the rule." It is thus that "a new order of things and a new creation begin." Humanity will have "to make itself what it still ought to become." In this way the human species finds itself "in the midpoint of its life on earth." After this turning point, it must become a "new human race."[6] What in Germany was speculation, in France had been the goal of plans backed by the real power of the revolutionary state.

The project was seeking a type. Thus Cabanis sought to bring the species closer to a "perfect type." Not a summit, but an average model at once perfectly intelligible and perfectly docile.[7] In the industrial era, the domination of technology produced a specific human type, the worker. This is what Ernst Jünger saw in a 1932 book to which Heidegger devoted a seminar.[8] "The total character of work is the way in which the figure of the worker begins to penetrate the world. . . . Life is related to the sole power today capable of conferring dominion, the figure of the worker. . . . The technological will can appear as the specific expression of the will of a superior race." But technology itself is the figure of a "metaphysical power." Behind it, one must discern "the reign of the figure . . . who puts at his service the meaning of the type—that is, that of the worker."[9] Technology, however, not only has the dominion of the human type, the worker, for its consequence. It more decisively produces the dominion of the type over man himself. Only what corresponds to the type counts as human. The rest is devalued.

We possess literary illustrations of the type even before Jünger, in the Zola of *The Human Beast* (1890) and in Jünger's French contemporary, Saint-Exupéry, in *Night Flight* (1931). Putting himself at the service of the machine, man comes to think in a mechanistic way of the moral qualities (cleanliness, efficiency, permanent availability) required to ensure the machine's continued functioning. And what Günther Anders called "promethean shame" can even develop: to feel inferior to the perfection of one's products.[10]

The Domination of Man by Man

The idea of the "great man" remains symbolic. But the translation to political realization is never far away. The domination of man over nature turns into a domination of man over man, and certain thinkers acknowledged it, beginning with Francis Bacon. In truth, this means the domination of certain human beings over others, the domination of those who best represent the type "man" over the others. Humanism also means that "man represents the highest authority for man," with its ominous overtones. Husserl notes that progress in the knowledge of the universe also includes "mastery over humanity as belonging to the real surrounding world—that is, mastery over himself and his fellow man." From this should come an increased power over his fate and thus a more complete happiness, a word that Husserl, however, puts in quotation marks.[11]

In the nineteenth century, Auguste Comte provided a good example of this enterprise of domination. He deplored that the action of man on nature was limited to the inorganic realm; from now on technology should also aim at becoming political and moral.[12] He exhorted his disciples to a conquest of the world that he likened to the one that Muhammad had promised his believers or that Cromwell had promised the saints. They are "to govern the world." To the souls of an elite, wrote Comte, belonged "a general empire": "[To you] I deliver the world. . . . Take hold of the social world, for it belongs to you."[13] Positivism will take control of the government before conquering society; however, it "will be, for a generation at least, the religion of the leaders before becoming that of the subjects." Comte is quite aware that this inverts the path followed by Christianity, which conquered the masses before converting the elites who persecuted it.[14] He, however, takes advantage of the freedom of thought of modern societies and expects the triumph of positivism simply because of its superiority in the free competition of ideas.[15] Nonetheless, he also speaks of submitting all intellects to "an exact, continual discipline." He dreams of remaking the medieval Catholic church, at least as he imagined it, but by augmenting its authority. Human beings will be emancipated, but at the same time subjected. "All the precepts of Catholicism concerning the submission of reason to faith are so many programs to achieve."[16] He even speaks of "the contemporary need of a worthy fanaticism," because "dedication ought to replace devotion." The word "fanaticism," which Voltaire had used in his well-known derogatory sense, here assumes a positive tone, as it will later with J. D. Bernal and André Breton.[17]

All the pedagogical projects contain an authoritarian aspect, if only because of their character as a blueprint. For the result to be controllable, it was best to withdraw the child from every other influence. Plato already took them from their parents; Gaspard Guillard de Beaurieu (d. 1795) wanted to totally isolate the student, so that nothing would come to corrupt the work of nature.[18] Rousseau formed the project of an absolute control of the child by the educator, which would be even more effective as the educator was to remain invisible to his charge: "Let him [the student] believe that he is always the master, and let it be you who always are. *There is no subjection more perfect than that which maintains the appearance of liberty*; thus one captures the will itself. . . . No doubt he [the child] ought not do anything but what he wants; but he ought not to want anything but what you want him to do; he ought not to take a step that you have not foreseen; and he ought not to open his mouth, without you knowing what he is going to say."[19] Under the revolution, then under the empire, this idea was developed and put into practice by the first psychiatrists. It was also adopted by legislators. The latter, far from having confidence in man disabused of "prejudices" and restored to his adult status, had a rather dark view of him. They treated the citizen as a big child whom one must lead to "happiness" despite himself.[20]

Dominion would not be to the benefit of the masters, but the subjects. At bottom, though, it is done above all for mastery itself, which determines its subjects in function of its project. This leads to the same paradox as we find in Plato's *Republic*: the guardians ensure the overall happiness of the city, but they themselves are not happy. The full deployment of justice in the city rests on an injustice toward those who are to administer it. It is the same in Dostoyevsky, in the "Legend of the Grand Inquisitor": the masters make the masses happy, but they themselves suffer. In turn, Nietzsche raised the question of the domination of the earth and of the ruling class that is adequate to the task. The "masters of the Earth are *to replace* God and to ensure the deep and unconditional confidence of the dominated." However, those who are subjugated also have to renounce happiness and comfort. And in the same way, in a more recent scientific utopia we read that "the man of the future will probably have discovered that happiness is not a goal of life."[21]

In the more tranquil climate of liberal societies, the project of a manipulation of human beings by the more competent among them appeared in the more subdued form of *social engineering*. The phrase comes from Karl Popper, who uses it with a pejorative meaning. The attempts it designates are represented by the behaviorism of J. D. Watson, for example in the American penal system, which wants not so much to punish as to "reeducate." Reeducation by work also remained the program of the Soviet and Chinese camps. The American psychologist B. F. Skinner (d. 1990) recognized that human being's action on itself in reality signifies the action of certain persons on others. Some have seen in behaviorism as a whole a way of safeguarding the dream of the omnipotence of man, at the price of renouncing human interiority. In any case, the avowal is quite candid in Skinner, and first of all in his utopia *Walden*

Two (1948), a visit to an ideal community, interspersed with didactic discussions. In them, the creator of the community unfolds the project of a technology of human behavior and states specifically: "When we ask what Man can make of Man, we don't mean the same thing of 'Man' in both instances. We mean to ask what a few men can make of mankind. And that's the all-absorbing question of the twentieth century. What kind of world can we build—those who understand the science of behavior?"[22] And more than twenty years later, the same author, in *Beyond Freedom and Dignity* (1971), proposes a "technology of behavior." Putting it in place requires that one renounce the illusion of the autonomous subject, master of his decisions, for the sake of a control of the environment that controls him. To those who fear an "abolition of man," he responds that only "the autonomous man, the inner man, the homunculus, the possessing demon," is abolished, so that "science does not dehumanize man, it dehomunculizes him, and it must do so if it is to prevent the abolition of the human species. To man qua man we readily say good riddance. . . . Only then can we turn from the inferred to the observed, from the miraculous to the natural, from the inaccessible to the manipulable." The little book ends on a trumpet blast explaining what the 1948 novel only sketched: "We have not yet seen what man can make of man." The proposition is no longer attributed to a fictional character, but assumed by the author.[23]

Defeated by His Conquest

Where action (*praxis*) is reduced to making (*poiēsis*), man loses what he alone was able to do, since he alone "acts" in the strict meaning of the term.[24] There is therefore no longer any reason for which he could exempt himself from production, and he must himself become its object.

Man cannot escape from a comparison with his own products, and this is not necessarily in his favor. Nothing prohibits man from being dominated by his creations. They are artificial and not human, or human solely by their origin, but an origin that they hasten to reject. It is not surprising, therefore, that machines taking over is a recurring nightmare. That machines would function without human intervention was previously a dream: if the shuttles wove by themselves, one could do without slaves. The poet Antipater of Thessalonica praised the windmill that allows servants to sleep.[25] With the industrial revolution, however, the dream turned into a nightmare, because mechanization puts artisans out of work—for example, the weavers alluded to above. They reacted by destroying the new textile machines, a movement called "Luddism" after the name of its first representative.[26] In a first phase, the idea appeared according to which man would be dominated by the very instruments that allowed him to dominate nature, that is, machines. In fact, the idea perhaps appeared earlier than mechanization itself, since pre-Colombian paintings showed weapons fighting men and defeating them.[27]

The rise to authority of the Darwinian model for the explanation of life gave new strength to the myth. Thus in 1863, the young Samuel Butler wrote a brief essay, "Darwin among the Machines." As the title indicates, it is located in the evolutionist wave seeking to extrapolate from Darwin's theories that had appeared a few years before and which quickly had great success. Moreover, the application of Darwinian hypotheses to technological objects did not remain isolated. Marx already wished that a history of mechanical technologies would develop in parallel with that of nature's techniques written by Darwin, and his wish did not remain without resonance.[28] Butler sees in the perfecting of machines by man an equivalent to natural selection and sees in the machines themselves the answer to the question: "What sort of creature is man's successor in supremacy over the earth?"[29]

In his best-known work, *Erewhon* (1872), Butler creates a negative utopia. A civil war opposes proponents and opponents of machines. The opponents having triumphed, every invention dating from the last two hundred years was banished. The narrator cites a "Book of Machines" that showed that they differ from man only by degree. In fact, they calculate faster than man and are never tired. The current defects of machines are due to their still-rudimentary state. Their future evolution will allow them to surpass man, who will become a sort of parasite on them. They already "act upon man and make him man," because technological progress has permitted population growth. The day will come when man will be to the machines what the animals are to man. But we doubtlessly will be happier when we are domesticated: "There is reason to hope that the machines will use us kindly, for their existence will be in a great measure dependent upon ours; they will rule us with an iron rod, but they will not eat us; they not only will require our services in the reproduction and education of their young, but also in waiting upon them as servants; in gathering food for them, and feeding them; in restoring them to health when they are sick; and in either burying their dead or working their deceased members into new forms of mechanical existence."[30] The image of a manipulation of man by superior powers is not new. In the *Laws* Plato compares man to a marionette whose strings are held by the gods, and Jean Paul had already made man a machine put in motion by angels.[31] But here man is not overarched by anything that, in itself, is better than he; he is overcome by his own creation.

The nightmare of the sorcerer's apprentice, drawn from a work of Lucian, reemerged in Goethe's ballad, *Der Zauberlehrling* (1797). An analogous idea is implicit in the Jewish stories of the golem first thought to serve his master but rendered dangerous by his incessant growth.[32] In the modern West, the fear of technology under the form of machines appears perhaps for the first time with Jean Paul Richter, in 1782–83. It develops in the writing of E. T. A. Hoffmann, where a young man falls for a beauty who turns out to be an automaton. In 1909, E. M. Forster evoked a world in which human life was entirely governed by an omnipresent Machine, in a short story written "in reaction to one of the paradises H. G. Wells had just described." Human beings live under the earth and are not interested in the stars. "The Machine," says the hero, "proceeds—but not to our goal. We only exist as the corpuscles that course though its arteries, and if it could function without us, it would let us die." Technology is like clothing. Finery for man as long as he can take it off and put it on at will, it ends by suffocating him by making him neglect his body.[33]

With the Czech writer Karel Čapek and his *R.U.R.* (1920), the idea of "robot" took up residence in the collective imagination. The word, formed from the Slavic root for "to work," entered into all the European languages. In the book, the scientist Rossum imagined, and his son perfected and commercialized, artificial workers that were intelligent and indefatigable but incapable of feelings: "Rossum's Universal Robots" (hence the acronym of the title, "R.U.R."). The father wanted to dethrone God by science; his successors only wanted to liberate man from the slavery of work and to make him the master of creation. With all of their needs satisfied, human beings no longer had to work, but they ceased to reproduce. The robots, however, revolted and killed the humans. Their leader proclaimed: "The time of man is over. A new world begins. The reign of robots."

However, the secret of their manufacture disappeared with the death of the last human beings. In the third act, on the scene there are only robots and the "last man," the only one spared, but one who does not know how to manufacture life. Life would disappear forever if two robots did not discover—one knows not by what miracle—love for each other. At the end of the story, they depart to become the Adam and Eve of a new world, while the last man reads the story of Adam's creation and intones a hymn to life and love that ends with the *Nunc dimittis*.[34] The play, even though it is Grand Guignolesque, saw worldwide success. Ever since then, the theme of the revolt of robots haunts popular novels and films.

The same year, 1920, the French novelist Claude Farrère published a novel of anticipation, *Useless Hands*. The plot is set in motion by the invention of "hands-machines," which are capable of liberating humanity from all labor except intellectual. They can direct the work of a gigantic factory-city which provides the American continent with bread and pasta, thus making workers useless. The boss installs these machines by taking advantage of a workers' strike, rendering them useless with the new equipment. They revolt and want to destroy the new machines. The boss and his assistants kill them by the thousands, thanks to an invention capable of destroying all life but leaving intact the minerals. The explanation of the facts is borrowed from Darwin. The workers were not able to adapt and thus are condemned to death; hence the French title of the work, *Les condamnés à mort*. The cynical inventor of the weapon justifies himself in the name of the "Most Holy Selection, . . . a Moloch, but a natural Moloch, therefore inevitable." By the same token, responsibility and guilt evaporate: "We were merely the representatives of the power of Force. It was not we who killed, but the Law that killed by means of us."[35]

To leave the mineral domain intact and to eliminate the living is also a recurring dream. In it, the one-on-one encounter between man and the mineral world would ensure absolute domination by the latter. Visions of an entirely mineral world abound in modern poetry at least since Baudelaire.[36] They found their partial realization in the Crystal Palace of the universal Exposition in London (1851), which quickly became a symbol. But the dream changed into the domination of man by the mineral. The theme recently received new currency with the advent of machines with such a capacity to compute that it would not be absurd to attribute "thought" to them. The idea has been put forth that in the amplitude of evolution, life would culminate with man, but now as the constructor of thinking machines. The immense history of the organic would thus only be a grand detour allowing the mineral to arrive at thought. With J. H. Rosny Senior, the form of life that develops when man disappears is represented by the "ferromagnetals." In this way, "the mineral, defeated by the plant and the beast for thousands of years, would take definitive revenge." However, "the new reign could . . . not come to be except thanks to the human milieu."[37] Today, thinking machines would be on the verge of taking over. At most we can hope that they will tolerate us like domestic animals, writes George B. Dyson in a book whose title reprises that of Butler's essay.[38]

18

Man Remade

Man leaves his place as the subject of creation to also become the object of creation. Collective or virtual subjects appear, which subject other men deemed their inferiors. They aim to remedy everything that falls short of them and to remake man in their image.

The Man to Remake

The project of remaking man first of all presupposes that he is indefinitely malleable, and thus manipulable at will. One therefore sees doctrines appear that justify this plasticity and show man as being what he is only by chance.[1] During the Renaissance, L. B. Alberti had taken up the ancient discussion of the respective roles of nature and education, emphasizing the importance of habit and exercise. In Great Britain, the Puritans as well as John Locke supposed the total malleability of the human species.[2] But the idea became systematic among the French materialists of the late eighteenth century, who exploited the image of wax and its equivalents: "Would that I could knead them . . . like an excellent dough!" (La Mettrie).[3] The Bible compared the Creator to the potter modeling the clay (Jeremiah 18:1–6); for Helvétius and d'Holbach, the educator plays the role of the Creator: "Education can do everything," "one makes of man everything one wants." Who is this "one"? The answer is found in Abbé Raynal (although the passage may come from Diderot): "*The human race is what one wants it to be*; it is the way one governs it that decides it for good or for evil. . . . Human beings are what *the government* makes them."[4]

At the moment of the French Revolution, as viewed by Wordsworth, political practitioners as well as utopians saw in man a plastic being to fashion at will. This presupposes that nature is mastered first of all at the conceptual level. Man *must lack* any nature. Herder had already located the nature of man in the fact of being an "indeterminate nothing," and Fichte saw in plasticity what is proper to man. At the end of the century, Oscar Wilde still affirmed this during his flirtation with socialism. "Human nature will change. The only thing that one really knows about human nature is that it changes. Change is the only quality we can predicate of it."[5]

This perspective leads logically to the idea of "human material" given over to the hands of those who can make it a masterpiece. These will be conceived on the model of artists. The sovereignty of the artist thus prepared the arbitrariness of the politician or the social engineer. Failed artists—painters or calligraphers—will provide revolutionaries, first fictional ones like the Évariste Gamelin of Anatole France, then real ones like Hitler and Mao.[6]

The project of remaking man next presupposes that such a transformation, being possible, is also desirable. Therefore the existence of man and his qualities must be a purely contingent datum, the product of the interplay of blind circumstances. Man conceived as the result of the benevolence of a God who created him in his image and who calls him into a free communion with him would ill suit the enterprise of a total remaking. To be sure, the economy of salvation requires an energetic treatment to heal man, but it does not claim to replace him. Above all, it does so by appealing to the liberty of man, who can choose or not choose his regeneration. Therefore, as dreamed of by the modern project, the re-creation of man must be prepared by a rise of a "gnostic" sensibility, one that only seems to be without any connection with the different technologies that can lead to this transformation. By presenting the existence and properties of individuals as pure chance, one denies the value of the concrete state in which they find themselves; thus nothing can oppose its being replaced by others. The image of life as something into which one is thrown without one's consent is found in antiquity, for example in the metaphor of the shipwreck. It returned in force in the period from the 1820s to the 1840s, from one end of Europe to the other. Thus on 26 May 1828, his birthday, Pushkin composed a short poem in which he asked "why this unmerited and fortuitous gift, life, had been made to him?," and why life, "by a mysterious fate," was thus "condemned to the death penalty?" One sees the same accents in the young Flaubert, then in Kierkegaard. For a character in Chekhov, life is a "regrettable trap."⁷ Nothing, therefore, stands in the way of what was botched being sent back to be recast.

The idea that a new birth is needed to save man is found in the New Testament (John 3:3–7). It took on a new cast with the Calvinist interpretation of the fall as a *total* corruption of man. For Catholic doctrine, human nature remained stable and preserved the "image" of the Creator; it therefore can serve as a foothold to regain the lost "likeness." In the new view, grace must remake man from top to bottom. Unless a secularized pedagogy assumes the task. The idea of a remaking of man appeared for the first time in a nonreligious form in Galileo, who wished "to remake the brains of men."⁸ If the literal formulation is mainly a joke, it is interesting as a symptom of a project that does not limit itself to replacing false ideas, but wishes to remake the subject that produces them, the ultimate goal being that knowledge of the truth would become spontaneous, not by putting an errant liberty back on the right path, but by replacing the henceforth useless liberty with an impulsion that is as irresistible as it is unreflective. One finds the same intention transposed onto the plane of action by Robespierre: "The perfection of society would be to create in him [i.e., the citizen], in moral matters, a rapid *instinct* that, *without the tardy assistance of reasoning*, would prompt him to do the good and avoid evil."⁹ In Christianity, the transformation of man was the work of the grace (*charis*) of God. With Kleist, the perfection of action becomes in man, like in the other animals, instinctual action, activity returned to an unselfconscious state, which confers an inimitable grace (*Anmut*) on all deeds.¹⁰ Closer to us, André Malraux summed up the spirit of the century: "The only problem is to know in what form we can re-create man."¹¹ To name this re-creation, several words have been coined, with varying degrees of success. The biologist Julian S. Huxley (d. 1975), the brother of the novelist, a very feted person (for example, the first president of UNESCO), ventured the term "transhumanism." "The human species can, if it wishes, transcend itself—not just sporadically, an individual here in one way, an individual there in another way, but in its entirety, as humanity. We need a name for this new belief. Perhaps 'transhumanism' will serve: man remaining man, but transcending himself, by realizing new possibilities of and for his human nature." The intention of promoting an improved human coexists with distrust toward the unrefined version. Everything that can limit the proliferation of the latter, including the tsetse fly, would be welcome.¹²

Ever since then, the dream of such a transformation haunts Western consciousness. Sometimes it takes on caricatural forms, but it gains in seriousness and plausibility with the advances of various technologies that can serve more radical and definitive changes than simple reparative treatment. Pharmacology, genetics, surgery, electronics, and information technologies make us envisage a transformation of man such that one would no longer stand before the same species.[13]

The Artificial Man

A further step is taken with the dream of an artificial man, now no longer a product of nature, but of technology. Man thus finds himself supplanted by something that pertains to the human because it is produced by him, but that leaves it behind insofar as it is no longer natural.

The idea of an artificial man is ancient. According to Polybius, Nabis, king of Sparta, possessed an animate statue by which he dismembered debtors who refused to pay him back.[14] The first occurrence in the Middle Ages is in an Arabic version of the legend of Salaman and Absal. A pseudo-Platonic text, the *Laws of Plato* or *Book of the Cow*, gives directions for fabricating a rational animal, but it seems that it is a demon, not a human. In a passage that "contains the oldest mention of a human-automaton," the several alchemists writing in Arabic, whose works are known under the nom de plume of Jabir, calmly explained how to make living beings of all sorts, human beings included. The idea of a creation of an artificial man might come from the Egyptian theory of the fabrication of "gods"—in truth, statues.[15] Paracelsus is said to have sought to create a homunculus, and a work attributed to him provides plans. According to a legend hardly found before the nineteenth century, but which knew a literary amplification, Rabbi Loew (the MahaRaL) of Prague supposedly created a golem; in fact, the oldest testimony concerns Elyahou of Helm and dates from the 1730s. The production of a homunculus, for which human semen is needed, is a kind of in vitro fertilization which assists biological processes; on the other hand, the golem replaces them with exclusively linguistic procedures.[16]

The idea of the artificial production of the living was made thinkable by the synthesis of urea by Friedrich Wöhler (1828). A little while later, an English researcher, Andrew Crosse, had the surprise of (believing he was) seeing dust-mites form in the water through which a current of electricity passed. In this way spontaneous generation, an ancient belief, passed from nature to technology, thanks to electricity. People then tried, for example, to reanimate the corpse of a hanged criminal by means of electrical shocks.[17]

Thanks to Mary Shelley, the daughter of the reformer William Godwin, and her *Frankenstein, or The Modern Prometheus* (1818), the dream of an artificial man saw a novelistic version. The story rapidly became a modern myth, which circulated in various versions, often embellished, but not always faithful to their source. Like her hero, the story escaped its author.[18] The chemist Victor Frankenstein succeeded in animating a being of great size, but with repulsive features. Confronting the horror of his deed, he fled. Left to himself, the monster awakens to consciousness, and the reader observes the progressive development of his mental faculties (depicted in the spirit of the evolutionary psychology of the time). The monster then learns to speak by observing a nearby family, from whom, however, he hides. But when he shows himself, his ugliness causes them to chase him away.[19] Despairing of making himself accepted, and having decided to revenge himself, he kills the relatives of his creator, who then pursues him to the North Pole, where he dies en route. The monster then immolates himself by fire on an ice flow.

The lesson of this "gothic" novel is a warning against curiosity and the dangers of knowledge. The experience of Frankenstein is to serve as an object lesson to the sailor who found him, who is ready to pay with a human life "for the dominion [he] should acquire and transmit over the elemental foes of [the human] race."[20] Earlier, the science of the chemist was not disinterested, but aimed at acquiring power over nature. His readings, in fact, were more magic than scientific, and his argument in favor of modern science that of Bacon: "The powers of the [ancient science] were chimerical, while those of [modern science] were real and practical."[21]

The point of the work lies in the moral convictions of the eighteenth century. Wickedness is the result of unhappiness—the monster cries out: "Misery made me a fiend!" It was his deformity that caused him to choose evil as his good. The sovereign good being happiness, a creator has the duty of ensuring the happiness of his creatures, and Frankenstein's fault is to have created a man without making him happy.[22] Nowhere is it suggested that Frankenstein has encroached on the Creator's prerogatives. The chemist invokes the earth just as much as God, who, moreover, is not named, except as a character in Milton. It was in *Paradise Lost* that the monster learned to read, and it was what allowed him to formulate his own fate. Created alone as an Adam that God then abandoned, he changed himself into a Satan. The creature thus turns against his creator and ends by mastering him: "You are my creator, but I am your master." "My reign is not yet over," writes the monster to his pursuer.[23] But the revolt of the creature comes solely from the fact that his creator did not completely fulfill his duties towards him.

In 1886, the French writer Villiers de l'Isle-Adam published a novel, *The Future Eve*, which recounts the fabrication of an artificial woman. The young Lord Ewald has fallen in love with a young woman with a perfect body, similar to the (complete!) Venus de Milo. Alas, her soul is vulgar, base, "bourgeois," a word that sums up all the disgust of the impoverished aristocrat.[24] The inventor Edison, who is a real and quite famous person, offers to manufacture an exact replica of Lord Ewald's beloved, one provided with a soul worthy of her lover. The operation succeeds, but the passenger ship in which Lord Ewald brings back the beloved automaton with him (in his baggage hold!) catches fire and sinks. Villiers recounts in detail the construction of the mechanical body of the future Eve, but recoils before the idea of creating an artificial soul. The one that inhabits it, that of a real woman, is "superadded" to it. Edison exclaims: "Unknown to me, a Soul was superadded to my work.... In this new work of art, a being beyond Humanity suggested itself, where a mystery, inimitable until now, is irrevocably located." Technology is thus completed by spiritualism, in a combination that is quite revealing of the period. The awareness of a rivalry with God, creator of the first Eve, is expressed several times. "I claim the power ...," cries the inventor, "to bring from the silt of the current Human Science a Being *made in our image*, and which will be to us, consequently, WHAT WE ARE TO GOD."[25]

It is not surprising that the young lord is overtaken with scruples: "But to undertake the creation of such a being ... , it seems to me that this would be to tempt ... *God*." Edison responds: "Without knowing it, every man has the name 'Prometheus'—and none escapes from the beak of the vulture."[26] Two things lie hidden beyond Edison's rhetoric: "The first, the love of Humanity. The second, one of the most violent cries of despair—the coldest, most intense, most prolonged to the Heavens, perhaps!—which has ever been uttered by a living thing." As for the first, it is a matter of creating an automaton that, different from earlier attempts, can truly "give Man the sentiment of his power."[27] As for the second, Villiers borrows from Chateaubriand or Musset the term "disenchantment": The heaven is empty, "*God has withdrawn from the song.*" Villiers even attributes the forgetting of faith to industry: "In twenty-five years, five hundred thousand puffs of locomotives have sufficed to plunge your 'enlightened souls' into the deepest doubt about all that was the faith of more than six thousand years of humanity."[28]

We Are Remade!

Beyond the projects and the dreams, beyond the putting into place of the conditions that will allow their realization, one already observes attempts at realization. They proceed by quotas, by "improvement," by selection of the best and elimination of the others.

The first taking control of himself by man is quantitative. From the moment when the humanity of man can vary, the people who do not satisfy certain requirements escape from the shelter that, until then, was assured by the love of humanity. As early as 1725, the idea appeared in Francis Hutcheson that it would be legitimate to eliminate useless old people, or even "a deform'd or weak race that could never, by Ingenuity and Art, make themselves useful to Mankind, but should grow an absolutely unsupportable Burden, so as to involve a whole State in Misery."[29]

The entrance into life is also subjected to a calculation to determine how many children will be produced. In itself, contraception is an ancient practice, with a variety of means. It saw a turning point in the middle of the eighteenth century in France, where, until then, it was above all practiced by the upper classes. An antinatalist attitude was not rare among them, reinforced by the very real risk of dying in childbirth. Madame de Sévigné regretted the multiple pregnancies of her daughter. Toward 1750, contraception spread among the people, although no one knows, or will ever know, why. The drop in fecundity was perceived and began to be worrisome. In 1764, Voltaire wrote: "The past few years people speak a lot about population." Some recalled to nineteenth-century Europe, despite the considerable demographic expansion it then enjoyed, that ancient Greece declined because of its dearth of men.[30] Next, contraception entered into the realm of technology. The ancient methods were perfected. Latex condoms appeared; new ones acted directly on biological processes. The American biologist Gregory Pincus, financed by the Rockefeller Foundation, invented the contraceptive pill (1956), which was commercialized in 1960.

In the final analysis, this endeavor rests on the decision to place life under conditions, because it has less value than happiness. This is a distant consequence of the separation of the transcendentals: being is no longer intrinsically good, but only in certain cases. Voltaire had already subordinated concern for population growth to the concern for happiness. A generation later, Condorcet is even clearer: "If they [human beings] have obligations toward beings who do not yet exist, these obligations do not consist in giving them existence, but happiness; they have for their object the general well-being of the human species or the society in which they live, the family to which they are attached, and not the puerile idea of loading the earth with useless and unhappy beings."

Even more radical ideas were ascribed to the geographer Alexander von Humboldt. Marriage would be stupidity, even a crime, since it brings into the world beings whom one cannot guarantee will be happy.[31] Bergson shared the obsessive fear of overpopulation and predicted war "if one did not 'rationalize' the production of man himself, as one commences to do so with his work." The quotation marks attenuate what the verb contains that could trouble, even in the mouth of an inoffensive thinker. But the word is there, and with it the double shift it implies. First, one makes the human enter into the sphere of production; then, once man has become no longer a subject but the *object* of production, everything invites to subject him to rationalization like every other product. Other philosophers acknowledge the possibilities offered by advances in chemistry and biology, without always accepting them. Thus Heidegger indicates that a day will perhaps come when one will be able to produce the human on command; and in our day, Peter Sloterdijk has pointed out possibilities of this sort, without taking a position in their favor.[32]

After quantity, quality. The French revolutionaries did not want to content themselves with cosmetic adjustments, and already spoke of "modifying the substance of man." According to Auguste Comte, the "new philosophy" has for its goal "the continuous improvement, not only of our condition, *but also and above all, our nature.*" The idea could be found in germ from the beginnings of modern political philosophy. The Leviathan, the collective man of Hobbes, is artificial, as is Rousseau's citizen.[33] The "remade" man first knew an aesthetic version, thus rather anodyne. For example, the dandy in Baudelaire. In contemporary art, the artist becomes more important than the work, not only because he would be its proud subject (although always ready to detach himself from it by irony) but also because he is the first object of artistic creation, the first work of art.[34] In this connection, Charles Fourier very concretely proposed increasing man's size and furnishing him with an "archibras," a supple tail at the end of which is a hand. It is not surprising that the idea gave rise to caricatures and heavy-handed jokes.[35]

In daily life, the effort to remake oneself is also present, under forms as trivial as bodybuilding or cosmetic surgery (which first appeared in order to repair the "disfigured faces" of the Great War). Initially gymnastics aimed at the health or physical strength of the warrior, as with the guardian of Plato's ideal city, then was adopted by modern nations subject to obligatory military service, by France, Germany, and Sweden with Amoros, Jahn, and Ling. The appearance of a purely aesthetic plastic surgery and physical culture therefore mark a qualitative leap.

In this context, the idea of a new man takes on a central value.[36] In itself, the idea has been known since St. Paul (Ephesians 2:15; 4:24). In the Middle Ages, Alain de Lille named the perfect creature fabricated by the virtues the *homo novus*.[37] In the eighteenth century, the idea took on a new inflection, first in the Russia of Catherine the Great, which the "Philosophers" envisaged as the country for the experimentation of their utopias. Charged with founding schools, Count Ivan I. Betzky had the Tsarina say: "Behold the sole means to use to fulfill our maternal views in this regard: regenerating our subjects by means of an education founded on these principles, *we will create* (in a manner of speaking) *new human beings*, new parents, new citizens, who will inspire their children with the principles of honor, moral goodness, and justice on which they have been raised." It has been observed that "for the first time, one spoke of the 'new man' in terms of 'production' and 'breeding': a fine future will be promised this usage."[38] Auguste Comte said of future poets that they would be able "to worthily sing the new man in the presence of the new god." The two (the human and the divine) tended to coincide. The idea of a new man became a veritable obsession in the twentieth century. For example, in the word "surrealism," one hears the "super" in "superman" resonate. To go beyond reality, to surpass it, meant "first of all to efface man in order to make room for the new Man."[39]

All this was true to various degrees—and varying according to country—for all of Europe. Fascism centered its project on the regeneration of the Italian "race." For Mussolini, this "anthropological revolution" allowed for the creation of a new Italian "in our image and likeness," by changing the country into a "vast field of human experimentation," allowing for the creation of "generations produced in the laboratory."[40] Russia represents a particular case, because it was the first to have the experience—at what a price!—of "utopia in power." The idea of a "new Man" had entered its literature in 1863 with the subtitle of Chernyshevsky's novel, *What Is to Be Done?*, from which Lenin borrowed his ideal of humanity.[41] Dostoyevsky places the expression in the mouth of Kirillov in *Demons* (1872), then Ivan's in *The Brothers Karamazov* (1880).[42] Aleksandr Blok used it in a conference of 1919.[43] It belonged to official Soviet discourse.[44] At the end of a short story by Yuri Olesha in 1928, the hero cries out: "Long live the reconstruction of human material, the universal engineering of the new world!"[45] Stalin declared in 1935, between the Ukrainian Holodomor and the Great Purge, that man—above all, the party cadre, the avant-garde of humanity—is the most precious capital.[46] However, because the remaking of man was deemed to have been realized (or at least to be in the process of being realized, thanks to the Party), the expression rather quickly gave way to that of "Soviet man."[47]

The synthesis of quantity and quality occurred in the idea of selection, since it is the possession of certain qualities that determines the type to be retained and, conversely, the cast-offs to eliminate. Thus for Aleksandr Blok in 1919, the new man ought to result from a "new selection."[48] The idea of an application to man of the selection practiced on animals was already sketched in Plato.[49] In the Renaissance, it resurfaced in the Spanish doctor Juan Huarte, who in 1575 showed that the diversity of temperaments prevents obtaining a human being capable of all the professions; at most one can select the type most endowed for a specific profession. Campanella observed that we select the races of dogs and horses, while we neglect the human race.[50] The same remark is found in writers of the Enlightenment, minor ones like Faiguet de Villeneuve (d. 1781) or major ones like Maupertuis or Cabanis.[51] The idea of human stud farms appeared in La Beaumelle (d. 1773). "Princes have stud farms of horses; they ought to have them for subjects. When one prevents the mixing of the races, one will be sure to have excellence in horses and in men." The idea will develop into the *Lebensborn* of Nazi Germany.[52]

Certain contemporaries and disciples of Darwin developed visions of the future in which a new, superior race would form by the elimination of weaker races. This is the case in England with Alfred Russel Wallace, who calmly wrote: "The superior races—those that are more intellectual and moral—ought to replace the inferior and degraded races." A little later in Germany, Ludwig Büchner, brother of the author of *The Death of Danton*, expects an equalization of the level of humanity by the "annihilation of weaker races" and the improvement of the most intelligent.[53] The disappearance of the first is still left to nature, however.

The term "eugenics" appeared in 1883 with Francis Galton, used to designate "the science of improving stock, which is by no means confined to questions of judicious mating, but which, especially in the case of man, takes cognizance of all influences that tend in however remote a degree to give to the more suitable races or strains of blood a better chance of prevailing speedily over the less suitable than they otherwise would have had." Galton had accepted the ideas of his cousin Darwin on natural selection. He worried about the way in which civilization would not allow the elimination of the weakest, but tolerated their survival. It was therefore necessary to replace what nature did without knowing or willing it with the concerted action of man. Until then, evolution had proceeded without intelligence or scruples. It was time that man became aware of his advantageous position and actively promoted the great work of evolution. Henceforth he ought to consider himself as free, capable of giving form to the future course of humanity, and not as the subject of a despotic government.[54] Here, too, Cabanis was a precursor, who wanted "to take hold of future races in advance and . . . sketch the regime of humankind."[55] In practice, the most merciful method, according to Galton, would consist in identifying the superior races or lines and favoring them in such a way that their descendants would outnumber the older ones and end by replacing them. He encouraged the races most suited to occupy the earth to marry young and to avoid the biological equivalent of the "misalliances" of nobles. He did not mention the less gentle forms of eugenics. At most, he observed that he had "not spoken of the repression of the rest [of the races], believing that it would ensue indirectly but as a matter of course [from the favor shown to the better adapted races]."[56] Others, however, will have less scruples, and are found just about everywhere in the industrialized world, and not only in Nazi Germany.

The reverse of selection is the fate reserved to the "slag." The idea of the extermination of inferiors was already found in the utopians like Fontenelle, and even in Thomas More.[57] The doctrinaires of the French Revolution proposed the elimination, pure and simple, of their opponents, with the fate of the Vendeans serving as a good example.[58] In the industrial era, the idea took on a very concrete aspect. Thus, the German anarchist Johann Most (d. 1906) reassured us that it is not necessary to eliminate more than 5 percent of the inhabitants of so-called civilized countries, because, happily, there does not exist more than that of these "riff-raff owners," even counting their accomplices. He added: "Out of fear of awakening a misplaced compassion, may they be eliminated in the most *humane* and scientific way possible, for example, by means of electricity. We do not recommend cruelties, but only the *necessary*." Most thus took literally the "execution en masse of this parasitical population" that Proudhon recommended in a joking way and which, playing on the financial meaning of the term, he called "liquidation," a word that was to have a very real future in the totalitarian systems.[59]

With Nietzsche, the thought of the eternal return of the same is itself conceived to be selective: those who cannot bear the thought eliminate themselves. But the philosopher also does not flinch before the thought that millions of human beings who are too weak have to disappear, nor before the idea of aiding them in doing so.[60] In Russia, certain Nietzschean themes, simplified and exaggerated, could have influenced the Bolsheviks or their precursors.[61] The Russian utopians at the beginning of the Soviet regime coldly envisaged the liquidation of inferior beings. Konstantin Tziolkovsky (d. 1935), known as a pioneer of astronautics, considered it a necessity, even a duty, to eliminate all the forms of imperfect life. It was therefore necessary to cleanse the earth of all the animals and the majority of plants, without counting defective human beings.[62] The same utopia of selection and liquidation is encountered in a novel of anticipation by the biologist Konstantin Merezhkovski (d. 1921), who we know was read by Jörg Lanz von Liebenfels (d. 1954), one of Hitler's inspirations.[63] For Valerian N. Muravyov (d. 1932), humanity ought to become a single social body guided by a supreme council of science; the peoples that resist this endeavor have no right to live.[64] The English communist physicist J. D. Bernal (d. 1971), in a utopia, says the same thing with exquisite understatement. Once certain people are improved by science, "the better organized beings will be obliged in self-defense *to reduce the numbers* of the others, until they are no longer seriously inconvenienced by them."[65] At bottom, this is only the logical consequence of the rejection of any essential difference between man and the animal. Every argument in favor of human experimentation on animals can serve to justify the experimentation of superior human beings on inferior ones, however one may conceive their difference in level.[66]

In addition to the obvious meaning of the verb "refaire" (to remake, to do over), there is its slang sense in French. We are "refaits" when we are caught in our own trap, or, as the saying has it, "caught like rats." These expressions capture the dialectic contained in the project of a new anthropology.

19

Man Surpassed and . . . Replaced

Before the Enlightenment, humanism considered man as he was. It exalted his grandeur and dignity without dreaming, and even less projecting, that he could change to the point of exiting the human. In any case, an elevation of man above his present status could only be the work of the Creator and Redeemer. With modern times, the question of the subject of the domination was posed rather quickly. That it was still a human being ceased to go without saying.

To Fulfill or to Surpass?

In the eighteenth century, the idea of a surpassing of man was present, but the Enlightenment tended to reject it and to remain within the human. Lord Monboddo was an exception, who attempted to justify the millenarian forecasts of the Apocalypse; for him "the human species must come to an end in a few generations" in order to give way to a new race of saints.[1] The term "superhuman," even "overman," appeared in this context as one of two poles (the other being the "inhuman") between which it was appropriate to locate the golden mean of a human perfection that remained human. Thus with Herder: "All your questions concerning the progress of our race . . . receive a response that can be summed up in a word: humanity. If the question were to know if man could and ought to become more than a man, an overman or beyond-man, any line written on this subject would be one too many."[2] Thus one remained within a thought of the immanent perfection of the human.

The humanism of triumphant modernity assumed a dynamic form. It was a matter of liberating man from what shackled him.

On the nature of the chains to remove, however, there was no accord. In the eighteenth century, it was a matter of getting rid of the deception of "priests" and the oppression of "tyrants." At the Restoration, one rose up against empires, "prisons of the peoples," against the conditions of sanitation and cities that multiplied diseases and deaths, or an economic situation condemned by the development of productive forces. All the reformers agreed on one point: once these inhibiting factors were removed, man would attain his full measure, which the utopians bent every effort to evoke in order to encourage the effort. In all cases, however, man was simply to pass from potency to act or, in chronological terms, from prehistory to history, capitalism being but the last stage of prehistory.[3] It was not yet a question of surpassing man.

However, once man was placed in a becoming that produced and encompassed him, one could not avoid asking if this becoming had said its last word concerning him. The question was intimated before Darwin; after him it became burning. Even before Darwin's theory of evolution, eighteenth-century "Philosophers" fascinated by biology had dreamed of a future evolution of humanity, thus presaging the question.[4] In a nineteenth century steeped in a vulgarized Hegelianism, some insisted on the idea of the Spirit and saw in it a subject capable of taking over the reins from man and pursuing an ascent beyond its provisional incarnation in man. Thus as early as 1827, Edgar Quinet congratulated Herder for having seen that the subject of history is not man, but "universal thought, of which man is nothing but the docile expression"; and the Renan of 1848 wrote: "One must elevate oneself to humanity, or, better put: one must surpass humanity and raise oneself to the supreme being, where everything is reason and everything is reconciled." Renan sometimes calls this supreme being (written in lower case) God, but prefers to speak of "this mysterious *to pan* [Greek: "the all"], which will still exist when humanity will have disappeared."

Two years later, the socialist Alphonse Esquiros (d. 1876) grounded this intuition in an evolutionary vision of the world inspired by geology and biology. "When the created beings, man at the head, have exhausted the series of progressive developments limited by their organs, in order for man and the animals to rise to a more perfect existence it will be necessary for a new revolution in the present form of things."[5] Auguste Comte distinguishes man and humanity, and grants primacy to the latter. "Man properly speaking is, at bottom, only a pure abstraction; there is nothing real but humanity."[6] The context invites an initial distinction between the individual and the collectivity. But the difference that separates them is not merely quantitative. Humanity concerns the three dimensions of time—past, present, and future—in the continuity of generations. The individual man is not so much submerged in the species as pervaded by his ancestors and drawn toward his posterity. In that way, man is measured by a reality whose heights he is not always capable of attaining.

Ten years later, Darwin founded the theory of evolution on observation and gave it its canonical form. It then became tempting to extend the history of living things with a chapter that explained how man either would perfect himself or would be surpassed by a superior species. Darwin himself had discreetly suggested this in the final sentences of his second masterwork. "Man may be excused for feeling some pride at having risen, though not through his own exertions, to the very summit of the organic scale; and the fact of his thus having risen, instead of having been aboriginally placed there, may give him hope for a still higher destiny in the distant future." And in the same way: "Believing as I do that man in the distant future will be a far more perfect creature than he is now, it is an intolerable thought that he and all other sentient beings are doomed to complete annihilation after such long-continued slow progress." A. R. Wallace, who had the same intuition as Darwin and at the same time, has similar formulations.[7] The popularizers of evolutionism jumped on these ideas, which provided their intuitions with a scientific guarantee. In this way, having man descend from other species, or rather, having him arise from them, was the opposite of the humiliation some wanted to see in it. It was a source of pride.[8] Moreover, far from representing a wound to human narcissism, this hardly flattering picture of the ascent of man could, in the view of Darwinism, be compensated for with the perspective of a glorious posterity. The domination of nature thus turned into the domination of man by a nature that posed him as a provisional stage, but capable of being surpassed by a more perfect type. The product of this transfiguration could claim to be better than the species from which it came, but it no longer could bear the name "man."

In 1871, the same year as *The Descent of Man* was published, the English writer Edward Bulwer-Lytton published a short novel entitled *The Coming Race*. The author who had recounted the adventures of the last representatives of a city now evokes the possibility of a posthuman future.[9] A speleologist becomes lost and discovers a subterranean world inhabited by humanoids, among whom an elite people has discovered a universal energy, the *vril*, which constitutes "the unity of the energetic agents of nature,"[10] from which they derive their name, Vril-ya. The description of this fictive race extrapolates from the data of real science, and also from the theory of races then in fashion, according to which these beings "have descended from the same ancestors as the great Aryan family."[11] The Vril-ya constitute "the most perfect nobility that a political disciple of Plato or of Sidney could conceive as the ideal of an aristocratic republic." Only artistic innovation is lacking to them, as well as military and political grandeur.[12] In their subterranean abode, the Vril-yas do not hesitate to exterminate the human races inferior to them. Moreover, they know themselves "destined to return to the upper world and to supplant the inferior races that live there now. . . . If they ever left these lower retreats and saw the light of day . . . , they would destroy and replace the varieties of men who now exist." Returned to the surface, the hero says that he "ardently hopes that centuries will pass before those who will inevitably destroy us emerge into the light of the sun."[13]

At the end of the decade when Nietzsche had decreed that man has to be overcome and surpassed, Guy de Maupassant has one of his characters say: "The reign of man is finished." In a fantastic narrative, already marked by his madness, Maupassant imagined an invisible being, a sort of phantom who would not at all come from within man, but would possess him from without.[14]

The Full Extent of the Task

It is not enough to say that man will be dominated by his conquests, that the mechanical slave will turn against his master and enslave him in turn. Man is dominated by domination itself. The project of a kingdom of man ends with a dispossession of man, in the name of the kingdom to realize. Already in Butler the implicit criterion of the superiority of machines was the capacity to dominate. He asks, "[By creating machines,] are we not ourselves creating our successors *in the supremacy of the earth?*"[15] The decisive rupture, however, is represented by the work of Nietzsche, who takes the opposite of Bacon's call for man to dominate nature. He challenges all the earlier stages of humanism in declaring: "Man is something that must be overcome and surpassed." This "must" is formulated sometimes as a moral obligation (*sollen*), sometimes as an inevitable necessity (*müssen*).[16]

Nietzsche introduces the idea of the superman while employing the vocabulary of the Darwinism then in vogue. He describes the path taken from the worm to the ape, then to man; Alfred Jarry, who will read Nietzsche, will say twenty years later: "from the Indian pig to man," without seeing that man was going to become his own guinea-pig.[17] However, barely more than five years after *Zarathustra*, Nietzsche distanced himself from any and all biologisms.[18] Of this surpassing, he contented himself with saying, "Why not?" If life could evolve from the earthworm to the ape, then to man, why not go further? On the other hand, he remained rather discreet about the "why?" However, one can reconstruct it from scattered affirmations. Man is inadequate to the "domination of the earth." Nietzsche therefore addressed the future "lords of the earth" that his morality was to select. There must be several supermen, who will form a dominant race. However, the object of the domination exercised by them is not the "last man," nor anything precise; and the subject of the domination will form a distinct species, which will not concern itself with the other, following the example of Epicurus's gods.[19]

This task whose height man cannot attain is, nonetheless, his proper task. If it is true that "the will to power is the most intimate essence of being,"[20] the being of each thing must be defined by the way that the will to power deploys itself in it. Hence, to dominate is not an accidental characteristic of man, but his specific difference. Thus for modern times the will to power replaces what *logos* was for antiquity and the West until the nineteenth century, with liberty its flower. Man is therefore under the necessity of making himself the overman; if he does not do so, he will no longer be up to his own definition. Much earlier, certain Corypheans of the French Revolution had already given proof of a certain disappointment before man and balked before the expected regeneration. Madame de Staël remarks of Destutt de Tracy: "The human race displeased him . . . : one would say that he wished to deal with something other than human beings."[21] The disappointment will grow.

Indeed, until then domination had not taken the full measure of its proper object. Now, it will become a matter of dominating the earth *qua* earth. This first of all means, horizontally, envisaging the earth beyond the divisions among countries involved in the "great politics" to which the battle for the domination of the earth constrains one. In this way, Nietzsche puts himself back in the lineage of Bacon, who transcended the limits between political units to envisage the benefits that technology could bring to the entirety of humanity.[22] This also means, vertically, "remaining faithful" to the earth, without squinting toward some transcendence. To parody one more time a passage of the Gospels that Bacon already toyed with: it is not a matter of entering the kingdom of heaven, but of conquering the earthly kingdom.[23] According to Nietzsche, the most radical affirmation of immanence is "the eternal return of the same," which renders any evasion impossible. As we said, this thought is itself selective. Those who can bear it become by that very fact supermen; the others eliminate themselves. Hence Nietzsche's powerful image of the shepherd who bit off the head of the serpent that had introduced itself into his throat: he "is no longer a man."[24] Accomplishing this metamorphosis must divide history into a before and an after. Perhaps without knowing it, Nietzsche here echoes an idea prefigured by Fichte, then Feuerbach, and clearly formulated by Dostoyevsky's Kirillov.[25]

Nazism gives these ideas a bastardized version, based on a rudimentary biology. One idea remains. The selection of the masters takes place in view of the task of dominating the earth, and even acquitting oneself of the higher tasks that a unified earth presupposes, as in the "great politics" of Nietzsche. However, the access to a superior humanity no longer depends on a free decision; it is given from the beginning with biological membership in the race of masters, which will serve as a breeding ground for an even more severe selection that will not exempt anyone of German, or even "Aryan," origin.[26] In his manifesto, even if provisionally, Hitler alludes to these tasks to come. "The populist vision of the world corresponds to Nature's inner will, because it reestablishes the free play of forces that ought to lead to a durable and reciprocal selection of the highest [type], until the best human type, thanks to the possession of the earth it will have acquired, receives a free path to exercise its activity, in part above, in part outside of, the earth. We all feel that in a distant future problems will be posed to humanity that only a supreme race, a people of lords supported by the means and the possibilities of a unified earthly globe, will be called to address."[27]

The material domain is not the only one where man encounters a project he shows himself inadequate to realize. In an 1867 text concerning his own enterprise, Mallarmé doubts the capacity of man to bring it to completion. His poems are "of a purity that man has not attained—and perhaps will never attain—because it could happen ... that *the human machine is not perfect enough* to arrive at such results."[28] It is difficult to grasp precisely what experience the poet alludes to in this enigmatic letter. But the young Mallarmé thought he had emerged victorious from a battle with God. It therefore seems that the weight that man cannot carry is analogous to that which Nietzsche invoked fifteen years later.

It is equally revealing that the subject whose inability is suspected by the poet is characterized as a machine. To be sure, ever since Descartes, then Pascal, the image is banal. But that man should be understood as a particular species of the genus "machine," less perfect than the true machines, is rich in instruction. One thinks of what G. Anders called the "promethean shame" of the man of flesh and blood before the mineral perfection of the machines that, nonetheless, were made by him.[29] A certain repugnance makes itself felt toward what is now pejoratively called the "biological," a sort of shame for having a body that reconnects with Neoplatonism. The prime object of this disgust is the difference between sexes. Hence, while awaiting totally artificial reproduction, one finds the idea of a parthenogenesis, which renders the male superfluous. Perhaps for the first time it is found in Auguste Comte. He decouples marriage from procreation by making "the principal feminine office fully independent of all propagative function." He then ventures a "bold hypothesis": "If the masculine apparatus doesn't contribute to our generation except after a simple excitation derived from its organic destination, one can conceive the possibility of replacing this stimulant with one or several others, which the woman would freely employ."[30]

Man Replaced

The work to be realized would therefore be a combination of the human and the mechanical, the latter, to be sure, a human work. This new being—will it still be a human being, or better, but in any case different? The idea surfaces in the dreams of writers and in the plans of scientists.

In the years around the First War, science fiction and scientific popularization tended to merge into each other when they treated the theme. The production of this new man was no longer left to nature, but entered into the sphere of technology. In Italy, F. T. Marinetti, who in 1914 was to launch a "futurist" manifesto, in 1909 published a novel in French, *Mafarka the Futurist*. The context is furnished by wars between Arabs and "Negroes" in a land at once maritime and barren. The hero, Mafaka-el-bar, is an "Arab male . . . triumphant and domineering . . . by the almost supernatural perfection of his organism." His city knows mechanization and employs "giraffes of war" made of metal and wood. Mafarka has his blacksmiths and weavers fabricate a son, Gazourmah, whom he animates by imparting his own soul, hence at the price of his own death. This winged giant, a "hero without sleep," does not age and, a new messiah, represents "the most beautiful of the children of the earth."[31] The novel ends with the flight of the creature toward the infinity of heaven.

The meaning of this Grand Guignol story is given in chapter 9, entitled "The Futurist Discourse," which also explains the title of the novel. In it, one finds the boldest slogans of futurism, which will also be those of the fascism to which Marinetti will adhere: to despise death, "to nourish oneself on danger," "to believe in the absolute and invincible power of the will." What is important here is the technological dream. "Our will must go forth from us to take hold of matter and modify it as we will. We can thus fashion everything that surrounds us and renovate the face of the world without end." Even more remarkable is the renunciation of the living for the sake of the artificial. It is a matter of "giving birth" by a sort of masculine parthenogenesis—"without recourse to the vulva of the woman," which throughout the novel is the ambivalent object of a suspect fascination and disgust—a matter of "killing Love, and replacing it with the sublime pleasure of heroism."[32] Even in its highest form, the human, the living no longer suffices for this exacerbated will and must cede its place to artifacts. The "triumph of the will" demands the robot, and certain "transhumanists" today recognize in Marinetti a precursor.[33]

The response to the question of the human character of the new creatures given by a Soviet poet is clearer, and negative: "The earth is going to give birth to new beings, whose name will no longer be 'man.'"[34] Trotsky, ending a book on the cultural renewal promised by the revolution with a fanfare, reluctantly employs the term popularized by Nietzsche. "Man will endeavor to command his own sentiments, to raise his instincts to the heights of consciousness and render them transparent, to direct his will in the darkness of the unconscious. By that, he will lift himself to a higher level and create a superior biological and social type, an overman if you will. . . . It is as difficult to predict the limits of the self-mastery thereby attainable, as to foresee the extent to which one will be able to develop man's technological mastery over nature." The Copenhagen speech in 1932 preferred a more prosaic formulation: to replace "the man of today, filled with contradictions and disharmonies," by "a new and happier race."[35]

More than a century after Comte, in 1923 the Scottish Marxist biologist J. B. S. Haldane launched the idea (and the word) of "ectogenesis" or artificial gestation, which inspired the famous *Brave New World* of Aldous Huxley (1932). It also elicited a disillusioned response from Bertrand Russell entitled *Icarus*.[36] The American Hermann J. Muller, Nobel Prize winner in physiology in 1948, in 1935 published a book in which he defended a eugenics based on in vitro reproduction, an idea that he presented in 1936 to Stalin, who preferred the Lamarckian theories of Lysenko.[37]

The mass production of selected human types is part of Soviet utopian dreams, found for example in Valerian Murav'ev.[38] European communists of the same period were not far behind. Thus the British physicist J. D.

Bernal, who won the Lenin Prize in 1953, one of the last to defend Lysenko, treats the question of the future of man in a 1929 pamphlet, *The World, the Flesh and the Devil*. The title reprises the Anglican rite of baptism, where one prays that the baptized would defeat these three enemies. After a chapter on spatial conquest ("The World") comes one on "The Flesh."[39] Bernal understands thereby the human body as it exists today, but not without playing on the Pauline resonances of the term. He envisages ways of lessening the infirmities—here entirely physical—of man by technological means, and on this subject he proposes a "fable." Man will be produced by ectogenesis and initially will lead a "normal" life. Then his brain will be placed in a nourishing solution and inserted in an artificial "body." New senses will be "incorporated" into the human "body," making the "new man" a "mechanical man." In that way he will be much more "plastic" and capable of evolving than the "normal man." The beings thus produced will have such an intensity of communication among themselves that individuality will exist only in a weakened version and death will hardly have any meaning for them. The terminal stage of this evolution will be, perhaps, a humanity "that has completely become ether . . . [, that has] become masses of atoms in space communicating by radiations, and finally, perhaps, resolving themselves entirely into light." It is noteworthy that Bernal, in passing, named this process "dehumanization."[40]

The idea of a hybrid of cybernetics and organism was thus launched. The word to designate it, "cyborg," was coined in 1960 by two American engineers in an article of popularization.[41] To extend the domain of the unconscious regulations of the organism would allow the liberation of man from slavery to machines which required the maintenance of an artificial milieu. Beyond the technical details, the article contains an interesting idea. It is more logical to adapt man to his environment than to seek to transport his environment to him. The conquest of space presupposes that man begins by submitting himself, even his body, to the conditions of space. In truth, however, this is only an extreme example of what has been said a thousand times, ever since Thoreau, in 1854, complained that man was becoming "the instrument of his instruments." The fact that man must henceforth adapt himself to the rhythm of machines was named "inverse adaptation." The idea took on a grotesque cast—no doubt intentionally humorous—in J. B. S. Haldane, who dreamed of giving men organs adapted to the tasks of interplanetary exploration.[42]

The most sublime reality that human beings commit themselves to construct can be called "God." The idea is not absent from the fantasies of the nineteenth century. The object of the religion projected by Auguste Comte does not bear this name, but rather that of Humanity. He, however, does not hesitate to designate it by expressions that the eighteenth century had made traditional for God: "Great Being" and "Supreme Being." This being, "composed of its own worshipers," has the advantage of being "relative, modifiable and perfectible."[43] In the German realm, in 1899 Rilke deploys the metaphor of the collective construction of a vast edifice that is at once a cathedral, the world, and the god who inhabits it.[44] The idea equally appears in Russia in the tendency that Maxim Gorki, at the end of a story of 1908, calls "the construction of God," a phrase that remained in vogue until the revolution and even beyond.[45] It is found in the philosophers. In England, Samuel Alexander defined "Deity" as "the next higher empirical quality to mind, which the universe is engaged in bringing to birth." The idea is found a little later in Germany, in the later Max Scheler.[46] In France, Bergson speaks of the great mystic: "If all human beings, if many of them, could mount as high as this privileged man, it is not at the human species that nature would have stopped, because in reality he is *more than man*."[47] For Bergson, however, the surpassing of the human species is not the work of man, but of the élan vital, which does not proceed by fabrication. At the origin, the élan aimed higher, but for lack of better, had to stop at man—although not without pursuing its ascent within the human species, thanks to great religious geniuses. Far from it being the case that man transcends himself in a superhuman machine, it is the universe which is "a machine to make gods."

❁

Exclusive humanism had defined itself against the biblical God. Mallarmé believed that he had divested himself of the "old and nasty feathers."[48] He, however, returns, under a new figure. God is henceforth the object of a construction. According to what plan, though? Is this divinity "the *good* Lord"? Or an idol that demands human sacrifices? At this point, one wants to quote Augustine: "By worshiping the works of his hands, man may more easily cease to be man than the works of his hands can become gods through his worship of them."[49]

20

Checkmate?

The modern project of a kingdom of man rested on foundations that one must qualify as "metaphysical." More or less consciously, those working at this project preserved the medieval doctrine of the "convertibility" of the "transcendentals," according to which, in the last analysis, Being, the True, and the Good coincide. They did so by postulating that progress in knowledge must improve the lot of man. But with the revocation of God also postulated by exclusive humanism, Being is severed from the Good. Nothingness (*le néant*) can now receive a positive value. This is one of the meanings of "nihilism" (from the Latin *nihil*, "nothing"), which was named at the end of the eighteenth century and which the following century increasingly worried about.[1] The young Flaubert spoke of "that profound love of nothingness that the poets of our age carry in their bowels."[2]

Reversal of Values

The divorce of Being and the Good produces a new vision of Nature, while the divorce of the True and the Good leads to a devaluation of the truth to the benefit of illusion, even to the point of denying the value of life itself.

In the name of Nature, the Enlightenment protested against institutions that supposedly betrayed it. It was necessary to scrape off the additions from nature that the sciences after Galileo revealed. They showed that reality, as it were, skips over the conventional border between good and evil. By stripping away the imaginary garments of "superstition," science unveils Nature and shows that it is not intrinsically lovable. The frontispiece of the *Encyclopedia*, a weapon in the Enlightenment campaign, implicitly acknowledges this. The frontispiece illustrates a Petrarchan commonplace on the ornamentation of style: "It is the task of the poet to decorate the truth of things with beautiful veils."[3] The frontispiece shows poetry hastening to clothe with a dazzling cloak the Nature that science just stripped. One glimpses that there is something to hide. But reality shows itself, and in more insightful thinkers Nature becomes a cold monster, cruel in its very indifference. Literature underscores this. What seems peace and harmony is in fact a field of battle where the law of the strongest rules.[4]

It is not surprising that the Romantics reacted in the name of what had been lost. They in contrast presented the idyll of communion with nature and protested against the sciences which, by objectifying reality, deprive it of all charm. At a dinner, Charles Lamb and John Keats raised a toast against the mathematicians, guilty of having destroyed the poetry of the rainbow.[5] Newton, the idol of the Enlightenment, became the whipping boy of the Romantics, and William Blake maliciously annotated the *Essays* of another Enlightenment totem, Francis Bacon.[6]

The Enlightenment wanted to base itself on knowledge of the truth, to bid adieu to the superstitions fed by ignorance. "Life spent for truth" was Rousseau's motto. But if reality is without value, a knowledge that would be perfectly adequate to it, as such and without its practical consequences, would be too. The suspicion dawned: perhaps truth is ugly, even terrible. Byron spoke of a "fatal truth," and Renan asked: "Would truth be sad?" At this point, one can ask, with the Spanish king depicted by Claudel, whether one might not need a belief in creation in order not to agree with the thought.[7] Absent that belief, it is necessary to prefer illusion to truth. After a few rare ancient prefigurations, perhaps Cervantes's *Don Quijote* was the first work concerning the impossibility of acting without illusions.[8] The Enlightenment, too, had sensed that the intention to enlighten was costly, and no one better than d'Alembert, who wrote in 1757: "There is hardly any new knowledge we acquire except to *disabuse* ourselves of some agreeable illusion, and our knowledge is almost always at the expense of our pleasures." But there is a compensation: "If this knowledge can diminish our pleasures, at the same time it flatters our *vanity*."[9]

That is a profound acknowledgment. Behind the propaganda in favor of happiness, "a new idea in Europe," the ultimate goal of Enlightenment was not the joy that one finds in what is, but the pleasure of the subject in not being duped. The being "disabused" of the "philosopher," however, is not the *desengaño* of the Spanish Golden Age, in particular that of Quevedo. In fact, it is diametrically opposed. The latter aims to detach us from the things of here-below in order to show us the path to heaven, which the Enlightenment, to the contrary, had blocked. The Spanish moralists had as their goal to show the ultimate vanity of the created vis-à-vis the unshakable fidelity of the Creator.[10] The Enlightenment compensates us by "flattering our vanity," a word whose semantic evolution is itself revealing. The absence of any foundation for human works becomes the capacity for the subject to rely on nothing other than himself.

Other Enlightenment authors speak of the utility of illusion. In Germany, Wieland in 1768 wrote verses that have remained proverbial. "An illusion that makes my happiness / Is more valuable than a truth that oppresses me." Note once again that it is the idea of value that makes the true and the false commensurable. In a similar way, Burke regrets that the empire of Light and Reason destroys the "pleasing illusions" that make for the charm of society.[11] But it seems that it was not until the first half of the nineteenth century that the poets caused the scales to tip decidedly in favor of illusion. Thus in Italy, as early as 1818, with Leopardi: for him, the poet, fighting against the Romantic pretension to truth, *ought* to deceive. Why? Reason destroys the illusions without which man cannot live, and thus leads to its own contrary, barbarism. The logical result of a total destruction of illusions would be suicide.[12] In Russia, Pushkin, the exact contemporary of the Italian, will say ten years later that he prefers the heroic legend of Napoleon to the banal image yielded by historical criticism, and "the deception that elevates us" to the vulgar reality. For the Edison of Villiers de L'Isle-Adam's novel, one must "from now on prefer a positive, prestigious and always faithful Illusion to the lying, mediocre, and always changing Reality," since "without illusion, everything perishes."[13] In contrast, those who prefer the truth in its ugliness cultivate a new virtue, which the Victorians call "virility" and Nietzsche "intellectual probity."[14] Now, this virtue can enable one to bear life, but can it promote it?

Life, the being of the living, is drawn into the devaluation of Being.[15] Life—deemed to pervade everything that is, therefore the human, with a constantly renewed dynamism, carrying it toward an ever more decided affirmation—is not, however, when it is self-conscious, immune from uncertainty concerning its own value. The question of whether life is worth the trouble to be lived was posed as early as the Egypt of the Pharaohs. Talmudic Judaism discussed it when addressing the question, Did God do well in creating man?[16] In contrast, the Enlightenment of Winckelmann and Lessing, then the humanism of the Weimar poets, presented the ancient world in the rosy image of the peaceful serenity of the Olympians.

The nineteenth century destroyed this legend. The decisive moment was likely 1835, when the Bavarian classicist Ernst von Lasaulx devoted his dissertation to "the dominion of death [*de mortis dominatu*] in the ancients." In it he gathered all the classical passages, as well as a few extracts from Hindu authors, who expressed a preference for death. A Catholic, he contrasted this pessimism with the Christian experience of salvation.

In turn, Nietzsche subtitled his essay on the origin of tragedy "Hellenism and pessimism," and in this same spirit Jacob Burckhardt wrote his *History of Greek Civilization* (published posthumously in 1900).[17] Earlier, Schopenhauer had inaugurated a period of doubt on this score. He concluded his reflections on the value of life with a negative balance sheet. His work had a belated success, which made him the most influential philosopher among artists, writers, and musicians. His rule over European sensibilities lasted from the middle of the nineteenth century to the First World War and left profound traces thereafter.[18] The question of the value of life was thus posed, and people sought in every direction to respond to Schopenhauerian pessimism.

Thus in Germany, Eugen Dühring wrote *The Worth of Life* (1865) against "the spirit of the times"—that is, against Schopenhauer, Wagner, Darwin, and, before them, Byron.[19] In 1879, in England, William Hurrell Mallock broached the same topic in his *Is Life Worth Living?* Rather than directly answer the question, he showed that "positive" thought—that is, the scientific thought of Mill and Huxley—did not have the means of keeping its promise of promoting the dignity and morality which make for the value of human life. For that one needs a hope that transcends this life.[20] In France, Léon Ollé-Laprune published in 1894 his *Price of Life*.[21] In the United States, William James posed the same question in a lecture of 1895, republished in *The Will to Believe*.[22] Rudolf Eucken, with his *The Meaning and Worth of Life* in 1908, the year of his Nobel Prize, already seemed a johnny-come-lately.[23] That the response of these various authors was affirmative does not surprise; and the reasons for their reply do not need to occupy us. What is important is that the question was posed and that it was not without widespread impact. Thus Nietzsche summarized Dühring's work at length.[24] As for the negative response, it was to find an illustrious advocate in Clarence S. Darrow, the American lawyer who was later to defend Leopold and Loeb, the two young Nietzschean kidnappers and murderers, then the Darwinist instructor in the famous "Monkey Trial." Twice he debated the question, "Is life worth living?," and each time he answered no.[25]

Conclusive Experiment?

We have seen how modern science understood itself as resting on experimentation, and how it summarizes its approach in the phrase "experimental method."[26] This became the criterion allowing one to decide what is true, by eliminating the falsehood incapable of standing up to examination. The idea of experimentation took on a metaphysical dimension in German idealism, first of all with Kant, who reflected on the Baconian method. Schelling saw in experimentation the confirmation of the idealist position. In 1799 he interpreted Fichte's philosophy, beginning with the idea that every experiment is a question addressed to a nature forced to respond. But, he adds, "every question contains a hidden a priori judgment; every experiment which truly is an experiment is a prophecy; the very practice of experimentation is a production of phenomena."[27]

The decisive point, however, was when the idea of experimentation went beyond its original domain, the sciences of nature, where it finds its rigorous application, and invaded human life in general, transposed from theory to practice. Politics is the first dimension that was affected. For the authors of *The Federalist Papers* (1787–88), the young American republic is an "experiment."[28] Renan himself comes close to the idea of life as an experiment. "What would happen, therefore, if one joined the *practical experimentation of life* to scientific experimentation?" Ten years later, the liberal ethics of John Stuart Mill (1859) encouraged "experiments in living." In 1873, Walter Pater said it directly: "Not the fruit of experiment, but the experiment itself is the end."[29]

Nietzsche ennobled the idea of experimentation even more, making it the highest human activity. The philosophical endeavor is a series of attempts "to arrive at a form of life that we have not yet attained."[30] In our day, the idea finds a cancerous development in the aesthetic domain, and perhaps even more so in the search for originality and eccentricity in daily life at all costs.[31] Someone, therefore, has summarized our contemporary situation as follows: "We must constantly remember that what we are living is an experiment, and that we are an exception."[32] In all these cases, the experiment is a project that man undertakes because he decided to do so. As a consequence, he continues to occupy the place of the master.

It is entirely otherwise when man is considered not as the experimenter but as the object on which "one" experiments. Then the very existence of man is supposed to be nothing other than an essay conducted by a superior power. The idea is not without ancient roots. An enigmatic verse of the book of Job asks: "Is there not a service on earth for man?" The Septuagint translated it as, "Is not the life of man on the earth a *trial*?"; and Augustine, following the ancient Latin translation, had "a temptation [*tentatio*]."[33] Maimonides interpreted the biblical narrative of the temptation of Abraham as a test by means of which the obedience of the man toward God is made manifest not to God himself, who knows all things, but to the man who becomes conscious of his own capacities.[34] All of that, however, remains contextualized by the idea of a benevolent deity.

The atmosphere changes when the experimenter takes on the impersonal character of the indifferent Nature of the moderns. In 1768 Jean-Baptiste Robinet published a work that considered the graduated forms of life—from the minerals that resemble the organs of the body to the ape, passing through the plants—as so many *essays* of nature, sketches before it arrives at its masterpiece.[35] The *Future Eve* of Villiers de l'Isle-Adam represents an intermediate stage. In it, Edison recalls to his silent partner: "Both of us are parts of the experiment in question."[36] Human beings are still agents; but they are drawn into their own experiment.

The idea of man as the purely passive object of Nature's experimentation appears in Goethe. "Let one think of Nature standing before a gaming table and constantly crying: 'Double or nothing!'—that is, in all the domains of its activity constantly venturing what it has already gained in order to gain more, and so on to infinity. Stone, animal, plant—all of that, after a few fortunate tosses, is constantly wagered again. Who knows whether man himself is not a toss aimed at a higher goal?" More recently, the idea is found in Hans Jonas, in a book, however, that counsels prudence vis-à-vis any utopian adventure. In it he speaks of the "ontological experiment that Being undertook with man."[37] Earlier, the fictional materialist suicide, whose farewell letter Dostoyevsky composed, asks: "What if man had not been put on earth except as a kind of insolent experiment, solely to see if a being thus made would succeed in living or not?" The saddest thing is "that there is no particular being who had attempted the experiment, no one even to curse, but everything occurred simply according to the laws of inert nature." The novelist subtly presents an analogous idea four years later in the famous legend of the Grand Inquisitor, when Ivan Karamazov characterizes human beings as "unfinished beings, experimental, created for derision."[38]

Humanity as a whole is itself an experiment of life. The idea is found in a poem written by Rilke in Muzot, 4 June 1924, commentary on which Heidegger made the center of his essay on Rilke. "We are a risky venture." The sober prose of the biologist Julian Huxley later echoes the poet's song. "[Humanity] is an experiment of the universe in rational self-consciousness. . . . The only significance we can see attaching to man's place in nature is that he is willy-nilly engaged in a gigantic evolutionary experiment by which life may attain to new levels of achievement and experience."[39] Humanity, wrote another British scientist, by increasing its wisdom, knowing more and willing more, will risk more, including its own destruction. But "this daring, this experimentation, is really the essential quality of life."[40] The Marxist thus joins an unexpected companion, Nietzsche, who made the "attempt" (*Versuch*) the very figure of truth.[41] In this way, modernity conceives history as an experiment.

But rare are those who squarely confront the obvious consequence of this passing of man under the yoke of the experimental, the rather simple fact that if a laboratory experiment can be conclusive, it can also fail. It is as if a remnant of faith in Providence continued to nourish the confidence in experimentation and forbade any serious attempt at considering the possibility of failure. From time to time, however, one does encounter the acknowledgment that the experiment could *have already failed*. I found this said for the first time in the private correspondence, conveyed in a joking tone, of Alexander von Villers, a Franco-Austrian diplomat with a smattering of Kant and Schopenhauer. "I hold man for a failed experiment of nature, which it is going to abandon very soon."[42]

The idea will not depart Western consciousness. Thus, for example, the German sculptor and dramatist Ernst Barlach (d. 1938), for whom "one can very well consider man as an essay of nature which has failed, in the same way as there exists a series of forms that it has abandoned."[43] Nietzsche was perhaps the first to have had the courage to consider the possibility of failure in an experiment that was voluntarily undertaken and to have assumed the risk. In a passage that remained unpublished, he has his Zarathustra say: "We conduct an experiment with the truth! Perhaps humanity will disappear as a result! Let's do it!"[44] This does not lack nobility. But what happens if, in fact, the experiment fails? What happens if man adopts ways of conduct that in the long run compromise his survival?

To Life and to Death

A self-destructive dialectic is thus unleashed. The project of a radical immanence ends by reversing the project of a domination *of* nature *by* man into a domination *by* nature *over* man. Once the passive material of human activity, nature is hypostasized into an active authority whose omnipotence is acknowledged and whose wisdom is postulated. Initially aided by human knowledge and ingenuity, Life ends by substituting for them.[45] How, then, to distinguish it from death?

This dialectic is illustrated in a novel by Emile Zola, *Doctor Pascal*. Published in 1893, it was intended to recapitulate and conclude the entire cycle of the Rougon-Macquart. The doctor devotes himself to the search for a treatment, even more than to his patients. Injections of tissues would constitute a universal panacea allowing for the reconstruction of "a new and superior humanity. . . . When all will be healthy, strong, intelligent, there will only be a superior people, infinitely wise and happy." The goal of medicine is "to heal suffering humanity, to make it healthy and superior, to hasten happiness, [to bring about] the future city of perfection and felicity. . . . With science, one is going to penetrate the world's secret and realize the perfect happiness of humanity."[46] Rather than achieve the happiness of humanity as it is, however, one must redefine humanity in such a way that it cannot not be happy. "Humanity can be remade, finally healthy and superior . . . in good health and higher."[47] The accumulation of scientific knowledge "will end by giving man an incalculable power, and serenity, if not happiness." This "incalculable power," whose mention strikingly recurs in the story, is explained in a formulation that recalls Comte and Bacon: "to accept everything, to employ everything for happiness, to know all and to foresee all, to reduce nature to being nothing but a servant." This, however, is but "the most beautiful of dreams."[48]

"Dr. Pascal had but one belief, belief in life. . . . Life, that was God." Echoing Schopenhauer, the doctor thinks that "in the world there is no other will than this force which pushes everything to life, to a life that is ever more developed and higher."[49] However, the final triumph of life is compromised by the very science that believes that it leads to that triumph. "To correct nature, to intervene, to modify it and to run counter to its goal, is this a praiseworthy work? . . . To dream of a healthier humanity, strong, modeled on our idea of health and strength, do we have the right? . . . To want to heal everything, to regenerate everything, is a false ambition of our egoism, a revolt against life." Henceforth convinced that "life suffices, being the sole maker of health and strength," the doctor begins injecting his patients only with water. "The sole wisdom was to let nature evolve, to eliminate dangerous elements, to merely assist its labor of health and strength. . . . Every revolt against natural laws is bad. . . . The only wisdom is not to intervene, to let nature operate."[50]

Zola takes up the idea that Renan had sketched against Schopenhauer. "Life, even if it appears awful, must be great and good, because one applies to life a will that is so tenacious, for the sake, no doubt, of this very will and of the great unknown work that it accomplishes. . . . One must live for the effort of living, for the stone contributed to some distant and mysterious work."[51] Zola comes close to the idea of the Dionysian acceptance of the tragedy of life that Nietzsche, whom he did not know, had formulated a little while before. Knowing himself condemned, the doctor mounted "yet another degree in the faith in life, to this summit of serenity where life appears totally good, even with the fatal condition of suffering, which perhaps is its wellspring? Yes! To live all of life, to live and suffer all without rebellion, without believing that one makes it better by making it painless, that shone brightly . . . as great courage and great wisdom."[52]

The principal intrigue of the novel, the incestuous love of the doctor and his niece, provides a practical illustration of this dialectic, one that Zola himself was then experiencing in his private life. The doctor is very conscious of the weight of heredity, whose theory he wants to support with the example of his own family. However, he does not accept the death that he knows is very close until *after* having learned that his niece is pregnant. Previously he has ironically exclaimed: "Does one have the right to bring unfortunates into the world? One must kill bad heredity, kill life." Now he thinks: "The child is going to be, what matters what it will be! Provided that it is the continuation, life handed on and perpetuated, another oneself!"[53] This is very touching, but is it coherent?

An almost exact contemporary of Zola, Nietzsche, extolled this life as well; he even composed the music of a hymn addressed to it. But more powerful than life is death, which inevitably ends it: the life of the individual; of the species, according to Darwin; and finally, on the far horizon, the "thermal death" of the universe. A rigorous logic is at work, which leads to the divinization of death. The "madman," then the Zarathustra brought on stage by the philosopher, announce it: "God is dead."[54] God, the Living in person, could not defeat the "final enemy" (1 Cor. 15:26). On the contrary, death was able to defeat even God, and thus show itself more powerful than he. If ever since nominalism God was defined as the All-Powerful, and if, therefore, power is the measure of the divinity, the death that triumphed over God is the sole true and definitive god. After the death of God, it is not the kingdom of man that comes, but that of the last god, which is Death. The French expression which is the title of the present chapter (*échec et mat*) echoes a Persian phrase that means "The king is dead." It thus would be inverted: "Death is king."

The idea perhaps first surfaces in the sixteenth century, in a famous painting by Holbein, *The Ambassadors* (1533), and is conveyed by the mysterious skull presented in anamorphosis. It convicts of vanity the attributes of the humanist culture arranged complacently around the two figures.[55] In any case, Europe began to take clear cognizance of this divinization of death in the nineteenth century, first of all in the most lucid writers. Thus in a lengthy short-story written the same year as *Zarathustra*, C. F. Meyer (d. 1898) has the condottiere who is the hero of the story, the only one who knows that the wound that he suffered is lethal, speak of his death as "his divinity."[56] The "divinization of death" permeates, implicitly or explicitly, large swaths of nineteenth-century European literature.[57] And later, for Wolfgang Borchert (d. 1947), death is "the Old Sir in whom no one believes any more," the last avatar of the biblical "Ancient of Days" (Dan. 7:13), who himself identifies the gravedigger (death) as his successor.[58]

Fate had already reigned victorious over the gods of Homer. Christianity had exorcized it, in that way representing an experience of liberation for ancient man. It returns to service in the nineteenth century. In a letter of 1854, Wagner summarizes the message of his tetralogy: "To will what is necessary and to achieve it." Two years later, the old Auguste Comte spoke of "glorifying fatality" and flirted with the idea of a "worship of fate." And Nietzsche reprised the Stoic formulation of *amor fati* as the final word of his wisdom.[59] In this way, the modern movement of an extension of liberty received an ironic counterpoint. What good is liberty, if it exhausts itself in the affirmation of what in any case must be?

21

Lights Out

A dialectic is put in place by which the ambition of man to total dominance leads to his own effacement. Enlightenment thus finds its apotheosis in an extinction. The socialist deputy René Viviani, president of France's Council of State at the declaration of war in 1914, had declared in 1906: "All of us together, our fathers, our forebears, we ourselves, committed ourselves in the past to the work of irreligion. We severed men's minds from belief. When an exhausted human being, worn out by the weight of the day, went to his knees, we raised him up, we told him that behind the clouds there were only chimeras. Together—and with a magnificent gesture—*we extinguished the lights* in heaven, which will never be relit."[1] This unwitting humor, which people did not fail to note, still had symptomatic value.

From Humanism to Antihumanism

As is often the case, the first domain in which one observes the working-out of the self-destructive dialectic of humanism was not at the level of conceptual reflection but in aesthetic experience. In poetry, a dehumanization of the lyrical subject showed itself with Baudelaire ("*quidquid humani a me alienum puto*. My function is extra-human!"), was accentuated in Mallarmé ("I want nothing of the human"), and finally gained all of European poetry.[2] In the plastic arts, one notes an effacement of the human starting with cubist art. Some artists had already stated the little interest they had in nature. Heinrich Füssli refused to paint landscapes or portraits. "Nature takes away all my means."[3] But among natural realities, for certain artists at the beginning of the twentieth century man is the object of a special disgust. During the classical age, he was the highest subject of art, whose supreme task was to represent him in the best way possible. At the beginning of the Great War, however, the German painter Franz Marc wrote: "Very early on, I experienced man as 'ugly.'"[4] In 1918, Berdyaev noted that art no longer had need of nature or man.[5] The human face disappeared from paintings. José Ortega y Gasset summed up this movement in the formula "the dehumanization of art," the title of a little book of 1925.[6]

The Russian historian of art and essayist Vladimir Weidle perfectly expressed the dialectical character of this movement. "At first sight, one could believe that once art had become a docile instrument in man's hands, it would at the very least put man on the first rung.... In reality, it was the opposite that occurred. The art which man disposes of absolutely, that no longer has any secrets for him, and does not reflect anything outside his will and reason, such an art, precisely, is an art without man, an art that knows neither how to express him nor how to represent him.... To the art that sees nothing beyond and above man, it is man himself who, inevitably, will one day be missing.... What is divinized today, is man dehumanized."[7]

In 1913, Guillaume Apollinaire wrote that "the modern school of painting ... wants to depict the beautiful severed from the delectation that man causes man." He adds: "Too many painters still worship plants, stones, the wave and *human beings*.... It is time to be *masters*."[8] The last formulation is very interesting. It continues the critique of the humanist self-idolatry begun almost a century earlier.[9] But it is not done to reorient the perverted instinct of the "worshiping animal" (Baudelaire) toward its only legitimate object, the Lord of Creation, but for the benefit of the artist himself. The subject of this mastery is not explicated. He is not defined by his humanity, because one would thus fall back into the adoration of man, passing from one idolatry to another. More radically, this subject is identified on the basis of the injunction to be the master. More essential to the subject than even his humanity is his capacity to dominate. The model of domination dominates man himself. Modernity is thus the "passage from the reign of the human to that of the inhuman."[10]

The immediate postwar period saw an antihumanist crisis which lasted until the 1920s. It did not always get to the bottom of things. For example, in Germany, one had the anthology of lyric poetry published in 1920 by Kurt Pinthus, *The Twilight of Humanity*, which brought together poems by writers one would call "expressionists." In his preface, the editor sees the poets as constrained "to fight against the humanity of an epoch that comes toward its end, but also to prepare it, and to demand with impatience a new and better humanity." The young generation "cries out toward a man more noble and more human. . . . All the poems . . . have as their source lamentation over humanity, nostalgia for humanity. . . . Man cannot be saved except by man, not by the world the surrounds him. It is not derivative arrangements, inventions or laws, that are the essential and determinative factor, but man! . . . Nothing remains but hope in man and belief in utopia." The title is therefore ambiguous: the scattered light (*Dämmerung*) of twilight can also be a dawn.[11] In no way, therefore, do we have an attack against humanism, but rather a defense of it.

It was not without reason, therefore, that the same Pinthus, presenting the reedition of his anthology forty years later, proceeded to a retraction in good form. He especially claimed a kinship with the humanism of the Renaissance. "The expressionists were disappointed humanists. . . . One could say that the socialist or utopian demands of expressionism came . . . from humanism."[12] In 1919 in Russia, the poet Aleksandr Blok gave a lecture that contained, perhaps, the first occurrence of the word "antihumanism."[13]

At the same period, Martin Heidegger represented a much more profound level of reflection. The work in which his first period culminates, *Being and Time* (1927), begins with this bold statement: In the same way that the first figure of "the object" is not "the thing," but rather "gear for . . ." (*Zeug*), the first figure for the "subject" is not man, but *Dasein*. The book on Kant attacked the idea of a philosophical anthropology and concluded: "More original than man is the finitude of *Dasein* in him."[14] In a winter course of 1929–30, one reads: "The philosophical concept [*Begriff*] is an attack [*Angriff*] against man. . . . The aggressor is not man . . . but it is the *Dasein* in man that directs, in philosophical activity, that attack on man." To restore a central place to affective tonality (*Befindlichkeit*) to the detriment of reason as the specific difference of man should lead to "a total upheaval in our conception of man."[15] This conception can be called "humanism." However, Heidegger does not name it in this way until the 1930s, in particular in the 1938 essay on "the age of the world-picture." Being tied to the transformation of the world into a world picture, humanism could not have appeared in Greece or the Middle Ages, but only in the modern period.[16]

The starting point of the *Letter on Humanism* (1946) is the question, "How to restore meaning to the word 'humanism'?," which presupposes that the meaning has been lost. Heidegger sketches a genealogy of the humanist idea from the transposition of the Greek idea of *paideia* in Cicero and its recovery in the Renaissance. Humanism is care for the humanity of man, who should not depart from his essence. However, all humanism remains metaphysical, as all metaphysics is humanist. Metaphysics thinks of the being in its being, but not the difference between being and Being. Incapable of thinking the truth of being, it also does not think of man's belonging to this truth, for which Heidegger proposes the term "ek-sistence."[17] Metaphysics limits itself to insufficient determinations of the two elements of the traditional definition of man, "animality" and "rationality." As a consequence, "one does not make enough of the essence of man." It is necessary therefore "to rethink the essence of man" and to "experience it in a more original way." Humanism is still incapable of "experiencing the authentic dignity of man. . . . It does not yet place the *humanitas* of man high enough."[18]

But this height allowing one to think worthily of what makes man man leads to a paradox. It is not a matter of elevating man to the point of making him the "center," even less the "master," of what is, according to the Renaissance and Cartesian characterizations of human superiority, but to decenter the human vis-à-vis itself. "Thus, the determination of the humanity of man as ek-sistence implies that it is not man who is the essential, but rather Being, as the dimension of what ek-sistence has of ec-static." As a result, "*humanitas* is valuable in the service of the truth of Being, but without humanism in the metaphysical sense." The recast humanism is one which "thinks the humanity of man beginning from the proximity to Being." Hence the metaphors of man as "the shepherd of Being" or its "neighbor."[19] Heidegger therefore rejects neither the term "humanism" nor the idea it implies. One would be wrong to place him among the adversaries of "humanism." However, one must recognize that Heideggerian humanism takes a paradoxical form. His central thesis would indeed be that "the essence of man is essential to the truth of Being, specifically in such a way that the word does not pertain to man simply as such."[20] In any case, this thesis constitutes an invitation not to content oneself with lazy thinking about what makes man man.

A generation later, the rejection of humanism appeared on the epistemological plane in the reflection of the human sciences on themselves. For Claude Lévi-Strauss, "the final goal of the human sciences is not to constitute man, but to dissolve him." He defends the radical project of a "resolution of the human into the nonhuman," a particular case of a global enterprise "to reintegrate culture into nature, and finally, life into the ensemble of its physico-chemical conditions." Louis Althusser polemicized against an interpretation of Marx he characterized as "humanist." Michel Foucault, in turn, reprised the idea with a flamboyant metaphor. He ends the book that made him famous, *The Order of Things*, with the idea of a "death of man," an ambiguous expression that he later had to explain. Jacques Derrida sought an interpretation of interpretation that allowed one "to go beyond man and humanism."[21] With respect to a sociology aiming at a "theory of society," some have spoken of an "abolition of man," whom the theory would deprive of his liberty, his individuality, his morality, his culture.[22] In all these cases, the death of man is an image, acknowledged as such or left in obscurity. It designates less a disappearance, pure and simple, of man than the loss of a characteristic of the human judged to be fundamental. However, it could be that the expression needs to be taken more seriously.

Drama of Atheistic Humanism?

The nineteenth century was not without critiques of the project of atheistic humanism. Historians recalled that doubt concerning religion was the sign, and perhaps the cause, of the decadence of civilizations, an argument that was repeated a hundred times by apologists.[23] The end of the worship of God leads less to a progress than a regression toward a primitive religiosity, idolatry, which henceforth focuses upon man himself. Chateaubriand described the task of a renewed Christianity "in the midst of a dreadful idolatry, the idolatry of man himself."[24] Flaubert contented himself with imprecations. "The modern torpor comes from the unlimited respect that man has for himself. I say respect, but other words are better—worship, fetishism. . . . It is a curious thing, how, to the extent that it worships itself, humanity becomes stupid. . . . The adoration of humanity for and by itself, . . . this worship of the belly [*ventre*] . . . engenders wind [*vent*]."[25] Baudelaire coined the term "self-idolatry," but seems to have given it a positive meaning, as the expression of the ideal of the "worship of oneself" which he proposed for himself in poetry, as well as in life.[26] In England, Lewis Carroll noted the lassitude brought about by the worship of Nature, Reason, and Humanity, and saw in the adoration of the self the most refined of the religions produced by his century.[27]

In Spain, Donoso Cortés sketched a genealogy of modern errors, in which he sees heresies deriving from the denial of original sin and belief in the "immaculate conception of man." The absence of God makes necessary a god "armed with a single attribute, omnipotence, and [who is the] vanquisher of the three great weaknesses of the Catholic God: goodness, love and mercy."[28]

Naissant sociology, first with Louis de Bonald, then Émile Durkheim, insisted upon the indispensable character of religion for social life. But not without recalling that its true object is not a transcendent being, but society itself. In that way it collectivized and transposed into a positive key the idea of self-idolatry.

The impossibility of affirming man in a world without God became a constant theme in the polemics against modern atheism. However, it no longer was a matter of the banal idea that religion is good for society, its decline a cause and symptom of a weakening of the life of a civilization. Henceforth it is the very possibility of man's existence that is attached to religious faith. Thus the idea of a death of man appeared, as the ineluctable consequence of the death of God. After a few precursors such as the young Siegfried Lipiner in his *Der entfesselte Prometheus* (1876),[29] Leon Bloy was perhaps the first to pose the thesis in all its radicality. "It is quite permitted to ask if, in truth, the image is not as absent as the prototype, and if there can be human beings in a society without God."[30] After the Great War and the Bolshevik Revolution, this impossibility was recalled by Berdyaev. "The true nature of humanism is also revealed and unmasked, [this humanism] that at other periods seemed so innocent and sublime. If there is no God, there is no man either—behold what the experience of our time shows."[31] Other authors, this time agnostics, therefore not to be suspected of apologetic aims, take up the same theme. For example, in 1926 the young André Malraux formulated a logical consequence when he had a Chinese character say to a European: "For you, the absolute reality was God, then man; but *man is dead*, after God, and you anxiously seek someone to whom you could confide your strange heritage. Your little efforts at creating structures for moderate nihilisms, however, do not seem to me to be destined for a long existence."[32] One could look for a proof of this logic in real history; thus in 1930 Étienne Gilson wrote that "in losing God, the Renaissance was going to lose man himself."[33]

A last stage represents a transposition in the idea of humanity, now revised downward, as much in theory as in practice. As for theory, Jean-Paul Sartre hammers away that there is no human nature. The reason given is strange, however: "because there is no God to conceive it." Greek philosophy, however, had no need of a divine to ensure the existence and even the fixity of living species. And the divine from which Aristotle suspended the world knew nothing of its content. Nonetheless, Sartre continues: If there is no human nature, "man is nothing other than what he makes of himself." However, man "did not create himself."[34] How could one bring this irreducible contingency back under control? Sartre cites the word of Ivan Karamazov: "If God does not exist, all is permitted." But "God does not exist, and ... one must draw the consequences. ... Existentialism is nothing but the effort to draw all the consequences of a coherent atheistic position."[35] But is it really? Sartre ends his lecture with an unexpected pirouette. "Even if God existed, that would change nothing."[36] How then would his negation change anything?

As for practice, a youthful article of Sartre's friend, Michel Leiris, is exemplary. "Humanity ... has nothing to do with happiness, nor with goodness; here we are very far from any idea of charity: the most atrocious visions as well as the cruelest pleasures are entirely legitimate if they contribute to the development of such a humanity."[37]

Suicide

The negation of man is not confined to the ether of theory, but takes on a quite concrete dimension. Absolute liberty leads to self-destruction. One can see actual examples of this logic in the lives of several leading figures of late modernity, such as Alfred Jarry or Antonin Artaud.[38] Suicide took on relevance as a problem by entering into a "metaphysical" dimension. Until then, it was a private matter. An individual had recourse to it in order to escape what he could not bear, heartbreak or dishonor. It is true that it had already acquired its literary titles of nobility. First of all with the Swede Johann Robeck, who, after having written a monograph in favor of suicide in 1736, drowned himself. Then it appeared again in the eighteenth century, as a polemical topic between "Philosophers" who rehabilitated it and others who maintained its condemnation by Christian thinkers. Finally, it became a subject of scientific treatment, for the first time in 1761 in an Italian monograph. The series of studies of suicide has not ceased to our day, and their list includes famous authors, including Émile Durkheim.[39] Suicide then became the subject of works of fiction. In his *Sorrows of Young Werther* (1774), which had enormous success and led to actual suicides, the young Goethe argued for and against. He made the act as inevitable, and therefore as excusable, as a disease. But the expression "the burden of life" had already appeared. In France, Alphonse Rabbe (d. 1829) reprised the traditional apology for suicide and spoke of the "misfortune of living" before killing himself, and Alfred de Vigny put the problematic on stage in *Chatterton* (1835). The thought of the young poet was Stoic, but it was "society," incapable of understanding genius, that was responsible.[40]

In a fragment of 1797, Novalis sees in suicide "the authentic philosophical act . . . alone corresponding to all the conditions and marks of transcendent action." A little while later, his friend Friedrich Schlegel wrote: "The destiny of man is to destroy himself. But for that, he must first of all have become worthy; and he is not yet that." These formulations are probably to be understood on the basis of a graduated conception of life, according to which one must leave a lower level in order to attain higher states. It is in this sense that Fichte could write in the same year: "It is not death that kills, but more vital life."[41] Remarkably, the destruction in question would echo the formulations by which the ascetics of the patristic period transposed the experience of the martyr onto another level—"To give his blood and receive the spirit"—or the formulations of the Neoplatonic exegetes of the *Phaedo*, describing the suicide of the philosopher as training for death: "Die by your will and you will live by nature."[42] Schopenhauer too, on the basis of his negative vision of life, spoke of suicide. But he rejects it as contradictory. Whoever "ends his life" in reality suppresses not the will-to-live which is life's essence, but only one of its particular manifestations, one's body.[43]

From the 1820s, one saw appear across Europe an idea of suicide that had no other reason than the irreformable state of the world. This is how suicide is represented in Carlyle at the moment when the hero, largely inspired by the author, passes through a crisis of despair. In Germany, one sees it in the Danton put on stage by Georg Büchner, who allows himself to be brought up short by lassitude before life, which "is not worth the work that one must do to maintain it." The formulation echoes Schopenhauer's on life as "a business that does not cover its expenses." Friedrich Theodor Vischer sent to Mörike the account of a dream in which a suicide found no other excuse than the nothingness of all things.[44] In *The Future of Science*, the young Renan returned four times to formulations like the following: "If life were without suprasensible value, from one's first serious reflection it would be necessary to commit suicide."[45]

Such a suicide became a literary theme. Martin Decoud, a secondary character in *Nostromo*, a major novel by Joseph Conrad, represents a case of suicide by "lack of faith in himself and in others." At loose ends, he loses, along with the capacity for action, the illusion of an independent existence, and drowns himself in the immense indifference of things. In a novel by the American Kate Chopin, the heroine "was beginning to realize her position in the universe as a human being and to recognize her relations as an individual to the world within and around her"; she ends by losing all interest in her family and, after the failure of an illusory love, swims out to sea until she is exhausted, "extended towards the unlimited in which she could lose herself."[46] In his *Philosophy of the Unconscious*, which appeared in 1869 and was constantly reworked in subsequent re-editions, Eduard von Hartmann sees in suicide the necessary consequence of the end of illusions. The young Vladimir Soloviev put Hartmann at the center of his 1874 thesis, because he sees in Hartmann the logical conclusion of the evolution of modern philosophy, but also the impasse in which it finds itself. He critiques it, but without laying bare the immanent logic of the position. If one follows Max Stirner, "the sole means of defending my self-affirmation, my independence, against the natural law is suicide." And in Hartmann, "the isolated, individual suicide is replaced by the general, collective suicide."[47]

In his last novels, Dostoyevsky returns obsessively to suicide. He does so in *Crime and Punishment* (1866), in *The Idiot* (1868) with Hippolyte, in *The Adolescent* (1875) with Versilov, and in *The Brothers Karamazov* with Smerdyakov.[48] But his reflections culminate in *Demons* (1871–72) and touch on metaphysics with his character Kirillov. In killing himself, Kirillov wishes to prove that with God not existing, he himself is god.[49] In a passage of the *Journal of a Writer* (1876), the novelist imagines the arguments of a materialist who killed himself out of boredom. His vision of the world is a synthesis of the positivistic ideas in vogue in Russia, and his fictional letter was inspired by real confessions.

In a later installment, however, the writer had to clear up misunderstandings by setting out his personal position, albeit without argumentation. He puts the idea of immortality at the center, but nowhere mentions the idea of God. In the same way, the inhabitants of the idyllic world described in the "Dream of a Ridiculous Man," published in the April 1877 issue of the *Journal*, are firmly convinced of "eternal life"; in contrast, nothing indicates that they believe in God. One reads:

> It is indispensable and inevitable to have the conviction of the immortality of the human soul. . . . Lacking faith in his soul and in the immortality of this soul, the existence of man is against nature, inconceivable and intolerable. . . . In this world, there is only one supreme idea, and this is the idea of the immortality of the human soul, because all the other 'high' ideas that can cause man to live only derive from this one alone. . . . The love of humanity is not even conceivable, comprehensible, nor possible without concomitant faith in the immortality of the human soul. . . . Once the idea of

> immortality is lost, suicide becomes an absolute necessity and even inevitable for every man who is even a little intellectually above the beast. On the contrary, immortality, promising eternal life, binds man more strongly to earthly life."

The passage recalls the ideas that Ivan Karamazov will defend a few years later before a stall of quite proper ladies, without, however, believing a single word.[50]

In a little book of 1907, the French biologist and popular philosopher Félix Le Dantec observed that the "logical atheist" cannot have any interest in life: this would be true wisdom. But it is a wisdom that goes too far. Dantec himself said that he rejoiced that he possessed, in addition to his logical atheism, a moral conscience, the result of countless "ancestral errors," which dictated his conduct where his reason would let him drown himself. In a society of genuine atheists, "anesthetic suicide" would be the rule; and society would disappear.[51] This type of suicide was debated before the First War. It was authorized by the society that R. H. Benson imagined in a novel about the end of time, *Lord of the World*, which appeared the same year. It expressed the fears that the evolution of English society inspired in him. One can put to the side the nostalgia of a conservative, but the question remains asked. Thus, J. H. Rosny Senior, in a novel that appeared a little later, describes a humanity in which "euthanasia" is a common, even eagerly sought, practice.[52]

One can take Émile Durkheim's thesis concerning suicide (1897) as the involuntary metaphor for the state of Western culture.[53] In a 1942 essay that had enormous success, Albert Camus saw in suicide the only serious philosophical problem.[54] But he immediately narrowed the perspective by explaining: "Is life worth the trouble of being *lived*?" The question does not attain its full intensity for the individual, who is already "embarked" on life, and is thus party and judge. It does so only at the level of the species. The species constantly loses individuals carried away by death. It therefore cannot subsist unless living individuals call forth others to life, in whose place, therefore, they have to decide.

Why would they do so? One can see in human beings nothing more than playthings destined to amuse divine creators in their boredom, and see in sexual activity nothing but a trap, that of pleasure, guaranteeing that humans continue to turn like squirrels in their cage. In which case, why would these marionettes want to produce others? These themes, current since Schopenhauer, are much more ancient and are found in authors who perhaps have inspired the German thinkers, directly or not.

Thus, Milton presents an Adam who, after the fall, despairs of producing a posterity contaminated by his sin and condemned to death, and Byron represents Cain struck with the same hesitation. In Germany, the "pre-Romantic" writers have similar formulations. Klinger has his Zeus say that without the pleasure and enticement attached to the act of procreation, human beings would deprive him of his playthings.[55] Supposing, therefore, that "making babies" is, as a character of Sartre says, "an extreme stupidity,"[56] one can ask how an "enlightened" humanity, delivered from every "stupidity," could have much of a future?

Conclusion

At the conclusion of this journey, I can summarize my aim and give an overview of the path traveled.

The first part showed that a humanism was possible, and in fact had been realized, without therefore taking the form of the modern project. In the premodern world, man enjoyed a tranquil superiority, which did not prevent him from realizing technological advances, but which did not imply any intention of dominating the world, even less of making man independent of every external instance, natural or divine. In a second part, I followed the development of the modern project. I divided the study into several stages, where each period also corresponded to a specific idea whose appearance or apogee characterized it. None of these stages entailed or necessarily assumed the following. On the contrary, each resulted from a deliberate choice to go further. The third part showed how modernity not only runs up against an external critique, which one could call "reactionary," but involves an internal self-destructive dialectic, by which the modern project ends by producing something other than it believed it wanted, in fact its exact opposite.

There is no stage of the formulation, then the realization, of the modern project that is not accompanied, as its shadow, by an "antimodern" objection, often formulated in the same period and constituting its bad conscience. This is the case since Rousseau's *Discourse on the Sciences and Arts* (1750), the most striking manifesto of primitivism, even if Jean-Jacques himself was "not an anti-modern, but a disappointed modern." And even more since the conclusion of the *Scienza nuova* (1744), where a few years earlier Vico had evoked "the barbarism of reflection" alongside the crudeness of primitive mores.[1] Later the Scotsman Adam Ferguson took into account Rousseau's criticisms. In his *Essay on the History of Civil Society* (1767), he is quite conscious of the dangers represented by Enlightenment. He makes it known that man is not moved solely by considerations of interest, but by the free play of all his forces, which permits "civil society," understood as an equivalent of the ancient polis. He praises civic virtues and the concern for liberty, pleads for everything that can counterbalance "our effemination," and exhorts the dawning discipline of political economics not to reduce man to the aspect of his activity that it studies.[2]

Ever since Edmund Burke, conservatives have recalled with nostalgia all the riches that have been lost by the systematization of human relations, and above all the rupture in the fabric of history implied by the desire for a radical beginning. Hence the wish to save what can still be saved.[3] In our days, ecological consciousness does not fail to draw attention to the high price of the industrial domestication of nature—a most heavy burden on the living kingdom—as well as the risks that industry represents for the existence of man.

The image of light, chosen by the Enlightenment itself, contains an ironic counterpoint. Light can turn into a destructive fire, according to a small fable published in 1784 in the *Berlinische Monatsschrift*. In it, an ape lights a forest on fire and then congratulates itself on having illumined the countryside. From similar reflections, Leopardi drew a wise maxim. "Reason is a light. Nature wishes to be illumined by reason, but not set on fire by it."[4]

During the course of this investigation, I chose to cite only tangentially the objections of "conservatives," "reactionaries," and "obscurantists" of various stripes. In contrast, I granted a large place to expressions of the internal dialectic of the modern project, by citing others as often as possible and intervening but rarely. At most I sometimes underscored the formulations where this dialectic surfaces with particularly clarity. My intention was limited to recounting, in that way letting the modern project run freely to its self-destruction. However, my personal hope as an individual of a living species, the grateful heir of a civilization, and the loyal citizen of a political community, is obviously to counter this tendency.

※

Even so, is hope a duty? Must one truly defend man against what in the modern project puts him in danger? Thus the question is posed that I have elsewhere called the "legitimacy of the human."[5] It surfaces in what

I call the *paradox of the good*. The modern project is perfectly fine when it comes to producing *goods*: material, cultural, and moral goods, which it makes a point of providing to human beings; for that, it has no need of anything but the resources it finds in man. On the other hand, however, it seems to be incapable of explaining why it is *good* that there are human beings to enjoy the goods that are thus put at their disposal.

Here I would borrow a thought from John N. Gray. "At the period of late modernity in which we live, the Enlightenment project is affirmed principally because we fear the consequences that its abandonment would entail. . . . Our cultures are Enlightenment cultures not by conviction, but by default."[6] That is why we are so careful to maintain the specter of "obscurantism" and keep vigilant watch to ensure that credible "reactionaries" are around to play the role of foils that can justify an Enlightenment that has become incapable of defending itself.

Our humanism, in other words, is an *anti-antihumanism*, rather than a direct affirmation of the goodness of the human. Born in a revolutionary context, it has lost the initiative and now only constitutes a reaction against the antihumanism that it perhaps secretly produces. "Antihumanism: thunder against," Flaubert would have said, and our moderns, be they in the manner of Bouvard or Pécuchet, do not fail to become indignant. It is less easy, however, to explain what "humanism" means exactly, and why one should favor it.

The two sources of Western culture, "Athens" and "Jerusalem," insist on the fact that the human comes forth from a foundation that it does not produce, but which, on the contrary, produces it.

As for Greece, it was Aristotle who expressed the thought the best. "Man engenders man," he says about twenty times. One time, however, we read the developed formulation which the other ones abridge. "Man engenders man, *with the sun*."[7] By that he understands that a concrete human being, not the Platonic idea of humanity, engenders another concrete human being. But it is precisely because it is a matter of concrete individuals that one must recall, at the horizon of every generation, the presence of the sun which causes seeds to germinate and returns the season for mating.[8] In short, man becomes man against the background of realities of which he does not dispose. To name them, the Greeks found the key philosophical term "nature" (*physis*). This is why Aristotle observes that politics does not produce human beings, but receives them from nature.[9]

The other source of our culture, the Bible, did not explicitly develop the notion of nature and did not coin a term to express it. However, one can find its equivalent, less as a concept than as a narrative theme.[10] As for the necessity of a context for human action, Deuteronomy expresses it in its own way. "Do not say to yourself, 'My power and the might of my own hand have gotten me this wealth.' But remember the LORD your God, for it is he who gives you power to get wealth, so that he may confirm his covenant" (Deut. 8:17–18 NRSV).[11] What is possessed comes from another, and, more radically, everything that allows one to acquire is itself received. The exterior element here is not the constant presence of the natural, but the historical intervention of God. The covenant takes the place of nature, but without reducing itself to the latter.[12] Nothing is more tempting than to forget this external origin and to arrogate to oneself the merit of what one has acquired. It was already to such an arrogance that the person succumbed who said "in his heart" that it was he who acquired the promised land.

Remarkably, the awareness of and concern for the origin are confided to a labile instance like memory, which must be constantly maintained. They are guarded by a difficult virtue, what the Romans called "piety" (*pietas*).

❦

Modernity repudiated these two origins, natural and divine. For modernity, it is man who engenders man, and in order to do so he has need neither of the sun nor of the nature it symbolizes, nor of the God of the covenant. The project of autonomy leads to the idea according to which man is born by spontaneous generation, an idea with which the young Marx flirted.[13] At the other extreme, that of the ultimate destiny of man, the idea of a metamorphosis takes on a new meaning, even when the same image is used. In Dante, the caterpillar becomes a butterfly in order "to fly toward justice with no veil between" and to delight in its contemplation; in Wordsworth he uses his wings to be his own lord.[14]

But the creation of oneself by one's self, real or metaphorical, is only a species of a much larger genus, that of the *determination* of the self by the self. And nothing proves that it is the highest form. It takes a thousand efforts and a lot of time to modify one's physical appearance, to rise up the social ladder, even more to improve oneself morally. Does not self-destruction represent a quicker solution, one that is more total and, one might say, more economical? Suicide is "simpler and easier" than life, to reprise a formulation by which Leibniz expressed the advantage of "nothing" over "something."[15] To be sure, the suicide of the individual is unpleasant for the one who decides to commit it. That is why, as for its moral value, it can be blameworthy without ceasing to be respectable. In contrast, by displacing the problem from the individual to the species, demographic suicide does not have this inconvenience, even if it becomes a mass phenomenon. One should note, however, that it loses simultaneously what made it reprehensible (for *to whom* have I done wrong?) and what made for its relative dignity.

※

In a previous work, *On the God of the Christians*, I attempted to show that Christianity had this distinctive peculiarity, that it did *not* propose any other morality than that which is always valid for every human being. The human problem is not the ignorance of the law, but the inability to fulfill it. The divine aid consists in pardoning transgressors and giving repentant sinners the strength to will and accomplish the good.[16] Modernity retained this idea of a common morality, but believes that it can do without mercy, as well as grace.

The question is not to know if man can know on his own how he ought to live and live well. It is rather to know if he can *will to survive* without a superior instance to affirm him, without someone who has not only granted him his humanity—by breathing into him a soul or, more prosaically, by ensuring the conditions for an evolutionary emergence of superior mental functions ("mind")—but also granted him *legitimacy*. On his own, man cannot pronounce on his own value; he cannot be party and judge. Sartre said it in his sarcastic way: "One cannot allow a man to pass judgment on man."[17] There needs to be a neutral arbiter between human beings and the animals, like the "king of the Jinns" in the tale recounted in the encyclopedia of the "Sincere Brethren."[18]

Or it needs to be the One who declared on the sixth day of creation that everything was "very good."

Notes

Translators Foreword

1. Rémi Brague, *The Wisdom of the World*, trans. Teresa Lavender Fagan (Chicago: University of Chicago Press, 2003); Brague, *The Law of God*, trans. Lydia G. Cochrane (Chicago: University of Chicago Press, 2007).

2. Rémi Brague, *The Legitimacy of the Human*, translated with an introduction by Paul Seaton (South Bend, IN: St. Augustine's Press, 2017).

3. The quote within the quote comes from Guy Beaujouan, "Réflexions sur les rapports entre théorie et pratique au Moyen Âge," in *The Cultural Context of Medieval Learning*, ed. J. E. Murdoch and D. Sylla (Dordrecht: Reidel), 437–84.

4. See Manent, *An Intellectual History of Liberalism*, trans. Rebecca Balinski (Princeton: Princeton University Press, 1994); Manent, *A World beyond Politics?*, trans. Marc LePain (Princeton: Princeton University Press, 2006); Manent, *Metamorphoses of the City*, trans. Marc LePain (Cambridge, MA: Harvard University Press, 2013).

5. Jerry Z. Muller, *The Mind and the Market: Capitalism in Western Thought* (New York: Anchor Books, 2003).

6. For Brague's fuller treatment of the biblical message, see *On the God of the Christians (and on One or Two Others)*, trans. Paul Seaton (South Bend, IN: St. Augustine's Press, 2013), and the last two chapters of *Legitimacy of the Human* (see n. 2).

Preface

1. Rémi Brague, *Wisdom of the World*; Brague, *Law of God*.

Introduction

1. Following an image of Plato's *Republic*, Leo Strauss speaks of the three "waves" of modern thought. Strauss (1975).

2. Curtius (1953), 256–61; Freund (1957), 113, then Armogathe (2001), 803.

3. Schelling, *Die Weltalter: Urfassungen*, ed. M. Schröter (1946), 11, cited in Jauss (1970), 15; on the dialectic of project/reject, see Lachterman (1989), 2; on the "Middle Ages" see Brague (2006a), 40–41.

4. Jürgen Habermas (1980), 444–64, esp. 452–53; Dupré (1993), 101, 119, 126, 160; Dupré (2004), 4; Manent (2010a), 9–11.

5. Koyré (1966a), 213–23 (Galileo), 376–86 (Pascal); Rey (2003), 61. Koyré defended an extreme position, which was subsequently nuanced; see Shea (2003).

6. Ferrarin (2001), 189–96, esp. 191.

7. Descartes, letter to Mersenne, March 1636 (*OC* 1:339). Comte speaks of "the great philosophic renovation, projected by Descartes and Bacon." *Cours*, 58th lesson (2:639).

8. Nietzsche, frag. 25 [290], Spring 1884 (*KSA* 11:85).

9. Defoe, *Essay*, 186, then 188.

10. Swift, *Gulliver*, pt. 3, chaps. 5–6, pp. 216–33; confession to having been "a sort of projector," chap. 4, p. 215; also see Adam Smith, cited in Gay (1969), 354; on the Abbé de St. Pierre, see Becker (1932), 39–41; Glanvill, *PU*, 8; Shelley, *F*, chap. 24, p. 204.

11. Fichte, *Grundlage des Naturrechts* [1796], II, #6, η (*AW* 2:83). For the context, see below, p. 104; Heidegger, *Being*, para. 30, p. 142; Heidegger, *Vom Wesen des Grundes* [1929], III (*Wegmarken*, 59–64); Heidegger, *Humanism*, 169; Sartre, *EH*, 55; see also 23, 69–70; Rawls (1971), 407–16; critique in Larmore (1999).

12. A. Maier (1951), 114–20.

13. E. de Las Cases, *Mémorial de Sainte-Hélène*, 19 August 1816 (Paris: Dépôt du Mémorial et al., 1824), 3:274; the passage attracted the attention of Jacob Burckhardt in *Weltgeschichtliche Betrachtungen*, chap. 5 (*Geschichtswerk* 1:935); on the image, also see Nietzsche, *Also sprach Zarathustra*, pt. 3, Vom Gesicht und Rätsel (*KSA* 4:198).

14. Brague (2002b), 76–78. For more details, see below, 131, then Brague (2008c), 152–53.

15. Leiss (1972), 52–53, 80.

Chapter 1. The Best of the Living Things

1. See above, 6.

2. Kant, *Kritik der reinen Vernunft*, A804–5/B832–33; "Begriff von der Philosophie überhaupt," sec. 3 of the introduction to *Vorlesung über Logik* (*Werke*/Berlin 9:25); letter 574, to Carl Friedrich Stäudlin, 4 May 1793.

3. Plato, *Theaetetus* 174b; Varro, in Augustine, *City* 19.3 (2:436); Boethius, *Consolation* 1, pr. 6 (p. 168); Colotes, in Plutarch, *Adversus Colotem* 20, *Moralia* VI-2, ed. M. Pohlenz (Leipzig, Teubner, 1959), 196; De Koninck (1995), 43.

4. Seneca, *Consolation to Marcia* 11.3 (*Dialogues*, 25–26).

5. Homer, *Iliad* 17.446; Homer, *Odyssey* 18.130–31; Brague (1988), 208.

6. Merikare 46 (pp. 83–85); *Teaching of Ani* 10.7–10, in Ockinga (1984), 87; Hornung (1967), 136, 153.

7. Ovid, *Metamorphoses* 1.83.

8. Xenophon, *Cyropaedia* 8.3.49; *Mahabharata* 12.288.20d [*non vidi*], in De Koninck (1995), 21.

9. Linck (1999), 77.

10. Aristotle, *Politics* 1.3.1253a31–33; Alexander of Aphrodisias, *Aporias and solutions* 4, 1st ethical aporia: Against those who say that life is not a good, in *Scripta*, 119, 31–36; Brague (1988), 210.

11. Aristotle, *Nicomachean Ethics* 6.7.1141a33–b2; Chrysippus in Cicero, *Gods* II, vi/16 (p. 590), and III, x/26 (p. 1017); Pascal, *Pensées*, frag. 347 (as a reminder).

12. Xenophon, *Memorabilia* 1.4.14; Aristotle, *Protrepticus*, frag. 10c, in *Fragmenta*, 42.

13. Sophocles, *Antigone* 332–75, esp. 365–66; Cicero, *Gods* II, lx–lxi/150–53 (pp. 939–49).

14. Job 28:1–11; Aeschylus, *Prometheus Bound* 500–503; Linck (1999), 82.

15. *Contra* Castoriadis (1999), 29–30, 43; on autodidacticism as inspiration, see Homer, *Odyssey* 22.347–48.

16. Protagoras, in DK, B 1, frag. 80. See *HWPh*, s.v. "Homo-mensura-Satz" (vol. 3, cols. 1175–76; by C. Grawe). On the uncertain character of the text, see Neumann (1938). For an interpretation, see Heidegger, *Holzwege*, 94–98.

17. Nicholas of Cusa, *De beryllo*, chap. 5 (*PTW* 3:6).

18. Plato, *Laws* 4.716c4–6; echo in Taubes's (1991) epilogue, 193.

19. Cicero, *Officiis* 1.30.106 (p. 36).

20. Baker (1961), despite his title, does not mention the idea of dignity in the first part of his book: "The Classical View of Man," 3–105, a second-hand survey of classical thought. In contrast, see the excellent syntheses in Bruch (1981) and Kobusch (1993).

21. Augustine, *De vera religione* 16.30 (BA 8:62–64); Gregory of Nyssa, *On the Creation of Man*, chaps. 3, 5 (*PG* 44:133c, 136cd).

22. St. Leo the Great, *Christmas Sermon* 1, para. 3 (SC 22, 2nd ed., p. 7); 7, para. 6 (p. 160); Bernard, *Sermon on the Nativity of the Lord* 2.1 (*Opera* 4:252); Guillaume, *Commentaire*, para. 54, p. 80.

23. Thomas Aquinas, *ST* III.1.2, corpus. The passages from Augustine and Leo cited in the previous notes are found in Thomas. See also Thomas Aquinas, *SCG* IV.54 (p. 513a).

24. Dales (1977), 572, whom I closely follow.

25. Maximus the Confessor, *Ambigua* (PG 91:1305a); Chenu (1955), 115–24.

26. Aristotle, *De la noblesse*, frag. 4, in *Fragmenta*, 59–60.

27. Dante, *Convivio*, bk. 4, chap. 20 (pp. 303–6); Eckhart, *Vom edlen Menschen* (*DW* 5:109–19).

28. See, for example, Averroës, *Tahâfut* 3.139–40, 161, 217, 226. Curiously, the connection with Eckhart is not in Flasch (2006).

29. Libera (1991), 334.

30. Du Toit (1997), 402, 405.

31. Denzinger (1908), para. 148, p. 66.

32. Benz (1937).

33. See the cruel note by Schaeder (1925), 253.

34. Schimmel (1989).

35. Rig Veda 10.90 (pp. 498–500); Plato, *Timaeus* 42bc; Idel (1992), 170.

36. Schenke (1962), 155; Rudolph (1978), 101–2, 111.

37. Nag Hammadi codex II 3 Gospel of Philip, 71 (119), 35–72 (120), 4 (*NHC II*, 1:186–87).

38. E. Swedenborg, *De Coelo et ejus Mirabilibus, et de Inferno, ex Auditis et Visis* [1758], para. 79; see C. Milosz, *La Terre d'Ulro: Méditation sur l'espace et la religion*, trans. Z. Bobowicz (Paris: Albin Michel, 1985), para. 27 (p. 171), cited by Dupré (2004), 331.

39. *Poimandres* (I), para. 31 (*CH* 1:18); *The Key* (X), 4, 15 (*CH* 1:114, 120); *Asclepius* 41 (*CH* 2:352). I follow closely Fowden (1986), 104–7; *Poimandres* (I), 15 (*CH* 1:11); Treatise 9.4–5 (*CH* 1:97–98); Extracts from Strobaeus 2A.6 (*CH* 3:5); *The Key* (X), 9 (*CH* 1:117); note of Nock and Festugière, *CH* 1:23n47.

40. *Asclepius* 6 (*CH* 2:301–2); Bernard, *Sermon on the Psalm "Qui habitat"* 14.1 (*Opera* 4:469): *magna res est homo*.

41. *Poimandres* (I), 12–13 (*CH* 1:10); Treatise 3.3 (*CH* 1:45); *The Key* (X), 18 (*CH* 1:122).

42. Mulsow (2003), 744, 751–55.

43. *EI*, s.v. "al-Insân al-kâmil" (3:1239; by R. Arnaldez); Schaeder (1925); Massignon (1948), besides its obscurity, in fact only treats the eschatology.

44. *Theology of Aristotle*, chap. 10, para. 71, in Badawi, *Aflutin*, p. 145, lines 2–3; see the context in Schaeder (1925), 222–26.

45. "Sincere Brethren," *Letter of the Animals*, in *R*, II, 8 [22] (vol. 2, p. 376).

46. Ibn Arabi, *Gems*, chap. 1 (Adam), p. 7; Schaeder (1925), 237–45; Takeshita (1987); Ibn Arabi, *Gems*, chap. 25 (Moses), p. 163. The formulation of Genesis is attributed to Muhammad in an often-cited but uncertain hadith; see Ibn Arabi, *Gems*, chap. 1 (Adam), p. 8, 12; the image of the ring reappears in chap. 12 (Shu'aiyb), p. 80; chap. 4 (Idris), p. 33.

47. Jîlî, *Perfect man*; excellent synthesis in Nicholson (1921), 77–142. See Jîlî, *Perfect man*, chap. 60, p. 249, translated in Nicholson (1921), 86; chap. 24, p. 129, line 16, and chap. 69, p. 253, line 25, translated in Nicholson (1921), 118n9, 106; chap. 69, p. 252, translated in Nicholson (1921), 105; chap. 15, p. 103, line 26, and chap. 69, p. 254, lines 20–22, translated in Nicholson (1921), 130, 107; chap. 72, p. 270, lines 8–11, translated in Nicholson (1921), 121n6.

48. On the *Asclepius*, see below, 45.

49. Shmuel Ibn Naghrela, *Ben Qohelet*, in Shmuel, *Diwan*, 302–3, no. 315; more easily available in Alvar and Talens (2009), 152–54. The Castilian translator does not render the crucial word "whole"; on Ibn Ezra, see Wolfson (1990).

Chapter 2. Domination

1. Needham (1951), 229–30; on the question of why modern science did not appear outside of Europe, see H. Cohen (1994), 348–488; on the reasons for its appearance in Europe, see Baechler (2002), 329–40.

2. In Passmore (1974), 26.

3. Chan (1963), 122. See also Fung (1983), 285–86; Ivanhoe and Van Norden (2001), 272–73; Machle (1993), 125–28.

4. *Xunzi*, bk. 17, pp. 20–21. See also Linck (1999), 89.

5. Linck (1999), 95.
6. See Pritchard (1954): regarding hunting and animals, nn. 182–90, pp. 56–60 (commentary, pp. 270a–271a); queen of wild beasts, Minet el-Beida, n. 464, p. 160 (commentary, p. 303b); hero holding a lion, Khorsabad, n. 615, p. 201 (commentary, p. 323b).
7. Christou (1968), 176, then Nunn (2012), 175n102, 179.
8. Hornung (1971), 96.
9. *Merikare* 46 (pp. 83–85).
10. Porphyry, *De l'abstinence* 4.9.2 (p. 14).
11. On the significance of anthropomorphism in the representation of the divine, see Manetti, *Dignity* 3, #11, p. 72; #18, p. 76, lines 17–19; Hegel, *Ästhetik*, 420–22; Feuerbach, *Vorläufige Thesen zur Reform der Philosophie*, #22 (*KS*, 129).
12. Empedocles, in DK, B 31, frag. 111; Xenophon, *Memorabilia* 1.1.15; Plato, *Theaetetus* 180c7–d5; Strauss (1959), 96.
13. See, for example, Theophrastus, *Enquiry into Plants* 3.2.2–3 (ed. A. Hort [Loeb, 1916], 1:166).
14. See, for example, Pseudo-Aristotle, *Mechanics*, preface, 847a11–21.
15. Pappus, *Collectionis* 8.2 (3:1024); Pappus, *Mathématique* 3:810–11; Cassiodorus, letter to Boethius [in 507], in *Variarum* 1.45, ed. A. J. Fridh, CCSL 96, p. 51; cited in Sternagel (1966), 14; Newman (2004), 22–23.
16. Anonymous, *Papyrus de Stockholm*, #18, in Halleux (1981), 116; Newman (2004), 28.
17. Ovid, *Metamorphoses* 1.76–78; Cicero, *Gods* II, lx/152 (p. 945); A. S. Pease's commentary on this passage in Cicero only refers to a commonplace on "habit, second nature."
18. See Pseudo-Apollonius, *Geheimnis* 2.5.13 (p. 169); German trans., p. 97; commentary, p. 187; *Geheimnis* 5.2.2 (p. 396); trans., p. 128; *Geheimnis* 6.1.1 (p. 424); trans., p. 135; commentary, p. 213; *Geheimnis* 6.2.5 (p. 430); trans., p. 136; commentary, p. 219.
19. Republished in White (1968), 75–94; discussion in Thomas (1984), 22–23; more detailed in Barr (1972), then Groh and Groh (1991), 11–71.
20. Hegel, [Der Geist des Judentums], in [Der Geist des Christentums und sein Schicksal], in *Werke* 1:274; for the context, see Brague (2005), 127.
21. Firmicus, *L'Erreur*, 3.4, then 8.3 (p. 83, then 98); Hadot (2004), 122.
22. Augustine, *City* 22.24 (2:838–40); 7.23.1 (1:458); H. Maier (1999), 91–95; Augustine, *Genesi* 8.1 (p. 243), in Whitney (1990), 44.
23. I follow Westermann, *Genesis* 1:218–20, 222.
24. See above, 10.
25. Ockinga (1984), 153–54.
26. Qur'an 31:19/20; 45:12/13; 22:64/65; Brague (2008c), 137.
27. I paraphrase the conclusion of J. Cohen (1989), 309–10; see also Passmore (1974), 27; H. Maier (1999), 93; Bossi (2003), 427.
28. ACCS 1:40–41: Gregory of Nyssa, *De la création de l'homme* 18.1–2 (SC 6, pp. 167–68); John Chrysostom, *Homélies sur la Genèse* 10.9; Augustine, *Sur la*

Genèse contre les Manichéens 1.8, 29 (PL 34:187); John of Damascus, *On the Orthodox Faith* 4.24.

29. Irenaeus, *Heresies* 5.33.4 (p. 420).
30. Origen, *Homilies* 1.12 (pp. 13–14).
31. Gregory of Nyssa, *Homilies* 4.1 (SC 416, pp. 226–28).
32. Basil of Caesarea, *Sur la création de l'homme* 1.19, in Groh (2003), 272. Augustine, *Genesi* 3.20 (p. 86); then Augustine, *City* 14.21 (1:972).
33. John Philoponus, *Opificio* 6.6 (p. 240); on this scene, see Brague (2008a), 196–98; the interesting misinterpretation of Hobbes, *Leviathan* 1.4.18.
34. Basil, *Homilies* 9.5.11 (p. 290); see also "Sincere Brethren," *R*, II, 8 [22] (vol. 2, p. 216).
35. Maimonides, *Guide* 3.13 (p. 327; p. 94 in Munk's trans.); Nachmanides, commentary on Gen. 1:26 in *MG*, p. 8c; Gersonides, *Peyrush RLBG' al ha-Torah*, ed. J. L. Levy (Jerusalem: Mosad Rav Kook, 1992), 43.
36. Dodds (1965), 22; Matthew Hale, *The Primitive Origination of Mankind Considered according to the Light of Nature* (London, 1677), pt. 4, chap. 8, toward the end, cited in Black (1970), 56–57, and Passmore (1974), 30, who sees rather an exception; Augustine, *De vera religione* 35.65, (BA 8:118–20).
37. Emmanuel de Bénévent (?), commentary on (and in the margin of) *Ma'arekhet* 4 (p. 50).
38. See the dossier in Lovejoy and Boas (1935), chap. 13, "The Superiority of the Animals"; Plato, *Statesman* 263d; Plutarch, *Moralia* 6.1, "Bruta ratione uti" (pp. 76–93); Machiavelli, *L'Asino* 8 (O-2011, 850–53); Paparelli (1983), 184–87; Montaigne, *Essays*, bk. 2, chap. 12 (2:186–214, 218, 329–49); Apuleius, *Metamorphoses* (or, *The Golden Ass*) 4.4–5; 7.15–23; 8.30; 9.11–14; Bonaventure, *Cymbalum*, 3rd Dialogue (pp. 31–32); Jean de La Fontaine, "L'homme et la couleuvre," in *Fables* 10.1.
39. "Sincere Brethren," *R*, II, 8 [22] (vol. 2, pp. 178–377); Brague (2013), 89–103; *Iggeret*; Steinschneider (1893), para. 530, pp. 860–62; Turmeda, *Ass*.
40. "Sincere Brethren," *R*, II, 8 [22] (vol. 2, p. 376).
41. See below, 162–63.
42. Turmeda, *Ass*, 138–39.
43. Isa. 24:21–22; 1 Enoch 90.24–25.
44. Guillaume, *Nature* 2.103–4 (pp. 192–95; PL 180:721d); Thomas Aquinas, *ST* I.93.3; Dante, *Convivio*, bk. 4, chap. 19, pt. 6 (p. 302).
45. Qur'an 2:30; Brague (2002b), 92; Cragg (1968), chap. 2, "God Is, and Man Is His Caliph," is false starting with its title.
46. L.-C. de Saint-Martin, *L'Homme de désir* [1790/1802], para. 65 (*Oeuvres* 3:142).
47. Augustine, *City* 22.1 (2:748); Bernard, *Homélie pour la fête de saint Michel* 1.4 (*Opera* 5:296–97). The idea can also be found in Jacob Boehme; see Dupré (1993), 235. It is striking in Milton, *PL*, bk. 2, line 834 (p. 49); bk. 3, lines 678–79 (p. 75); bk. 7, line 152 (p. 163); bk. 7, lines 188–91 (p. 164); bk. 10, lines 147–51 (p. 201).

48. Anselm, *Cur Deus homo* 2.16 (PL 158:417–18); Honorius Augustodunensis, *Libellus octo quaestionum de angelis et homine* 1 (PL 172:1185b–1187a); Chenu (1957), 52–61.

49. Metz (1962), 47, 50, 110.

Chapter 3. Three Incomplete Prefigurations

1. Bacon, *Instauratio Magna*, frontispiece (*Organon*, bk. 1, para. 93 [p. 206]); commentary in Groh (2010), 399–402.

2. Bacon, *Temporis Partus Masculus sive Instauratio Magna imperii humani in Universum* [ca. 1604] (*Works* 3:527–39).

3. Bickermann (1937).

4. Brague (2006a), 145–46, 150.

5. b. Berakoth 34b; b. Shabbat 63a.

6. Schlier (1959).

7. In Clement, *Stromata* 4.13.89 (PG 8:1297a).

8. Xenophon, *Memorabilia* 1.4.14; Aristotle, *Protrepticus*, frag. 10c, in *Fragmenta*, 42.

9. *Merikare* 20 (p. 33).

10. Sarcophagus no. 20 in Wreszinski, *Inschriften*, III.2, C, line 21, p. 160 (line 3 in German trans.); the editor translates, "*das Gewissen des Mannes ist sein eigener Gott*," and adds, "*wohl sprichwörtlich.*" 170–71.

11. Habicht (1970) and Nock (1930), 50; on the ritual, see Zanker (2004); Seneca, *Apocolocyntosis*, 436–82; Vespasian, in Suetonius, *Lives of the Twelve Caesars*, Vespasian 23; on the absence of the votive offering, see Veyne (1983), 99; Lucian, *Kataplus è tyrannos* 16 (*Opera*, 191); Benz (1961a), 143–44.

12. Hippocrates, *Decorum*, chap. 5, para. 1; compare with Sir. 38:1: the doctor merits respect, because he is created by God. See also Epicurus, *Letter to Menoeceus* 135; Epictetus, *Discourses* 2.19.27.

13. Plato (?), *Theages* 125e–126a; Nietzsche, frag. 25 [137], Spring 1884 (*KSA* 11:50); Plato, *Theaetetus* 176b; Alexander of Aphrodisias, foreword to *Commentary on the Prior Analytics*, ed. M. Wallies, CAG, vol. 2, bk. 1, p. 6, lines 8–10.

14. Boethius, *Consolation* 3, pr. 10 (p. 280); Averroës, *Anima* 3.36, lines 607–22 (p. 50). Among the Christians, Albert the Great, *De quindecim problematibus* 1 (AMOO/Geyer, vol. 17, pt. 1, p. 33b62–69); *In De Anima* 3, cap. 11, sec. 3 (AMOO/Geyer, vol. 7, pt. 1, p. 222b79–85); *De intellectu et intelligibili* 2, tractatus unicus (AMOO/Borgnet, vol. 9, p. 517); *Metaphysica* 11, tractatus 2, cap. 11 (AMOO/Geyer, vol. 16, pt. 2, p. 498, lines 50–54). For the context, see Flasch (2006), 67–85.

15. Damascius, *Treatise* 3.100 (3:64); al-Biruni, *Tahqīq*, chap. 3 (p. 29).

16. See, for example, Lamennais, in Bénichou (2004), 683; in our day Schabert (1990), 17, and all of Huyn (1988).

17. Augustine, *Confessions* 2.6.14 (BA 13:354); see also *City* 19.12 (BA 2:470); *De vera religione* 45.84, 239 (BA 8:150); *Commentary on the First Epistle of St. John* 2.2.14 (SC 75, p. 180). See also Donoso Cortés, *Ensayo sobre el catolicismo, el protestantismo y el socialismo* [1851] 1.4 (*Obras*, 374).

18. Athanasius, *On the Incarnation of the Word* 54.3 (SC 199, p. 458); see also Irenaeus of Lyon, *Adversus haereses*, 3.19.1 (SC 34, p. 332); Pseudo-Augustine, *Sermon 128*, 1 (PL 39:1997c); Dionysius the Areopagite, *Ecclesiastical Hierarchy* 1.3 (PG 3:376a); Andia (1996). See the synthesis of N. Russell (2004); on the historical career of the idea, see Christensen and Wittung (2007), then N. Russell (2009).

19. Maximus the Confessor, *Questions to Thalassius* 22 (PG 90:321a); taken up again in Maximus, *Diversa capita* 1.76 (PG 90:1212a); Maximus, *Theological and polemical opuscula to Marinos*, "That one cannot say that there is only one will in Christ" (PG 91:33c); Maximus, *Letter 2, to John the Cubicular*, on charity (PG 91:393b); and see Maximus, *Mystagogy* 5 (PG 91:680c); Maximus, *Diversa capita* 1.42 (PG 90:1193d).

20. Basil, cited by Gregory of Nazianzus, *Oratio 43 – In laudem Basilii magni* 48 (PG 36:560a). My italics.

21. Dante, "Paradiso," canto 1, line 70, in *Commedia*; perhaps a reminiscence of Alain of Lille, *Anticlaudianus* 1, line 333 (p. 248)? The word struck the French historian Jules Michelet; see his journal entry of 14 February 1849, in *Journal*, ed. P. Viallaneix (Paris: Gallimard, 1962), 2:286, in Bénichou (2004), 946.

22. Alain of Lille, *Anticlaudianus* 1, line 333 (*Works*, p. 248); 6, line 366 (p. 422); 8, line 148 (p. 474); Tauler, according to Duby (1966), 78a.

23. In Vasoli (1984), 198–227; cited from 222–23, then 199.

24. Luther, *Disputatio contra scholasticam theologiam* (1571), xvii (*Studienausgabe* 1:22); see Lachterman (1989), 23.

25. Ammer (1988), 12–19; Ehlen (2000); Rifel (2013).

26. Plato, *Republic* 9.589ab.

27. Plato, *Laws* 10.96a; Aristotle, *De anima* 3.4.429a19; Marcus Aurelius 6.8 (p. 98); Plotinus VI.8[39].13 (O 3:290–93).

28. Gregory of Nyssa, *Life of Moses* 2.3 (SC 1, p. 108); Gregory, *Homilies on Ecclesiastes* 6.5 (SC 416, p. 318).

29. Frag. 21 [Zosime], pt. 3, chap. 49, on the appliances and stoves, para. 4 (*CAAG* 2:230 [Greek]; 3:222–23 [French]; *CH* 3:118 [Greek], 120–21 [French]).

30. Mauss (1936); Séris (1994), 132–33; Nabokov, *Pnin*, chap. 2, sec. 4, p. 35.

31. Augustine, *City* 14.24 (1:980). [Joseph Pujol (1857–1945) was a famous French flatulist and pantomime (translator's note).]

32. Dodds (1965), 29–36; for example, John Cassian, *Collationes* 7.7 (PL 49:673b); Glacken (1967), 302–9; H. Maier (1999), 64–71, 82–90.

33. Gobineau (1987), 367–73, cited from 370.

34. Séris (1994), 115.

35. Groethuysen (1928), 56–57; Foucault (1984), 53–85.

36. Aristotle, *Politics* 1.5.1254b20–23; Locke, *STG*, chap. 4, paras. 22–23 (pp. 13–14); Hegel, *Phänomenologie* B, IV, A (pp. 145–46).

37. Schuhl (1947), 10–11; Koyré (1971a), 296–98.

38. Aristotle, *Politics* 1.10.1258a21–23; Cicero, *Finibus* 4.13.34 (p. 135); then 5.9.24–26 (pp. 166–68); the expression is taken in the negative sense apropos to Claudius, of whom his mother would have said, *nec absolutum a natura, sed tantum inchoatum*. Suetonius, *Divus Claudius* 3.2.

39. Plotinus I.6[1].9.13 (O 1:116).
40. Eliot, *Monarchie* 2:10, 135, 141, 207, 226–27; Aristotle, *Politics* 1.5.1254b4–6.

Chapter 4. Metaphorical Dominations

1. Lachterman (1989), 6, 148; Taylor (1989), 144.
2. Archimedes, Letter to Dositheus, preface to *Sphere*, 1:8, 18–20, 9, 8–11; in Lachterman (1989), 75, 122.
3. Aristotle, *Metaphysics* Θ, 9.1051a31–32; the passage is not cited in Lachterman (1989).
4. Averroës, *Tafsir*, Tta' C20, I (p. 1218); Thomas Aquinas, *Metaphysicorum* 10.10, #1894 (p. 454b); Alexander of Aphrodisias, *Commentarius in Metaphysicam Aristotelis*, ed. M. Hayduck, CAG 1:597; Augustini Niphi Medici Philosophi Suessani, *Metaphysics*, 509b.
5. Fonsecae, *Commentariorum* 3:664–65.
6. Hobbes, epistle dedicatory to *Lessons*, 183–84; see also *Leviathan*, pt. 4, chap. 46, p. 435.
7. Kant, *Kritik der reinen Vernunft*, A725/B753; Kant, *Judgment*, para. 68, end (p. 248); letter to J. S. Beck, 1 July 1794, no. 351 [634] (*Briefwechsel*, 676); letter to J. Plücker, 26 January 1796, no. 382 [692] (*Briefwechsel*, 714); Kant, *Logik*, 2394 (p. 344); 2398 (p. 345).
8. J. Cardan, *De arcanis aeternitatis*, chap. 20, in *Opera Omnia*, ed. Charles Spon (Lyon, 1663), 10:43a, in Rüfner (1955), 273; Maïmon, *Progressen*, 42.
9. R. Dedekind, letter to H. Weber, 24 January 1888, in *Gesammelte mathematische Werke*, ed. R. Fricke et al. (Braunschweig: Vieweg, 1932), 3:89, cited in Lachterman (1989), 44.
10. Galileo, *DMS*, First Day, p. 110; Marion (1981), 203–27; Kepler, letter to Herwart von Hohenburg, 9–10 April 1599, in *Gesammelte Werke*, p. 309, lines 173–83; Groh & Groh (1991), 28.
11. Proclus, *Republic* 4 (1:235, lines 18–19); Lachterman (1989), 90; John Scotus Eriugena, *De divisione naturae* 2.24 (PL 122:579b–580a), in Rüfner (1955), 259, and [An anonymous commentary on the *De Trinitate* of Boethius] in Parent (1938), 197.
12. Nicholas of Cusa, *De Beryllo*, #6 (*PTW* 3:8); *Asclepius* 1.6a, 8; then Koyré (1971b), 97, 99, then 90; Cardan, *De arcanis aeternitatis*, chap. 4 (*Opera Omnia*, 10:4b).
13. Vico, *De antiquissima Italorum sapientia* 1.1 (MM, 194), then *De nostri temporis studiorum ratione*, chap. 4 (MM, 82); Löwith (1986); Valéry, *Léonard et les philosophes* [1929], in *Oeuvres* 1:1245; Shattuck (1968), 327–28.
14. Marx, *Capital*, bk. 1, sec. 3, chap. 5, #1 ("Arbeitsprozess", p. 158); see also Comte, *Ensemble*, chap. 5, p. 394.
15. Bettetini (2004), 97–158.
16. Courtine (1999), 31–43.
17. Bodin, *République* 1.8 (pp. 122–61).

18. Hesiod, *Theogony* 27; Solon, in Hiller and Crusius, *Anthologia*, frag. 27 (p. 42); Augustine, *De ordine* 2.14.40 (BA 4:432); Isidore of Seville, *Etymologies* 19.16.1; John of Salisbury, *Policraticus*, 1:186; Alain of Lille, *Anticlaudianus* 1, line 125 (p. 234); Rüfner (1955), 265; Dante, *Convivio*, bk. 2, chap. 1, pt. 3 (p. 66); Leopardi, *Zibaldone*, 2386 (4 April 1822), quoting Heliodorus, *Ethiopica* 1.26.6, ed. R. M. Rattenbury and T. W. Lumb (Paris: Les Belles Lettres, 1960), p. 38.

19. Sketch in Kantorowicz (1961), 357–60; development in Bredekamp (2008), 9–23, 68–79.

20. Berlin (1999), 51.

21. Aristotle, *Physics* 2.8.199a15–17; see also Aristotle, *Protrepticus*, frag. 11, in *Fragmenta*, 44 (= #13 During).

22. Pliny the Elder, *Natural History* 35.65.

23. Kaufmann (1993), 174–94, esp. 181–82, 185.

24. Anonymous (Francis Bacon?), *Speeches of the Six Councillors*, extract in *Gesta Grayorum*, in *Works*, vol. 8, bk. 1, p. 335; cited in Kaufmann (1993), 184.

25. Baudelaire, *Salon de 1846*, sec. 4 (*OC*, 891).

26. Dion of Prusa (Dio Chrysostom), *Oratio 12: Olympikos* 82–83 (*Discourses 2*, 84); see also Epictetus, *Discourses* 2.8.19; Democritus, in DK, B 68, frag. 21 (*kosmos epeon*); Macrobius, *Saturnalia* 5.1.19 (1:243); and see Rüfner (1955), 258; Theodore of Mopsuestia, in John Philoponus, *Opificio* 6.14 (p. 256), and in Panofsky (1962), 171n48; Thomas Aquinas, *ST* I.45.8; Dante, "Inferno," canto 11, lines 103–5, in *Commedia*; Meung, *Rose*, line 16210 (p. 436); Rüfner (1955), 280.

27. Delacroix, *Journal*, 9 August 1859 (3:222); Manzoni, "Dialogo dell'invenzione" [1850], (*Opere*, 983–1022 [cited from 984, 994]); Mallarmé, "La musique et les lettres" [1894] (*OC*, 647).

28. Curtius (1953), 400–404; Bouwsma (1993), 18–19, 25, 32.

29. Plotinus V.8[31].1.35–38 (*O* 2:376); see, for example, Petrarch (who could not yet read Plotinus), letter to Boccaccio of 28 October 1366, *Ad familiares*, sec. 23, letter 19, paras. 11–13 (*Prose*, 1018–19). Seneca had already developed the metaphor of the bee; see *Lucilius*, bk. 11, letter 84, paras. 3–5 (pp. 285–86); see Reckermann (1993), 116–17, 131–32.

30. Landino, "Che cosa sia poesia e poeta e della origine sua divina e antichissima," in *Proemio al commento dantesco* [1461] (*Scritti* 1:142); see Buck (1952), 92–93; Tigerstedt (1968).

31. Leonardo da Vinci, *Trattato della pittura* 2.65 (*S*, 62); Panofsky (1922), 121n303; Eberle (1980), 58–64; Fehrenbach (1997), 60–64. The liberty of the painter is already underscored by C. Cennini (ca. 1398), *Arte*, 62. Compare with Plato, *Sophist* 233d–234b; Leonardo da Vinci, *Trattato della pittura* 1.9 (*S*, 24); I cite the version of Farago found in Leonardo da Vinci, *Paragone* 13 (p. 194). A reader replaced the word *dio* in the manuscript with *creatore*, the reading of the current edition. Dürer, *Die Lehre von der menschlichen Proportion* [Der große ästhetische Exkurs am Ende des 3. Buches], #57 (*Nachlass*, 356n24); then A. Dürer, *Lehre von der menschlichen Proportion*, #55 (*Nachlass*, 295b).

32. Shaftesbury, *Advice to an Author*, pt. 1, sec. 3 (*Characteristics* 1:135–36); Tigerstedt (1968), 455–56.

33. Berlin (1999), 133–34; Duchesne (2013).
34. Vico, *De antiquissima Italorum sapientia*, 1.7.4 (*MM*, 288).
35. Bénichou (2004), 393–96; Manent (2010b), 139–40; Besançon (1994), 508; Chesterton, *Heretics*, chap. 17 (pp. 130–32); De Keyser (1965), 173b; Compagnon (1990), 135–36; and Jouannais, *Artistes*.

Chapter 5. The New Lord of Creation

1. Couzinet (2007), 8, basing herself on Garin (1969), 28, 35.
2. Plato, *Republic* 10.617d–621b; Gregory of Nyssa, *Life of Moses* 2.3 (SC 1, p. 108); *Homilies* 6.5 (SC 416, p. 318); on the traditional character of the theme reprised by Pico, see de Lubac (1974). On the contrary, one has seen here the first form of the idea of a *regnum hominis*; see, for example, G. Gentile (1916), 66.
3. Van Engen (1980), 150–51; Whitney (1990), 12.
4. Landes (1969), 555.
5. Augustine, *De opera monachorum* (PL 40:547–82); synthesis of the fathers in Salamito (1996); Arendt (1958), 316; Gauchet (1985), 92–113; cited from 100.
6. "Sincere Brethren," *R*, I, 8 [8] (vol. 1, p. 290); Marquet (1961), 230; Pinès (1996a).
7. See the dossier collected in Mulsow (2002). On the influence of Hermeticism on modernity, see the synoptic view of Faivre (1988); introduction to the edition of the *Asclepius* in *CH* 2:264–75.
8. *Asclepius* 8 (*CH* 2:305–6).
9. *Asclepius* 9 (*CH* 2:307), 10 (*CH* 2:308p); on the idea, see Brague (2002b), 196–98; *Asclepius* 11 (*CH* 2:310).
10. Seznec (1980), Gay (1966).
11. Raimundus Sabundus, *Theologia* 64 (p. 83); see Faye (1998), 59.
12. See above, 12, and Garin (1938).
13. Lotharii, *Miseria*.
14. Printed in Sandeus, *Regibus*, 149–68. On Facio, see the notice of Viti in *Dizionario* 44:113a–121a concerning *De excellentia hominis*, col. 117a. Facio is summarized in Trinkaus (1970), 215–29; extracts on 408–13.
15. Manetti, *Dignity* 4, #4, p. 102, lines 20, summarized by Trinkaus (1970), 230–58; 1, #3–12, pp. 6–12 (Cicero, *Gods* 2); 1, #14–32, pp. 12–22 (Lactantius, *De opificio Dei*); 1, #36, p. 23, lines 8–11.
16. Manetti, *Dignity* 2, #16, p. 45, lines 2–4; 2, #19, p. 47, lines 3–7; 3, #5, p. 67, lines 29–68, 1; 3, #5, p. 68, line 19; 3, #7, p. 69. Same idea in the Talmud: first one builds the banquet hall, then the invited come to occupy it; see Urbach (1979), 2:784–85n8; see also Calvin, *Institutes* 1.14.22; Manetti, *Dignity* 3, #35, p. 86, lines 14–16; see also 3, #22, p. 79, lines 12–13; 3, #45, p. 91, line 24. Descartes's formulation (see below, 71) follows that of Manetti. But nothing proves that it comes from him; see Manetti, *Dignity* 3, #30, p. 84, lines 1–2; 3, #37, p. 87, lines 21–25; 3, #20, p. 77, lines 18–19; 3, #27, p. 82, lines 1–13.
17. Manetti, *Dignity* 3, #9, p. 71, lines 15–16; 3, #24, p. 80, lines 14–16; 3, #56, p. 97, lines 8–25; 3, #38, p. 88, line 5. See Thomas Aquinas, *ST* I.100.1, corpus.

18. Manetti, *Dignity* 4, #20, p. 113, lines 18–29; then 3, #59, from p. 98, line 23, to p. 99, line 2; and 3, #58, p. 98, lines 16–22. See Duns Scotus, *Quaestiones in tertium librum Sententiarum* 3, d. 7, q. 3, scholia 2 (*OO* 14:354b); *Reportata Parisiensia* 3, d. 7, q. 4, scholia 2 (*OO* 23:302b–303a). Already in Rupert, *Gloria* 13 (p. 415), and Honorius Augustodunensis, *Libellus octo quaestionum de angelis et hominis* 2 (PL 172:1187a–1188b).

19. Manetti, *Dignity* 3, #23, p. 79, lines 21–80, 2; then 4, #58, p. 135, lines 14–16; finally, 4, #73, p. 142, lines 22–143, 4.

20. Manetti, *Dignity* 2, #36, p. 58, line 1; 3, #20, p. 78, line 14; 2, #37, p. 58, lines 18–26; 2, #38–40, pp. 59–60; 2, #21, p. 47, lines 28–48, 3; see Lactantius, *Institutiones* 7.9, 13–14 (p. 613, 6–19).

21. Summary of Poggio in Trinkaus (1970), 258–70; extracts in Latin, 428–33; for the other two point-counterpoints, 271–321; list of minor treatises on the same themes, 391–392n16.

22. Oliva, *Diálogo*, 85–130; cited from 85, 130; Boaistuau, *Discours*.

23. Ficino, *Théologie* 13.3 (pp. 1224–36); repeated in 14.4 (p. 1306). See Trinkaus (1970), 482–84, 784–86; connection with Francis Bacon in Kristeller (1972), 19–20; Avicenna, *Soul* 5.2 (pp. 209–21).

24. Ficino, *Théologie* 14.1 (p. 1276); then 14.4 (p. 1306); 10.4 (p. 852); 11.5 (p. 1006).

25. Ficino, *Théologie* 13.3 (p. 1232).

26. Charles de Bovelles, *De sapiente*, chap. 24, in Cassirer (1927), 350–51; see also Bovelles, *Sage*, 172. The translation of the quoted phrase is inadequate.

27. Alberti, *I libri della Famiglia*, prologue to *Opere volgari*, 3–12, esp. 5, 6, 9.

28. Machiavelli, *Il Principe* 25 (*O*, 78–79, 81). See Strauss (1958), 246; Rosen (1969), 69. There is a curious parallel with Wang Tingxiang, a Chinese contemporary of Machiavelli; see Linck (1999), 107.

29. G. Bruno, *Spaccio della bestia trionfante*, 3rd dialogue in *DFI*, 601–602; Moscovici (1968), 168–69. Cf. Plato, *Statesman* 272cd.

30. See above, 36.

31. Campanella, *Senso* 2, chap. 25 (p. 94).

32. Kepler, *In Dioptricen Praefatio: De usu et praestantia perspicilli nuper inventi* (*Werke* 4:344); cited in Blumenberg (1988), 437, but with an erroneous reference to *De macula in sole observata*, which in fact is by Fabricius.

Chapter 6. Attempts and Temptations

1. Aristotle, *Physics* 2.8.199a17; Galen, *De constitutione artis medicae ad Patrophilum* (*Opera* 1:303); *Ars Medica* (*Opera* 1:378); Vitruvius, *Architecture* 10.1.4 (pp. 460–62); Cervantes, *Quijote*, pt. 2, chap. 16, p. 667.

2. Shakespeare, *The Winter's Tale* 4.4.89–92; on the context, see Tayler (1964), 121–41, and Hansen (1978), 486; an analogous formulation (*ars naturam ipsa natura superat*; "art overcomes nature by means of nature herself") in the paraphrase of Archimedes by Guidobaldo del Monte (1588), cited by Stöcklein (1969), 123n45. See also Eamon (1983), 184, 198.

3. Qur'an 3:49; 5:110.
4. Avicenna, "Actions et Passions," in *Traités*, 225; *Genèse* 3.20.1–2, (pp. 120–21); *Gloses*, p. 129, lines 15–17, then p. 48, lines 8–10. Would Avicenna's source be al-Biruni? Chapter 17 of al-Biruni's book on India (*Tahqīq*) is vague on this. See also Avicenna, *États de l'âme*, ed. Ahwani, p. 124, in Michot (1986), 142n3; *Vingt-deux questions*, in Michot (1986), 142n3; *Livre*, 220, lines 1–2, trans. Goichon, p. 521; Michot (1986), 141–53.
5. Roger Bacon, *Opus tertium* 26 (*Opera* 1:96); Hadot (2004), 99. See Avicenna, *De animalibus* 7.7, "De moribus animalium," in *Avicenna*, fol. 40, col. C.
6. Albert, *Animalibus* 22, treatise 1, chap. 5, "De naturalibus proprietatibus hominis et divinis," #9 (p. 1353); *De intellectu et intelligibili* 2, cap. 11 (AMOO/Borgnet, vol. 12, p. 519b).
7. Ficino, *Théologie* 13.4 (pp. 1238–62).
8. Agrippa, *Occulta* 1.6 (p. 414); Hadot (2004), 158; Reuchlin, *Verbo* 1 [. . .] (p. [27]).
9. Exod. 22:18; Lev. 19:26, 31; 20:6; Deut. 18:10; Maimonides, *Guide* 3.37 (pp. 397–99); Fogen (1997) and Flint (1991), 400–401.
10. Agobard, *Liber contra insulsam vulgi opinionem de grandine et tonitruis*, in *Opera*, 3–15. See Job 37:22.
11. Thomas Aquinas, *ST* I-II.102.5, ad 4; *HDA*, vol. 7, s.v. "Schmetterling," 4, col. 1246; Taylor (1989), 192.
12. Porphyry, *Life of Plotinus* 10; Plotinus, *O* 1:16; Iamblichus, *Mystères* 2.11 (pp. 95–96); Julian, Letter 12 to Priscus, in *Oeuvres*, I-2, p. 19; Proclus, *Théologie platonicienne* 63, following Iamblichus, *Mystères*, 10.4–8 (pp. 212–15); see Dodds (1951), appendix 2 (pp. 282–311); Olympiodorus, *Commentaire* 2, #170 (p. 123, lines 3–11).
13. Newman (2004), 32; *Picatrix* 4.3.1 (pp. 315–16); "Picatrix," 310.
14. Lewis (1954), 5–13; Eamon (1983), 172; Muray (1999), 159; Koyré (1966a), 50–51; (1971b), 80, 83, 94; citation of Jacques Lacan, in *Scilicet* 2/3 (1970): 83, cited in Muray (1999), 578; Berlin (1999), 47–48; and all of Muray (1999).
15. Idel (1992), 238; Gregory (2012), 317.
16. Roger Bacon, *In libro sex scientiarum* . . . , in *Retardatione*, 183–84. See also Bacon, *Opus majus* 2, pp. 204–13; *Opus tertium*, ed. A. G. Little, 45–54; *Epistula*, chap. 7. On the condemnation of Bacon, see Thorndike (1923–58), 2:628–29.
17. Mensching (1993), in particular 165, 170, 179.
18. William of Auvergne, *Universo* 2.3.21 (1:1058H).
19. Sternagel (1966), 45–47; Stöcklein (1969), 60; on the rehabilitation of the word "mechanical," see Moscovici (1968), 248–49, 483.
20. Koyré (1971b), 82; Paracelsus, *Die bücher von den unsichtbaren Krankheiten* [1531/1532] 5.13, in *Werke*, ed. K. Sudhoff (Munich-Planegg: Otto Wilhelm Barth, 1925), ser. 1, vol. 9, p. 341, in Benz (1961a), 54.
21. Stöcklein (1969).
22. Plotinus IV.4 [28].40–45; Arab equivalent in *Theology of Aristotle*, chap. 6, paras. 13–75, in Badawi, *Aflutin*, pp. 74–83.
23. C. Agrippa, *De vanitate scientiarum*, chap. 42.

24. Browne, *Religio* 1.31 (p. 51); Campanella, *Senso* 4.19.

25. Francis Bacon, *De augmentis scientiarum* 3.5 (*Works* 1:571 [in the title *Expurgatio vocabuli magiae*] and 573); *Progress* 2.7.1 (*Works* 1:106); 2.8.3 (*Works* 1:118); see Lewis (2000), chap. 3, pp. 77–78; Forbes (1968), 10.

26. In *L17* (1:137–380).

27. Proclus, *Republic* 2:234, lines 17–26. Critiques: Dante, "Inferno," canto 29, line 49, in *Commedia*; Chaucer, "The Canon Yeoman's Tale," in *Tales*, 257–66.

28. Eliade (1956), 178.

29. Meister Eckhart, *Sermon* no. 38, *In illo tempore* (*DW* 2:228).

30. See the remarks by Henry (1976), 1:139–40.

31. Olympiodorus, *Sur l'art sacré*, #9 (*CAAG* 3:73–74; French trans., 2:80). I cite Kraus (1942), 99; Jâbir, *TC*, p. 221, line 15, and p. 445, line 1: see the manuscripts cited by Idel (1992), 249, 262.

32. Avicenna, *Congelatione*, 41 (English); 53 (Latin); 85, lines 9–10 (Arabic); Averroës, *Generatione* 1.1, in Aristotle, *Aristotelis Stagiritae Libri omnes ad animalium cognitionem attinentes cum Averrois Cordubensis variis in eosdem commentariis [. . .]*, 6:206v, col. A, lines 36–40, then 48–52; see also *Tahâfut*, Questions physiques 1.3 (p. 511); same argument in Thomas Aquinas, *Commentaire des Sentences* II, d. 7, q. 3, a. 1, ad 5m, in *Opera*, 145c.

33. Meung, *Rose*, lines 16096–101 (pp. 433–34); Obrist (1996), 218 (cited), 243. See also Oldrado da Ponte, in Migliorino (1981), 26.

34. Newman (1989), 443, 429, then 434, and Newman (2004), 69.

35. Obrist (1996), 258, 279.

36. *Secretum secretorum*, Latin (*Opera hactenus* 5:173); Ibn Khaldun, *Muqaddima* 6 (3:234); Niccolo Tedeschi (Panormitano), in Migliorino (1981), 37.

37. Gratian, *Decretum*, 2nd part, cause 26, q. 5, canon 12, in *Corpus Juris Canonici*, vol. 1, col. 1031; other texts in Newman (2004), 104, 11; Migliorino (1981), 15–16.

38. Bernard Palissy, *Traité des métaux et de l'alchimie*, in *Discours admirables [. . .]*, in *Oeuvres*, 2:105–6.

39. Yates (1964), 156.

40. Dédéyan (1955–64); *contra*, Faust would be the last medieval hero, the first modern hero being Hamlet; Armogathe (2007), 41; Landes (1969), 21, 24, 32.

41. C. Marlowe, *The Tragical History of Dr. Faustus*, scene 2, lines 52–63, then 76–77; for the context, see Gregory (2012), 56–59.

Chapter 7. The Formation of the Modern Project

1. White (1962) and (1968); the formulation constitutes Gimpel's title (1975).

2. Küster (2009), 41–42; *Comprendre et maîtriser la nature au Moyen Age* (1994), despite its title, includes nothing of the sort; Dante, "Inferno," canto 23, line 47, in *Commedia*; "Paradiso," canto 10, lines 139–48, in *Commedia*.

3. Bessarion, letter 13, to Constantin Paleologue, #18, in *Gelehrtenkreis*, 448; Gimpel (1975), 225–26.

4. Roger Bacon, chap. 4 of *Epistola de secretis operibus artis et naturae et de nullitate magiae* (*Opera* 1:533); for the long view, chap. 5 (1:534); Boll (1917).

5. White (1962), 56, in Black (1970), 67–68.
6. Federico, *Arte*, 2–4.
7. Guido d'Arezzo, *Micrologus*, ed. J. Smits Van Waesberghe (Rome: American Institute of Musicology, 1955), 223, in Beaujouan (1975), 439–40; Eamon (1983), 196, 201; John Dee, preface to a translation of Euclid [1570], in Debus (1978), 7.
8. Beaujouan (1991), 8, 11, 12; Niccolò Tartaglia, *Nova scientia* (Venice, 1537); Koyré (1966a), 117–18; Mittelstrass (1970), 175–77, Moscovici (1968), 325.
9. al-Farabi, *Catálogo*, 74 (Arabic), 104 (Gundisalvo); in Beaujouan (1975), 441.
10. Aristotle, *Metaphysics* A.2.982b29 and *Metaphysica* 1.1–4.4 (p. 10).
11. I paraphrase White (1978), 52–56; also see Forbes (1968), 19; Gimpel (1975), 123–24, 156. On perpetual movement, see Moscovici (1968), 349; Eamon (1983), 210n97; U. Friedrich (2003), 111–14; Rouvillois (2010), 388; Céline (1952), 406.
12. Hugh of Saint-Victor, *Eruditiones didascalicae* 1.6 (PL 176:745); Sternagel (1966), 85–87.
13. Ficino, *Théologie* 2.13 (p. 192); Eamon (1983), 174–79, 186–94; U. Friedrich (2003), 93–94.
14. Manetti, *Dignity* 3, #37, p. 58, lines 18–26 (navigation); Du Bellay, *Deffence* 1.9 (pp. 53–54); François Rabelais, *Tiers Livre*, 51, "Éloge du Pantagruélion"; Bodin, *Methodus ad facilem historiarum cognitionem*, chap. 7, end (*Oeuvres*, 227b–228a); Galileo, *DMS* [1632], First Day, p. 111; Campanella, *CS*, p. 54, lines 1237–38, or *De gentilismo non retinendo*, in Armogathe (2007), 102; Vair, *De la constance et consolation ès calamitez publiques*, in *Oeuvres*, bk. 3, p. 381–82; Louis Le Roy, *Of the Interchangeable Course or Variety of Things in the Whole World*, trans. "R. A." (London, 1594), fol. 127v [*non vidi*], in Eamon (1994), 273; Hadot (2004), 233; Rabelais, *Pantagruel*, chap. 8, p. 44; Cervantes, *Quijote*, pt. 1, chap. 38, p. 397; see the horror of the giants of Brobdingnag in Swift, *Gulliver*, pt. 2, chap. 7, pp. 158–59; in Milton it is the demons who invented artillery, and make use of it, *PL*, bk. 6, lines 482–91 (pp. 145–46).
15. Bacon, *Organon*, bk. 1, para. 129, p. 270; Séris (1994), 41–42; Bacon, *Advancement* 2.2.13 (p. 93), against Virgil, *Aeneid* 6.590.
16. Beaujouan (1975), 463–64.
17. Jonas (1954), 146–49, 223–33, 251–55, in Brague (2002b), 98.
18. Thomas Aquinas, *Sent* II, d. 9, q. 1, a. 8, arg. 3 (p. 152a); Blumenberg (1951), 259; Bacon, *Organon*, bk. 1, para. 51 (p. 114); Spinoza, *Letter lvi* to H. Boxel (O 4:192); Strauss (2001), 364–69.
19. Aristotle, *Nicomachean Ethics* 6.7.1141a33–b2; Ps. 8:5, and see above, 9.
20. Augustine, *City* 9.13.3 (1:588); Brague (2002a).
21. Kant, *Die Religion innerhalb der Grenzen der blossen Vernunft*, pt. 2, footnote (WW 4:743); Schopenhauer, *Preisschrift über die Grundlage der Moral*, pt. 2, para. 6 (WW 3:658); Brague (2006a), 125, with citation to de Tocqueville, letter to Eugène Stoffels, 3 January 1843, in *Inédites*, 1:449.
22. J. Maritain, *Trois Réformateurs: Luther, Descartes, Rousseau*, pt. 2 (Descartes), chap. 3, in Maritain (1984), 3:488; see also Balthasar (1956), 93.

23. Comte, *Cours*, 60th lesson (2:777) (my italics). Comte credits medieval Catholicism with the idea that "the saints prevailed over the angels" (*Synthèse*, introduction, 52). On the idea of "type," see *Esprit*, chap. 2, p. 208.

24. Bacon, *Sylva Sylvarum* 1, #100 (*Works* 2:383–84)—for the nature of a body to be changed, it must be completely annihilated, which is impossible; Rossi (1974), 54–62; Newman (2004), 264–65.

25. Bacon, *Progress* 1.5.11 (*Works* 1:41–43); *De augmentis* 3.5 (*Works* 1:571); nuanced by Bacon, *Organon*, bk. 1, para. 129 (p. 272); *Meditationes sacrae* 11, "De haeresibus" (*Works* 8:241).

26. Bacon, *Organon*, bk. 1, para. 129 (p. 270); and see above, 58; Brague (2002b), 306.

27. Bacon's subtitle for *Organon*: *Aphorismi de interpretatione naturae et regno hominis* (p. 80); *Organon*, bk. 1, para. 68 (p. 144); *Cogitata*, no. 18 (p. 208).

28. Bacon, *Organon*, bk. 2, para. 52 (pp. 610–12); on the idea of repairing the fall, see also *Advancement* 2.16.4 (p. 159); *Valerius Terminus of the Interpretation of Nature* (*Works* 3:222). See William Whiston cited in Groh and Groh (1991), 49; Groh (2010), chaps. 4–7.

29. Groh (2003), 157–58 (Ambrose) and 279 (John Chrysostom).

30. Hugh, *Didascalicon* 1.5, 20 (pp. 128, 192); Krolzik (1988), 83–93; Bonaventura, *De reduction artium ad theologiam* 2, in Stöcklein (1969), 37, 40–41. Synthesis in Whitney (1990), 74–127; rapprochement with Bacon, 127. In the modern era, still see Milton, *PL*, bk. 10, lines 1078–85 (p. 259).

31. Bacon, *Organon*, bk. 1, para. 129 (p. 270).

32. Bacon, *Progress* 2.7.6 (*Works* 1:112); *Cogitata*, no. 16 (p. 192); *Atlantis*, p. 288; Adams (1949), 387.

33. Bacon, *Parasceve ad historiam naturalem et experimentalem*, aphorism 5 (*Works* 1:399), then *Cogitata*, no. 16 (p. 194); "Distributio operis," in *Organon*, p. 56; Dilthey (1914), 259.

34. Hippocrates, *Art* 12.3 (p. 240); Hadot (2004), 131–32; Zosimus of Panopolis, *Mémoires authentiques* 10.7, in *Alchimistes*, vol. 4, pt. 1 (pp. 40–41); I interpret this doubtful text by following Newman (2004), 30.

35. Bacon, *Parasceve ad historiam naturalem et experimentalem*, aphorism 1 (*Works* 1:395).

36. Bacon, *Descriptio globi intellectualis et thema coeli*, chap. 2 (*Works* 3:730).

37. Narrative of Clerselier in Baillet, *Vie* 1:164–65; Descartes, letter to Mersenne, 23 December 1630 (*OC* 1:195–96); also see the letter to M. Descartes (from l'Abbé Picot?), preface to the *Traité des Passions* (*OC* 11:320).

38. Descartes, *Discours de la méthode* [1637], pt. 6 (*OC* 6:61–62; Latin, 574); on the expression "masters and possessors," see Manetti, *Dignity* 3, #35, p. 86, lines 14–16.

39. Koyré (1966b), 12; Séris (1994), 206; Kennington (2004), 123–44; Séris (1994), 154.

40. See above, 47.

41. Descartes, *Discours de la méthode*, pt. 3 (*OC* 6:25).

42. Descartes, *Meditationes de prima philosophia*, meditation 4 (*OC* 7:14), and *Réponses*, chap. 2 (*OC* 7:149); letter-preface of the *Principles* (*OC*, bk. 2 of vol. 9,

p. 4); *Regulae*, chap. 1 (*OC* 10:361); letter to Elisabeth, 6 October 1645 (*OC* 4:305); contra, *Traité des passions*, pt. 2, art. 142 (*OC* 11:434), and Hölderlin: "Und wenig Wissen, aber der Freude viel / Ist Sterblichen gegeben" (frag. 29, GSA 3:323); Descartes, *Discours de la méthode*, pts. 1, 3 (*OC* 6:10, 28).

43. Descartes, letter to Mersenne, 3 December 1640 (*OC* 3:249—my italics); *Traité des passions*, chap. 3, #152 (*OC* 11:445—my italics); parallel in the letter to Christine, 20 November 1647 (*OC* 5:84).

44. Seneca, *Consolation à Helvia* 5.2 (*Dialogues*, 63); the Buddha even says that the sage is the "envy of the gods": *Dhammapada* 7.94 and 14.181 (pp. 69, 87).

45. Descartes, *Traité des passions*, pt. 1, art. 50 (*OC* 11:370). See also I, #44 (*OC* 11:361); #47 (*OC* 11:365–66); #50 (*OC* 11:370); IV, #211 (*OC* 11:486); III, #156 (*OC* 11:448).

46. Spaemann (1996), 145; Irrgang (1986), 197; also see Janicaud (1985), 188–99; Taylor (1989), 147.

Chapter 8. The Beginnings of the Realization

1. G. M. Lancisi, "Del modo di Filosofar nell'Arte Medica, e si prova, che per la Medicina rationale e meglio servirsi della filosofia sperimentale che di qualunque altra," in *Galleria di Minerva* [1704], vol. 4, 3rd part, pp. 33–37; cited from pp. 35, 34; reference in Hazard (1989), 289.

2. Robitaille (2007), 165.

3. Hobbes, *De corpore*, bk. 1, chap. 1, #6 (*Opera* 1:6); R. Boyle, *The Christian Virtuoso*, 1st part 1 (*W* 5:514); Webster (1975).

4. R. Boyle, *Certain Physiological Essays [. . .]* (1661), chap. 1, "A Proëmial Essay [. . .] with Some Considerations Touching Experimental Essays in General [. . .]" (*W* 1:310–11), then *The Usefulness of Natural Philosophy*, 1st part (1663), essay 1, "Of the Usefulness of Experimental Philosophy, Principally as It Relates to the Mind of Man" (*W* 2:14–15).

5. Cowley, *A Proposition for the Advancement of Experimental Philosophy*, in *Essays*, 21–44; citations from 25–26, then 33–34.

6. Locke, *An Essay concerning Human Understanding* [1677] (*Political*, 260–65; cited from 261); Hazard (1989), 297, seems to have attributed the passage to Fontenelle.

7. Voltaire, *Le Siècle de Louis XIV*, chap. 31 (*Oeuvres h.*, 997).

8. Brown (1936), in particular 191–92.

9. Fontenelle, *Préface: Sur l'utilité des mathématiques et de la physique, et sur les travaux de l'Académie des sciences* (*Oeuvres* 1:30–38).

10. Spinoza, *Ethica*, pt. 4, preface (*O* 1:182); appendix, #26 (*O* 1:242); prop. 37, scolia 2, (*O* 1:209); *De intellectus emendatione*, chap. 5, 14–15, (*O* 1:6); *Ethica*, pt. 4, prop. 45, scolia, (*O* 1:216); see also Milton, *PL*, bk. 10, line 1084 (p. 259).

11. Leibniz, *Denkschrift über die Errichtung einer Churfürstlichen Societät der Wissenschaften* [1700] (*Deutsche*, 268); citation from *Andere Denkschrift* [25 May 1700] (*Deutsche*, 273). There is a title from Leibniz, *De utilitate scientiarum et verae eruditionis efficacia ad humanam felicitatem* (*Opuscules*, 218). See also *Nouveaux Essais*, pt. 4, chap. 3, para. 27 (*Philosophischen* 5:370); *Théodicée*, chap. 2, #147, p. 182.

12. Koyré (1968), 44.

13. Cuvier, *Rapport*, 387; C. G. J. Jacobi, letter to A. M. Legendre, 2 July 1830, in Borchardt "Correspondance," 273.

14. Voltaire, *Lettres*, chap. 12, pp. 60–66; Rousseau, *Discours sur les sciences et les arts*, chap. 2 (*OC* 3:29); d'Alembert, *Discours*, 92–96; Condorcet, *Esquisse*, 8th epoch, p. 210 (still moderate). Liebig sees that it was the French who made Bacon famous; see *Bacon*, 54, and Mittelstrass (1970), 353; Deleyre, *Analyse*; Ferrone (1989), 348; Comte, *Cours*, 58th lesson (2:739, 749).

15. Maistre, *Examen de la philosophie de Bacon* (*Oeuvres*, vol. 6); Liebig, *Bacon*, 9, 15, 36–37, 45, 48–49; C. Bernard, *Introduction*, pt. 1, chap. 2, sec. 6, p. 86; pt. 3, chap. 4, sec. 4, p. 310.

16. Schaffer (1983).

17. White (1978), 59–73; on the metaphor of elevation, see Starobinski (1964), 209a; Van Delft (2008), 187–93; Fischer (1985), 102. Proust, *Sodome et Gomorrhe*, pt. 3, in *Recherche*, 2:1029.

18. Diodorus, *Bibliothèque* 2.55–60 (pp. 257–66).

19. More, *Utopia*, 182; Adams (1949), 382, 384.

20. English translation in Yates's appendix (1972), 238–51 (*Fama*) and 251–60 (*Confessio*).

21. J. V. Andreae, *Reipublicae Christianopolitanae Descriptio*, chaps. 44–50 (pp. 112–24); Yates (1972), 30; Groh (2010), 509–32.

22. R. Bacon, in Newman (2004), 88; Gruman (1966), 62b–67b.

23. F. Bacon, *Valerius Terminus of the Interpretation of Nature*, chap. 1 (*Works* 3:222).

24. Descartes, *Traité de l'homme* (*OC* 11:223–24); Gruman (1966), 77a–80a.

25. Descartes, letter to Huygens of 25 January 1638 (*OC* 1:507); Letter to Chanut of 15 June 1646 (*OC* 4:441–42). The dream of Descartes is still alive at the end of his century (Rouvillois [2010], 226), and it continues in the European memory; see, for example, Bulwer-Lytton, *Race*, chap. 26, p. 116.

26. Mlle. de Saint-Quentin, "Traité pour établir la possibilité de l'immortalité corporelle," *Mercure*, November 1692, 31–64, and the responses to objections, *Mercure*, January 1693, 82–102; Rouvillois (2010), 226 (the reference is incorrect).

27. See Goethe, *Maximen*, #402 (pp. 82–83).

28. François Arago, "Carnot" (*Oeuvres* 1:511–633); citation from 523–24 (italics original).

29. Augustine, *City* 14.23 (1:974–76); Groh (2003), 376; Malebranche, *Recherche de la Vérité*, VIIIe Éclaircissement, paras. 5–6 (*O* 1:849–50). On pleasure, Thomas Aquinas, *ST* I.98.2, ad 3.

30. W. Godwin, *An Enquiry concerning Political Justice*, chap. 8, para. 7 (*Writings* 3:460, 465), then Leon Kass, cited in Robitaille (2007), 197. For the messianic tone, see Matt. 16:28.

31. Dostoyevsky, *Demons*, pt. 3, chap. 5, sec. 5 (p. 528).

32. Comte, *Ensemble*, chap. 4, p. 362; Renan, *Dialogues*, dialogue no. 3 (*OC* 1:626).

33. Fedorov, *Filosofija*; *What Was Man Created For? The Philosophy of the Common Task: Selected Works*; extracts in German in *NM*, 70–232. On the doctrine, see

the synthesis in Hagemeister (1989), 15–127. See also Heller and Niqueux (1995), 162–63 (citation); Fedorov is the most cited name in the index.

34. Heller and Niqueux (1995), citation from 215, then 163; Hagemeister (2005), 42.

35. Jakobson (1931), 387; Starr (1981), 249.

36. Seneca, *Quaestiones* 7.25.4–6 and 6.5.2–3 (pp. 326–27, 256–57); Macrobius, *In Somnium Scipionis* 5.10.6–8 (2:125–26); Tacitus, *Histories* 1.3 (p. 2); nothing like it in *Annales* 3.3, in Gay (1969), 94; Augustine, *City* 22.24 (2:839–40); Dodds (1973), 1–25.

37. Jâbir, texts translated in Kraus (1942), 54–58, 125–26; Abu Bakr Muhammad ibn Zakariyya al-Razi, *Shukûk*, p. 3; reported by his homonym Abu Hâtim al-Razi, in *Proofs* 1.2 (pp. 8–9).

38. Marie de France, prologue to *Lais*, ed. J. Rychner (Paris: Champion, 1983), line 16 (p. 1), in Jauss (1970), 21; on Judaism, see Zlotnik (1975); Guibert de Tournai, in Gimpel (1975), 141.

39. Nicholas of Cusa, *Idiota de mente* 13.148–49 (*PTW* 2:112).

40. Tuveson (1972), vi, 75, 134, 201, and elsewhere; on Pierre Jurieu, see Armogathe (2005), 197.

41. Bury (1932); Rouvillois (2010). On the Renaissance idea of degeneration, see Allen (1938), 211–13, 219–24.

42. Hobbes, *Leviathan*, pt. 1, chap. 11, p. 63; see his reinterpretation of the maxim *respice finem*, *Leviathan*, pt. 1, chap. 3, p. 15.

43. Voltaire, *Essai*; Becker (1932), 107; Gay (1969), 123–24. In Germany, Wieland, too, is reserved; see Gay (1969), 107–8.

44. *OED*, s.v. "progressive."

45. Comte, *Esprit*, chap. 2, p. 180. My italics.

46. Spencer, *Social*, pt. 1, chap. 2, #4, p. 65.

47. Lewis (1975), 74; see also Tenbruck (1984), 65–66.

48. Haeckel, "Über die Entwicklungslehre Darwins" [1863] (*GW* 5:3–32; cited from 28); Marx, *Deutsche Ideologie*, bk. 1 (*FS*, 430b).

49. J. Glanvill, *PU*; Dupré (1993), 155; Bury (1932), 79–91; Becker (1932), 132–33; Fumaroli (2001), 59–76.

50. Grimm, letter of 15 January 1757 (*Correspondance* 4:27); Dupré (2004), xii; see also Bayle, in Jauss (1970), 33; A. R. J. Turgot, "Tableau philosophique des progrès successifs de l'esprit humain," *ODC* 1:214–35; Goguet, *Origine*; Savérien, *Histoire*. See Ferrone (1989), 340–43; Venturi (1990), vol. 5, pt. 2, pp. 221–24.

51. Priestley, *Government*, 4–5; Becker (1932), 144–45; Bredvold (1961), 101; Price, *Evidence*, 25; Condorcet is cited on 51n. See Condorcet, *Vie de Turgot* [1786] (*Oeuvres* 5:14).

52. Buffon, *Époques de la nature*, 7th epoch (*OP*, 195b–196a).

53. Rey (2006), 143–44.

54. Mercier, *2440*, chap. 3, pp. 291–306, cited from pp. 298–99; chap. 40, p. 377; chap. 8, p. 115; chap. 14, pp. 146–47.

55. Mercier, *2440*, chap. 28, pp. 249–50, cited from p. 248. To burn books is an ancient practice. For ancient Rome, one has the case of Cremutius Cordus (Tacitus, *Annales* 4.35). It is associated with the "obscurantism" of "reaction." But

"progressivism" did not hesitate to suppress works tainted with "superstition." According to the Bible of Velislav (Bohemian, thirteenth century), it is the Antichrist who burns the books of philosophers and theologians (illustration in Armogathe [2005], facing p. 152; see also p. 265). Hume's sally, to burn the books of theology and metaphysics (*Inquiry*, pt. 12, chap. 3, #132 [p. 165]), was rendered more concrete during the Revolution by Urbain Domergue: "Portons le scalpel révolutionnaire dans les vastes depots de livres et coupons tous les membres gangrenés du corps bibliographique" (Ozouf [1989], 142–43). As for practice, one has the "purification" of the libraries of Bavarian convents that were secularized; see *Bayern*, 122.

56. Mercier, *2440*, chap. 12, pp. 136–37; chap. 15, pp. 148–49; chap. 29, p. 275 n. 6.

57. See the synthesis of Schwonke (1957); see below, 115–19.

58. Compagnon (1990), 49–50; see also Shattuck (1968).

Chapter 9. The Master Is There

1. Buffon, *Époques de la nature*, 4th epoch (*OP*, 160b, and see the text cited on 109).

2. Plato, *First Alcibiades* 130c; *Republic* 9.590a; *Phaedo* 248c; Plotinus I.1[53] (1:48–61); I.9.203 (1:56–57); I.7.16–17 (1:55).

3. Albert the Great, *Summa de homine*, conveniently, but only in part, accessible in *Menschen*; Nachmanides, *Kitvey* (2:11–311).

4. Montaigne, *Essays*, bk. 2, chap. 17 (2:605); Charron, *De la sagesse*, pt. 1, preface, first sentence; Bacon, *Progress* 2.9.1 (*Works* 1:123–24); Armogathe (2007), 74.

5. *HWPh*, s.v. "Anthropologie" (vol. 1, col. 373 [O. Marquard]), and Marquard (1973), 122–44, 213–48.

6. Van Delft (2008), 86; Hume, introduction to *Treatise*, xx; Gay (1969), 335; Comte, *Esprit*, chap. 1, p. 148; see also *Esprit*, chap. 3, p. 216; Comte, *Ensemble*, chap. 1, p. 70; Saint-Simon, preface to *Mémoire sur la science de l'homme* (*Oeuvres* 11:40).

7. Spinoza, *Ethica*, pt. 4, prop. 35, scholia (*O* 1:207); Malebranche, preface to *De la recherche de la Vérité* (*O* 1:13); Pope, *An Essay on Man*, 2nd epistle, st. 1, line 2; Comte, *Cours*, 57th lesson (2:761).

8. Voltaire, "Sur les Pensées de Pascal," pt. 3, chap. 25, in *Lettres* (pp. 191–92).

9. Augustine, *City* 19.6 (2:454–56); Brague (2008c), 242–43.

10. Kamen (1997), chap. 14, "Inventing the Inquisition" (305–20).

11. Bodin, *Démonomanie*. The book was translated into Latin and German the following year.

12. Spee, *Cautio*.

13. Gay (1969), 398; Beccaria, *Dei*; Verri, *Osservazioni*; Manzoni, *I promessi sposi*, chaps. 31–32 (*Opere*, 407–30), and *Storia della colonna infame* (*Opere*, 603–79).

14. Bakunin, *Fédéralisme, socialisme et antithéologisme*, pt. 1 (*Oeuvres*, 34); Rousseau, *Émile*, pt. 1 (*OC* 4:302); Schiller, *Das Eleusische Fest* (1798), line 49.

15. Macrobius, *In Somnium Scipionis* 1.8.7 (2:38); Isidore, *Etymologies* 10.116 (letter H); Thomas Aquinas, *ST* II-II.80.1. ad 2; again Erasmus, in Groethuysen

(1928), 186; Bacon, *Essays*, no. 13, "Of Goodness and Goodness of Nature" (*Works* 6:403); Voltaire, *Éléments de la philosophie de Newton* [1738], pt. 1, chap. 6 (*Oeuvres* 22:422; my italics); Beccaria, *Dei*, chap. 5, p. 43; chap. 28, p. 80; chap. 29, p. 88. These passages in Beccaria, *Dei*, contain ten other uses of *umano* in the sense of "human race." In the letter to Abbé Morellet of 26 January 1766, Beccaria recognizes his debt to Helvétius, who had opened his eyes to "the blindness and the misfortunes of umanity [sic]" (as translated in Venturi [1969–90], 1:677; see also Beccaria, *Dei*, chap. 46 [1:114] [sole use of the adjective]) (my italics); P. Verri, *Osservazioni*, #4, p. 78; #14, p. 147. Ten occurrences in the entire work, four of the adjective *umano*, once *inumanità*, #7, p. 108. On Jesus, #12, p. 134 (my italics).

16. W. A. Mozart, *Die Zauberflöte*, 1.12.

17. Rousseau, letter to M. de Franquières, 15 January 1769 (*OC* 4:136); Schalk (1966), 286; also see Schopenhauer, *Über die Grundlage der Moral*, chap. 3, #3 (*WW* 3:745). Barère, "Discours à la Convention," 7 prairial, year II (26 May 1794), *Archives parlementaires* 1 (91:38a); Carrier, in *Gazette nationale ou Le Moniteur universel*, no. 98 (28 December 1793), 57; the formulation became the title of Gérard's book (1999); Fritz Klein's response to Ella Lingens in Martin (2008), 114.

18. Lilla (1993), 16–23.

19. See the synthesis of Mercier (1960), Crocker (1959), 459; Spinoza, *Ethica*, pt. 5, prop. 36, scholia (*O* 1:267); prop. 42, scholia (*O* 1:273).

20. Rousseau, *Émile*, pt. 2 (*OC* 4:322); Boswell, *Johnson*, year 1766 (p. 320).

21. Voltaire, *Dictionnaire philosophique*, s.v. "Méchant" [wicked] (2:127); Gay (1969), 172. See above, 12.

22. Rousseau, in Gagnebin (1971), 42; Kant, *Mutmasslicher Anfang der Menschengeschichte* [1786] (*WW* 6:87–89). This way of looking at the matter is already refuted by Maimonides, *Guide* 1.2.

23. See above, 28–31; Koyré (1971b), 28; on the eclipse of divinization, see Taylor (2007), 224.

24. Gilbert, *Calejava*, bk. 2, 4th dialogue (pp. 15–16). The passage is cited in Hazard (1989), 141.

25. Rousseau, *Émile*, pt. 4 (*OC* 4:588).

26. Marquard (1981), 39–66.

27. Göchhausen, *Enthüllungen*; Barruel, *Mémoires*.

28. Poliakov (1968), 103–17 (Voltaire), 138–43 (d'Holbach), 165 (Mercier); Hitler, *MK*, pt. 1, chap. 11, pp. 317, 332. John Lukacs, in Negro (2009), 248.

29. Leroy (1992), 235–57.

30. Fichte, *Die Anweisung zum seligen Leben* [1806], 10th lesson (*AW* 5:260); Wordsworth, *Prelude*, bk. 8, lines 649–50. See (the critique in) Benson, *Lord*, bk. 2, chap. 7, sec. 2 (p. 200); Rousseau, *Confessions*, chap. 1 (*OC* 1:5).

31. E. Quinet, *Examen de la vie de Jésus par le Dr Strauss* [1838], in *Oeuvres* 8:211; Béranger, cited in Bénichou (2004), 879, then 814. Resurgence in Ferry (1996), 177; see also 245.

32. Michelet, *Peuple*, bk. 2, chap. 7 (p. 213); Bénichou (2004), 961; Swift, letter to Pope of 29 September 1725, no. 673, *Correspondence* (2:606–7); Mme. de Charrière, in Martin (2008), 251; Dostoyevsky, *Karamazov*, pt. 1, bk. 2, chap. 4, p. 60; see also Dostoyevsky, *The Dream of a Ridiculous Man*, chap. 5, p. 72;

symmetrical formulation in G. Sénac de Meilhan, *L'Émigré* [1794], letter 10, in Cheyron (1965), 1577.

33. Bénichou (2004), 310–13; Zilsel (1926), 203–8; Bonnet (1998), 206–9; E. Zola, *Lettres de Paris: Nouvelles artistiques et littéraires, Écrits sur l'art*, ed. J.-P. Leduc-Adine (Paris: Gallimard, 1991), 402, in Compagnon (1990), 55.

34. Collins, *Free-Thinking*, chap. 3, pp. 123–77; Hazard (1989), 245.

35. Kant, *Judgment*, paras. 46–50; Schaffer (1990); Goethe, *Dichtung und Wahrheit*, bk. 4, chap. 19 (*W* 5:680); Musil, *Mann*, bk. 1, chap. 13 (1:44); Arendt (1958), 210–11.

36. Jean Paul Richter, in Mulsow (2003), 739; Carlyle, *SRHW* (1840); Cassirer (1946), 189–223; see also Lasaulx, *PG*, chap. 5, pp. 90–99.

37. Robespierre, "Sur les rapports des idées religieuses et morales avec les principes républicains," 18 floréal, year II (7 May 1794), in *Discours*, pp. 279–80; Byron, *Don Juan*, canto 1, st. 1–5 (*SP*, 383–84); Zamoyski (2000), facing page 242.

38. On Lei Feng, see Leys (1998), 301, 324; on comrade Ogilvy, Orwell, *Nineteen Eighty-Four*, bk. 1, chap. 4, pp. 40–42.

39. Already in Comte, "Conclusion générale," in *Ensemble*, 472–76; then conclusion to 11th interview, tableau D, in *Catéchisme*, 339; Tenbruck (1984), 127–28.

40. Zamoyski (2000). On the Pantheon, see Bonnet (1998); Muray (1999); on Walhalla, see Assmann (1993). Bonald had a similar dream; see Burleigh (2005), 131.

41. Hagemeister (2005), 36–37; on Melnikov, see Starr (1981), 240–58.

42. Comte, *Ensemble*, chap. 2, p. 151, and "Conclusion générale," p. 474; prefiguration in *Plan*, 287. Analogous idea in Nodier, cited in Bénichou (2004), 207.

43. Burleigh (2005), 71.

Chapter 10. Moral Dominion

1. See above, 46–50.
2. See, for example, Merchant (1980).
3. Toulmin (1990), 121, 128; Boehme and Boehme (1983), 33–35; on the example of ballet, Lippe (1974).
4. Deuchler (1984); Eberle (1980), 33–39.
5. Gombrich (1953), 116–17.
6. Alain of Lille, *The Plaint of Nature* [*De planctu naturae*], chap. 7 (*Works*, pp. 84–89), in Raby (1959), 367–68n241; *Anticlaudianus* 2, lines 72–74 (*Works*, p. 266); Meung, *Rose*, lines 19505–32 (p. 517); Chaucer, *Tales*, "The Physician's Tale," line 20, in *Tales*, p. 175a.
7. Balthasar (1956), 31; Telesio, *Natura*; see Bacon, *De principiis atque originibus secundum fabulas cupidinis et coeli* (*Works* 1:79–118, esp. 114 [*novorum hominum primus*]).
8. Descartes, *Le Monde*, chap. 7 (*OC* 11:37); Nobis (1967).
9. Gómez Pereira, *Antoniana Margarita* [. . .] (1554); Descartes, letter to Henry More, 5 February 1649 (*OC* 5:276–79).
10. Boyle, *W* 1:15; in Passmore (1974), 11.

11. Spenser, *Faerie Queene*, bk. 7 ("Mutabilitie"), canto 7, st. 5–6 (2:441); cited in Armogathe (2007), 202; Brague (2002b), 285–86. Add Chekhov, *Step'* [1888], 6, beginning, in *Izbrannye* 133a; in French trans., 104; compare with Goethe, *Wilhelm Meisters Wanderjahre*, bk. 1, chap. 10 (*Werke* 8:119).

12. See below, 114–15. Prefiguration in Zwingli, in Groh (2003), 660.

13. Locke, *STG*, chap. 5, paras. 25–61 (pp. 14–27); Strauss (1953), 248; Manent (1994), 167, 174; Locke, *STG*, chap. 5, paras. 32 (p. 17), 35 (pp. 18–19). On the patristic interpretation of Genesis 1:26b, see above, 21–22; Locke, *STG*, chap. 5, paras. 27 (p. 15), 43 (p. 23); chap. 19, para. 222 (p. 110).

14. Vico, *Scienza nuova* [1744], bk. 1, sec. 3, para. 331 (*O*, 541–42); Brague (2002b), 322.

15. Rousseau, *Contrat social*, bk. 1, chap. 8 (*OC* 3:364); my italics. Rosen (1969), 77. On Marx, see below, 123. For Hobbes, the contractors are already humans: *Leviathan*, pt. 2, chap. 17, p. 112; Rousseau, *Émile*, first version (Favre Manuscript) (*OC* 4:1268).

16. Kant, preface to *Anthropologie in pragmatischer Hinsicht* (*WW* 6:399).

17. Homer, *Iliad* 9.498; Pindar, *Isthmian Odes* 5.6; Brague (1988), 207.

18. Cicero, *Finibus* 3.6.20 (p. 95).

19. Seneca, *Lucilius*, bk. 14, letter 1 (89), para. 14 (p. 328); Augustine, *De doctrina christiana* 1.27.28, ed. M. Moreau (BA, vol. 11, pt. 2, p. 112); Traherne, *Centuries*, bk. 1, poem 12 (p. 7); in Lewis (2000), chap. 1, p. 16.

20. Montaigne, *Essays*, bk. 1, chap. 14 (1:109).

21. Descartes, letter to Princess Elisabeth, 1 September 1645 (*OC* 4:284); *Les passions de l'âme*, pt. 2, chap. 138 (*OC* 11:431). My italics.

22. See above, 97; Buffon, "Première vue," in *La Nature* (*OP*, 33b–34b); Rousseau, *Émile*, pt. 4 (*OC* 4:582); Diderot, article "Encyclopédie," in *Encyclopédie* 5:641ab; Morelly, *Code de la nature*, pt. 3 (*OP*, 338); Schabert (1969), 60.

23. S. T. Coleridge, "Dejection: An Ode" [1802], st. 4, line 48.

24. Kant, *Judgment*, para. 86 (pp. 312–13 [410–12]); Séris (1994), 330–31.

25. Nietzsche, *Also sprach Zarathustra*, pt. 1, chap. 15, "Von tausend und einem Ziele" (*KSA* 4:75). Heidegger, *Humanism*, 179.

Chapter 11. The Duty to Reign

1. Starobinski (1964), 22.

2. Locke, *STG*, chap. 5, para. 34 (p. 18); Taylor (2007), 167.

3. The theme has become hackneyed since Max Weber. See Bollnow (1958), 31–65; Münch (1984); Wenzel (1960); Koyré (1971a), 311–29.

4. Maimonides, *Treatise on Ethics*, chap. 6.

5. Thomas à Kempis, *Imitation*, bk. 2, chap. 53, paras.13–14 (p. 242) (my italics); Chaucer, "The Parson's Tale," line 261, in *Tales*, p. 279b; Cervantes, *Quijote*, pt. 2, chap. 72 (p. 1093).

6. Corneille, *Cinna*, act 5, scene 3; Milton, *Defensio secunda pro populo anglicano*, in *Works* 8:214; Lachterman (1989), 203; for an ironic reversal of Corneille's formulation, see Bossi (2003), 359.

7. Descartes, *Traité des passions*, pt. 1, art. 50 (*OC* 11:370); Taylor (2007), 130, 133; Dupré (2004), 55–56; Rousseau, "Lettre à M. de Franquières" (1769) (*OC* 4:1143) (my italics); Hegel, *Jenaer*, 273.

8. Sartre, *Being*, pt. 4, chap. 1, secs. 1 and 3 (pp. 515, 639).

9. Kant, *KRV*, A534/B562; Berlin (1999), 76; *Judgment*, para. 83 (pp. 299–300 [390–391]); para. 84 (p. 304 [398], p. 305 [399] and n., p. 306 [399]).

10. Kant, *Judgment*, para. 83 (p. 303 [395]); Arendt (1958), 156; Kant, *Judgment*, para. 84 (p. 305 [398]).

11. Kant, "Appendix to the First Section: On a Pure Mysticism in Religion," chap. 1 in *Der Streit der Fakultäten* [1798] (*WW* 6:341).

12. Schiller, *Über das Erhabene* [around 1793] (*S*, 130); Berlin (1999), 80–81; Schiller, *Über die ästhetische Erziehung des Menschen in einer Reihe von Briefen* [1795], 25 (*S*, 269–73); Ritter, "Landschaft: Zur Funktion des Ästhetischen in der modernen Gesellschaft" [1963], in Ritter (1974), 158–61; Starobinski (1964), 205b; Séris (1994), 328.

13. Kant, *Opus postumum*, first file, fourth quire, p. 2 (*Nachlass*, 8:45); Lachterman (1989), 17.

14. Fichte, *Berichtigung*, bk. 1, chap. 1, p. 69; *Grundlage des Naturrechts* [1796], II, #6, η, and corollaria (*AW* 2:83–88). On these anthropological themes, see Brague (2002b), 135, 146–50.

15. Fichte, *Über die Würde des Menschen* [1794] (*Werke* 1:412–16).

16. Cicero, *Finibus* 4.13.34 (p. 135).

17. Pliny the Elder, *Historia naturalis* 7.preface.1–4.

18. Aristotle, *De anima* 3.4.429b31, and see a21.

19. Rouvillois (2010), 75.

20. Fichte, *Die Bestimmung des Menschen* [1800], bk. 1 (*AW* 3:288–89), then *Der geschlossene Handelsstaat* [1800], bk. 1, chap. 3 (*AW* 3:452); Berlin (1990), 227.

21. Fichte, *Die Staatslehre* [1813], sec. 3, "Deduktion des Gegenstands der Menschengeschichte" (*AW* 6:523–24). See also Schelling, *Neue Deduktion des Naturrechts* [1795], #7 (*AW* [1794–98], 128); Novalis, *Vorarbeiten 1798*, para. 124 (*WTB* 2:343): "The world ought to be as I will."

22. Koyré (1966a), 81. The rapprochement between positivism and Proclus's prudence is already found in Duhem, *Essai*, 23–24.

23. Bacon, letter to P. Redemptus Baranzano, 30 June 1622 (*Works* 14:375); Morelly, *Code de la nature*, pt. 4, "Law concerning Studies," then arts. 4 and 5 (*OP*, 369–70).

24. Locke, *An Essay concerning Human Understanding* [1677], in *Political*, 261; d'Holbach, *Système de la nature*, vol. 1, bk. 1, chap. 1, p. 2, in Lubac (1998), 163n1.

25. Comte, *Plan*, 283; without reference in Black (1970), 30, *Plan*, 255; Aristotle, *Nicomachean Ethics*, 9.9.1170b10–12.

26. Comte, *Plan*, 276, 277, 304, 318, and again 277. My italics. For a curious parallel in a Chinese contemporary of Descartes, Wang Fuzhi, see Linck (1999), 108.

27. Fourier, "Discours préliminaire," in *Théorie analytique de la chaleur* (Paris, 1822), 1, in Saint-Sernin (2007), 284.

28. Comte, *Esprit*, chap. 1, p. 138; *Cours*, 58th lesson (2:719–20, 727, 730, 736); 60th lesson 2:771); *Ensemble*, chap. 1, p. 78; *Ensemble*, "Conclusion générale," p. 544; *Système* 1:66–68; Lubac (1998), 168–69.

29. Comte, *Cours*, 2nd lesson (1:45); *Cours*, 49th lesson (2:165–66).

30. B. Russell (1992).

31. Comte, *Ensemble*, chap. 5, p. 415, and see chap. 1, p. 69; *Cours*, 58th lesson (2:707–8, 711, 715); 59th lesson (2:756, then 751; see also 757).

32. Bernard, introduction, pt. 1, chap. 1, sec. 4, p. 48; pt. 1, chap. 2, sec. 10, p. 130; pt. 3, chap. 4, sec. 3, p. 290. I do not know if it is a citation or a formulation by the modern scholar himself.

33. Bernard, *Introduction*, pt. 2, chap. 2, sec. 10, p. 209, then p. 202; pt. 2, chap. 2, sec. 9, p. 198 (my italics). The first sentence has strange syntax: "to gain ground on" (and not "for") signifies to diminish the power of something. I am tempted to correct: "to gain the sure ground of determinism."

34. Bernard, *Introduction*, pt. 1, chap. 1, sec. 2, p. 42 (my italics).

35. Bernard, *Introduction*, pt. 2, chap. 1, sec. 4, p. 107 (my italics).

36. See Nietzsche, frag. 15 [51], Spring 1888 (*KSA* 13:442); an analogous formulation, perhaps a memory, in Dupré (1993), 73. Prefiguration in Lichtenberg, in Gay (1969), 165. I have not found the original. See also Ferrarin (2001), 129.

37. Bernard, *Introduction*, pt. 1, chap. 2, [foreword], p. 60; pt. 1, chap. 2, sec. 6, p. 85 (italics original). C. Delsol tells me that the formulation is found in Valéry, *Regards sur le monde actuel*, in *Oeuvres*, 2:1105. This epistemology gives all its rigor to the formulation which characterizes the *anemelectroreculpedalicoupeventombrosoparacloucycle* of Z. Brioché, which uses "all the propulsive forces, known and even unknown." Christophe, *Idée*, eighth song (p. 155); my italics.

38. Descartes, *Meditationes de prima philosophia*, meditation 4 (*OC* 7:58).

39. Bernard, *Introduction*, pt. 2, chap. 1, sec. 4, p. 108; Bernard, appendix to *Leçons*, 397.

40. Augustinus Triumphus, *Summa de potestate ecclesiastica* [1326], chap. 32, para. 3 (Rome, 1585), p. 194 (in Wilks [1963], 170n2), which comes close to a declaration of Nero in Suetonius, *Nero* 32.3 (*Caesars* 2:146).

41. Bernard, *Introduction*, pt. 2, chap. 1, sec. 9, p. 126.

42. Bernal, *WFD*, chap. 5, p. 62 (my italics).

43. See, for example, Buddha, *Aggivacchagotta Sutta* (no. 72), in *Teachings*, 590–94, esp. 591–92; Shankara, *Svâtma-nirûpana*, 93, in Glasenapp (1948), 74–75; Epictetus, *Discourses* 1.8.4–10; Augustine, *De utilitate credendi* 9.22 (BA 8:256); Thomas Aquinas, *ST* II-II.166–67; Petrarch, *Ignorantia* 4 (p. 103).

44. Berlin (1999), 88–89.

45. F. C. S. Schiller, "The Definition of Pragmatism and Humanism," in *Studies*, 1–21; citations from 12, 16. *HWPh*, s.v. "Humanismus" (vol. 3, cols. 1217–30; by C. Menze, R. Romberg, and I. Pape), omits this English use. See also F. C. S. Schiller, *Humanism*; James, "Humanism and Truth" [October 1904], in *Meaning*, 52–53.

46. Rorty (1981).

Chapter 12. The Iron Rod

1. Kuhn (1977), 142; citation: Séris (1994), 210.
2. Moscovici (1968), 422–27; Saint-Sernin (2007), 182; on Liebig, see Gregory (2012), 352.
3. Russo (1986), 401–14, in Séris (1994), 30; see also the reflections on a huge power failure in North America in Anders (2002b), 121–22.
4. Moscovici (1968), 98–100; on Berthelot, cited in Moscovici (1968), 393, 399.
5. Bulwer-Lytton, *Race*, chap. 7, p. 21.
6. Comte, *Cours*, 60th lesson (2:786); my italics. The pronoun "I" refers to an unexpressed subject, "man," drawn from "each one"; *Esprit*, chap. 1, p. 162. On anticipation in baroque poetry, Friedrich (1964), 583, 660–61.
7. See, for example, Cicero, *Gods* 1.33.92 (p. 447); 2.22.57 (p. 684 and note p. 685a); 32.81 (p. 752 and note p. 752a); 57.142 (p. 919); Galen, *Facultés* 1.6 (p. 24) and 13.35 (p. 56); Close (1969); quotation of Marsilio Ficino, *Théologie* 4.12 (p. 258; see also pp. 146–47 and Joseph Addison, *The Spectator*, no. 414 [25 June 1742]).
8. Novalis, "Die Natur," chap. 2 in *Die Lehrlinge zu Sais* (*WTB* 1:210–11); letter of William Lovell to E. Burton, in L. Tieck, *William Lovell*, bk. 3, chap. 10 (*Werke* 1:333); other texts in Brague (2002b), 293–305.
9. On Mill, see Brague (2002b), 296–97; Schopenhauer, *Paralipomena*, chap. 9, #125 (*WW* 5:292–93). The fact is emphasized by Horkheimer (1967), "Die Aktualität Schopenhauers" [1961], p. 250. On the Romantic sources of Schopenhauer, see Hübscher (1973), 30–63 and 309–13.
10. Vigny, "La maison du berger" [1844], pt. 3, strophes 9–11 (prosopopoeia of nature), in *Les Destinées* (*PC*, 140–41).
11. Heine, *Lutezia* [1855], letter 17 of 5 May 1843 (*Frankreich*, 510).
12. Hawthorne, *The House of the Seven Gables* [1851], chap. 17. See also Hergé, *Lune*, 32, and P. G. Wodehouse, *Pigs Have Wings*, chap. 3, beginning; Adams, *Education*, chap. 25 [1900], pp. 317–26. Critical response: "The Dynamo and the Virgin Reconsidered," in White (1968), 57–73; Eckermann, *Goethe*, 21 February 1827 (pp. 599–600); Weber, *Entlastung*, 4.
13. Verne, *De la Terre à la Lune* [1864], chap. 28, last words of the chapter and the book; then chap. 7.
14. Verne, *Île*, pt. 1, chap. 6, pp. 65–66; pt. 1, chap. 9, p. 107; pt. 1, chap. 19, p. 259 (the quotation marks are in the text); pt. 3, chap. 15, p. 199.
15. Vernes, *Île*, pt. 2, chap. 14, p. 211; chap. 2, p. 27 (citation); pt. 3, chap. 11, p. 143, 146; pt. 1, chap. 4, p. 49; pt. 2, chap. 10, p. 151.
16. Verne, *Île*, pt. 1, chap. 20, p. 273; pt. 2, chap. 8, p. 119; pt. 3, chap. 8, p. 110.
17. Verne, *Les Cinq Cents Millions de la Bégum*, chap. 8; see also Benson, *Lord*, bk. 3, chap. 1, sec. 1 (p. 222).
18. Flaubert, *Bouvard et Pécuchet* (1881), extract of the plan (*OC* 2:300b–301a).
19. Wells, *Men*. The same title, in Russian, was used by the Soviet novelist S. Snegov (1966–68); Snegov is mentioned in Heller and Niqueux (1995), 253.
20. Wells, *Men*, bk. 1, chap. 5, pp. 55–56, 63; bk. 3, chap. 2, p. 186; chap. 4, p. 220; bk. 2, chap. 1, p. 127.

21. Wells, *Men*, bk. 3, chap. 4, p. 220; bk. 2, chap. 4, p. 166; bk. 1, chap. 6, p. 72; bk. 2, chap. 1, p. 125 (the term was not yet compromised by the "great [Stalinist] cleansing" [*bolšaya tšistka*] of 1936); bk. 3, chap. 2, p. 188.

22. Wells, *Men*, bk. 1, chap. 5, p. 57; see also bk. 2, chap. 1, p. 124; bk. 1, chap. 6, p. 81; bk. 1, chap. 5, p. 64; chap. 6, p. 74; bk. 2, chap. 1, p. 127, then bk. 2, chap. 2, p. 137; bk. 3, chap. 2, p. 203; bk. 1, chap. 6, p. 74.

23. Wells, *Men*, bk. 1, chap. 6, pp. 81–82; a character approximates Tennyson, *In Memoriam*, sec. 56. For the context, see Brague (2002a), 314. And see Wells, *Men*, bk. 2, chap. 3, p. 165 (allusion to the verse of A. E. Housman: "whatever brute or blackguard made the world").

24. Wells, *Men*, bk. 1, chap. 6, pp. 82–83.

25. Robitaille (2007), 127, and the letter to Mother Nature of "Max More" [1999] cited on 121.

26. For the context of the whole, before and after the revolution, Billington (1970), 478–92: *Prometheanism*; on the beginnings of the Soviet era, see Stites (1989); Hagemeister (1989), 241–61.

27. Lenin, *Les Tâches immédiates du pouvoir des soviets* [The immediate tasks of the Soviet government] [April 1918] (*Oeuvres* 27:245–87; here: chap. 5, p. 268).

28. M. Gorki, "O znanii," in *Arkhiv*, vol. 12, pp. 101–11, citation from p. 111; Anonymous, *Proletarskaja ētika* (1906) [*non vidi*], after Hagemeister (1983), 17; Rozkov, *Smyl'*, 19 [*non vidi*], Russian in Hagemeister (1983), 17. See above on Marsilio Ficino, 48; Murav'ev, *Domination du Temps* [The mastery of time], 103, in Hagemeister (2005), 53.

29. See the film *Experiments in the Revival of Organisms* (1940), http:www.archive.org/details/Experime1940; M. Bulgakov, *Coeur de chien* [1925]; Joravsky (1970).

30. Büchner, *Kraft*, 268, or the popular edition (1894), 157–58. The first edition dates from 1855. The chapter "Der Mensch," where the idea is found, is still missing in the 8th edition of 1864. Quotation is from Büchner, *Vorlesungen*, 253; Benz (1961a), 94.

Chapter 13. The New Meaning of Humanism

1. Stroh (2008), 535–38, 567–68.

2. Campana (1946) and Kristeller (1944–45). *OED*, s.v. "humanism," p. 1944b–c. Littré only records the historiographical meaning invented by the German historian H. Voigt (1859). On the history of the word, see *GG*, s.v. "Menschheit, Humanität, Humanismus" (3:1121–26 [H. E. Bödeker]), and *HWPh*, s.v. "Humanismus" (vol. 3, cols. 1217–30 [various authors]). See example in Duby's title (1966), and see 171–77 (glorification of the flesh).

3. Rüegg (1973), 186.

4. Feuerbach, *Grundsätze der Philosophie der Zukunft*, #15 (*KS*, 164–65); #54 (*KS*, 216); in Lubac (1998), 25n2 (italics original).

5. Feuerbach, *Kritik des 'Anti-Hegel'* [1835] (*KS*, 56); Hobbes, epistle dedicatory to *De cive* (*Opera* 2:135–36); Spinoza, *Ethica*, pt. 4, prop. 35, scholia (*O* 1:206);

for memory: *homo homini lupus* (Plautus, *Asinaria* 495). In another context, Bacon, *Organon*, bk. 1, para. 129 (p. 268).

6. Feuerbach, *Christianity*, bk. 2, chap. 7, "Schlußanwendung," p. 444; *Zur Kritik der Hegelschen Philosophie* (*KS*, 122); *Notwendigkeit einer Veränderung* [1842/ 43], marginal note, in *KS*, 223n1.

7. Tschižewskij (1930), 266; on the origin of the term in ancient Christianity, heretical (Montanus) and orthodox (Clement of Alexandria, Origen), see Benz (1961b).

8. Feuerbach, *Vorläufige Thesen zur Reform der Philosophie* [1842], [#1] (*KS*, 124); [#13], (*KS*, 126; *Grundsätze*, #12 (*KS*, 158).

9. Feuerbach, *Vorläufige Thesen*, [#49] (*KS*, 137). The adjective "theandric" is current from the time of Pseudo-Dionysius (*Letter IV to Gaius* [PG 3:1072c]); one finds *theandria* once in Pseudo-Methodius of Olympus and *theanthrōpotēs* in John Damascene, but these substantives remained without issue (see *PGL*, 615a–616a). The term "theandrism" (bogotšelovetsvo), which has become familiar in contemporary Orthodox theology, is not found before the lectures of Soloviev (1877), 2nd lecture, final words (*RO* 3:26). But in 1872, the Kirillov of Dostoyevsky already turned "man-god" into "god-man" (*Demons*, pt. 2, bk. 1, chap. 5, p. 218).

10. Feuerbach, *Grundsätze*, #1, then #52 (*KS*, 145, 214).

11. Marx, introduction to *Zur Kritik der Hegelschen Rechtsphilosophie* (*FS*, 283). On Marx's humanism, see M. Henry (1976), 2:84–120; first sentence of the preface to Engels, *Die Heilige Familie* (Marx/Engels, *WW* 2:7; 6:132, then 139); Marx, *Manuscripts*, no. 3, p. 86 (*FS*, 309). The mistake in the second sentence is in the original.

12. Marx, *Manuscripts*, no. 3, p. 98 (*FS*, 320; my italics); Engels, *Die Heilige Familie*, bk. 4, chap. 1, "Flora Tristan" (Marx/Engels, *WW* 2:20); Arendt (1958), 86; Rosen (1969), 201.

13. On Rousseau, see above, 98; Bakunin, *Fédéralisme, socialisme et anti-théologisme*, 2 (*Oeuvres*, 36); 3 (*Oeuvres*, 65–66, 85, 110).

14. Marx, *Manuscripts*, no. 3, p. 97 (*FS*, 319); see the severe pages of Voegelin (2004), 17–21.

15. Proudhon, prologue to *Système*, p. xxv; *Système*, vol. 1, chap. 5, pp. 253, 388–89, 397–98; Lubac (1998), 22.

16. Renan, *Avenir*, chap. 5, *OC* 3:809; Comte, "Conclusion générale," in *Ensemble*, 467, 470, 472.

17. Tchernychevski [Chernyshevsky], *Antropologičeskij*, 7:222–95; *Philosophiques*, 47–134, esp. pt. 1, p. 68 [Russian p. 240], and pt. 2, p. 132 [Russian p. 294]; Besançon (1977), 124–25.

18. Galileo, *DMS*, First Day, pp. 62–63; Brague (2006a), 283–84, and already Proclus, *Timée* 4 (3:141–44).

19. Bossi (2003), 112; Gutzkow, "Die Nihilisten," chap. 5; in *Selbsttaufe*, p. 305; Comte, introduction to *Synthèse*, 14; see also 23, 34, 50, 53–54, 107; Leroux, *Humanité*, bk. 5, chaps. 1–3 (pp. 173–79).

20. Heine, *Religion*, bk. 1, p. 83; bk. 2, p. 122; *Deutschland, ein Wintermärchen*, chap. 1, lines 37–48, cited from 46–48; *Sämtliche* 4:578. The verses are still cited by Freud, *Die Zukunft einer Illusion*, chap. 9, end (*Werke* 14:374); Marx, *Manuscripts*,

no. 3, pp. 136–37 (*FS*, 332); on this passage, see Granel (1972), 217. See reminiscence of Goethe in *Grenzen der Menschheit* [1789], lines 21–24: "Steht er mit *festen*, / Markigen Knochen / Auf der *wohlgegründeten*, / Dauernden *Erde*" (W 1:63; added emphasis indicates words of Goethe's poem echoed by Marx); Bakunin, letter to Varvara Alexandrovna of 9 March 1836, in Kornilov, *Molodye*, 187; Bakunin to Alexandrovna, 10 August 1836, in Kornilov, *Molodye*, 226–27, itself cited in Sarkisyanz (1955), 39; Nietzsche, preface to *Also sprach Zarathustra*, 3 (*KSA* 4:15); *Also sprach Zarathustra*, pt. 1, "Von der schenkenden Tugend," sec. 2 (*KSA* 4:99); Joyce, *A Portrait of the Artist as a Young Man* [1916], chap. 4, end, in *Essential*, 187.

21. A. K. Gastev, "My posyagnuli" [We encroached], in Rodov, *Proletarskie*, 231–33; Sarkisyanz (1955), 43; on Gastev, see Johansson (1983).

22. Venturelli (2008), 351–53; Keller, letter to Wilhelm Baumgarten of 27 March 1851 (*Briefe* 1:290).

23. Jacobsen, *Niels Lyhne*, chap. 9, end, *Samlede Vaerker*, ed. F. Nielsen (Copenhagen: Rosenkilde og Bagger, 1973), 2:129–30; German trans. A. Matthiesen, *Sämtliche Werke*, Leipzig, Insel, n.d., 468); cited in Rehm (1947), 225–26; Dostoyevsky, *The Adolescent*, pt. 3, chap. 7, sec. 3 (*Oeuvres* 8:597–98); Taylor (1989), 411; Dostoyevsky, *Karamazov*, pt. 1, bk. 1, chap. 5, p. 29.

24. Hofmann (2010), 53; on Marx, see above, 123.

25. Nerval, *Aurélia*, pt. 2, chap. 4, p. 167; Diderot, *Pensées détachées sur la peinture*, in *Oeuvres esthétiques*, 771; Starobinski (1964), 146a; see the poem by Gottfried Benn referenced by Blumenberg (1957), 171.

26. Benson, *Lord*, bk. 1, chap. 5, sec. 2 (pp. 87–88).

27. "Sincere Brethren," *Risâla*, 323; J. C. Lavater, *Aussichten in die Ewigkeit: Gemeinnütziger Auszug aus dem größeren Werk dieses Namens* (Zurich, 1781), 109, in Benz (1961a), 61; Fichte, *Sittenlehre* [1798], pt. 3, para. 18, sec. 4 (*AW* 2:623); the image is in a novel of Cather, *Archbishop*, bk. 9, chap. 4, p. 275.

28. Marx, *Manuscripts*, no. 1, p. 61; again in 1858 in the *Grundrisse*, chap. 5, p. 388; see also pp. 384, 391; *Manuscripts*, no. 1, pp. 65 and 58; *Introduction générale à la critique de l'économie politique*, in Karl Marx, *Oeuvres: Economie*, trans. M. Rubel, Bibliothèque de la Pléiade (Paris: Gallimard, 1965), 1:240; *Manuscripts*, no. 3, p. 95 (*FS*, 317); *Deutsche Ideologie*, pt. 1; *FS*, 42.

29. Marx, *Manifest der Kommunistischen Partei*, 1 (*FS*, 600); *Randglossen zum Programm der deutschen Arbeiter-partei* [1875], I, 1 (Marx/Engels, *WW* 19:15; French trans. in *Oeuvres: Economie*, 1:1413); *Capital*, pt. 5, chap. 14, p. 455 (*Oeuvres: Economie* 1:1005–6).

30. Engels, *Sozialismus*, chap. 3, pp. 84–85.

31. Renan, *Avenir*, chap. 4, *OC* 3:792, then chap. 10, *OC* 3:1049; see also chap. 2, *OC* 3:753.

32. Bergson, *Sources*, chap. 4, p. 329.

Chapter 14. The Sole Lord

1. Alfred Schmidt (1982) only poses the question in the title of his short essay.

2. Nelson (1967), 3; Webster (1975).

3. Strauss (1964), 42–44.
4. Voegelin (1952), 124–32, then (1968), 32, 40, 81.
5. Blumenberg (1988), 137–259; Brague (2013), 163–86; Wieland (1983), 270.
6. Fried (2001); Groh (2003), 449–50.
7. Garrigues (1982), 22–44, citation on 36; Brague (2008c), 397; Batut (2009), chap. 6, sec. 3, pp. 507–29.
8. See, to only cite an example of the highest distinction, Guillou, *Père*, 140; contra, Manent (2010b), 148–49.
9. Comte, *Esprit*, 1, p. 155; also see Nietzsche, frag. Autumn 1887, 10 [7] (*KSA* 12:457).
10. See above, 114.
11. Proudhon, *Système*, vol. 1, chap. 8, sec. 2, pp. 414–15; Mittelstrass (1970), 347.
12. Vega, *Anticristo*, line 159, pp. 425–56; Armogathe (2005), 247; Eichendorff, "Über die ethische und religiöse Bedeutung der neueren romantischen Poesie in Deutschland" [1847] (*Werke* 3:52, 54, 63).
13. Charles de Bovelles, *De sapiente*, chap. 8, in Cassirer (1927), 320; F. Bacon, *De sapientia veterum*, 26 (*Works* 6:668–76, esp. 675–76); Rossi (2007), 183–88; Ferrarin (2001), 29–65.
14. Vico, *Scienza nuova*, explanation of the frontispiece, para. 3 (*O*, 416); Hegel, *Vorlesungen*, pt. 2, sec. 2, subsection 2 (The religion of beauty), subsection B (The figure of the divine), item a (The struggle of the spiritual and the natural; *Vorlesungen* 16:106–9); Starobinski (1964), 146b; Fellmann (1976), 72–77; Blumenberg (1984), pt. 3; Dupré (1993), 113.
15. Diderot, *Réfutation de l'ouvrage d'Helvétius intitulé l'Homme* (*Oeuvres* 2:431–32); Marx, preface to *Differenz der demokritischen und epikureischen Naturphilosophie* [1841] (supplement to *W*, 1968, pp. 262–63); Landes (1969), title and 24.
16. Haldane, *Daedalus*, 46–48 and see 92.
17. See above, 86.
18. Cicero, *Gods* 2.6.16 (p. 590) and 3.10.26 (p. 1017); cited above, 10.
19. Bonaventure, "L'homme de bien," lines 10–13 (*Oeuvres*, 82); the expression that I italicize is cited, but without a reference, by R. Philippe in Baille (1963), 491a.
20. Feuerbach, *Vorläufige Thesen*, #69 (*KS*, 144 [last words]); Lautréamont, *Chants*, no. 5, sec. 3 (p. 279); context in Carrouges (1948), 79.
21. Ignatius of Loyola, *Ejercicios espirituales*, 2nd week, #169–88 (*OC*, 231–35).
22. Descartes, *Discours de la méthode*, pt. 2 (*OC* 6:13–14); on the transformation of the principle into a social rule, see Gregory (2012), 115, 164, 171, 215, 217.
23. See, for example, Themistius, *In libros Aristotelis "De anima" paraphrasis* 5.4, ed. R. Heinze, pp. 92, 13–29 (*CAG* 5:3).
24. Dionysius the Areopagite, *Hiérarchie céleste* [Celestial hierarchy] 3.2 (PG 3:165bc).
25. See *HWPh*, s.v. "Vorurteil," in vol. 11 (2001), cols. 1250–63 (K. Reisinger, O. R. Scholz); Descartes, *Principia Philosophiae*, pt. 1, art. 71 (*OC* 8:35–36); Letter to M. C. L. R. [Clerselier], 12 January 1646 (*OC*, vol. 9, pt. 1, p. 204).

26. Spinoza, *Ethica*, pt. 1, appendix (*O* 1:67); Malebranche, *De la recherche de la Vérité*, bk. 2, pt. 2, chap. 7, sec. 1 (*O* 1:230).

27. See, already, H. B. de Longepierre, *Discours sur les Anciens* [1687], in *QAM*, 286–290; then Burke, *Revolution*, 76; J. de Maistre, "4ième Lettre d'un royaliste savoisien," in *Écrits*, 35; Wordsworth, *Prelude*, bk. 8, lines 322–27 ("prepossession"); Taine, *Origines*, pt. 1, *L'Ancien Régime*, bk. 3, chap. 2, sec. 2 (1:155–58).

28. Tenbruck (1984), 252.

29. Locke, *Essay concerning Human Understanding*, ed. P. Nidditch (Oxford: Clarendon Press, 1975), bk. 3, chap. 5, para. 3 (p. 429); Manent (1994), 168.

30. Marx, *Capital*, pt. 1, chap. 1, sec. 4, p. 70.

31. Defoe, *Robinson*, 81, 93; 80, 84, 88, 138; 84–85, 133; 83; 87, 182; 178–82.

32. Defoe, *Robinson*, 104; 90, 112, 127, 192, 246.

33. Ozouf (1989), 117; Schabert (1971), from whom I borrow the expression.

34. Chastellux, *Félicité* (2:313); Becker (1932), 93–94.

35. Ozouf (1989), 155.

36. The formulation was proposed by Charles Thomson on 20 June 1782. It comes from Virgil, *Bucolics* 4.5, which lacks the chief adjective *novus*. *Rerum novus nascitur ordo* seems to be an invention of Diderot (or a memory failure), in *Rêve de D'Alembert* (*Oeuvres philosophiques*, 300). The verse figures in an interesting passage of Bayle, *Nouvelles Lettres critiques sur l'histoire du calvinisme* [1685], vol. 2, p. 274b (*Oeuvres* 2:274b), but the tone of the context is not that which Schabert assumes (1971), 14. See also Arendt (1963), 211–15.

37. Paine, *Common Sense*, appendix (*Rights*, 299); then *Rights of Man*, pt. 2, chap. 4 (*Rights*, 153). The two texts are cited in Ozouf (1989), 126n1; Jared Eliot, in Glacken (1967), 692.

38. See, for example, Plato, *Laws* 3.702d; Ibn Khaldun, introduction to *Muqaddima* (1:52, lines 8–10).

39. Saint-Étienne, *Considérations*, 1–105, citation from #1, p. 11; Fichte, *Berichtigung*, bk. 1, chap. 1, pp. 64–82; Wordsworth, *Prelude*, bk. 6, line 341.

40. Chénier, "Discours"; Boissy d'Anglas, "Quelques idées sur les arts, sur la nécessité de les encourager, adressées à la Convention nationale et au Comité d'instruction publique" (*Procès-verbaux* 3.637–56), Billaud-Varenne, *Réimpression de l'Ancien Moniteur* 20:263; Ozouf (1989), 125n1, 133, 140.

41. Mirabeau, *Premier discours, De l'instruction publique ou de l'organisation du corps enseignant*, in Baczko (1982), 81; Ozouf (1989), 128; Burke, *Revolution*, 27; Maistre, *Considérations sur la Révolution française*, pt. 5 (*Écrits*, 134).

42. Paine, *Rights of Man*, I, 1 (*Rights*, 35, 37), then *Common Sense* (*Rights*, 257–60); Brague (2008c), 79–84.

43. Paine, *Rights of Man*, I, 1 (*Rights*, 35).

44. Robespierre, "Sur la nouvelle Déclaration des droits," 24 April 1793, in *Discours*, p. 128; Arendt (1951), 380.

45. Marx, preface to *Differenz der demokritischen und epikureischen Naturphilosophie* [1841]; cited above, 131.

46. See, for example, F. Engels, "Die Lage Englands" (review of Carlyle, *Past and Present*) [1843] (Marx/Engels, *WW* 1:545); Nietzsche, *Die fröhliche Wissenschaft*, pt. 4, aphorism 285 (*KSA* 3:528).

47. See appendix A, no. 355, William Steele to Jonathan D. Steele, September 1825, in Farrand, *Convention* 3:472–73; to the contrary, James Madison, on Thursday, 28 June, reports nothing of the sort; see Farrand, *Convention* 1:451–52.

48. Comte, *Cours*, 58th lesson (2:712); *Ensemble*, "Conclusion générale," 452, 457, 500; *Cours*, 57th lesson (2:664); Leo XIII, encyclical *Libertas praestantissimum*, 20 June 1888, para. 15; *Acta Santae Sedis*, 20 (1887), pp. 893–913, cited from p. 900.

49. Kant, *Opus Postumum*, first file, second quire, p. 4 (Werke/Berlin 21:25); first file, eleventh quire, p. 2 (21:144–45); seventh file, tenth quire, p. 2 (22:120), and seventh file, tenth quire, p. 4 (22:130); Schwarz (2004). *Est deus in nobis* is in Ovid, *Fastes* 6.5.5, or *Ars Amatoria* 3.5.549; Schiller, *Über Anmut und Würde* (S, 188); Berlin (1990), 220; N. de Bonneville, *Appendices de la seconde édition de l'Esprit des religions [. . .]* (Paris, 1792), #45, "L'homme est Tout," p. 95; cited (without the capital "T") in Bénichou (2004), 75. See also #46, p. 97.

50. See, for example, Jean Paul, *Clavis Fichtiana seu Leibgeberiana* [1800], Anhang zum 1. Komischen Anhang des Titans (Werke/Miller 3:1011–56), in particular *Clavis*, #6, "Aseitas" (Werke/Miller 3:1033).

51. Heine, *Berichtigung* [1849] (Werke 7:354); letter to Heinrich Laube, 12 October 1850 (9:363); letter to Saint-René Taillandier, 3 November 1851 (9:447); *Geständnisse* [1854] (7:127); Rosen (1987), 106, and (1999), 273, 277.

52. Heine, *Religion*, preface to the second edition [1852], 59; *Religion* [1833/34], bk. 2, p. 124; Topitsch (1973), 37; Péguy, "Un poète l'a dit" [1907] (*Oeuvres* 2:855).

53. Baudelaire, "Le poème du Haschich," pt. 4, "L'Homme-Dieu," in *Les Paradis artificiels* (OC, pp. 372–83); Arendt (1951), 279 (Cecil Rhodes); Dostoyevsky, *Demons*, pt. 1, bk. 3, chap. 8, pp. 103–8; pt. 2, bk. 1, chap. 5, pp. 212–21; pt. 3, bk. 5, chap. 5, pp. 527–28; pt. 3, bk. 6, chap. 2, pp. 544–59. Nietzsche, frag. 11 [331], [334], [337], November 1887–March 1888 (*KSA* 13:141–42, 143–44, 146); Camus, *Le Mythe de Sisyphe*, in *Essais*, ed. L. Faucon and R. Quilliot (Paris: Gallimard, 1965), 182–88; Kojève (1947), 517–18n1. One will note the reference to Jacob Klein; however, I found nothing in his work.

54. See, for example, Benson, *Lord*, prologue, p. 9; bk. 2, chap. 2, sec. 4 (p. 126).

55. Comte, letter 587 to P. Laffitte, Thursday, 11 Descartes 61 [18 October 1849] (*Correspondance* 5:98).

56. Opponents: Benson, *Lord*, bk. 1, chap. 5, sec. 1 (p. 177); for the disciples, see Sternhell (1985), 306–9.

57. Comte, *Ensemble*, "Conclusion générale," p. 452, then *Système*, "Conclusion totale" (4:531); see also *Dynamique sociale*, chap. 7 (*Système* 3:618); *Catéchisme*, conclusion, 12th talk, p. 381; "entirely to eliminate God," in *Testament*, 9; Prefiguration in *Cours*, 58th lesson (2:715).

58. Comte, *Ensemble*, 4, p. 365—my italics; see also introduction to *Synthèse*, 17.

59. Comte, *Système*, "Conclusion totale" (4:531) (my italics); in Lubac (1998), 170.

Chapter 15. Kingdom or Wasteland?

1. Renan, *Dialogues*, dialogue no. 3 (*OC* 1:615); Russell (1962), chap. 17, pp. 263–264; on *power-thought*, chap. 3, p. 83, and chap. 10, p. 175. The allusion to Alberich of *The Ring of the Nibelung* is clear. At the same moment, Freud speaks of an "aggression against nature," in *Das Unbehagen in der Kultur* [1930], II (*Studienausgabe* 11:209).

2. Osterhammel (2000), 36, 39, 50.

3. Aristotle, *Politics* 1.5–6; Bodin, *République*, bk. 1, chap. 5, pp. 46–47.

4. Locke, *STG*, chap. 4, paras. 22–23 (pp. 13–14); *Epistola*, 132–34.

5. Dienel (1992) and (1995).

6. Goethe, *Faust*, pt. 2, act 5 (Offene Gegend) (*W* 3:371–78). The poem that made Paul Celan famous, "Todesfuge," perhaps contains an allusion to this episode, seen as prefiguring the Shoah. Shattuck (1996), 101.

7. A. Guépin and E. C. Bonamy, *Nantes*; Villermé, *Tableau*; A. de Villeneuve-Bargemont, *Économie politique chrétienne, ou Recherches sur la nature et les causes du paupérisme en France et en Europe, et sur les moyens de le soulager et de le prévenir*, 3 vols. (Paris, 1834), in Burleigh (2005), 391; Engels, *Die Lage der arbeitenden Klasse in England: Nach eigner Anschauung und authentischen Quellen* [1845] (Marx/Engels, *WW* 2:225–506); Charles Dickens, *Oliver Twist* [1839].

8. Porphyry, *De l'abstinence*; Sorabji (1993), pp. 170–94. See above, 23.

9. Bentham, *Principles*, ed. W. Harrison (Oxford: Basil Blackwell, 1960), chap. 17, sec. 4, para. 1, note b (pp. 411–12).

10. Tuveson (1972), 193; Thomas (1984), chap. 4, "Compassion for the Brute Creation" (pp. 143–91); chap. 3, "The Dethronement of Man" (pp. 165–72); Schopenhauer, *Preisschrift über die Grundlage der Moral*, pt. 3, para. 19, sec. 7 (*WW* 3:777–80).

11. Michelet, *Peuple*, II, 6 (p. 203); in Muray (1999), 396; Schopenhauer, *Paralipomena*, chap. 15, "Über Religion," #177, "Über das Christentum" (*WW* 5:437–45).

12. Darwin, *Descent*, chap. 2, p. 432.

13. Groh (2010), 564, 590, 620; E. von Weber, *Folterkammern*; Carroll, "Vivisection as a Sign of the Times" and "Some Popular Fallacies about Vivisection" [1875] (*Works*, 1089–92 and 1092–1100); Bossi (2003), 10n2.

14. Rousseau, letter to Voltaire, 18 August 1756 (*OC* 4:1061).

15. See Dienel (1992), 102–8.

16. Vigny, "La maison du berger" [1844], pt. 1, strophes 10–18, in *Les Destinées* (*PC*, 134–36).

17. Hawthorne, *Stories*, 218–38. Does the chemist owe his name to Eilmer of Malmesbury, the first to have attempted to fly? White (1978), 59–73.

18. Forbes (1968), 92.

19. I. Svevo, *La coscienza di Zeno* [1923], last paragraph.

20. Plato, *Critias* 111c; Theophrastus, cited by Seneca, *Quaestiones* 3.11.3, ed. P. Oltramare, Paris, Les Belles Lettres, 1929, p. 126; on Liu An, Linck (1999), 82; Columella, *Rustica* 1.preface.1–3 (1:2); in Black (1970), 13–14; Pliny, *Histoire*, bk. 36, chaps. I(1)–III(3) (pp. 48–50); *L'Etna*, lines 256–58 (pp. 20–21); Hadot (2004), 194.

21. Gimpel (1975), 82–83.
22. Columbus, in Thompson (1980), Grove (1995), 30–31, 67; Ronsard, Élégie 34 [towards 1576, published in 1584] (*Oeuvres* 2:408–9); English parallels in Thomas (1994), 212–23.
23. Küster (2009), 66.
24. Fabre, *Torrents*, pt. 1, sec. 2, para. 3 (pp. 144–45); Glacken (1967), 698–702.
25. Rauch, *Régénération*; Arndt, *Pflegung*; see Radkau (2011), 40, 46, 48, 49.
26. Schneevogel, *Iovis*, 5–38; citations from 20, 29, 33; Bredekamp (1984), Fischer (1985), 105–6, and in *EN*, s.v. "Anthropozentrismus" (vol. 1, cols. 430–33 [J. Sieglerschmidt]); Spenser, *The Faerie Queene*, referred to, but without attribution, in Hadot (2004), 437n20; Milton, *PL*, bk. 1, lines 684–88 (p. 22); Calvin, *Commentary on Genesis*, commentary on 3:18, in *Opera Omnia*, vol. 23, cols. 73–74, in Groh (2003), 739.
27. Buffon, "Le boeuf" [1749], in *Histoire* 4:440; then "Les animaux carnassiers" [1758], in *Histoire* 7:3; Glacken (1967), 678.
28. James Thomson, *The Seasons*, "Spring," line 241 (*Poems*, 12).
29. Marsh (1965), esp. chap. 1, "Introductory," 7–52; cited from 36–37.
30. E. Haeckel, *Natürliche Schöpfungs-Geschichte: Gemeinverständliche wissenschaftliche Vorträge über die Entwicklungslehre* [1868], 30th conference (*GW* 2:793); in Black (1970), 2.
31. Marx, *Capital*, bk. 3, sec. 6, chap. 23 (*Oeuvres* 2:1385–86).
32. Engels, *Dialektik der Natur*, "Anteil der Arbeit an der Menschwerdung des Affen" (*WW*, 20:452–53).
33. Rossi (1979); Taylor (1989), 349–50; W. Krauss (1987), 27–31; Kant, *Zum ewigen Frieden* [1795], sec. 2, 1st addition (*WW* 6:220); Buffon, *Époques de la nature*, 3rd epoch (*OP*, 151b); cf., for example, with M. Weber, *Die protestantische Ethik und der Geist des Kapitalismus* [1905], pt. 2, sec. 2, in *Gesammelte Aufsätze zur Religionssoziologie* (Tübingen: Mohr, 1965 [= 1920]), 1:203; Dienel (1992), 95–101; Verne, *Île*, 2:161–63; A. A. Cournot, *Considérations sur la marche des idées et des événements dans les Temps modernes*, ed. A. Robinet (Paris: Vrin, 1973), bk. 5, chap. 6, p. 422, in Saint-Sernin (2007), 132; see also Renan, *Dialogues*, dialogue no. 2 (*OC* 1:589).
34. Fontenelle, *Entretiens sur la pluralité des mondes*, 5th evening, (*Oeuvres* 2:108–13); Buffon, *Époques de la nature*, 5th epoch (*OP*, 169b); 6th epoch (184b); Byron, *Darkness* (*SP*, 64–66).
35. Thomson, "Tendency"; "Heat."
36. Balthasar (1998), 130.
37. Heller and Niqueux (1995), 167.
38. Saint-Simon, *Mémoire sur la science de l'homme* (*Oeuvres* 11:294–95); Rosny, *MT* [1910].
39. Secchi, *Soleil*. Translated into German and Spanish.
40. F. Engels, *Dialektik der Natur*, Einleitung (Marx/Engels, *WW* 20:324); see also Dostoyevsky, *Demons*, pt. 1, bk. 2, chap. 2, p. 240; Marinetti, *Mafarka*, chap. 2, p. 49.
41. Flammarion, *Fin*.
42. D'Holbach, *Nature*, bk. 1, chap. 6 (p. 105); Dupré (2004), 33.

43. Muray (1999), 248. It does not seem that Charles Fourier feared a reversal of the equatorial poles, as Muray seems to believe. Panorama in Godin (2003), 72–86.

44. Comte, *Cours*, 60th lesson (2:774); *Ensemble*, "Conclusion générale," p. 489; *Dynamique sociale* (*Système* 3:72–73); Bakunin, *Fédéralisme, socialisme, antithéologisme*, 3 (*Oeuvres*, 124).

45. See Hofmann (2010), 70, who probably bases himself on Silvestre, *Histoire*, 123.

46. Arendt (1951), 226.

47. Cousin de Grainville, *Dernier*; Stafford (1994), 201–5; Michelet, *Histoire*, pt. 3, chap. 10 (pp. 91–109).

48. Stafford (1994), 261–88.

49. E. Boratysnski, "Poslednjaja smert'" (*Stikhotvorenija*, 68–71).

50. See above, 117–19.

51. Wells, *Mind*, sec. 1, p. 5; sec. 4, pp. 18–19; then sec. 8, p. 30.

52. References in Brague (2002b), 143–44; add [Anonymous] *Songe*, pt. 2, chap. 260, sec. 3 (2:222); Black (1970), 98; Machiavelli, *Discorsi*, bk. 2, chap. 5 (*O*, 248); on Vico, see Fellman (1976), 119–20; Malthus, *Population*, 1st ed. (1798), chaps. 1–2, pp. 5–17; 2nd ed. (1803), bk. 4, chaps. 1–3, pp. 477–500; Galton, *Inquiries*, 207.

53. Flaubert, *Mémoires d'un fou* [1838], chap. 7 (*OC* 1:234b).

54. See above, 100, and Comte, introduction to *Synthèse*, 12.

55. W. S. Blunt, in Passmore (1974), 180; for A. Döblin and D. H. Lawrence, see Brague (2013), 26–27.

56. Dubos, *Réflexions*, pt. 2, sec. 33 (2:476–77 [259a]); more accessible in *QAM*, 648; cited, in part, in Hazard (1989), 379. On the positive evaluation of prejudice, see above, 132–33.

57. Rousseau, "La profession de foi du vicaire Savoyard," in *Émile*, pt. 4 (*OC* 4:632–33; my italics).

58. Taguieff (2000) and Godin (2003).

59. See the entire chap. 8 of Black (1970), 109–24.

60. Dante, *Monarchia* 1.1 (p. 60).

61. Hakewill, *Apology*, I, ii, 4, p. 21; cited without reference in Black (1970), 114.

62. Diderot, letter to Falconet, letter no. 4, February 1766; or *Le pour et le contre*, in *Oeuvres*² 15:33; Becker (1932), 147; Robespierre, discourse of 11 January 1792 at the Jacobins Club (*Oeuvres* 8:110); Becker (1932), 142–43; Roland, *Appel*.

63. Mill, "Auguste Comte and Positivism" [1865], chap. 2 (*Essays*, 334); Black (1970), 115.

64. Burke, *Revolution*, 29; Tocqueville, *Démocratie*, vol. 2 (1840), pt. 2, chap. 2 (p. 614).

65. Böckenförde, "Die Entstehung des Staates als Vorgang der Säkularisation" [1967] (*Recht*, 112); Brague (2000), 51–52.

66. Renan, *Dialogues*, chap. 2 (*OC* 1:589, 598); Nietzsche, frag. 14 [226], Spring 1888 (*KSA* 13:398); C. Péguy, "De la situation faite au parti intellectuel dans le monde moderne devant les accidents de la gloire temporelle" [6 October 1907]

(*Oeuvres* 2:725); "Note conjointe sur M. Descartes et la philosophie cartésienne" [1914], in *Oeuvres en prose*, ed. M. Péguy (Paris: Gallimard, 1961), 1512; Chesterton, "Is Humanism a Religion?" (*Thing*, 16–17); Brague (2014), 19–22.

Chapter 16. Man, Humiliated

1. Rey (2003), 309, 146.
2. See, for the example of the purported Copernican wound, Brague (2006b), 263–65.
3. See above, 46.
4. Brague (1993), 132–33; add Flaubert, *Mémoires d'un fou*, chap. 20 (*OC* 1:244b).
5. Blumenberg (1975), 723–47.
6. Galileo, *Diversi frammenti attenenti al trattato delle cose che stanno su l'acqua* (*Opere* 4:24); *DMS*, First Day, pp. 107–8; Arendt (1958), 114n63.
7. M. Henry (1985) and Gauchet and Swain (1992).
8. Freud, "Eine Schwierigkeit der Psychoanalyse" [1917] (*Werke* 12:3–12, esp. 11). On the eighteenth century, see Crocker (1959), 219–25—who mentions Freud.
9. See above, 23.
10. See the synthesis in W. Krauss (1987), 136–75.
11. *Theophrastus Redivivus* [1659], 6th treatise, sec. 2 (*L17* 2:247–90); Cyrano de Bergerac, *Empire de la lune* [1657] (*L17* 1:961–63).
12. P. Bayle, "Rorarius (Jerome)," in *Dictionnaire*, 4:76–87.
13. Spinoza, *Ethica*, pt. 1, appendix (*O* 1:67); Thomas (1984), 165–72.
14. Fromm (1999).
15. Echo in Bonaventura, *Nachtwachen*, 72–74 (8th vigil [?]).
16. Buffon, "De la manière d'étudier et de traiter l'histoire naturelle" (1749) (*OP*, 10a).
17. La Mettrie, *Le Système d'Épicure*, para. 32 (*OP*, 240); *L'Homme plante*, chap. 3 (*OP*, 201).
18. D'Holbach, *Système de la nature* (1770), pt. 1, chap. 7 (1:93–94); pt. 2, chap. 3 (1:67); Sade, *Boudoir*, 238, 242–43, in Godin (2003), 122.
19. Ferguson, *Civil Society*, pt. 1, sec. 1, p. 11; Gay (1969), 175n4.
20. Kondylis (1986), 285.
21. Comte, *Cours*, 45th lesson (1:842n1); Martin (2008), 345.
22. Maupassant, *Sur l'eau* [1888], Cannes, 7 April, 9 hrs. at night (p. 45).
23. For the epithet used here (*salaud*) in the case of Sade, see the police report of 18 January 1766 in Farge (1989), 84–85: impatient at a traffic jam, the marquis plunged his sword into the belly of a horse. For Maupassant, see his reaction to the death of the office clerk, a simpleton, whom he had hazed so cruelly that he was suspected of having killed him: letter [to an unknown] (1879) in *Correspondance*, 307–8. The pedophile tastes of Buffon are attested to by Hérault de Séchelles in his *Voyage à Montbard* [1785], cited in Gaillard, *Buffon*, 150–51, 156. (Translator's note: the French word employed by Brague [*salaud*] is rather stronger than "jerk"; it typically means "bastard.")

24. Swift, *Gulliver*, pt. 4, pp. 271–375; Machiavelli, *Il Principe*, chap. 18 (*O*, 55); on the contrary, Maistre, *Soirées*, second night (p. 64); on expressionism, Osterkamp (2010), 7–44.

25. La Mettrie, *Le Système d'Épicure* (1750), para. 2 (*OP*, 234); Martin (2008), 10, 164, 248–49, 324.

26. Sade, *Les Cent Vingt Journées de Sodome, ou L'École du libertinage*, bk. 1, chap. 23 (*Oeuvres* 1:255). The passage is cited in Hadjadj (2008), 16; his commentary, while different from mine, has its own interest and I recommend it.

27. Pascal, *Pensées*, 434; on Voltaire, see 86.

28. See 110.

29. Marx, "Zur Judenfrage" (*FS*, 254); Spaemann (2001), 187, 480.

30. Kierkegaard, *Postscriptum définitif et non scientifique aux Miettes philosophiques* [1846], pt. 2, sec. 2, chap. 3, para. 4, trans. P.-H. Tisseau and E.-M. Jacquet-Tisseau (*Oeuvres*, 55); Rehm (1947), 53.

31. Flaubert, letter to Louise Colet, 14 December 1853 (*Correspondance* 2:478).

32. Dostoyevsky, *Carnet*, pt. 2, chap. 10 (pp. 376–77); Musil, *Mann*, pt. 1, sec. 2, chap. 72, pp. 303–4 (cited by Rey [2003], 270–71); *Mann*, pt. 1, sec. 2, all of chap. 53 (pp. 269–77).

33. Statius, *Thébaïde* 11.469–70, in Lewis (1963), 96; Sade, *Boudoir*, 108; Rostand, *Pensées*, 87; Martin (2008), 107; Brague (2013), 140.

34. See, for example, Guardini (1949), 44; Crocker (1959), 73, 78; Starobinski (1964), 203; Fukuyama (1992), 296–97; Kinneging (2000), 140.

35. Balthasar (1956), 206; Weaver (1948), 7; Brague (1998), 226.

36. Lewis (1963), 56.

37. Hume, "On Suicide," in *Essays*, 587, 590; Crocker (1952), 70–72.

38. Soloviev, *Čtenija o bogočelovečestve*, lesson 2 (*RO* 3:20); *Leçons*, 31.

39. Bentham, "Anarchical Fallacies: Being an Examination of the Declaration of Rights Issued during the French Revolution" (*Works* 2:501); Gregory (2012), 224; Arendt (1951), 369–79.

Chapter 17. The Subjugated Subject

1. Sextus Empiricus, *Contre les Logiciens* 1.284–91; Plotinus V.3[49].

2. H. Maier (1966); Foucault (1975); Plato, *Protagoras* 319b–c.

3. Crocker (1959), 455.

4. Schabert (1969), 24–28; Morelly, *Code de la nature*, pt. 1 (*OP*, 291).

5. Kant, *Über Pädagogik* (*WW* 6:693–761, cited from 699); Comenius, *De rerum humanarum emendatione consultatio catholica* (*Opera*, ser. 19, vol. 1, p. 447, col. 721, in Groh [2010], 537–38).

6. Fichte, *Reden an die deutsche Nation*, 2 (*AW* 5:387, 393), then 3 (*AW* 5:416–17); see also 4 (*AW* 5:422); 9 (*AW* 5:511); 11 (*AW* 5:539) and 13 (*AW* 5:587), then 4 and 11 (*AW* 5:422 and 547–48).

7. Pierre-Jean-Georges Cabanis, *Rapports*, 298; Martin (2008), 214 and 242–43; see also Léonard Bourdon, cited in Martin (2008), 156.

8. Heidegger, *Über Ernst Jünger*, ed. P. Trawny (*GA*, 90).

9. Jünger, *Worker*, sec. 31, p. 110; sec. 66, p. 252; sec. 77, p. 307; sec. 35, p. 126; see also sec. 37, p. 138, sec. 41, p. 153.

10. Balthasar (1956), 158–61 and esp. 160; Anders (2002a), 23.

11. See above, 32; Lewis (1943), 55; on Bacon, see Groh (2010), 461, 463; citation in Sloterdijk (1999), 45; Husserl, *Krisis*, sec. 12 (p. 67).

12. Comte, *Cours*, 58th lesson (2:727).

13. Comte, *Système* 1:90; preface to *Synthèse* (p. xxx); letter 1083 to C. de Blignières, Thursday, 3 César 68 [24 April 1856] (*Correspondance* 8:250; letter 1054 to M. Papot, Thursday, 10 Moses 68 [10 January 1856] (*Correspondance* 8:211); letter 696 to C. de Blignières, 27 Dante 63 [11 September 1851] (*Correspondance* 6:140), in Lubac (1998), 261.

14. Comte, letter 821 to C. de Blignières, 26 Frédéric 64 [29 November 1852] (*Correspondance* 6:440); letter 693 to B. Profumo, 24 Dante 63 [8 August 1851], (*Correspondance* 6:128); "Préface: Essor empirique du républicanisme français" (17 June 1852), in *Dynamique sociale* (*Système* 3:xliii); Lubac (1998), 262.

15. Comte, *Ensemble*, chap. 2, pp. 172, 177.

16. Comte, *Cours*, 46th lesson (2:28, end); in Lubac (1998), 256; letter 1062 to H. Dix-Hutton, Tuesday, 1 Homère 68 [29 January 1856] (*Correspondance* 8:215).

17. Comte, letter 655 to A. Leblais, 15 Moses 63 [15 January 1851] (*Correspondance* 6:11; Lubac (1998), 24; J. D. Bernal, *WFD*, chap. 3, p. 43, and chap. 6, p. 70; André Breton, "Trois interventions à *Contre-Attaque*," III, 8.12.1935; *Oeuvres complètes*, ed. M. Bonnet et al., Paris, Gallimard, t. II, 1992, p. 609; Clair (2003), 138.

18. G. Guillard de Beaurieu, *L'Élève de la nature* [1763], in Bredvold (1961), 89; Lewis (1943), 59–60.

19. Rousseau, *Émile*, chap. 2 (*OC* 4:362–63; my italics); in Martin (1994), 271. The passage is still cited with approval by Skinner, *Beyond*, pt. 2, pp. 37–38.

20. Gauchet and Swain (1980), 138–44; Martin (1994): massive pessimism, 218; big babies, 255, 275.

21. Plato, *Republic* 4.419a and 5.465e; Dostoyevsky, *Karamazov*, pt. 2, bk. 5, chap. 5, p. 263; Lubac (1998), 342; Nietzsche, frag. 39[3], August–September 1885 (*KSA* 11:620); Lubac (1998), 341; Bernal, *WFD*, chap. 5, p. 63.

22. Skinner, *Walden Two*, chap. 33, p. 279. The capital letter in "Man" is in the original. Richter (1979), 75–79.

23. Skinner, *Beyond*, chap. 1, p. 19; chap. 2, p. 39; chap. 3, p. 54; chap. 9, pp. 175, 186, 189; then chapter 9, p. 191. He has C. S. Lewis (2000) in mind, and names him in chap. 9, pp. 191, and 197. The homunculus is not the alchemist's artificial man, but rather the inner "little man" postulated by certain psychological doctrines, and already found in Plato, *Republic* 9.589ab. Finally, chap. 9, p. 206.

24. Aristotle, *Nicomachean Ethics* 6.2.1139a20.

25. Aristotle, *Politics* 1.4.1253b33–1254a1; Antipater of Thessalonica, in *Greek Anthology* 9. Paton, *Épigrammes*, no. 418 (3:232). The poem is cited by Marx, *Capital*, pt. 4, chap. 13, sec. 3, para. b, p. 367; Séris (1994), 167.

26. Moscovici (1968), 253; Séris (1994), 96–97.

27. Example given by White (1962), 175 (note 1 on p. 129), referring to Krickeberg (1928), 386–88, and referring to Seler, *Gesammelte* 5:127 on p. 132, fig. 4.

28. Marx, *Capital*, pt. 4, chap. 13, sec. 3, para. b, p. 334, in Séris (1994), 168–69; then Séris (1994), 35, 80.

29. Butler, "Darwin among the Machines," in *Note-Books*, 42–47, preceded by an explanatory note, 39–42; the text alone is reprinted in *Works*, 208–13; quotation from p. 210.

30. Butler, *Erewhon*, chap. 9, p. 57; chap. 22, p. 139; chap. 25, pp. 162–63; then chap. 25, p. 157; chap. 24, p. 146; finally chap. 25, pp. 158–59.

31. Plato, *Laws* 1.644c–645a; Jean Paul [Menschen sind Maschinen der Engel] (*Sämtliche*, ser. 2, vol. 1, pp. 1028–31).

32. See Lucian, *Philopseudeis*, chap. 35–36, pp. 102–4; on the reception, see E. Ribbat, "'Die ich rief, die Geister . . .' Zur späten Wirkung einer Zaubergeschichte Lukians," in Lucian, *Philopseudeis*, pp. 183–94; Idel (1992), 274 and 284.

33. Jean Paul, "Der Maschinen-Mann nebst seinen Eigenschaften," in *Auswahl aus des Teufels Papieren, Dritte Zusammenkunft mit dem eben so müden als beliebten Leser*, sec. 10 (*Sämtliche*, ser. 2, vol. 2, pp. 446–53); Hoffmann, "Die Automate," in *Die Serapionsbrüder*, II, pt. 3 (*Werke* 3:328–54); Forster, "The Machine Stops," in *Stories*, 115–58; cited from vii, then 141 and 157.

34. Čapek, prologue to *RUR*, pp. 22 and 38, then act 2, p. 73; act 1, pp. 51, 54, then act 2, p. 90; act 3, p. 92. On the theme, see 147–48 in this volume; see also act 3, pp. 104–5.

35. Farrère, *Condamnés*, I, 2, p. 9b; I, 5, p. 18ab; III, 6, p. 50b; then I, 2, p. 10b; I, 5, p. 19a; IV, 3, p. 60b; IV, 8, p. 73a; a related idea in Anders (2002b), 98–99; finally Farrère, *Condamnés*, IV, 8, p. 73a; IV, 12, p. 78a, and Qur'an 8:17; Hauser (2004), 411.

36. Baudelaire, *Les fleurs du mal*, no. 102, "Rêve parisien" (*OC*, 96–98); other texts in Carrouges (1948), 132–41; see the ideas of professor Filostrato in C. S. Lewis, *That Hideous Strength*, chap. 8, sec. 3.

37. Rosny, *MT*, chap. 2, pp. 110, 112.

38. Dyson (1998).

Chapter 18. Man Remade

1. See Passmore (1965); Crocker (1959), 183, 188.

2. Alberti, *Famiglia*, bk. 1, pp. 58–62; Taylor (2007), 121, 127.

3. La Mettrie, *Anti-Sénèque ou Discours sur le Bonheur* [1750] (*OP*, 331); Martin (2008), 155–56.

4. Helvétius, *De l'homme* [1772], sec. 10, chap. 1 (*Oeuvres* 2:566); d'Holbach, *Social* [1773], pt. 1, chap. 1, p. 28; Raynal, *Histoire*, bk. 19, chaps. 35 and 47 (7:256, 421; my italics). Imprecise citation in Strauss (1953), 271.

5. Wordsworth, *Prelude*, bk. 11, line 138; Herder, *Unterhaltungen und Briefe über die ältesten Urkunden* [1771–72] (*Werke* 6:152); on Fichte, see above, 104–5; Wilde, "The Soul of Man under Socialism" [1891], in *Profundis*, 48.

6. Martin (2008), 315–16; Lewis (2000), 74; Arendt (1958), 188; Berlin (1990), 194; A. France, *Les dieux ont soif* [1912].

7. Pushkin, *Dar naprasnyj, dar slučajnyj* . . . (*O*, 317a). It was very much an execution (*kazn'*), not merely a death (*smert'*), as in the parallel in *Ocen'*, strophe 6, line 3 (*O*, 374a); Flaubert, *Mémoires d'un fou*, chaps. 2, 10, and 20 (*OC* 1:231b, 237b, 244b); Kierkegaard in Brague (2002b), 313; A. Chekhov, *Salle 6*, 80 (my translation).

8. Galileo, *DMS*, First Day, p. 61.

9. Robespierre, "Sur les rapports des idées religieuses et morales avec les principes républicains," 18 floréal, year II (7 May 1794), in *Discours*, p. 264 (my italics); Martin (2008), 249–50.

10. Kleist, "Über das Marionettentheater" [1810] (*Werke*, 805–7).

11. Malraux, "L'homme et la culture artistique" [1946], in Malraux (1996), 56; Friedrich (1955), 3.

12. Huxley, "Transhumanism," in *Bottles*, 13–17, cited from 17, then *Memories*, 181; Radkau (2011), 108–9.

13. Fukuyama (2002); Robitaille (2007).

14. Newman (2004), chap. 4, "Artificial Life and the Homonculus," pp. 164–237; see also the anthology of Völker (1971); then Kraus (1942), 119–21; finally Polybius, *History* 13.7 (pp. 18–19).

15. Pinès (1996b); then Newman (2004), 177–81, and Pingree (1993), 141; finally Jâbir, *TC*, 343–91, translated or summarized in Kraus (1942), 103–34, cited here from p. 111.

16. Scholem (1992); Idel (1992), 271–72, then 255–57.

17. Secord (1989); Hauser (2004), 226.

18. See, for example, Heine, *Religion*, bk. 3, p. 149: the creature asks his creator to give him a soul. Against the movie adaptations, see Winner (1977), 306–17.

19. Shelley, *F*, chap. 5, p. 55; then chaps. 11 and 12. Condillac, *Traité des sensations*, Dessein de cet ouvrage (*Oeuvres* 1:222a, and see the editor's note); finally, Shelley, *F*, chap. 15.

20. Shelley, *F*, letter 4, pp. 27–28; chap. 4, p. 51; chap. 24, pp. 203 and 210.

21. Shelley, *F*, chap. 2, p. 37; chap. 3, p. 45.

22. Shelley, *F*, chap. 17, p. 140; then chap. 24, p. 212; the reminiscence of Milton's Satan, *PL*, bk. 4, line 110 (p. 80), is obvious; that of Shakespeare, *Richard III*, 1.1, is possible; finally, Shelley, *F*, chap. 10, p. 97; chap. 17, p. 141; chap. 24, p. 209. Compare with Condorcet, *Esquisse*, 10th epoch, p. 282, cited below, 175–76.

23. Shelley, *F*, chap. 22, p. 184, and chap. 24, p. 196; then chap. 10, p. 96; chap. 15, p. 125; finally chap. 20, p. 162; chap. 24, p. 198.

24. Villiers, *Eve*, bk. 1, chap. 6, p. 148; Bénichou (2004), 396–98.

25. Villiers, *Eve*, bk. 5, chaps. 1, 3, 5, 8, 13–15; then bk. 6, chap. 12, p. 405; bk. 6, chap. 13, p. 406; finally bk. 2, chap. 4, p. 190. I reproduce faithfully the neologisms, improprieties, italics, and superfluous capitals which burden this overwrought text.

26. Villiers, *Eve*, bk. 2, chap. 5, p. 191, and bk. 2, chap. 6, p. 195.

27. Villiers, *Eve*, bk. 5, chap. 4, p. 301, then bk. 2, chap. 4, p. 184.

28. Villiers, *Eve*, bk. 2, chap. 4, p. 187; bk. 6, chap. 4, p. 371. Chateaubriand, *Génie*, pt. 2, bk. 3, chap. 9, p. 714; Musset, *Confession*, pt. 1, chap. 2, p. 37; then pt. 5, chap. 4, p. 301, and pt. 3, chap. 4, p. 237; finally pt. 5, chap. 16, p. 332.

29. F. Hutcheson, *Inquiry concerning the Original of Our Ideas of Virtue or Moral Good*, sec. 4, para. 138, in Selby-Bigge, *British Moralists*, 1:122; on Haeckel, see Arendt (1951), 235.

30. Voltaire, Letter to the *Gazette littéraire de l'Europe*, October 1764, D 12144, in *Oeuvres*/Besterman, vol. 28, *Correspondence*, 165; then Lasaulx, *PG*, 7, pp. 101–2.

31. Condorcet, *Esquisse*, 10th epoch, p. 282; also see Diderot, in Gay (1969), 13; then Humboldt, *Memoiren* 1:365–66, who cites as his source the journal of a countess de B., born Mlle. de R. In it, she recounts a conversation that one of Humboldt's friends allegedly had with Humboldt in Paris in 1812. It was a forgery, however; see Biermann (1990), 262. The passage is cited, but without any indication of its source, in Duviols and Minguet (1994), 116. Brague (2011), 90–91.

32. Bergson, *Sources*, chap. 4, p. 309; then Heidegger, "Überwindung der Metaphysik," para. xxvi [1942] (*Vorträge*, 91); finally, Sloterdijk (1999), 46–47.

33. L.-M. de La Révellière-Lepeaux, in Martin (2008), 162–63; Comte, *Esprit*, 2, p. 180 (my italics). See also Comte, *Esprit*, 1, p. 60; Negro (2009), 31–32, 57, 66, 75, 78, 114.

34. Baudelaire, *Le Peintre de la vie moderne*, chap. 9 (*OC*, 1177–80); Brague (2008b), 117–26; see above, 41; see Shattuck (1968), 39, apropos to Alfred Jarry.

35. The passage referring to Fourier, which his disciple V. Considérant had censored, was only published in *La Brèche: Action surréaliste*, no. 7, December 1964, pp. 69–71. Witticisms: H. de Balzac, *Monographie de la presse parisienne* [1843]; Le Blagueur, in Balzac, *Oeuvre*, 14:603; Reybaud, *Jérôme*, chap. 9. Tails promised to humanity, pp. 167–83.

36. *HWPh*, s.v. "Mensch" (neuer, vol. 5, cols. 1112–17; by M. Arndt/U. Dierse), and Negro (2009).

37. Alain of Lille, *Anticlaudianus* 6, line 331 (*Works*, p. 420); 7, line 74 (p. 436); Negro (2009), 300–301.

38. Betzky, *Plans* 2:3 (my italics). Heller and Niqueux (1995), 68, alluded to the text, but with no citation or specific reference.

39. Comte, *Ensemble*, "Conclusion générale," 469; then A. Baring, Schönhauser Gespräche, no. 7, 1999, p. 30 [*non vidi*], in H. Maier (2001), 24n60. Also see Negro (2009), 191; Clair (2003), 77, 110, 113.

40. On the Hispanic world, Wentzlaff-Eggebert (1999) hardly keeps the promises of his title. For Italy, see E. Gentile (2002), 235–64; quotations from 249 (with the blasphemous allusion to Gen. 1:26), 253, 254.

41. See Chernyshevsky [Tchernychevski], *What*; Heller and Niqueux (1995), 142–45; on Rakhmetov as a model for Lenin, see Besançon (1977), chap. 7.

42. Dostoyevsky, *Demons*, pt. 1, chap. 3, para. 8, p. 106; *Karamazov*, pt. 4, bk. 11, chap. 9, p. 651, in Lubac (1998), 330.

43. A. Blok, *Effondrement*, sec. 7, p. 114; "Le naufrage de l'humanisme" (*Oeuvres*, 414–32).

44. See Kheveshi, *Tolkovij*, s.v. "novyi sovietskii tchelovek," p. 105, and "sovietskii tchelovek," pp. 141–42. Attwood and Kelly (1998) study the means of propaganda (literature for children, cinema), without reflecting on the central notion in the title.

45. Olesha, *Čelovečeskiy material*, in *Povesti*, 214–45, cited from 245; in French trans., 67–71, cited from 71. Also see Heller and Niqueux (1995), 237.

46. Discourse pronounced in the palace of the Kremlin on the occasion of the promotion of the students of the Academy of the Red Army (4 May 1935), http://www.communisme-bolchevisme.net/download/Staline_Le_capital_le _plus_precieux.pdf.

47. See the *Pravda* of 17 May 1934, in Negro (2009), 347.

48. Blok, *Effondrement*, sec. 7, p. 114.

49. Plato, *Statesman* 308c, e; Sloterdijk (1999), 47–55.

50. Huarte, *Examen*; Mulsow (2003), 754–55; Campanella, *CS*, p. 10, lines 149–51.

51. Joachim Faiguet de Villeneuve, *L'Économie politique: Projet pour enrichir et perfectionner l'espèce humaine* (Paris, 1763), pt. 2, pp. 115–53, in Martin (1994), 170–71; Maupertuis, *Vénus physique* [1745], pt. 2, chap. 3 (*Oeuvres* 2:110–11); Martin (2008), 232; Cabanis, *Rapports du physique et du moral de l'homme* [1805, 2nd ed.], conclusion of the 6th memorandum (*OC* 1:356–57).

52. La Beaumelle, *Pensées*, para. lxxxiv, p. 64; Martin (2008), 234.

53. A. R. Wallace, "The Development of Human Races under the Law of Natural Selection" [1864], in *Contributions*, 302–31, citation from 329; L. Büchner, *Die Stellung des Menschen in der Natur in Vergangenheit, Gegenwart und Zukunft, oder Woher kommen wir? Wer sind wir? Wohin gehen wir? Allgemein verständlicher Text mit zahlreichen wissenschaftlichen Erläuterungen und Anmerkungen* (Leipzig, 1869), 239, in Benz (1974), 385.

54. Galton, *Inquiries*, 17n1 and 199, 197–98, then 218.

55. Cabanis, *Rapport fait au Conseil des Cinq-Cents sur l'organisation des écoles de médecine* (*OC* 1:367); in Martin (2008), 268.

56. Galton, *Inquiries*, 199–200, 210, 216, 219.

57. Fontenelle, *République*, chap. 8, p. 93; More, *Utopia*, bk. 2, p. 210; Rouvillois (2010), 347.

58. Martin (2008), 104–12.

59. Most, *Gesellschaft*, 71. The idea is not found in the polemical appendix (77–102). The synonymy between "humane" and "scientific" is interesting. Proudhon, *Manuel*, pt. 1, chap. 7, para. 5, conclusion (p. 171); Berlin (1990), 198–99.

60. Nietzsche, *Die fröhliche Wissenschaft*, pt. 4, aphorism 341 (*KSA* 3:570); *Der Antichrist*, aphorism 2 (*KSA* 6:170).

61. Kline (1969); Rosenthal (2002); on Gorki, see Günther (1993), 14–18, and bibliography, 231–34.

62. Hagemeister (2005), 59–61, and the text translated in *NM*, 336–37; also see Murav'ev, *Domination du Temps*, 104–5, translated in *NM*, 439; the novelistic transposition by C. S. Lewis, *That Hideous Strength* [1945], chap. 8, para. 3.

63. Hagemeister (2005), 62n126; on Lanz von Liebenfels, see Hauser (2004), 422.

64. Murav'ev, *Domination du Temps*, chap. 7, para. 3, p. 110; German in *NM*, 447.
65. Bernal, *WFD*, chap. 6, p. 73 (my italics).
66. C. S. Lewis, "Vivisection," in Lewis (1985), 82.

Chapter 19. Man Surpassed and . . . Replaced

1. Burnett, *Metaphysics*, bk. 7, chap. 9, p. 319; Tuveson (1972), 190.
2. Herder, *Briefe zur Beförderung der Humanität*, 2nd collection [1793], sec. 25 (*Werke* 17:115); Benz (1961a), 68; Mulsow (2003), 758.
3. Marx, preface to *Zur Kritik der politischen Ökonomie* [1859] (Marx/Engels, *WW* 13:9).
4. Gay (1969), 99–100.
5. Quinet, *Introduction à la philosophie de l'histoire de l'humanité*, in *Oeuvres*, vol. 8, *Premiers travaux*, p. 39; Bénichou (2004), 878; then Renan, *Avenir*, chap. 17, *OC* 3:991; see also chap. 2, *OC* 3:1125, n. 14; chap. 10, *OC* 3:883; chap. 12, *OC* 3:905; chap. 18, *OC* 3:1037–38; finally Esquiros, *Future*, bk. 1, chap. 4, p. 77, Muray (1999), 234; on the background, Bénichou (2004), 856n26; writing after Darwin, whom he cites, Bakunin is more prudent: *Fédéralisme, socialisme et antithéologisme*, 3 (*Oeuvres*, 93).
6. Comte, *Cours*, 58th lesson (2:715, 748); see also 60th lesson (2:780).
7. Darwin, *Descent*, chap. 21, p. 920; then *Autobiography*, 92. On Wallace, see Rouvillois (2010), 372.
8. See, for example, Strauss, *Glaube*, pt. 3, para. 62, p. 199; Benz (1974), 378.
9. See above, 147–48, and Stafford (1994), 297.
10. Bulwer-Lytton, *Race*, 7, p. 21. The author bases himself on Faraday, *Researches*, 19th series, para. 26, sec. 1, n. 2146 (3:1–2). The idea of *vril* remained alive in certain occultist circles.
11. Bulwer-Lytton, *Race*, 15, pp. 51–52. Darwin is not named. The transmission of acquired characteristics seems presupposed in chap. 22, p. 90, and chap. 23, p. 94; Bulwer-Lytton, *Race*, 27, p. 119.
12. Bulwer-Lytton, *Race*, 19, p. 82. It refers to Algernon Sidney (d. 1683). See also 17, p. 67 (and 5, p. 13); 27, p. 118.
13. Bulwer-Lytton, *Race*, 18, p. 76; 15, p. 52, and 27, p. 119; 29, p. 128.
14. Guy de Maupassant, *Le Horla* [1887], in *Contes et nouvelles* 2:913–28, cited from 933; the first version, Maupassant, *Le Horla*, 822–30, contains an analogous idea on 829, but without the formulation.
15. Butler, *Erewhon*, chap. 24, p. 149 (my italics).
16. Nietzsche, *Also sprach Zarathustra*. With *sollen*: prologue, 3 (*KSA* 4:14); pt. 1, "Vom Krieg und Kriegsvolke" (*KSA* 4:60); with *müssen*: pt. 1, "Von den Freuden- und Leidenschaften" (*KSA* 4:44); "Vom Freunde" (*KSA* 4:72); pt. 3, "Von alten und neuen Tafeln," 3 (*KSA* 4:248) and 4 (*KSA* 4:249); pt. 4, "Der hässlichste Mensch" (*KSA* 4:332). Also see the question: "how to overcome man?" in pt. 4, "Vom höheren Menschen," 3 (*KSA* 4:357).
17. Jarry, *La Dragonne* (around 1905); Shattuck (1968), 40, 193.

18. Nietzsche, *Der Antichrist*, #3 (*KSA* 6:170); also see frag. 11 [413], November 1887–March 1888 (*KSA* 13:191), and 15 [120], Spring 1888 (*KSA* 13:481); Bossi (2003), 114n11.

19. Nietzsche, frag. 25 [137], Spring 1884 (*KSA* 11:50); 37 [8], June–July 1885 (*KSA* 11:582); 2 [57], Autumn 1885–Autumn 1886 (*KSA* 12:87); frag. 35 [72], May–July 1885 (*KSA* 11:541); frag. 7 [21], Spring–Summer 1883 (*KSA* 10:244); and 16 [85] (*KSA* 10:529).

20. Nietzsche, frag. 14 [80], Spring 1888 (*KSA* 13:260).

21. Staël, *Considérations*, 363; Martin (2008), 324.

22. Nietzsche, *Jenseits von Gut und Böse*, VI, aphorism 208 (*KSA* 5:140); see above, 69.

23. Nietzsche, *Also sprach Zarathustra*, pt. 4, "Das Eselsfest," 2 (*KSA* 4:393).

24. Nietzsche, *Die fröhliche Wissenschaft*, pt. 4, aphorism 341 (*KSA* 3:570); *Also sprach Zarathustra*, pt. 3, "Vom Gesicht und Rätsel," 2 (*KSA* 4:202); frag. 10 [47], June–July 1883 (*KSA* 10:378); 15 [10] (*KSA* 10:482); 26 [283], Summer–Autumn 1884 (*KSA* 11:224–25).

25. Nietzsche, Ecce Homo: *Warum ich ein Schicksal bin*, para. 8 (*KSA* 6:373); letter 1176 to A. Strindberg, 8 December 1888, in *Briefe* 8:509. See Fichte, *Reden an die deutsche Nation*, 3 (*AW* 5:416–17); see above, 162; Dostoyevsky, *Demons*, pt. 1, chap. 3, para. 8, p. 107.

26. Arendt (1951), 533.

27. Hitler, *MK*, pt. 2, chap. 1, p. 422.

28. Mallarmé, letter to Henri Cazalis, 14 May 1867, in *Correspondance*, 343 (my italics). For the context, see Carrouges (1948), 46.

29. G. Anders (2002a), 21–95.

30. Comte, *Ensemble*, 4, p. 325, then *Système*, vol. 4, chap. 1, p. 68; in Muray (1999), 149.

31. Marinetti, *Mafarka*, chap. 3, p. 102; chap. 4, p. 118; chap. 3, pp. 91–93; chap. 12, pp. 281–82, 297. Pss. 121:4; 45:3.

32. Marinetti, *Mafarka*, chap. 9, pp. 213 and 215. The majuscule beginning the word for "Love" is in the original, as is the interesting lapsus "to give birth," while one would expect "to engender." On this usage, see also *Mafarka*, p. 219.

33. Robitaille (2007), 213.

34. A. K. Gastev, poem cited above, 125; cited in Sarkisyanz (1955), 44.

35. L. Trotski, *Literatura i revolyusiya* [1924], chap. 8, end; "Eine Vision der Zukunft" [German original], in *Denkzettel*, chap. 20, essay 58, pp. 420–23, citation from p. 423.

36. J. B. S. Haldane, *Daedalus*, 63–68; Haldane is named in Bernal, *WFD*, chap. 3, pp. 33 and 37. On the discussion, see Squier (1994), 66–99; on Haldane, 69–73; on Bernal, 86–89; B. Russell, (1924).

37. Muller (1935); Shattuck (1996), 203–5. Letter to Stalin in Glad (2003), 307–19.

38. Murav'ev, *Domination du Temps*, chap. 7, para. 1, p. 105; translated in *NM*, 439; Hagemeister (2005), 54.

39. Bernal, *WFD*, chap. 3, pp. 32–46. On the work, see Kohn-Waechter (1995).
40. Bernal, *WFD*, chap. 3, pp. 35, 38, 41, 42, 46. Regarding the same dream of a transformation into light in Tziolokovsky, see Hagemeister (2005), 59; *WFD*, chap. 5, p. 60.
41. Clynes and Kline (1970). The word "cyborg" is proposed on p. 31a.
42. Thoreau, "Economy" (*Walden*, 80); Janicaud (1985), 200; more general, Guardini (1949), 61; Winner (1977), 229; Haldane, "Biological Possibilities for the Human Species in the Next Ten Thousand Years," in *Man*, 337–61, cited from 354–55; Gloy (1996), 202–3.
43. See Comte, *Ensemble*, "Conclusion générale," 452–53, then 488, 500, 540.
44. Rilke, *Das Stunden-buch*, bk. 1, *Das Buch vom mönchischen Leben* (*Werke* 1:9–57).
45. Gorki, *Ispoved'* [1908] (*Sobranie* 8:215–378). See also Heller and Niqueux (1995), 171–72; details in Sesterhenn (1982).
46. Alexander, *Space*, bk. 4, chap. 1 (2:347); Scheler, *Stellung*, 91–93; Shattuck (1968), 40–41.
47. Bergson, *Sources*, III, p. 226 (my italics); then IV, p. 338.
48. Mallarmé, letter to Henri Cazalis, 14 May 1867 (*Correspondance*, 342).
49. Augustine, *City* 8.23 (1:544); Brague (2013), 30–34 and 200–205.

Chapter 20. Checkmate?

1. On the history of the word and concept, see the synthesis of Volpi (1996); Rehm (1947).
2. G. Flaubert, *L'Éducation sentimentale* [1845], chap. 21 (*OC* 1:323a); Nodier, in Bénichou (2004), 319.
3. Petrarch, *Invective contra medicum*, bk. 1, toward the end.
4. See the texts cited or referred to in Brague (2002b), 298–305.
5. Haydon, *Diary* 1:269 [VIII, 28 December 1817]; in Armogathe (2007), 231–32.
6. Blake, "Annotations to Bacon's Essays Moral, Economical and Political" (*Complete*, 620–32).
7. Byron, *Manfred* [1817], 1.1.10–12 (*SP*, 309); Renan, "De la Métaphysique et de son avenir" [1860], III (*OC* 1:714); Claudel, *Le Soulier de satin*, first day, scene 6 (*Théâtre*, 2:687).
8. See the interpretation by Carroll (2008), 47; Epictetus, *Discourses* 1.4.27; 2.20.8.
9. D'Alembert, *Réflexions sur l'usage et sur l'abus de la philosophie dans les matières de goût* (*Oeuvres* 4:333; my italics).
10. See Quevedo, *La cuna y la sepultura para el conocimiento propio y desengaño de las cosas ajenas* [1634] (*Obras* 1:1190–1226, esp. chaps. 1 and 4); Starobinski (1964), 86b.

11. Martin (1994), 267–70; Wieland, *Idris und Zenide*, song 3, strophe 10 (*Werke* 4:242); Burke, *Revolution*, 67. Already Proclus, *Republic* 6 (1:116).

12. G. Leopardi, *Discorso di un italiano intorno alla poesia romantica* [1818] (*Opere*, 968–96, cited from 973b); see also *Zibaldone*, 21–22 (*Opere*, 20b); 216 (18–20 August 1820) (*Opere*, 83b).

13. Pushkin, "Geroy" [29 September 1830], lines 63–64 (*O*, 362b). For an allusion in Gorki, see Heller and Niqueux (1995), 239; Villiers, *Eve*, V, 16, p. 333; then V, 2, pp. 287–88. Also see V, 11, p. 322.

14. See Nietzsche, frag. 1 [145], Autumn 1885–Spring 1886 (*KSA* 12:44); Taylor (1989), 404.

15. Aristotle, *Protrepticus*, frag. 14, #86 (*Fragmenta*, 50); *De anima* 2.4.415b8.

16. Barta, *Gespräch*; Pinès and Harvey (1984).

17. Lasaulx, *Mortis*; Burckhardt, *Griechische Kulturgeschichte*, 5. Abschnitt [sec. 5], in *Geschichtswerk*, 2:396–444. Burckhardt, who cites Lasaulx, *PG*, abundantly in his *Weltgeschichtliche Betrachtungen*, does not mention him in his work on Greek history.

18. Schopenhauer, *Die Welt als Wille und Vorstellung*, bk. 4, chap. 46, "Von der Nichtigkeit und dem Leiden des Lebens" (*WW* 2:733–54); on the reception, see the panorama of A. Henry (1989); for Germany: I. Krauss (1931); on Beckett and Borges: Wellbery (1998); on Klages, Ernst Bloch, Heidegger, Adorno: Pauen (1994).

19. Dühring, *Werth*.

20. Mallock, *Worth*, 31, 33, 44–45.

21. Ollé-Laprune, *Prix*.

22. James, "Is Life Worth Living?" (*Will*, 32–62).

23. Eucken, *Sinn*.

24. Nietzsche, frag. 9 [1], Summer 1875 (*KSA* 8:131–81).

25. "*Is Life Worth Living?*" *Debate; Affirmative: Prof. George B. Foster; Negative: Clarence S. Darrow*, 11 March 1917 (Chicago: Higgins, 1917); *Great Public Debate on the Question: "Is Life Worth Living?," Yes: Frederick Starr, No: Clarence S. Darrow*, 28 March 1920, Chicago [*non vidi*].

26. See above, 2, 109–10.

27. Kant, *Kritik der reinen Vernunft*, preface, Bxii–xiv; then Schelling, *Einleitung zu dem Entwurf eines Systems der Naturphilosophie*, para. 4 (*AW* [1799–1801], 276).

28. Cooke, *Federalist*, 88–89; Gay (1969), 566.

29. Renan, *Avenir*, chap. 8, *OC* 3:1133, n. 68; Mill, *On Liberty*, chap. 3 (*ULRG*, 115; also see 122); and see 4 (*ULRG*, 137); Walter Pater, conclusion to *Studies in the History of the Renaissance*, in Shattuck (1996), 318.

30. Nietzsche, frag. 6 [48], Summer 1875 (*KSA* 8:115–18).

31. Shattuck (1986), 78–81.

32. Lilla (2007), 308 as well as 5–6 and 12; also see Shattuck (1996), 27, 289, 309.

33. Job 7:1a. The classical Jewish commentators all understand the passage as a reminder of the brevity of life. It is the same with the translators of the Autho-

rized Version. The Vulgate (*militia*) and Luther (*im Dienst stehen*) chose the idea of "service"; Augustine, *Confessiones* 10.28.39 (BA 14:210).

34. Maimonides, *Guide* 3.24 (from p. 361, line 27, to p. 362, line 5; p. 189 in Munk's trans.).

35. Robinet, *Vues*.

36. Villiers, *Eve*, bk. 2, chap. 4, p. 187.

37. Goethe, conversation with Johann Daniel Falk (no. 1185), 14 June 1809 (*Gespräche* 2:41); Hadot (2004), 263; then Jonas (1979), 188; also see 280.

38. Dostoyevsky, *Journal*, October 1876, issue no. 1, art. 4, p. 322; on the theme "nobody to curse," see the passage by S. Crane, in Brague (2002b), 286; then *Karamazov*, pt. 2, bk. 5, chap. 5, p. 265. The phrase is presented as a citation (in quotation marks!). The word "experimental" disappears in the translation of H. Mongault. Beyond the echoes of Psalm 104:26, or of Shakespeare, *Richard III*, 1.1.20, there is no doubt an allusion to N. N. Strakhov, criticizing the thinkers according to whom man would only be a transitory form, an essay of nature bound to be supplanted by a superior being; see Čyževśkyj (1936), 70. I owe this reference to B. Harress (Leipzig).

39. R. M. Rilke, "Wie die Natur die Wesen überlässt . . ." (*Gedichte*, 324); Heidegger, "Wozu Dichter?" (*Holzwege*, 248–95). The word "risk" is also in Jonas (1979), 247; Huxley, *WDIT?*, chap. 5, pp. 150–51, 177.

40. Bernal, *WFD*, chap. 5, p. 64 (last words of the chapter).

41. Nietzsche, *Morgenröte*, III, aphorism 187 (*KSA* 3:160); V, aphorism 432 (*KSA* 3:266); aphorism 453 (*KSA* 3:274); aphorism 501 (*KSA* 3:294); *Die fröhliche Wissenschaft*, I, aphorism 51 (*KSA* 3:415–16); III, aphorism 110 (*KSA* 3:471); IV, aphorism 324 (*KSA* 3:552); *Jenseits*, V, aphorism 203 (*KSA* 5:126).

42. Alexander von Villers, letter to Warsberg, 30 April 1873 (*Briefe*, 245).

43. Schult, *Barlach*, 22 (June 1921). Cited without reference in Sedlmayr (1948), 157.

44. Nietzsche, frag. 25 [305], Spring 1884 (*KSA* 11:88). The exclamation *wohlan!* has the value of a concept.

45. See Arendt (1958), 307; Starobinski (1964), 145; M. Henry (1987), 94–95—with another concept of life.

46. Zola, *Pascal*, chap. 2, pp. 97, 94; chap. 8, p. 304; chap. 4, p. 159.

47. Zola, *Pascal*, chap. 6, pp. 222, 228; also see chap. 8, p. 305, and above, p. 171.

48. Zola, *Pascal*, chap. 2, p. 102; the formulation is reproduced identically in chap. 14, p. 497, then chap. 14, p. 501; same formulations in a manuscript sketch, reproduced in the dossier at the end of the cited edition, pp. 542–45.

49. Zola, *Pascal*, chap. 2, pp. 93, 102.

50. Zola, *Pascal*, chap. 8, pp. 305, 307; chap. 9, pp. 312, 341; chap. 12, pp. 427, 449.

51. Zola, *Pascal*, chap. 2, p. 116; chap. 5, p. 214; on Renan, see Brague (2014), 310.

52. Zola, *Pascal*, chap. 12, p. 443.

53. Zola, *Pascal*, chap. 6, p. 242; chap. 12, p. 434.

54. Nietzsche, *Die fröhliche Wissenschaft*, pt. 3, aphorism 125 [1882] (*KSA* 5:480–82); *Also sprach Zarathustra*, prologue, 2 (*KSA* 4:14); *Die fröhliche Wissenschaft*, pt. 5, aphorism 343 [1887] (5:573).

55. See Carroll's interpretation (2008), 29–34, esp. 32; on Shakespeare's *Hamlet*, 43.

56. Meyer, *Versuchung*, chap. 3, p. 72; chap. 4, pp. 83, 106; chap. 5, pp. 109–10. See Meier (2003), 79–80.

57. Title of the third volume of the *Apokalypse der deutschen Seele* of H. U. von Balthasar (1939). The same expression (smertobožnitšestvo) is the title of an anonymous Russian brochure of 1926, inspired by Fedorov; in it, Christianity is reproached for having deified death by renouncing fighting it technologically, thereby agreeing to yield to the power of nature; see Scheibert (1967).

58. W. Borchert, prologue to *Draussen vor der Tür* [1946] (*Gesamtwerk*, 104–5).

59. Wagner, letter to August Rockel, 25 January 1854; Comte, introduction to *Synthèse*, 18; Nietzsche, *Die fröhliche Wissenschaft*, pt. 4, aphorism 276 (*KSA* 3:521 [*amor fati*]).

Chapter 21. Lights Out

1. René Viviani, Discours à la Chambre des députés of 8 November 1906, in *Journal officiel de la République française*, 9 November 1906, p. 2433c (my italics). Remarks by Péguy, *Oeuvres*, 550–59.

2. Baudelaire, *Théophile Gautier*, sec. 6 (*OC*, 699–700); Mallarmé, *Hérodiade*, scene 2 (*OC*, 47); Friedrich (1967), 37, 69, 106.

3. H. Fussli, in Knowles, *Fuseli*, chap. 15 (vol. 1), p. 404.

4. Winckelmann, *Erinnerung über die Betrachtung der Werke der Kunst* [1759] (*Schriften*, 151); Marc, letter to his wife on 12 April 1915 (*Briefe*, 63); Sedlmayr (1948), 156–59.

5. Berdyaev, "Krizis isskustva" [1918] (*Filosofia* 2:408–9; in Marcadé [2008], 567). Also see Bulgakov, "Trup krassoty: Po povody kartin Picasso" [1914] (*Tikhie*, 26–39); partial trans. in Pain, Bulgakov, 67–72.

6. Godin (2003), 114–16; on the neo-iconoclast context, see Besançon (1994), 3rd pt.; Ortega y Gasset, *La deshumanización del arte* (*Obras*, 353–86).

7. Weidlé (2002), 233–34, then 403. Weidlé knew Ortega y Gasset's work, and cites pages 357–58 (p. 134).

8. G. Apollinaire, "Sur la peinture," in *Méditations esthétiques: Les peintres cubistes* [1908] (*Oeuvres*, sec. 7, p. 17, then sec. 1, p. 5 [my italics]).

9. See, below, the texts of Chateaubriand and Flaubert, 205.

10. M. Henry (1987), 85.

11. Pinthus, preface to *MD* (1919), 23, 25, 27, 32, then postface (1922), 35.

12. Pinthus, *MD*, "Nach 40 Jahren" (1959), 15.

13. Blok, *Effondrement*, sec. 7, p. 114, and also see sec. 3, p. 97; Brague (2013), 112–30. Since the original edition of the book cited above, I discovered an earlier use of the word "antihumanism" in Scheler, *Ressentiment*, sec. 4, p. 76.

14. Heidegger, *Being*, para. 10, p. 46; Brague (2006b), 124–26; Heidegger, *Kant*, para. 37, 188–93. Citation from para. 41, p. 207.

15. Heidegger, *Die Grundbegriffe der Metaphysik: Welt-Endlichkeit-Einsamkeit*, ed. F. W. von Herrmann (*GA*, vol. 29/30, pp. 31, 93); *Vom Wesen der menschlichen Freiheit: Einleitung in die Philosophie*, ed. H. Tietjen (*GA*, vol. 31, p. 127).

16. Heidegger, "Platons Lehre von der Wahrheit" [1931] (*Wegmarken*, 142); *Hölderlins Hymnen "Germanien" und "Der Rhein,"* winter semester, 1934–35 (*GA*, vol. 39, pp. 47–48, 50); "Die Zeit des Weltbildes" [1938] (*Holzwege*, 86).

17. Heidegger, *Humanism*, 147, 175, then 151–53, 155.

18. Heidegger, *Humanism*, 154–55, 175, 161.

19. Heidegger, *Humanism*, 183, 172; 164, 183, 173; 162, 172; 173.

20. Heidegger, *Humanism*, 176.

21. Lévi-Strauss, *Pensée*, 326–27; L. Althusser (1964), reprinted in Althusser (1965); Foucault (1966), 396–98 (image); foundation in Nietzsche, 353 and see 232; "Is Man Dead?" [June 1966], in Foucault (1994), vol. 1, no. 39, pp. 540–44; the interpretation of Taylor (2007), 635 (Foucault attacks the "civilizing" side, the repressive side, of humanism), seems to me to be too kind; Brague (2013), 133–59; Derrida (1967), 427.

22. Tenbruck (1984), 230–43.

23. Lasaulx, *PG*, 4, pp. 73–74; 6, p. 106.

24. Chateaubriand, *Mémoires*, pt. 4, bk. 44, p. 1791; Bossi (2003), 7 and 114 ("anthropolatry").

25. Flaubert, letter to Louise Colet, 2 March 1854 (*Correspondance* 2:529); cited without reference in Muray (1999), 505; then Flaubert, letter to Louise Colet, 26 May 1853 (*Correspondance* 3:334); in Muray (1999), 587.

26. Baudelaire, *Fusées*, sec. 11 (*OC*, 1256).

27. Carroll, "Vivesection as a Sign of the Times" [1875] (*Works*, 1091–92).

28. Donoso Cortés, Carta al Cardenal Fornari [19 June 1852] (*Obras* 2:613–30, cited from 617 and 621, then 623).

29. Trousson (1964), 2:427.

30. Bloy, *Le Fils de Louis XVI* [1900], chap. 3, "L'absence de Dieu" (*Oeuvres* 5:98–103, cited from 99).

31. Berdyaev, *Novoe*; see French trans., 21; Bloy and Berdyaev are both cited in Lubac (1998), 62.

32. Malraux, *Tentation*, 128.

33. Gilson (1955), 192.

34. Sartre, *EH*, 20, 22, 52, 67, then 23, 55, 69–70; 37.

35. Sartre, *EH*, 36, then 33–34, then 94. The word attributed to Dostoyevsky, under the form of "all is permitted," is placed by him in the mouth of Ivan Karamazov; see *Karamazov*, pt. 1, bk. 2, chap. 6, p. 73.

36. Sartre, *EH*, 95.

37. Leiris, "Homme," 266; Carrouges (1948), 214 and 377.

38. Shattuck (1968), 216–17; Clair (2003), 155.

39. Robeck, *Exercitatio* [*non vidi*]; mentioned, among others, by Voltaire, *Candide*, chap. 12, and Rousseau, *La Nouvelle Héloïse*, pt. 2, letter 21 (*OC*, 378); Crocker (1952); Cromaziano, *Istoria*; Durkheim, *Le Suicide* [1879].

40. Goethe, *Die Leiden des jungen Werther*, pt. 1, letter of 12 August (*W* 4:41–45, cited from p. 43); Rabbe, *Album d'un pessimiste*, followed by *Portefeuille*, 33–59,

cited from 40; Vigny, *PC*, preface, then act 2, scene 5 (The Quaker) (pp. 205, then 235).

41. Novalis, *Hemsterhuis und Kant-Studien* [1797], Fragmentblatt, para. 20 (*WTB* 2:223; commentary, *WTB* 3:330–31). It is perhaps to this passage that J. S. Mill alludes in *Utilitarianism*, chap. 2 (*ULRG*, 12); Schlegel, *Philosophische Fragmente*, first period, sec. 3 [1800.2], no. 585 (*Ausgabe*, 174); also see nos. 589 and 592 (*Ausgabe*, 175); Fichte, *Die Bestimmung des Menschen*, bk. 4, sec. 4 (*AW* 3:413).

42. See *Apophtegmes des Pères du desert*, 5th apophthegm of Father Longin (PG 65:257b); cited, incorrectly, by al-Farabi, *State*, pt. 6, chap. 19, para. 6, p. 320; commentary, p. 500 and Vallat (2005), 56n2; Elias, *Prolegomena Philosophiae*, 5, ed. A. Busse (*CAG*, vol. 18, pt. 1), pp. 13, 25–27.

43. Schopenhauer, *Paralipomena*, chap. 13, paras. 157–60 (*WW* 5:316–67).

44. Carlyle, *Sartor Resartus* [1836], bk. 2, chap. 7 (*SRHW*, 122, 126); G. Büchner, *Dantons Tod* [1835], act 2, scene 1 (*Werke*, 30); also see act 3, scene 4 (*Werke*, 48); Schopenhauer, *Die Welt als Wille und Vorstellung*, bk. 2, chap. 28, and bk. 4, chap. 46 (*WW* 2:457 and 734); Vischer, "Ein Traum: Mitgeteilt von Robert Scharff" (*Briefwechsel*, 259–303).

45. Renan, *Avenir*, chap. 1, *OC* 3:734; chap. 8, *OC* 3:858; chap. 17, *OC* 3:988; chap. 19, *OC* 3:1056. Renan cites the case of Chatterton in chap. 10, *OC* 3:1048.

46. Conrad, *Nostromo*, pt. 3, chap. 10, pp. 412–16; on the theory of action implied here, see pt. 1, chap. 6, p. 86; Chopin, *The Awakening*, chaps. 6, then 39 and 10 (*Complete*, 654–55, then 535 and 552).

47. Hartmann, *Philosophie*, pt. C, "Metaphysik des Unbewußten," chap. 13, 3rd stage of illusion (2:373); Soloviev, *Krizis zapadnoy filosofii (Protiv positivistov)*, pt. 4 (end) (*RO* 1:125, 127; in French trans., 305, 308).

48. Paperno (1997), 123–61.

49. See above, 137.

50. Dostoyevsky, *Journal*, October 1876, issue no. 1, art. 4, pp. 321–22; in French trans., 725–28. On the context, see Paperno (1997), 162–84; see the texts cited there: Kramer, 134, Russian, 285; N. N., 168–69, Russian, 294–95; "The Dream of a Ridiculous Man," chap. 4 in Fache, *Nouvelles*, 62; Dostoyevsky, *Journal*, December 1876, issue no. 1, art. 3, pp. 387–91; in French trans., 811–15; *Karamazov*, pt. 1, bk. 2, chap. 6, p. 73.

51. Le Dantec, *Atheism*, 101 and 106.

52. Benson, *Lord*, bk. 3, chap. 4, sec. 1 (p. 260); J. H. Rosny Senior, *La Mort de la Terre* [1910].

53. Carroll (2008), 181.

54. Camus, *Le Mythe de Sisyphe* (*Essais*, esp. 99).

55. Jacobi, "Sylli an Clerdon," chap. 4 in *Allwills* (4:58); Milton, *PL*, bk. 10, lines 979–91 (p. 256); Byron, *Cain: A Mystery* [1821], act 2, scene 1 (*SP*, 356–57); F. M. Klinger, *Der verbannte Göttersohn* [1777], in Rieger, *Klinger*, 234; Bonaventura, *Nachtwachen*, 118 (14th vigil); Hof (1970), 57; Brague (2011), 90–98.

56. Sartre, "La Nausée" (*Oeuvres*, 187); in Godin (2003), 159.

Conclusion

1. Rousseau, *Discourse on the Sciences and the Arts*; the felicitous formulation I cited is from Lilla (2007), 112; Vico, *Nuova scienza*, "Conclusion," para. 1106 (O 1:967); Lilla (1993), 209–17. On the essential, see M. Henry (1987).
2. Ferguson, *Civil Society*, pt. 3, sec. 6, then pt. 3, sec. 4, pp. 149 and 140.
3. Schabert (1990), 43–44.
4. In Pütz (1978), 31–32; Leopardi, *Zibaldone*, 21–22 [not dated, between 1817 and 1818], p. 20b; also see Donoso Cortés, *Ensayo sobre el catolicismo, el liberalismo y el socialismo* [1851], bk. 1, chap. 1 (*Obras* 2:349).
5. Brague (2002a), 74, and more recently Brague (2013).
6. Gray (1995), 144.
7. Aristotle, *Physics* 2.2.194b13; Hermann Bonitz, *Index aristotelicus* [1870], 59b40–45; on the meaning of the formulation, see Oehler (1963), 37–65, esp. 55n46; Cervantes, *Quijote*, pt. 2, chap. 45, p. 887.
8. Aristotle, *On generation and corruption* 2.10, in particular 336b17–18; also see *Metaphysics*, Lambda, 5, 1071a13–17.
9. Aristotle, *Politics*, cited above, 34.
10. Brague (2008a), 184.
11. The classical commentators are rather reticent, except Nachmanides, who, however, only paraphrases (*MG*, 28b–29a); for the fathers of the church, see *ACCS* 3:289 (Ambrose, *Hexameron* 6.8.53 [PL 14:264cd]; Clement of Alexandria, *Stromata* 2.18, 96, 4 [SC 38, pp. 107–8]). Biblical parallels: Ezek. 28:4 and Isa. 10:13–14.
12. Maimonides, *Guide* 3.12, p. 322, lines 6–7 (p. 77 in Munk's trans.); Brague (2008c), 341–42.
13. Marx, *Manuscripts*, no. 3, p. 97; see above, 123.
14. Dante, "Purgatorio," canto 10, lines 124–25, in *Commedia*, and Wordsworth, *Prelude*, bk. 11, lines 251–54.
15. Leibniz, *Principles*, para. 7, p. 45.
16. Brague (2008c), 434–35.
17. Sartre, *EH*, 91–92; also see B. Russell (1962), chap. 5, p. 122.
18. "Sincere Brethren," *R*, II, 8 [22] (2:204), and see above, 23–24.

Bibliography

In the primary sources, where two sets of publication information are provided, the later edition is the one that has been cited in this book.

Primary Sources

ACCS = *Ancient Christian Commentary on Scripture*. Edited by T. C. Oden. Downers Grove, IL: InterVarsity Press, 2001–.
BA = Bibliothèque Augustinienne. Paris: Desclée De Brouwer, 1949–.
CAAG = *Collection des anciens alchimistes grecs*. Edited by M. Berthelot and C. E. Ruelle. 3 vols. Paris: Steinheil, 1888.
CAG = *Commentaria in Aristotelem Graeca*. Berlin: Reimer, 1882–1909.
CCCM = Corpus Christianorum: Continuatio Mediaevalis. Turnhout: Brepols, 1969–.
CCSL = Corpus Christianorum: Series Latina. Turnhout: Brepols, 1953–.
CH = *Corpus Hermeticum*. Edited by A. D. Nock and A. J. Festugière. 4 vols. Paris: Les Belles Lettres, 1946–54.
DK = *Die Fragmente der Vorsokratiker*. Edited by H. Diels and W. Kranz. Zurich and Berlin: Weidmann, 1964.
GCS = Die griechischen christlichen Schriftsteller der ersten [drei] Jahrhunderte.
EI = *Encyclopédie de l'Islam*. 2nd ed. Leiden: Brill; Paris: Maisonneuve et Larose, 1960–89.
Loeb = Loeb Classical Library. Cambridge, MA: Harvard University Press.
MG = *Miqraot Gedolot*. Jerusalem: Eshkol, 1976.
NHC II = *Nag-Hammadi Codex II, 2–7*. Edited by B. Layton. Leiden: Brill, 1989.
NM = *Die neue Menschheit: Biopolitische Utopien in Russland zu Beginn des 20. Jahrhunderts*. Edited by B. Groys and M. Hagemeister. Frankfurt: Suhrkamp, 2005.
PF = *Philosopher par le feu: Anthologie de textes alchimiques occidentaux*. Edited by F. Bonardel. Paris: Seuil, 1995.
PG = Patrologia Graeca. Edited by J.-P. Migne. 162 vols. Paris, 1857–86.

PL = Patrologia Latina. Edited by J.-P. Migne. 217 vols. Paris, 1844–64.
QAM = La Querelle des Anciens et des Modernes. Edited by A.-M. Lecoq. Paris: Gallimard, 2001.
SAC = Barocchi, P., ed. Scritti d'arte del cinquecento. Vol. 1, Generalia, Arti e scienze, Le arti. Turin: Einaudi, 1977.
SC = Sources chrétiennes. Paris: Editions du cerf, 1941–.

Adams, Education = Adams, H. The Education of Henry Adams. Edited by I. B. Nadel. Oxford: Oxford University Press, 1999.
Agobard, Opera = Agobard of Lyon. Opera Omnia. Edited by L. Van Acker. Corpus Christianorum: Continuatio Mediaevalis 52. Turnhout: Brepols, 1981.
Agrippa, Occulta = Agrippa of Nettesheim. De occulta philosophia libri tres. Edited by V. Perrone Compagni. Leiden: Brill, 1992.
Alain of Lille, Works = Alain of Lille, Literary Works. Edited by W. Wetherbee. Cambridge, MA: Harvard University Press, 2013.
Albert, AMOO/Borgnet = Albert the Great. Alberti Magni Opera Omnia. Edited by Auguste Borgnet. Paris: Vivès, 1890–99.
Albert, AMOO/Geyer = Albert the Great. Alberti Magni Opera Omnia. Edited by Bernhard Geyer. Münster: Aschendorff, 1975–.
Albert, Animalibus = De animalibus. Edited by H. Stadler. Münster: Aschendorff, 1920.
———, Menschen = Über den Menschen: De homine. Edited by H. Anzulewicz et al. Hamburg: Meiner, 2006.
Alberti, Famiglia = Alberti, Leone Battista. I libri della famiglia. Edited by F. Furlan. Turin: Einaudi, 1994.
———, Opere = Opere volgari. Edited by C. Greyson. Bari: Laterza, 1960.
al-Biruni, Tahqīq = al-Biruni. Tahqīq li-'l-Hind min maqūla maqbūla fi'l-'aql aw mardūla. Edited by A. Safa. Beirut: 'Alam al-kutub, 1983.
Alchimistes = Les Alchimistes grecs. Edited by M. Mertens. Paris: Les Belles Lettres, 1995.
Alexander, Space = Alexander, S. Space, Time and Deity [. . .]. London: Macmillan, 1927.
Alexander of Aphrodisias, Scripta = Alexander of Aphrodisias. Scripta minora. Supplementum aristotelicum 2.2. Edited by I. Bruns. Berlin, 1892.
al-Farabi, Catálogo = al-Farabi. Catálogo de las ciencias. Edited by A. Gonzalez Palencia. Madrid: CSIC, 1953.
al-Farabi, State = al-Farabi [al-Farabi]. On the Perfect State. Edited by R. Walzer. Oxford: Oxford University Press, 1985.
al-Razi, Abu Bakr Muhammad ibn Zakariyya, Shukûk = Abu Bakr Muhammad ibn Zakariyya al-Razi. Kitâb Al-Shukûk 'Alâ Jâlinûs. Edited by M. Mohaghegh. Tehran: Institute of Islamic Studies, 1993.
al-Razi, Abu Hâtim, Proofs = al-Razi, Abu Hâtim. The Proofs of Prophecy. Edited by T. Khalidi. Provo, UT: Brigham Young University Press, 2011.
Andreae, Reipublicae = Andreae, J. V. Reipublicae Christianopolitanae Descriptio. Edited by R. van Dülmen. Stuttgart: Calwer Verlag, 1972.
Apollinaire, Oeuvres = Apollinaire, G. Oeuvres en prose complètes. Edited by P. Caizergues and M. Decaudin. Paris: Hermann, 1991.

Arago, *Oeuvres* = Arago, François. *Oeuvres complètes*. Edited by J. A. Barral. Paris: Gide, 1854.

Archimedes, *Sphere* = Archimedes. *De la sphère et du cylindre*. Edited by C. Mugler. Paris: Les Belles Lettres, 1970.

Aristotle, *Fragmenta* = Aristotle. *Fragmenta selecta*. Edited by W. D. Ross. Oxford: Oxford University Press, 1955.

———, *Metaphysica* = *Metaphysica: Translatio Jacobi sive "Vetustissima."* Edited by G. Vuillemin-Diem. Aristoteles Latinus XXV, 1–1a. Brussels and Paris: Desclée De Brouwer, 1970.

Arndt, *Pflegung* = Arndt, E. M. *Ein Wort über die Pflegung und Erhaltung der Forsten und der Bauern im Sinne einer höheren d. h. menschlichen Gesetzgebung*. Schleswig, 1820.

Augustine, *City* = Augustine. *Der Gottesstaat/De civitate Dei*. Edited by C. J. Perl. 2 vols. Paderborn: Schöningh, 1979.

———, *Genesi* = *De Genesi ad litteram*. Edited by J. Zycha. Corpus Scriptorum Ecclesiasticorum Latinorum 28/1. Prague: Tempsky, 1894.

Augustini Niphi Medici Philosophi Suessani, *Metaphysics* = Augustini Niphi Medici Philosophi Suessani. *Expositiones in Aristotelis libros Metaphysices [. . .]*. Frankfurt: Minerva, 1967. First published in Venice, 1559.

Averroës, *Anima* = Averroës [Ibn Rushd]. *Commentary on the De Anima*. Edited by F. S. Crawford. Cambridge, MA: Medieval Society of America, 1953.

———, *Tafsir* = *Tafsir ma ba'd at-tabi'at*. Edited by M. Bouyges. Beirut: Dar al-Mashreq, 1983.

———, *Tahâfut* = *Tahâfut al-Tahâfut*. Edited by M. Bouyges. Beirut: Dar el-Machreq, 1987.

Avicenna, "Actions et Passions" = Avicenna. "Actions et Passions." In *Traités*. Qom: Bîdâr, n.d.

———, *Avicenna* = *Avicenna [. . .] opera in lucem redacta [. . .]*. Frankfurt: Minerva, 1961.

———, *Congelatione* = *Avicennae de congelatione et conglutinatione lapidum, Being Sections of the Kitâb al-Shifâ; The Latin and Arabic texts [. . .]*. Edited by E. J. Holmyard and D. C. Mandeville. Paris: Geuthner, 1927.

———, *Genèse* = *Genèse et retour*. Edited by A. Nurani. Teheran: n.p., 1984.

———, *Gloses* = *Gloses*. Edited by A. Badawi. Cairo: G.E.B.O., 1983.

———, *Livre* = *Le livre des théorèmes et des avertissements*. Edited by J. Forget. Leiden, 1892. Translated by A.-M. Goichon. Paris: Vrin, 1951.

———, *Soul* = *Avicenna's "De anima": Being the Psychological Part of "Kitāb al-Shifā'."* Edited by F. Rahman. London: Oxford University Press, 1959.

Bacon, *Advancement* = Bacon, Francis. *The Advancement of Learning and New Atlantis*. Edited by T. Case. London: Oxford University Press, 1969.

———, *Atlantis* = *New Atlantis*. London: Oxford University Press, 1969.

———, *Cogitata* = *Cogitata et Visa*. In *Récusation des doctrines philosophiques et autres opuscules*, edited by G. Rombi and D. Deleule, 146–215. Paris: Presses Universitaires de France, 1987.

———, *Organon* = *Neues Organon*. Latin-German. Edited by W. Krohn. 2 vols. Darmstadt: Wissenschaftliche Buchgesellschaft, 1990.

———, *Works* = *Works*. Edited by J. Spedding, R. L. Ellis, and D. D. Heath. London: Longman, 1858–74.

Bacon, R., *Epistula* = Bacon, Roger. *Epistula de secretis operibus artis et naturae*. Edited by J. S. Brewer. London, 1859.

———, *Opera* = *Opera quaedam hactenus inedita*. Edited by J. S. Brewer. London, 1859.

———, *Opera hactenus* = *Opera hactenus inedita Rogeri Baconi*. Edited by R. Steele. 16 vols. Oxford: Oxford University Press, 1905–40.

———, *Opus majus* = *Opus majus*. Edited by J. H. Bridges. 3 vols. Oxford: Clarendon, 1897–1900.

———, *Opus tertium* = *Part of the "Opus tertium" of Roger Bacon: Including a Fragment Now Printed for the First Time*. Edited by A. G. Little. Aberdeen: Aberdeen University Press, 1912.

———, *Retardatione* = *De retardatione accidentium senectutis [. . .]*. Edited by A. G. Little and E. Withington. Vol. 4 of *Opera Hactenus Inedita*. Oxford: Clarendon Press, 1928.

Badawi, *Aflutin* = Badawi, A. *Aflutin 'inda al-'Arab*. 3rd ed. Kuwait: Waqālat al-maṭbū'āt, 1977.

Baillet, *Vie* = Baillet, Adrien. *Vie de M. Des Cartes*. 1691.

Bakunin, *Oeuvres* = Bakunin, Mikhail. *Oeuvres: "Fédéralisme, socialisme et anti-théologisme"; "Lettres sur le patriotrisme"; "Dieu et l'État."* 1895.

Balzac, *Oeuvre* = Balzac, Honoré de. *L'Oeuvre de Balzac*. Edited by A. Béguin and J. A. Ducourneau. Paris: Club français du livre, 1966.

Barruel, *Mémoires* = Barruel, Augustin. *Mémoires pour servir à l'histoire du jacobinisme*. 5 vols. Hamburg, 1798–99.

Barta, *Gespräch* = Barta, W., ed. *Das Gespräch eines Mannes mit seinem Ba (Papyrus Berlin 3024)*. Berlin: Hessling, 1969.

Basil, *Homilies* = Basil of Caesarea. *Homélies sur l'Hexaemeron*. Edited by M. Naldini. Milan: Mondadori, 1990.

Baudelaire, *OC* = Baudelaire, Charles. *Oeuvres complètes*. Edited by Y.-G. Le Dantec and C. Pichois. Paris: Gallimard, 1961.

Bayern = *Bayern ohne Klöster? Die Säkularisation 1802/03 und ihre Folgen; Eine Ausstellung des Bayerischen Hauptstaatsarchivs*. Munich: Generaldirektion der Staatlichen Archive Bayerns, 2003.

Bayle, *Dictionnaire* = Bayle, Pierre. *Dictionnaire historique et critique*. 5th ed. Amsterdam, 1740.

———, *Oeuvres* = *Oeuvres diverses*. Edited by E. Labrousse. Hildesheim: Olms, 1965. First published in The Hague, 1727.

Beccaria, *Dei* = Beccaria, Cesare. *Dei delitti e delle pene*. Edited by A. Burgio. Milan: Feltrinelli, 1991. First published in 1764.

Benson, *Lord* = Benson, Robert Hugh. *Lord of the World*. New York: Dodd, Mead and Co., 1907. Reprint, South Bend, IN: Saint Augustine's Press, 2001.

Bentham, *Principles* = Bentham, J. *An Introduction to the Principles of Morals and Legislation.* Edited by J. H. Burns and H. L. A. Hart. London: Athlone Press, 1970.

———, *Works* = *Complete Works.* Edited by J. Bowring. Edinburgh: Tait, 1843.

Berdyaev, *Filosofia* = Berdyaev, N. *Filosofia tvorčestva, kultury i isskustva.* Moscow: Iskusstvo, 1994.

———, *Novoe* = *Novoe Srednevekov'e: Razmýslenie o sud'be Rossii i Evropy.* Berlin: Obelisk, 1924. http://krotov.info/library/02_b/berdyaev/1924_24_21.html. Translated into French by J.-C. Marcadé and S. Siger as *Le Nouveau Moyen Âge [. . .].* Lausanne: L'Âge d'Homme, 1985.

Bergson, *Sources* = Bergson, Henri. *Les deux Sources de la morale et de la religion.* Paris: Alcan, 1932.

Bernal, *WFD* = Bernal, John Desmond. *The World, the Flesh and the Devil: An Inquiry into the Future of the Three Enemies of the Rational Soul.* London: Jonathan Cape, 1929. Reprint, Bloomington: Indiana University Press, 1969.

Bernard, *Introduction* = Bernard, Claude. *Introduction à l'étude de la médecine expérimentale,* edited by F. Dagognet. Paris: Garnier-Flammarion, 1966.

———, *Leçons* = *Leçons sur les phénomènes de la vie communs aux animaux et aux végétaux.* Paris, 1878.

Bernard, *Opera* = Bernard of Clairvaux. *Opera.* Edited by J. Leclercq et al. Rome: Editiones Cistercienses, 1957–.

Bessarion, *Gelehrtenkreis* = Cardinal Bessarion. *Aus Bessarions Gelehrtenkreis: Abhandlungen, Reden, Briefe [. . .].* Edited by L. Mohler. Aalen: Scientia, 1967. First published in 1942.

Betzky, *Plans* = Betzky, Ivan I. *Les Plans et les Statuts des différents établissements ordonnés par sa Majesté Impériale Catherine II pour l'éducation de la jeunesse et l'utilité générale de Son Empire.* Originally published in Russian. Translated into French by "Mr. Clerc." Amsterdam, 1775.

Blake, *Complete* = Blake, W. *The Complete Poetry and Prose.* Edited by D. V. Erdman. Berkeley: University of California Press, 1982.

Blok, *Effondrement* = Blok, Aleksandr. "Крушение гуманизма" [The foundering of humanism]. In *Собрание сочинений* [*Collected Works*], Moscow: Editions d'État de littérature d'art, 1962, t. 6: проза 1918–1921, 93–115.

———, *Oeuvres* = *Oeuvres en prose, 1906–1921.* French translation by J. Michaut. Lausanne: L'Âge d'homme, 1974.

Bloy, *Oeuvres* = Bloy, Léon. *Oeuvres.* Edited by J. Bollery and J. Petit. Paris: Mercure de France, 1966.

Boaistuau, *Discours* = Boaistuau, Pierre. *Bref discours de l'excellence et dignité de l'homme.* Edited by M. Simonin. Genève: Droz, 1982.

Bodin, *Démonomanie* = Bodin, Jean. *De la démonomanie des sorciers.* Paris, 1580.

———, *Oeuvres* = *Oeuvres philosophiques.* Edited by P. Mesnard. Paris: Presses Universitaires de France, 1951.

———, *République* = *Les six livres de la République.* 1583. Reprint, Aalen: Scientia, 1961.

Boethius, *Consolation* = Boethius. *De consolatione philosophiae.* Edited by H. F. Stewart et al. Loeb, 1973.

Boissy d'Anglas, *Procès-verbaux* = Boissy d'Anglas, F. A. *Procès-verbaux du Comité d'instruction publique de la Convention*. Edited by J. Guillaume. Paris, 1897.
Bonaventura, *Nachtwachen* = Bonaventura [E. A. F. Klingemann]. *Nachtwachen*. Edited by W. Paulsen. Stuttgart: Reclam, 2003.
Bonaventure, *Cymbalum* = Bonaventure des Périers (?). *Cymbalum mundi*. Edited by P. H. Nurse. Geneva: Droz, 1983.
———, *Oeuvres* = Bonaventure des Périers. *Oeuvres françoises de B. des P.* [Edited by] L. Lacour. Paris, 1856.
Boratysnski, *Stikhotvorenija* = Boratysnski, E. *Stikhotvorenija, Poēmy*. Kemerovo: Éditions littéraires, 1984.
Borchardt, "Correspondance" = Borchardt, C. W. "Correspondance mathématique entre A. M. Legendre et C. G. J. Jacobi." *Journal für die Reine und angewandte Mathematik* 80 (1875): 205–79.
Borchert, *Gesamtwerk* = Borchert, W. *Das Gesamtwerk*. Hamburg: Rowohlt, 1949.
Boswell, *Johnson* = Boswell, J. *The Life of Samuel Johnson*. Edited by C. Rawson. New York: Knopf, 1992.
Bovelles, *Sage* = Bovelles, Charles de. *Le livre du sage*. Edited and translated by P. Magnard et al. Paris: Vrin, 1982.
Boyle, *Enquiry* = Boyle, Robert. *A Free Enquiry into the Vulgarly Received Notion of Nature*. Edited by E. B. Davis. Cambridge: Cambridge University Press, 1996.
———, *W* = *Works*. Edited by T. Birch. 6 vols. London, 1772. Reprint, Hildesheim: Georg Olms Verglagsbuchhandlung, 1966.
Breton, *OC* = Breton, André. *Oeuvres complètes*. Edited by M. Bonnet et al. Paris: Gallimard, 1992.
Browne, *Religio* = Browne, T. *Religio medici*. Edited by W. A. Greenhill. London: Macmillan, 1950.
Bruno, *DFI* = Bruno, Giordano. *Dialoghi filosofici italiani*. Edited by M. Ciliberto. Milan: Mondadori, 2000.
Büchner, *Kraft* = Büchner, L. *Kraft und Stoff oder Grundzüge der natürlichen Weltordnung: Nebst einer darauf gebauten Moral oder Sittenlehre. In allgemeinverständlicher Darstellung*. 15th ed. Leipzig, 1883.
———, *Vorlesungen* = *Sechs Vorlesungen über die Darwin'sche Theorie von der Verwandlung der Arten und die erste Entstehung der Organismenwelt*. Leipzig, 1868.
Büchner, *Werke* = Büchner, G. *Werke und Briefe*. Edited by W. R. Lehmann et al. Munich: Hanser, 1980.
Buddha, *Teachings* = Buddha. *The Teachings of Buddha: A New Translation of the Majjhima Nikāya*. Translated by B. Ñāṇamoli. Boston: Wisdom Publications, 1995.
Buffon, *Histoire* = Buffon, Georges-Louis Leclerc, Comte de. *Histoire naturelle, générale et particulière, avec la description du cabinet du roi*. Paris, 1749–1804.
———, *OP* = *Oeuvres philosophiques*. Edited by J. Piveteau. Paris: Presses Universitaires de France, 1954.
Bulgakov, *Tikhie* = Bulgakov, S. *Tikhie dumy*. Moscow: Respublika, 1996.
Bulwer-Lytton, *Race* = Bulwer, Edward, Lord Lytton. *The Coming Race*. 1871. Santa Barbara, CA: Woodbridge, 1989.

Burckhardt, *Geschichtswerk* = Burckhardt, Jacob. *Das Geschichtswerk*. 2 vols. Frankfurt: Zweitausendeins, 2007.
Burke, *Revolution* = Burke, Edmund. *Reflections on the Revolution in France*. 1790. Reprint edited by J. G. A. Pocock. Indianapolis: Hackett, 1987.
Burnett, *Metaphysics* = Burnett, James, Lord Monboddo. *Antient Metaphysics: Volume Fifth, Containing the History of Man in the Civilized State*. Edinburgh, 1797.
Butler, *Erewhon* = Butler, Samuel. *Erewhon*. 1872. Reprint edited by D. MacCarthy. London: Dent, 1962.
———, *Note-Books* = *The Note-Books of Samuel Butler [. . .]*. London: Fifield, 1913.
———, *Works* = *The Shrewsbury Edition of the Works of Samuel Butler*. Edited by H. F. Jones and A. T. Bartholomew. Vol. 1, *A First Year in Canterbury Settlement, and Other Early Essays*. London: J. Cape; New York: Dutton, 1923.
Byron, *SP* = Byron, Lord [George Gordon]. *Selected Poems*. London: Oxford University Press, 1947.
Cabanis, *OC* = Cabanis, Pierre-Jean-Georges. *Oeuvres complètes*. Paris, 1823.
Calvin, *Institutes* = Calvin, John. *Institutes of the Christian Religion*. Edited by John T. McNeill. Translated by Ford Lewis Battles. Philadelphia: Westminster, 1960.
———, *Opera Omnia* = *Joannis Calvini opera quae supersunt omnia*. Edited by Edouard Cunitz, Johann Wilhelm Baum, and Eduard Wilhelm Eugen. Braunschweig, 1863.
Campanella, *CS* = Campanella, Tommaso. *La città del Sole*. 1623. Reprint edited by L. Firpo. Bari: Laterza, 1997.
———, *Senso* = Campanella, Tommaso. *Del senso delle cose e della magia*. Edited by G. Ernst. Bari: Laterza, 2007.
Camus, *Essais* = Camus, Albert. *Essais*. Edited by R. Quilliot and L. Faucon. Paris: Gallimard, 1965.
Čapek, *RUR* = Čapek, Karel. *R.U.R.* 1920. French edition translated by J. Rubeš. La Tour d'Aigues: L'Aube, 1997.
Carlyle, *SRHW* = Carlyle, Thomas. *Sartor Resartus: On Heroes and Hero-Worship*. Edited by W. H. Hudson. London: Dent, 1973. First published in 1833–34.
Carroll, *Works* = Carroll, Lewis [Charles Dodgson]. *Works of Lewis Carroll*. Edited by R. L. Green. Feltham: Hamlyn, 1965.
Cather, *Archbishop* = Cather, W. *Death Comes for the Archbishop*. New York: Vintage, 1990. First published in 1927.
Cennini, *Arte* = Cennini, C. *Il libro dell'arte*. Edited by F. Frezzato. Vicence: Neri Pozza, 2003.
Cervantes, *Quijote* = Cervantes, Miguel de. *Don Quijote*. Edited by F. Rico. Madrid: Prisa, 2012.
Chastellux, *Félicité* = Chastellux, Francois Jean de. *De la Félicité publique, ou Considérations sur le sort des hommes dans les différentes époques de l'histoire*. Bouillon, 1776. First published in 1772.
Chateaubriand, *Génie* = Chateaubriand, François-Auguste-René, vicomte de. *Génie du christianisme*. Edited by M. Regard. Paris: Gallimard, 1978.
———, *Mémoires* = *Mémoires d'outre-tombe*. Edited by P. Clarac. Paris: Le Livre de Poche, 1973.

Chaucer, *Tales* = Chaucer, Geoffrey. *The Canterbury Tales*. In *The Complete Works of Geoffrey Chaucer*, edited by F. N. Robinson, 19–314. London: Oxford University Press, n.d.

Chekhov, *Izbrannye* = Chekhov, Anton. *Izbrannye Sotchinennya*. Moscow: Gosudarstvennoe Izdatel'stvo Khudoğestvennoï literatury, 1946. First published 1888.

———, *Salle 6* = *Salle 6/Palata n. 6*. Edited by E. Parayre and L. Denis. Paris: Gallimard, 2006.

Chénier, "Discours" = Chénier, Marie-Joseph. "Discours à la Convention nationale 15 Brumaire an II." *Le Moniteur Universel* 18 (1793): 351–52.

Chernyshevsky [Tchernychevski], *What* = Chernyshevsky [Tchernychevski]. Что делать? Из рассказов о новых людях [What is to be done? From narratives about new people]. French translation by D. Sesemann. Paris: Editions des Syrtes, 2000.

Chesterton, *Heretics* = Chesterton, G. K. *Heretics*. Mineola, NY: Dover, 2006. First published in 1905.

———, *Thing* = *The Thing*. London: Sheed & Ward, 1946. First published in 1929.

Chopin, *Complete* = Chopin, K. *Complete Novels and Stories*. Edited by S. M. Gilbert. New York: Library of America, 2002.

Christophe, *Idée* = Christophe. *L'Idée fixe du savant Cosinus*. 26th ed. Paris: Colin, 1957.

Cicero, *Finibus* = Cicero. *De finibus bonorum et malorum*. Edited by T. Schiche. Stuttgart: Teubner, 1915.

———, *Gods* = Cicero. *De natura deorum*. Edited by A. S. Pease. 2 vols. Loeb, 1958.

———, *Officiis* = *De officiis*. Edited by C. Atzert. Leipzig: Teubner, 1973.

Claudel, *Théâtre* = Claudel, P. *Théâtre*. Edited by J. Madaule. Paris: Gallimard, 1965.

Collins, *Free-Thinking* = Collins, A. *A Discourse on Free-Thinking*. Edited by G. Gawlick. Stuttgart: Frommann, 1965.

Columella, *Rustica* = Columella. *De re rustica*. Edited by H. B. Ash. Loeb, 1941.

Comenius, *Opera* = Comenius, Jan Amos. *Opera omnia*. Edited by O. Chlup et al. Prague: Academia, 1966.

Comte, *Catéchisme* = Comte, Auguste. *Catéchisme positiviste ou Sommaire exposition de la religion universelle*. Edited by P.-F. Pécaut. Paris: Garnier, n.d.

———, *Correspondance* = *Correspondance générale et confessions*. Edited by P. E. de Berrédo Carneiro, P. Arnaud, and P. Arbousse-Bastide. 8 vols. Paris: EHESS et Vrin, 1973–90.

———, *Cours* = *Cours de Philosophie positive*. Vol. 1, *Leçons 1 à 45*, edited by M. Serres et al. Paris: Hermann, 1998. Vol. 2, *Leçons 46 à 60*, edited by J.-P. Enthoven. Paris: Hermann, 1975.

———, *Ensemble* = *Discours sur l'ensemble du positivisme*. Edited by A. Petit. Paris: Flammarion, 2008.

———, *Esprit* = *Discours sur l'esprit positif*. In *Philosophie des Sciences*, edited by J. Grange, 127–225. Paris: Gallimard, 1996.

———, *Plan* = *Plan des travaux scientifiques nécessaires pour réorganiser la société*. Paris: Gallimard, 235–347.

———, *Synthèse* = *Synthèse subjective ou système universel des conceptions propres à l'état normal de l'humanité.* vol. 1 [the only volume published], containing *Système de logique positive, ou Traité de philosophie mathématique.* Paris: Chez l'auteur et Dalmont, 1856.

———, *Système* = *Système de politique positive ou Traité de sociologie, instituant la religion de l'humanité.* 4 vols. Paris: Mathias, 1851–54.

———, *Testament* = *Testament d'Auguste Comte avec les documents qui s'y rapportent [. . .].* Paris, 1884.

Condillac, *Oeuvres* = Condillac, Étienne Bonnot de. *Oeuvres philosophiques.* Edited by G. Le Roy. Paris: Presses Universitaires de France, 1947.

Condorcet, *Esquisse* = Condorcet, Jacques Caritat de. *Esquisse d'un tableau historique des progrès de l'esprit humain.* Edited by A. Pons. Paris: Garnier-Flammarion, 1988.

———, *Oeuvres* = *Oeuvres.* Edited by A. Condorcet O'Connor and F. Arago. Paris, 1847.

Conrad, *Nostromo* = Conrad, J. *Nostromo: A Tale of the Seaboard.* Edited by M. Seymour Smith. London: Penguin Classics, 1988. First published in 1904.

Cooke, *Federalist* = Cooke, J. E., ed. *The Federalist*, no. 14 (James Madison). Middletown, CT: Wesleyan University Press, 1961.

Corpus Juris Canonici = *Corpus Juris Canonici.* Edited by E. Friedberg. Graz: Akademische Verlagsanstalt, 1955.

Cournot, *IETM* = Cournot, Antoine-Augustin. *Considérations sur la marche des idées et des événements dans les Temps Modernes.* Edited by A. Robinet. Paris: Vrin, 1973.

Cousin de Grainville, *Dernier* = Cousin de Grainville, J.-B. F. X. *Le Dernier Homme.* 2 vols. Paris, 1805. New ed., Paris: Payot, 2010.

Cowley, *Essays* = Cowley, A. *The Essays and Other Prose Writings.* Edited by A. B. Gough. Oxford: Clarendon Press, 1915.

Cromaziano, *Istoria* = Cromaziano, Agatopisto [Appiano Buonafede]. *Istoria critica e filosofica del suicidio.* Annotated by A. C. Lucques, 1761.

Cuvier, *Rapport* = Cuvier, G. *Rapport historique sur les progrès des sciences naturelles depuis 1789 et sur leur état actuel [. . .].* Brussels: Culture et civilisation, 1968. First published in Paris by Imprimerie impériale, 1810.

d'Alembert, *Discours* = d'Alembert, Jean Le Rond. *Discours préliminaire de l'Encyclopédie.* Edited by F. Picavet. Paris: Colin, 1894.

———, *Oeuvres* = *Oeuvres.* Paris, 1822.

Damascius, *Treatise* = Damascius. *Treatise on the first principles.* Edited by L. G. Westerink. Paris: Les Belles Lettres, 1991.

Dante, *Convivio* = Dante, *Il Convivio.* Edited by P. Cudini. Milan: Garzanti, 2005.

———, *Monarchia* = *De Monarchia.* Edited by R. Imbach. Stuttgart: Reclam, 1989.

Darwin, *Autobiography* = Darwin, Charles. *The Autobiography of Charles Darwin, 1809–1882.* With original omissions restored. London: Collins, 1958.

———, *Descent* = *The Descent of Man and Selection in Relation to Sex.* New York: The Modern Library, n.d.

———, *Origin* = *The Origin of Species by Means of Natural Selection, or The Preservation of Favored Races in the Struggle for Life*. New York: The Modern Library, n.d.
Defoe, *Essay* = Defoe, Daniel. *An Essay upon Projects*. 1697. In *The True-Born Englishman, and Other Writings*, edited by P. N. Furbank and W. R. Owens. London: Penguin, 1997.
———, *Robinson* = *Robinson Crusoe: The Farther Adventures of Robinson Crusoe*. London: Collins, 1953.
Delacroix, *Journal* = Delacroix, E. *Journal*. Edited by A. Joubin. Paris: Plon, 1932.
Deleyre, *Analyse* = Deleyre, A. *Analyse de la philosophie du Chancelier François Bacon*. 2 vols. Amsterdam, 1755.
Descartes, *OC* = Descartes, René. *Oeuvres complètes*. Edited by P. Adam and J. Tannery. 11 vols. Paris, 1897–1913.
Dhammapada = *Dhammapada: Les Stances de la Loi*. Translated by J.-P. Osier. Paris: Garnier-Flammarion, 1997.
D'Holbach, *Nature* = D'Holbach, Paul-Henri Dietrich, Baron. *Système de la nature*. Paris, 1821. Facsimile reprint, Hildesheim: Olms, 1966.
———, *Social* = *Système social*. Paris: Fayard, 1994.
Diderot, *Oeuvres* = Diderot, Denis. *Oeuvres complètes*. Edited by J. Assezat. Paris, 1875.
———, *Oeuvres*² = *Oeuvres complètes*. Paris: Hermann, 1986.
———, *Oeuvres esthétiques* = *Oeuvres esthétiques*. Edited by P. Vernière. Paris: Garnier, 1959.
———, *Oeuvres philosophiques* = *Oeuvres philosophiques*. Edited by P. Verniere. Paris: Garnier, 1960.
Diodorus, *Bibliothèque* = Diodorus of Sicily. *Bibliothèque historique*. Edited by F. Vogel. 1888. Reprint, Stuttgart: Teubner, 1964.
Dion of Prusa, *Discourses 2* = Dio Chrysostom. *Discourses 12–30*. Edited and translated by J. W. Cohoon. Loeb, 1939.
Donoso Cortès, *Obras* = Donoso Cortes, Juan. *Obras completas*. Edited by J. Juretschke. 2 vols. Madrid: BAC, 1946.
Dostoyevsky, *Carnet* = Dostoyevsky, Fyodor. *Carnet du sous-sol*. Edited by M. I. Brudny. Paris: Gallimard, 1995.
———, *Demons* = Бесы [*Demons*]. Moscow: АСТ, 2005.
———, *Journal* = Дневник писателя 1876 год [*A Writer's Diary, 1876*], in Собрание сочинений [*Collected Works*], vol. 13. Saint Petersburg: Nauka, 1994. Translated into French by G. Aucouturier as *Journal d'un écrivain*. Paris: Gallimard, 1972.
———, *Karamazov* = Братья Карамазовы [*The Brothers Karamazov*]. Moscow: АСТ, 2006.
———, *Oeuvres* = *Oeuvres complètes en 15 tomes*. Leningrad: Nauka, 1990.
Du Bellay, *Deffence* = Du Bellay, Joachim. *La Deffence et Illustration de la Langue Francoyse*. Edited by H. Chamard. Paris: Didier, 1948. First published in 1549.
Dubos, *Réflexions* = Dubos, Abbé Jean-Baptiste. *Réflexions critiques sur la poésie et la peinture*. Paris, 1770. Facsimile reprint, Geneva: Slatkine, 1982.

Duhem, *Essai* = Duhem, P. *Essai sur la notion de théorie physique de Platon à Galilée*. Paris: Vrin, 1982. First published in 1908.
Dühring, *Werth* = Dühring, E. *Der Werth des Lebens: Eine philosophische Betrachtung*. Breslau, 1865. The last edition was published in 1922.
Duns Scotus, *OO* = Duns Scotus. *Opera Omnia*. Paris, 1894.
Dürer, *Nachlass* = Dürer, A. *Schriftlicher Nachlass*. Edited by H. Rupprich. Berlin: Deutscher Verlag für Kunstwissenschaft, 1969.
Eckermann, *Goethe* = Eckermann, J. P. *Gespräche mit Goethe in den letzten Jahren seines Lebens*. Edited by E. Beutler. Munich: dtv, 1976.
Eckhart, *DW* = Meister Eckhart. *Deutsche Werke*. Edited by J. Quint. Stuttgart: Kohlhammer, 1958–.
Eichendorff, *Werke* = Eichendorff, J. von. *Werke*. Munich: Winkler, 1976.
Eliot, *Monarchie* = Eliot, John. *The Monarchie of Man*. [Edited by A. B. Grosart.] N.p., 1879.
Encyclopédie = *Encyclopédie ou Dictionnaire raisonné des sciences, des art et des métiers*. Paris, 1755.
Engels, *Sozialismus* = Engels, F. *Die Entwicklung des Sozialismus von der Utopie zur Wissenschaft*. Berlin: Dietz, 1951.
Esquiros, *Future* = Esquiros, A. *De la vie future au point de vue socialiste*. Paris, 1850.
L'Etna = *L'Etna: Poeme*. Edited by J. Vessereau. Paris: Les Belles Lettres, 1961.
Eucken, *Sinn* = Eucken, R. *Der Sinn und Wert des Lebens*. Leipzig: Quelle & Meyer, 1908. 8th ed., 1921.
Fabre, *Torrents* = Fabre, Jean Antoine. *Essai sur la théorie des torrents et des rivières*. Paris, 1797.
Fache, *Nouvelles* = Fache, K., et al., eds. *Nouvelles et récits russes classiques*. Paris: Pocket, 2005.
Faraday, *Researches* = Faraday, M. *Experimental Researches in Electricity*. London, 1855. First published in 1845.
Farrand, *Convention* = Farrand, M., ed. *The Records of the Federal Convention of 1787*. New Haven: Yale University Press, 1941.
Farrère, *Condamnés* = Farrère, Claude. *Les condamnés à mort*. Paris: L'Illustration, 1920.
Federico II, *Arte* = Federico II di Svevia. *De arte venandi cum avibus: L'arte di cacciare con gli uccelli*. Edited and translated by A. L. Trombetti Budriesi. Bari: Laterza, 2000.
Fedorov, *Filosofija* = Fedorov, N. F. *Filosofija obšŝego dela*. 2 vols. Facsimile reprint, Lausanne: L'Âge d'Homme, 1985. First published in Moscow in 1906–13.
———, *Works* = *Selected Works*. Edited by E. Koutaissoff and M. Minto. London: Honeyglen; Lausanne: L'Âge d'Homme, 1990.
Ferguson, *Civil Society* = Ferguson, Adam. *An Essay on the History of Civil Society*. Edited by F. Oz-Salzberger. Cambridge: Cambridge University Press, 1995.
Feuerbach, *Christianity* = Feuerbach, Ludwig. *Das Wesen des Christentums*. Edited by W. Schuffenhauer. 2nd ed. Berlin: Akademie Verlag, 1984.
———, *KS* = *Kleine Schriften*. Edited by K. Löwith. Frankfurt: Suhrkamp, 1966.

Fichte, *AW* = Fichte, Johann Gottlieb. *Ausgewählte Werke*. Edited by F. Medicus. 6 vols. Darmstadt: Wissenschaftliche Buchgesellschaft, 1962.
———, *Berichtigung* = *Beitrag zur Berichtigung der Urteile des Publikums über die französische Revolution*. 1793. In *Schriften zur Revolution*, edited by B. Willms, 34–213. Cologne: Westdeutscher Verlag, 1967.
———, *Werke* = *Werke*. Edited by I. H. Fichte. Berlin: De Gruyter, 1971.
Ficino, *Théologie* = Ficino, Marsilio. *Teologia platonica*. Edited by E. Vitale. Milan: Bompiani, 2011.
Firmicus, *L'Erreur* = Firmicus Maternus. *L'Erreur des religions païennes*. Edited by R. Turcan. Paris: Les Belles Lettres, 1982.
Flammarion, *Fin* = Flammarion, C. *La Fin du monde*. Paris, 1894.
Flaubert, *Correspondance* = Flaubert, Gustave. *Correspondance*. Edited by J. Bruneau. 5 vols. Paris: Gallimard, 1973–2007.
———, *OC* = *Oeuvres complètes*. Edited by B. Masson. Paris: Seuil, 1964.
Fonsecae, *Commentariorum* = Fonseca, Pedro. *Commentariorum in Metaphysicorum Aristotelis Libros*. Hildesheim, Olms, 1964. First published in Cologne in 1615.
Fontenelle, *Oeuvres* = Fontenelle, Bernard le Bovier de. *Oeuvres complètes*. Paris: Fayard, 1991.
———, *République* = *La République des philosophes, ou Histoire des Ajaoiens [. . .]*. Geneva, 1768.
Forster, *Stories* = Forster, E. M. *Collected Short Stories*. London: Sidgwick & Jackson, 1947.
Freud, *Studienausgabe* = Freud, S. *Studienausgabe*. Frankfurt: Fischer, 1982.
———, *Werke* = Freud, S. *Gesammelte Werke*. Frankfurt: Fischer, 1947.
Gaillard, *Buffon* = Gaillard, Y. *Buffon: Biographie imaginaire et réelle*. Paris: Hermann, 1977.
Galen, *Facultés* = Galen. *Des facultés naturelles*. Edited by A. J. Brock. Loeb, 1916.
———, *Opera* = Galen. *Opera Omnia*. Edited by C. G. Kühn. Leipzig, 1821.
Galileo, *DMS* = Galilei, Galileo. *Dialogo sopra i due massimi sistemi del mondo*. 1632. Reprint edited by F. Flora. Turin: Mondadori, 2004.
———, *Opere* = *Opere*. Edizione nazionale, reprint. Florence: Barbèra, 1968.
Galton, *Inquiries* = Galton, Francis. *Inquiries into Human Faculty and Its Development*. Edited by E. Rhys. London: Dent, 1908.
Gilbert, *Calejava* = Gilbert, C. *Histoire de Calejava ou de l'Isle des hommes raisonnables*. Edited by M. S. Rivière. Exeter: University of Exeter Press, 1990.
Glanvill, *PU* = Glanvill, Joseph. *Plus Ultra, or The Progress and Advancement of Knowledge since the Days of Aristotle. In an Account of Some of the Most Remarkable Late Improvements of Practical, Useful Learning: To Encourage Philosophical Endeavours. Occasioned by a Conference with One of the Notional Way*. 1668. Reprint, London: Olms, 1979.
Göchhausen, *Enthüllungen* = Göchhausen, Ernst August Anton von. *Enthüllungen des Systems der Weltbürger-Republik in Briefen aus der Verlassenschaft eines Freymaurers [. . .]*. Rome, 1786.
Godwin, *Writings* = Godwin, W. *Political and Philosophical Writings of William Godwin*. Edited by M. Philp. London: Pickering, 1993.

Goethe, *Gespräche* = Goethe, Johann Wolfgang von. *Goethes Gespräche: Gesamtausgabe*. Edited by F. von Biedermann [. . .]. Leipzig: Biedermann, 1909.

———, *Maximen* = *Maximen und Reflexionen*. Edited by M. Hecker. Frankfurt: Insel, 1976. First published in 1822.

———, *W* = *Werke*. Edited by F. Apel et al. Edition of the Jubilee. 6 vols. Darmstadt: Wissenschaftliche Buchgesellschaft, 1998.

———, *Werke* = *Werke*. Edited by E. Trunz. Hamburg: Wegner, 1950.

Goguet, *Origine* = Goguet, A. Y. *De l'origine des lois, des arts et des sciences et de leurs progrès chez les anciens peuples*. Paris, 1758.

Gorki, *Arkhiv* = Gorki, M. *Arkhiv A. M. Gorkogo*. Moscow: Nauka, 1969.

———, *Sobranie* = *Sobranie sočineniy v tridśati tomakh*. Moscow: Gosudartsvennoe Izdatelstvo Khudojestvennoi Literatury, 1950.

Greek Anthology = *Greek Anthology*. Edited by W. R. Paton. Loeb, 1917.

Gregory of Nyssa, *Homilies* = Gregory of Nyssa. *Homélies sur l'Ecclésiaste*. Edited by F. Vinel. SC 416. Paris: Cerf, 1996.

Grimm, *Correspondance* = Grimm, F. M. *Correspondance littéraire*. Edited by U. Kölving. Ferney-Voltaire: Centre international d'études du XVIII siècle, 2010.

Guépin and Bonamy, *Nantes* = Guépin, A., and E. C. Bonamy. *Nantes au XIXe siècle: Statistique, topographique, industrielle et morale [. . .]*. Nantes, 1835.

Guillaume, *Commentaire* = Guillaume de Saint-Thierry. *Commentaire sur le Cantique des cantiques*. Edited by M.-M. Davy. Paris: Vrin, 1958.

———, *Nature* = *De la nature du corps et de l'âme*. Text established, translated, and commented on by M. Lemoine. Paris: Les Belles Lettres, 1988.

Gutzkow, *Selbsttaufe* = Gutzkow, K. *Die Selbsttaufe: Erzählungen und Novellen*. Edited by S. Landshuter. Passau: Stutz, 1998.

Haeckel, *GW* = Haeckel, Ernst. *Gemeinverständliche Werke*. Edited by H. Schmidt-Jena. 6 vols. Leipzig: Kröner; Berlin: Henschel, 1924.

Hakewill, *Apology* = Hakewill, George. *An Apology of the Power and Providence of God in the Government of the World, or An Examination and Censure of the Common Error Touching Natures Perpetual and Universal Decay*. Oxford, 1627.

Haldane, *Daedalus* = Haldane, J. B. S. *Daedalus, or Science and the Future: A Paper Read to the Heretics, Cambridge, on February 4th, 1923*. London: Kegan Paul, 1924.

———, *Man* = *Man and His Future*. Edited by G. Wolstenholme. London, Churchill, 1963.

Hartmann, *Philosophie* = Hartmann, E. von. *Philosophie des Unbewußten*. 11th ed. Leipzig: Haacke, 1904.

Hawthorne, *Stories* = Hawthorne, N. *"The Birthmark," "The Celestial Railroad" and Other Stories*. Edited by R. C. Murfin. New York: Penguin, 2006.

Haydon, *Diary* = Haydon, B. *The Diary of Benjamin Robert Haydon*. Edited by W. B. Pope. Cambridge, MA: Harvard University Press, 1960.

Hegel, *Ästhetik* = Hegel, G. W. F. *Ästhetik*. Edited by F. Bassenge. Frankfurt: Europäische Verlagsanstalt, 1955.

———, *Jenaer* = *Jenaer Realphilosophie: Vorlesungsmanuskripte zur Philosophie der Natur und des Geistes von 1805–1806*. Edited by J. Hoffmeister. Hamburg: Meiner, 1931.

———, *Phänomenologie* = *Phänomenologie des Geistes*. Edited by J. Hoffmeister. Hamburg: Meiner, 1952.

———, *Vorlesungen* = *Vorlesungen über die Philosophie der Religion*. Edited by H. Glockner. Stuttgart: Frommann, 1928.

———, *Werke* = *Werke*. Frankfurt: Suhrkamp, 1971.

Heidegger, *Being* = Heidegger, Martin. *Sein und Zeit*. 10th ed. Tübingen: Niemeyer, 1963.

———, *GA* = *Gesamtausgabe*. Frankfurt: Klostermann, 1975–.

———, *Holzwege* = *Holzwege*. Frankfurt: Klostermann, 1950.

———, *Humanism* = "Brief über den 'Humanismus.'" In *Wegmarken*, 145–94.

———, *Kant* = *Kant und das Problem der Metaphysik*. Frankfurt: Klostermann, 1965.

———, *Vorträge* = *Vorträge und Aufsätze*. Pfullingen: Neske, 1954.

———, *Wegmarken* = *Wegmarken*. Frankfurt: Klostermann, 1967.

Heine, *Frankreich* = Heine, Heinrich. *Schriften über Frankreich*. Edited by E. Galley. vol. 3 of *Werke*. Frankfurt: Insel, 1968.

———, *Religion* = *Zur Geschichte der Religion und Philosophie in Deutschland*. 1833/34. Reprint edited by W. Harich. Frankfurt: Insel, 1966.

———, *Sämtliche* = *Sämtliche Schriften*. Edited by K. Briegleb. Munich: Hanser, 1971.

———, *Werke* = *Werke und Briefe*. Edited by H. Kaufmann. Berlin: Aufbau Verlag, 1962.

Helvétius, *Oeuvres* = Helvétius, Claude-Adrien. *Oeuvres complètes*. Paris, 1818.

Herder, *Werke* = Herder, Johann Gottfried von. *Sämtliche Werke*. Edited by B. Suphan. Hildesheim, Olms, 1967. Facsimile reprint of the first publication, in Berlin, 1881.

Hergé, *Lune* = Hergé. *Objectif Lune*. Tournai: Casterman, 1953.

"Hermès Trismégiste," *CH* = *Corpus Hermeticum*. Text established by A. D. Nock and translated by A. J. Festugière. 4 vols. Paris: Les Belles Lettres, 1946–54.

Hiller and Crusius, *Anthologia* = Hiller, E., and O. Crusius, eds. *Anthologia lyrica* [. . .]. Leipzig: Teubner, 1913.

Hippocrates, *Art* = Hippocrates. *De l'art*. Edited by J. Jouanna. Paris: Les Belles Lettres, 1988.

———, *Decorum* = *Decorum* [*On Honorable Conduct*]. In *Hippocrates: Volume II*. Edited by W. H. S. Jones. Loeb, 1923.

Hitler, *MK* = Hitler, A. *Mein Kampf*. 665th ed. Munich: Zentralverlag der NSDAP, 1942.

Hobbes, *Lessons* = Hobbes, Thomas. *Six Lessons to the Professors of the Mathematics* [. . .]. In *The English Works*, edited by T. Molesworth, 7:183–356. London, 1845. First published 1656.

———, *Leviathan* = *Leviathan*. Edited by M. Oakeshott. Oxford: Blackwell, 1960.

———, *Opera* = *Opera latina*. Edited by W. Moleswort. London, 1839.

Hoffmann, *Werke* = Hoffmann, E. T. A. *Werke*. Munich: Hanser, 1968.
Hölderlin, *GSA* = Hölderlin, Friedrich. *Sämtliche Werke: Grosse Stuttgarter Ausgabe*. Edited by F. Beissner. Stuttgart: Kohlhammer, 1946–.
Huarte, *Examen* = Huarte de San Juan, J. *Examen de ingenios para las ciencias*. Barcelona: Linkgua, 2012.
Hugh, *Didascalicon* = Hugh of Saint-Victor. *Didascalicon de studio legendi/Studienbuch*. Edited by T. Offengeld. Freiburg im Breisgau: Herder, 1997.
Humboldt, *Memoiren* = Humboldt, Alexander von. *Memoiren Alexander von Humboldt's*. Leipzig, 1861.
Hume, *Enquiry* = Hume, David. *Enquiry concerning Human Understanding*. Edited by L. A. Selby-Bigge. Oxford: Clarendon Press, 1902.
———, *Essays* = *Essays, Moral, Political and Literary*. London: Oxford University Press, 1963.
———, *Treatise* = *Treatise on Human Nature*. Edited by L. A. Selby-Bigge. Oxford: Clarendon Press, 1965. First published in 1888.
Husserl, *Krisis* = Husserl, Edmund. *Die Krisis der europäischen Wissenschaften und die transzendentale Phänomenologie*. Edited by W. Biemel. The Hague: Nijhoff, 1954.
Huxley, *Bottles* = Huxley, J. S. *New Bottles for New Wine*. London: Chatto & Windus, 1957.
———, *Memories* = *Memories*. London: Allen & Unwin, 1970.
———, *WDIT?* = *What Dare I Think? The Challenge of Modern Science to Human Action and Belief*. London: Chatto & Windus, 1931.
Iamblichus, *Mystères* = Iamblichus. *Les Mystères d'Égypte*. Edited by E. Des Places. Paris: Les Belles Lettres, 1966.
Ibn Arabi, *Gems* = Ibn Arabi. *Fusûs al-hikam*. Cairo: Maktabat al-Thaqâfa al-dîniyya, 2005.
Ibn Khaldun, *Muqaddima* = Ibn Khaldun. *Muqaddima*. Edited by E. Quatremère. Paris: Didot, 1858.
Iggeret = *Iggeret ba'aley hayyim*. Edited by I. Toporowski. Jerusalem: Mosad Rav Kook, 1949.
Ignatius of Loyola, *OC* = Ignatius of Loyola. *Obras completas*. Edited by I. Iparraguirre. Madrid: Biblioteca de autores cristianos, 1963.
Irenaeus, *Heresies* = Irenaeus of Lyon. *Contre les hérésies*. Edited by A. Rousseau. SC 153. Paris: Cerf, 1984.
Jâbir, *TC* = Jâbir ibn Ḥayyân. *Essai sur l'histoire des idées scientifiques dans l'islam*. Volume 1, *Textes choisis*. Edited by P. Kraus. Cairo: el-Khandgi, 1935.
Jacobi, *Allwills* = Jacobi, F. H. *Eduard Allwills Briefsammlung*. Königsberg: Nicolovius, 1792.
James, *Meaning* = James, W. *The Meaning of Truth*. New York: Longmans, Green, 1914.
———, *Will* = *The Will to Believe, and Other Essays in Popular Philosophy*. New York, 1897.
Jean Paul, *Sämtliche* = Jean Paul. *Sämtliche Werke*. Edited by N. Miller and W. Schmidt-Biggemann. Munich: Hanser, 1974.

———, *Werke*/Miller = *Werke*. Edited by N. Miller. Munich: Hanser, 1961.
Jîlî, *Perfect man* = al-Ǧīlī, Abd el-Karīm b. Ibrāhīm. *Al-Insān al-Kāmīl fī ma'rifat al-awāḫir wa-l-awā'il*. Edited by A. al-Kayāli. Beirut: Dār al-kutub al-'ilmiyya, 2005.
John of Salisbury, *Policraticus* = John of Salisbury. *Policraticus*. Edited by C. C. J. Webb. Oxford: Clarendon, 1909.
John Philoponus, *Opificio* = John Philoponus. *De opificio mundi*. Edited by W. Reichardt. Leipzig, 1897.
Jouannais, *Artistes* = Jouannais, Jean-Yves. *Artistes sans oeuvres: I would prefer not to*. Paris: Hazan, 1997.
Joyce, *Essential* = Joyce, James. *The Essential James Joyce*. Edited by H. Levin. Harmondsworth: Penguin, 1965.
Julian, *Oeuvres* = Julian (emperor). *Oeuvres complètes*. Edited by J. Bidez. Paris: Les Belles Lettres, 1924.
Jünger, *Worker* = Jünger, Ernst. *Der Arbeiter: Herrschaft und Gestalt*. 1932. In *Werke*. Vol. 6, *Essays II*. Stuttgart: Klett, n.d.
Kant, *Briefwechsel* = Kant, Immanuel. *Briefwechsel*. Edited by R. Malter. Hamburg: Meiner, 1986.
———, *Judgment* = *Kritik der Urteilskraft*. Edited by K. Vorländer. Hamburg: Meiner, 1924.
———, *Logik* = *Logik*. Edited by E. Adickes. Vol. 3 of *Handschriftlicher Nachlass*. Berlin: Reimer, 1914.
———, *Nachlass* = *Kants Handschriftlicher Nachlass*. Berlin: De Gruyter, 1936.
———, *Werke*/Berlin = *Werke*. Akademieausgabe. Berlin and Leipzig: De Gruyter, 1923.
———, *WW* = *Werke in sechs Bänden*. Edited by W. Weischedel. Darmstadt: Wissenschaftliche Buchgesellschaft, 1983.
Keller, *Briefe* = Keller, G. *Gesammelte Briefe*. Edited by C. Helbling. Bern: Bonteli, 1950.
Kepler, *Werke* = Kepler, Johannes. *Gesammelte Werke*. Edited by M. Caspar. Munich: Beck, 1945.
Kheveshi, *Tolkovij* = Kheveshi, M. A. *Tolkovij slovar' ideologičeskikh I političeskikh terminov sovietskogo perioda*. Moscow: Mezhdunarodnye otnośenija, 2002.
Kierkegaard, *Oeuvres* = Kierkegaard, Søren. *Oeuvres complètes*. Paris: L'Orante, 1977.
———, *S* = *Skrifter*. Copenhagen: Gad, 1997–.
Kleist, *Werke* = Kleist, H. von. *Werke*. Edited by H. Sembdner. Munich: Hanser, 1966. First published in 1810.
Knowles, *Fuseli* = Knowles, J. *The Life and Writings of Henry Fuseli [. . .]*. London, 1831.
Kornilov, *Molodye* = Kornilov, A. A. *Molodye gody Mikhaila Bakunina: Iz istorij rysskogo romantisma*. Moscow: Sabaśnikov, 1915.
La Beaumelle, *Pensées* = La Beaumelle, Laurent Angliviel de. *Mes Pensées, ou Le qu'en dira-t-on*. Edited by C. Lauriol. Geneva: Droz, 1997. First published in 1752.

Lactantius, *Institutiones* = Lactantius. *Divinae Institutiones*. Edited by S. Brandt. CSEL 19. Prague, 1890.

La Mettrie, *OP* = Mettrie, Julien Offray de la. *Oeuvres philosophiques*. Edited by J.-P. Jackson. Paris: Coda, 2004.

Landino, *Scritti* = Landino, Cristoforo. *Scritti critici e teorici*. Edited by R. Cardini. Rome: Bulzoni, 1974.

Lasaulx, *Mortis* = Lasaulx, E. von. *De mortis dominatu in veteres: Commentatio theologico-philosophica*. Munich, 1835.

———, *PG* = *Neuer Versuch einer alten auf die Wahrheit der Tatsachen gegründeten Philosophie der Geschichte*. Vienna: Karolinger, 2002.

Lautréamont, *Chants* = Lautréamont. *Les Chants de Maldoror*. Edited by J.-L. Steinmetz. Paris: LGF, 2001.

Le Dantec, *Atheism* = Le Dantec, F. *L'Athéisme*. Paris: Alcan, 1907.

Leibniz, *Deutsche* = Leibniz, Gottfried Wilhelm. *Deutsche Schriften*. Edited by G. E. Guhrauer. Berlin, 1840. Facsimile reprint, Hildesheim: Olms, 1966.

———, *Opuscules* = *Opuscules et fragments inédits: Extraits des Ms. de la Bibliothèque royale de Hanovre*. Edited by L. Couturat. Paris: Alcan, 1903. Facsimile reprint, Hildesheim: Olms, 1961.

———, *Philosophischen* = *Die philosophischen Schriften von Gottfried Wilhelm Leibniz*. Edited by C. J. Gerhardt. 1882. Reprint, Hildesheim: Olms, 1960.

———, *Principles* = *Principles of Nature and Grace*. Edited by A. Robinet. Paris: Presses Universitaires de France, 1954.

———, *Théodicée* = *Essais de Théodicée*. Edited by P. Janet. Paris: Alcan, 1900.

Leiris, "Homme" = Leiris, M. "L'homme et son intérieur." *Documents* 5 (1930): 260–66.

Lenin, *Oeuvres* = Lenin, Vladimir. *Oeuvres*. Paris: Éditions sociales; Moscow: Editions en langues étrangères, 1961.

Leonardo da Vinci, *Paragone* = Leonardo da Vinci. *Leonardo da Vinci's Paragone: A Critical Interpretation with a New Edition of the Text in the Codex Urbinas*. Edited by C. J. Farago. Leiden: Brill, 1992.

———, *S* = Leonardo da Vinci. *Scritti*. Edited by J. Recupero. Santarcangelo di Romagna: Rusconi, 2009.

Leopardi, *Opere* = Leopardi, Giacomo. *Opere*. Edited by L. Felici. Rome: Newton Compton, 2007.

———, *Zibaldone* = Leopardi, Giacomo. *Zibaldone*. Edited by L. Felici. Rome: Newton Compton, 2007.

Leroux, *Humanité* = Leroux, P. *De l'Humanité*. Edited by M. Abensour and P. Vermeren. Paris: Fayard, 1985. First published in 1840.

Lévi-Strauss, *Pensée* = Lévi-Strauss, C. *La Pensée sauvage*. Paris: Plon, 1962.

Liebig, *Bacon* = Liebig, J. von. *Über Francis Bacon von Verulam und die Methode der Naturforschung*. Munich, 1863.

Locke, *Epistola* = Locke, John. *Epistola de Tolerantia*. Edited by R. Klibansky. Oxford: Clarendon Press, 1968.

———, *Political* = *Political Essays*. Edited by M. Goldie. Cambridge: Cambridge University Press, 1997.

———, *STG* = *The Second Treatise of Government (An Essay concerning the True Original, Extent and End of Civil Government)*. Edited by J. W. Gough. Oxford: Blackwell, 1966.
Lotharii, *Miseria* = Lotharii Cardinalis (Innocentii III). *De miseria humanae conditionis*. Edited by M. Maccarone. Lugano: Thesaurus Mundi, 1955.
L17 = *Libertins du xviie siècle*. Edited by J. Prévôt. Vol. 1, Paris: Gallimard, 1998. Vol. 2, Paris: Gallimard, 2004.
Lucian, *Opera* = Lucian. *Opera*. Edited by M. D. Macleod. Oxford: Clarendon Press, 1972.
———, *Philopseudeis* = *Philopseudeis è Apiston: Die Lügenfreunde, oder Der Ungläubige*. Edited by M. Ebner et al. Darmstadt: Wissenschaftliche Buchgesellschaft, 2001.
Luther, *Studienausgabe* = Luther, Martin. *Lateinisch-deutsche Studienausgabe*. Leipzig: Evangelische Verlagsanstalt, 2006.
Ma'arekhet = *Ma'arekhet ha-Elohut*. Mantua, 1558.
Machiavelli, *O* = Machiavelli, Niccolò. *Tutte le opere*. Edited by F. Flora and C. Cordié. Milan: Mondadori, 1968. Machiavelli, *O-2011* = *Tutte le opere storiche, politiche e letterarie*. Rome: Newton Compton, 2011.
Macrobius = Macrobius. *"Saturnalia" and "In Somnium Scipionis."* Edited by J. Willis. 2 vols. Leipzig: Teubner, 1963.
Maïmon, *Progressen* = Maïmon, Salomon. *Über die Progressen der Philosophie*. 1793. In *Gesammelte Werke*, edited by V. Verra, vol. 4. Hildesheim: Olms, 1970.
Maimonides, *Guide* = Maimonides. *Dalâlat al-Hâ'irîn*. Edited by Y. Joël. Jerusalem: Junovitch, 1929. French trans. by S. Munk, 1856–66. 3 vols. Reprint of Munk's trans., Paris: Maisonneuve, 1970.
Maistre, *Écrits* = Maistre, J. de. *Écrits sur la Révolution*. Edited by J.-L. Darcel. Paris: Presses Universitaires de France, 1989.
———, *Oeuvres* = *Oeuvres complètes*. Lyon, 1893.
———, *Soirées* = *Les Soirées de Saint-Pétersbourg*. Paris, n.d.
Malebranche, *O* = Malebranche, Nicolas. *Oeuvres*. Edited by G. Rodis-Lewis. Vol. 1, Paris: Gallimard, 1979. Vol. 2, Paris: Gallimard, 1992.
Mallarmé, *Correspondance* = Mallarmé, Stéphane. *Correspondance: Lettres sur la poésie*. Edited by B. Marchal. Paris: Gallimard, 1995.
———, *OC* = *Oeuvres complètes*. Edited by H. Mondor and G. Jean-Aubry. Paris: Gallimard, 1945.
Mallock, *Worth* = Mallock, William H. *Is Life Worth Living?* New York, 1899.
Malraux, *Tentation* = Malraux, André. *La Tentation de l'Occident*. Paris: Le Livre de Poche, 1976. First published in 1926.
Malthus, *Population* = Malthus, Thomas Robert. *An Essay on the Principle of Population, as It Affects the Future Improvement of Society, with Remarks on the Speculations of Mr. Godwin, M. Condorcet, and Other Writers*. 1798. Reprint, New York: Modern Library, 1860.
Manetti, *Dignity* = Manetti, Ianotii. *De dignitate et excellentia hominis*. Edited by E. R. Leonard. Padua: Antenore, 1975.
Manzoni, *Opere* = Manzoni, Alessandro. *Opere in prosa*. Edited by D. Monda. Milan: Rizzoli, 2009.

Marc, *Briefe* = Marc, Franz. *Briefe aus dem Feld*. Berlin: Rembrandt Verlag, 1941.

Marcus Aurelius = Marcus Aurelius. Edited by A. A. Farquharson. Oxford: Clarendon Press, 1968.

Marinetti, *Mafarka* = Marinetti, Francesco Tommasso. *Mafarka le futuriste: Roman africain*. Paris: Sansot, 1909.

Marx, *Capital* = Marx, Karl. *Das Kapital: Kritik der politischen Ökonomie*. Unabridged version based on the 2nd edition, published in 1872. Paderborn: Voltmedia, n.d.

———, *FS* = *Die Frühschriften*. Edited by O. Heins and R. Sperl. 7th ed. Stuttgart: Kröner, 2004.

———, *Grundrisse* = *Grundrisse der Kritik der politischen Ökonomie (Rohentwurf), 1857–1858*. Berlin: Dietz, 1953.

———, *Manuscripts* = *Ökonomisch-philosophische Manuskripte*. Edited by B. Zehnpfennig. Hamburg: Meiner, 2005.

———, *Oeuvres* = *Oeuvres*. Paris: Gallimard, 1968.

Marx/Engels, *WW* = Marx, Karl, and Friedrich Engels. *Werke*. Berlin: Dietz, 1956–.

Maupassant, *Contes* = Maupassant, Guy de. *Contes et nouvelles*. Edited by L. Forestier. Paris: Gallimard, 1979.

———, *Correspondance* = *Correspondance inédite de Guy de Maupassant*. Edited by A. Artinian and E. Maynial. Paris: Wapler, 1951.

———, *Eau* = *Sur l'eau*. N.p.: Minerve, 1989. First published in 1888.

Maupertuis, *Oeuvres* = Maupertuis, Pierre-Louis Moreau de. *Oeuvres [. . .]*. Lyon, 1756.

Mercier, *2440* = Mercier, Louis-Sébastien. *L'an 2440, ou Rêve s'il en fut jamais*. Edited by R. Trousson. Bordeaux: Ducros, 1971.

Mercure = *Mercure Galant*. Periodical published in Paris from 1672 to 1714.

Merikare = *Die Lehre für König Merikare*. Compiled by Wolfgang Helck. Wiesbaden: Harrasowitz, 1977.

Meung, *Rose* = Meung, Jean de. *Le roman de la rose*. Edited by D. Poirion. Paris: Garnier-Flammarion, 1974.

Meyer, *Versuchung* = Meyer, C. F. *Die Versuchung des Pescara: Novelle*. Stuttgart: Reclam, 1972. First published in 1886.

Michelet, *Histoire* = Michelet, J. *Histoire du XIXe siècle*. Paris, 1875.

———, *Peuple* = *Le Peuple*. Edited by R. Casanova. Paris: Julliard, 1965.

Mill, *Essays* = Mill, John Stuart. *Essays on Ethics, Religion and Society*. Edited by J. J. Robson. Toronto: University of Toronto Press; London: Routledge & Kegan Paul, 1969.

———, *ULRG* = *Utilitarianism, Liberty and Representative Government*. Edited by A. D. Lindsay. London: Dent, 1968.

Milton, *PL* = Milton, John. *Paradise Lost*. Edited by G. Teskey. New York: Norton, 2005.

———, *Works* = *The Works of John Milton*. New York: Columbia University Press, 1933.

Montaigne, *Essays* = Montaigne, Michel de. *Essais*. Edited by P. Villey. 3 vols. Paris: Alcan, 1930.

More, *Utopia* = More, Thomas. *Utopia*. Latin text and English translation by G. M. Logan et al. Cambridge: Cambridge University Press, 1995.
Morelly, *OP* = Morelly, Etienne-Gabriel. *Oeuvres Philosophiques*. Edited by J.-P. Jackson. Paris: Coda, 2004.
Most, *Gesellschaft* = Most, J. *Freie Gesellschaft: Eine Abhandlung über Principien und Taktik der kommunistischen Anarchisten; Nebst einem polemischen Anhang*. New York: Chez l'auteur, 1884.
Murav'ev, *Domination du Temps* = Murav'ev, V. Овладение временем как основная задача организации труда [The domination of time]. Moscow, self-published, 1924. Reprint with an introductory essay by M. Hagemeister, Munich: Sagner, 1983.
Musil, *Mann* = Musil, R. *Der Mann ohne Eigenschaften*. Edited by A. Frisé. Hamburg: Rowohlt, 1978.
Musset, *Confession* = Musset, Alfred de. *La Confession d'un enfant du siècle*. Edited by D. Leuwers. Paris: Garnier-Flammarion, 1993.
Nabokov, *Pnin* = Nabokov, V. *Pnin*. London: Penguin, 1980.
Nachmanides, *Kitvey* = Nachmanides. *Kitvey ha-RaMBaN*. Edited by H. D. Chavel. Jerusalem: Mosad Rav Kook, 1974.
Naudé, *A* = Naudé, Gabriel. *Apologie pour tous les grands personnages qui ont été faussement accusés de magie*. In *L17*, 1:137–380.
Nerval, *Aurélia* = Nerval, G. de. *Aurélia*. Edited by J. N. Illouz. Paris: Gallimard, 2005.
Nicholas of Cusa, *PTW* = Nicholas of Cusa. *Philosophisch-Theologische Werke*. Latin-German. 4 vols. Darmstadt: Wissenschaftliche Buchgesellschaft, 2002.
Nietzsche, *Briefe* = Nietzsche, Friedrich. *Sämtliche Briefe*. Kritische Studienausgabe. Munich: dtv/De Gruyter, 1986.
———, *KSA* = *Kritische Studienausgabe in 15 Bänden*. Edited by C. Colli and M. Montinari. Berlin: De Gruyter, 1980.
Novalis, *WTB* = Novalis. *Werke, Tagebücher und Briefe*. Edited by H.-J. Mähl. 3 vols. Darmstadt: Wissenschaftliche Buchgesellschaft, 1990.
Olesha, *Povesti* = Olesha, Y. *Povesti i rasskazy*. Moscow: Izdatelstvo khudojestvennaya literatura, 1965.
Oliva, *Diálogo* = Oliva, Fernán Pérez de. *Diálogo de la dignidad del hombre [. . .]*. Edited by J. L. Abellán. Barcelona: Ediciones de cultura popular, 1967.
Ollé-Laprune, *Prix* = Ollé-Laprune, L. *Le Prix de la vie*. Paris, 1894.
Olympiodorus, *Commentaire* = Olympiodorus. *Commentaire du Phédon*. Edited by W. Norvin. Leipzig: Teubner, 1913.
Origen, *Homilies* = Origen. *Homélies sur la Genèse*. Edited by W. A. Baehrens. GCS 29. Leipzig: Hinrich, 1920.
Ortega y Gasset, *Obras* = Ortega y Gasset, J. *Obras completas*. 2nd ed. Madrid: Revista de Occidente, 1950.
Orwell, *Nineteen Eighty-Four* = Orwell, G. *Nineteen Eighty-Four*. London: Penguin, 1954.
Pain, *Bulgakov* = Pain, J., and N. Zernov, eds. *A Bulgakov Anthology*. London: Westminster Press, 1976.

Paine, *Rights* = Paine, Thomas. *"Rights of Man"; "Common Sense."* Edited by M. Foot. London: Everyman, 1994.

Palissy, *Oeuvres* = Palissy, Bernard. *Oeuvres complètes.* Edited by M.-M. Fragonard et al. Mont-de-Marsan: Éditions InterUniversitaires, 1996.

Pappus, *Collectionis* = Pappus of Alexandria. *Collectionis quae supersunt.* Edited by F. Hultsch. Berlin, 1878.

———, *Mathématique* = Pappus of Alexandria. *La collection mathématique.* Translated by P. Ver Ecke. Paris: Desclée De Brouwer, 1933.

Pascal, *Pensées* = Pascal, Blaise. *Pensées.* Edited by Léon Brunschvicg. 3 vols. Paris: Hachette, 1921.

Paton, *Épigrammes* = Paton, W. R., ed. *Épigrammes.* Loeb, 1917.

Péguy, *Oeuvres* = Péguy, Charles. *Oeuvres en prose.* Edited by R. Burac. Paris: Gallimard, 1988.

Petrarch, *Prose* = Petrarch. *Prose.* Edited by G. Martellotti et al. Rome: Ricciardi, 1955.

———, *Ignorantia* = *De sui ipsius et de multorum ignorantia.* Edited by A. Buck. Hamburg: Meiner, 1993.

Picatrix = *Picatrix: Un traité de magie médiéval.* Translated by B. Bakhouche et al. Turnhout: Brepols, 2003.

"*Picatrix*" = Pseudo-Magrîtî. *Das Ziel des Weisen.* Vol. 1, *Arabischer Text.* Edited by H. Ritter. Leipzig: Teubner, 1933.

Pico della Mirandola, *OP* = Pico della Mirandola, Giovanni. *Oeuvres philosophiques.* Edited by O. Boulnois and G. Tognon. 3rd ed. Paris: Presses Universitaires de France, 2004.

Pinthus, *MD* = *Menschheitsdämmerung: Ein Dokument des Expressionismus.* Edited by K. Pinthus. Hamburg: Rowohlt, 1959.

Pliny, *Histoire* = Pliny the Elder. *Histoire Naturelle.* Edited by J. André et al. Paris: Les Belles Lettres, 1981.

Plotinus, *O* = Plotinus. *Opera.* Edited by P. Henry and H.-R. Schwyzer. 3 vols. Paris: Desclée De Brouwer; Brussels: L'édition universelle, 1951-73.

Plutarch, *Moralia* = Plutarch. *Moralia.* Edited by C. Hubert. Leipzig: Teubner, 1959.

Polybius, *History* = Polybius. *History.* Edited by E. Foulon. Translated by R. Weil et al. Paris: Les Belles Lettres, 1995.

Porphyry, *De l'abstinence* = Porphyry. *De l'abstinence.* Edited by M. Patillon and M. Bouffartigue. Paris: Les Belles Lettres, 1995.

Price, *Evidence* = Price, Richard. *Evidence for a Future Period of Improvement in the State of Mankind, with the Means and Duty of Promoting It.* London, 1787.

Priestley, *Government* = Priestley, Joseph. *An Essay on the First Principles of Government.* London, 1771.

Proclus, *Republic* = Proclus. *Procli Diadochii in Platonis Rem Publicam Commentarii.* Edited by W. Kroll. 3 vols. Leipzig, 1899.

———, *Timée* = Proclus. *Commentaire du Timée.* Edited by E. Diehl. Leipzig: Teubner, 1906.

Proudhon, *Manuel* = Proudhon, Pierre-Joseph. *Manuel du spéculateur en Bourse.* Paris, 1857.
———, *Système* = Proudhon, Pierre-Joseph. *Système des contradictions économiques, ou Philosophie de la misère.* Paris, 1846.
Proust, *Recherche* = Proust, Marcel. *À la recherche du temps perdu.* Edited by P. Clarac and A. Ferré. Paris: Gallimard, 1954.
Pseudo-Apollonius, *Geheimnis* = Pseudo-Apollonius von Tyana. *Buch über das Geheimnis der Schöpfung und die Darstellung der Natur (Buch der Ursachen)* [Sirr al-Halîqah]. Edited by U. Weisser. Alep: Institute for the Story of Arabic Science, 1979.
Pushkin, *O* = Pushkin, Alexandre. Сочинения [Works]. Paris: YMCA Press, 1991.
Quevedo, *Obras* = Quevedo, F., de. *Obras Completas.* Edited by F. Buendia. Madrid: Aguilar, 1966.
Quinet, *Oeuvres* = Quinet, E. *Oeuvres complètes.* Paris, 1882.
Rabbe, *Portefeuille* = Rabbe, A. *Portefeuille d'un pessimiste.* Edited by E. Roditi and J. R. Dahan. Paris: Jose Corti, 1991.
Rabelais, *Pantagruel* = Rabelais, François. *Pantagruel.* Edited by V.-L. Saulnier. Geneva: Droz, 1959.
Raimundus Sabundus, *Theologia* = Raimundus Sabundus. *Theologia naturalis seu liber creaturarum.* Photomechanical reprint of the edition published in Sulzbach in 1852. Edited by F. Stegmuller. Stuttgart-Bad Cannstadt: Frommann, 1966.
Rauch, *Régénération* = Rauch, F. A. *Régénération de la nature végétale [. . .].* 2 vols. Paris, 1818.
Raynal, *Histoire* = Raynal, Guillaume. *Histoire philosophique et politique des établissements et du commerce des Européens dans les deux Indes.* The Hague, 1774.
Renan, *Avenir* = Renan, Ernest. *Avenir.* In *OC*, 3:715–1151.
———, *Dialogues* = *Dialogues philosophiques.* In *OC*, 1:559–632.
———, *OC* = Renan, Ernest. *Oeuvres complètes.* Edited by H. Psichari. 10 vols. Paris: Calmann-Lévy, 1947–61.
Reuchlin, *Verbo* = Reuchlin, J. *De verbo mirifico.* Stuttgart: Frommann, 1964.
Reybaud, *Jérôme* = Reybaud, L. *Jérôme Paturot à la recherche de la meilleure des républiques.* Paris, 1848.
Rieger, *Klinger* = Rieger, M. *Klinger in der Sturm- und Drangperiode.* Darmstadt, 1880.
Rig Veda = Varenne, J., trans. *Le Veda: Premier livre sacré de l'Inde.* Verviers: Gérard, 1967.
Rilke, *Gedichte* = Rilke, R. M. *Gedichte, 1910–1926.* Edited by M. Engel and U. Fulleborn. Frankfurt: Insel, 1996.
———, *Werke* = *Werke in drei Bänden.* Frankfurt: Insel, 1966.
Robeck, *Exercitatio* = Robeck, J. *Exercitatio philosophica de eulogō exagōgē, sive morte voluntaria philosophorum et bonorum virorum etiam Judaeorum et Christianorum.* Rinteln, 1736.
Robespierre, *Discours* = Robespierre, Maximilien. *Discours et rapports à la Convention.* Edited by M. Bouloiseau. Paris: UGC, 1965.

———, *Oeuvres* = *Oeuvres de M. R.* Edited by M. Bouloiseau et al. Paris: Presses Universitaires de France, 1953.

Robinet, *Vues* = Robinet, J.-B. *Vues philosophiques de la gradation naturelle des formes de l'être, ou Les essais de la Nature qui apprend à faire l'homme.* Amsterdam, 1768.

Rodov, *Proletarskie* = Rodov, S., ed. *Proletarskie pisateli: Antologija proletarskoj literatury.* Moscow: Gosudarstvenno Izdat, n.d. [1924].

Roland, *Appel* = Roland, Jeanne Marie Philipon. *Appel à l'impartiale postérité [. . .].* Edited by L. A. G. Bosc. Paris, 1795.

Ronsard, *Oeuvres* = Ronsard. *Oeuvres complètes.* Edited by J. Céard et al. Paris: Gallimard, 1994.

Rosny, *MT* = Rosny, J. H., Senior. *La Mort de la terre.* Paris: Denoël, 1958.

Rousseau, *OC* = Rousseau, Jean-Jacques. *Oeuvres complètes.* Edited by B. Gagnebin and M. Raymond. 5 vols. Paris: Gallimard (Pléiade), 1959–95.

Rozkov, *Smysl* = Rozkov, N. A. *Smysl I krasota žizni.* Moscow: Kniga, 1923.

Rupert, *Gloria* = Rupert of Deutz. *De Gloria et honore filii hominis super Mattheum.* Edited by H. Haacke. CCCM 29. Turnhout: Brepols, 1979.

Sade, *Boudoir* = Sade, D. A. F. de. *La Philosophie dans le boudoir.* Paris: Gallimard, 1976.

———, *Oeuvres* = *Oeuvres.* Edited by M. Delon. Paris: Gallimard, 1990.

Saint-Étienne, *Considérations* = Saint-Étienne, Jean-Paul Rabaut. *Considérations sur les intérêts du Tiers-État adressées au peuple des provinces par un propriétaire foncier.* Paris, 1826. First published in 1788.

Saint-Martin, *Oeuvres* = Saint-Martin, L.-C. de. *Oeuvres majeures.* Edited by R. Amadou. Hildesheim: Olms, 1980.

Saint-Simon, *Oeuvres* = Saint-Simon, Henri de. *Oeuvres.* Edited by P. Enfantin. Paris: Dentu, 1876.

Sandeus, *Regibus* = Sandeus, F. M. *De regibus Siciliae et Apuliae [. . .].* Hanover, 1611.

Sartre, *Being* = Sartre, Jean-Paul. *L'Être et le Néant: Essai d'ontologie phénoménologique.* Paris: Gallimard, 1943.

———, *EH* = *L'existentialisme est un humanisme.* Paris: Nagel, 1946.

Savérien, *Histoire* = Savérien, A. *Histoire des progrès de l'esprit humain dans les sciences exactes, naturelles, intellectuelles et dans les arts qui en dépendent.* 4 vols. Paris, 1766–68.

Scheler, *Ressentiment* = Scheler, Max. *Das Ressentiment im Aufbau der Moralen.* Edited by M. S. Frings. Frankfurt: Klostermann, 1978. First published in 1912.

———, *Stellung* = Scheler, M. *Die Stellung des Menschen im Kosmos.* Bern: Francke, 1975.

Schelling, *AW* = Schelling, Friedrich Wilhelm Joseph. *Ausgewählte Werke.* Darmstadt: Wissenschaftliche Buchgesellschaft, 1980.

Schiller, *Humanism* = Schiller, F. C. S. *Humanism: Philosophical Essays.* London: Macmillan, 1903.

———, *Studies* = *Studies in Humanism.* London: Macmillan, 1907.

Schiller, *S* = Schiller, Friedrich. *Schriften.* Vol. 4, *Kleine Theoretische Schriften, Die großen Abhandlungen, Rezensionen, Historische Schriften.* Edited by H. Mayer and G. Mann. Frankfurt: Insel, 1966.

Schlegel, *Ausgabe* = Schlegel, F. *Kritische [. . .] Ausgabe.* Edited by E. Behler. Munich: Schöningh; Zurich: Thomas, 1963.
Schneevogel, *Iovis* = Schneevogel, Paul. *Iudicium Iovis, oder Der Gericht der Götter über den Bergbau: Ein literarisches Dokument aus der Frühzeit des Bergbaus.* Edited by P. Krendel. Berlin: Akademie Verlag, 1953.
Schopenhauer, *WW* = Schopenhauer, Arthur. *Werke.* Edited by E. von Lohneysen. 5 vols. Darmstadt: Wissenschaftliche Buchgesellschaft, 1982.
Schult, *Barlach* = Schult, F. *Barlach im Gespräch.* Leipzig: Insel, 1990.
Secchi, *Soleil* = Secchi, A. *Le Soleil: Exposé des principales découvertes modernes sur la structure de cet astre, son influence dans l'univers et ses relations avec les autres corps célestes.* Paris: Gauthier-Villars, 1870.
Selby-Bigge, *British Moralists* = Selby-Bigge, L. A., ed. *British Moralists.* Oxford, 1897.
Seler, *Gesammelte* = Seler, Eduard. *Gesammelte Abhandlungen zur amerikanischen Sprach- und Altertumskunde.* Berlin: Asher, 1902–23.
Seneca, *Apocolocyntosis* = Seneca. *Apocolocyntosis.* Edited by W. H. D. Rouse. Loeb, 1975.
———, *Dialogues* = *Dialogues.* Vol. 3. Edited by R. Waltz. Paris: Les Belles Lettres, 1923.
———, *Lucilius* = *Letters to Lucilius.* Edited by L. D. Reynolds. Oxford: Clarendon Press, 1965.
———, *Quaestiones* = *Quaestiones naturales.* Edited by P. Oltramare. Paris: Les Belles Lettres, 1929.
Shaftesbury, *Characteristics* = Shaftesbury, Anthony Ashley Cooper, 3rd Earl of. *Characteristics of Men, Manners, Opinions, Times.* Edited by J. M. Robertson. London: Grant Richards, 1900.
Shelley, *F* = Shelley, Mary. *Frankenstein, or The Modern Prometheus.* London: Penguin, 1994.
Shmuel, *Diwan* = Shmuel Ibn Naghrela [Samuel ha-Nagid]. *Diwan.* Edited by D. S. Sassoon. Oxford: Oxford University Press, 1934.
Silvestre, *Histoire* = Silvestre, T. *Histoire des artistes vivants français et étrangers: Études d'après nature.* Paris, 1856.
"Sincere Brethren," *R* = "Sincere Brethren." *Rasâ'il Ihwân as-Safâ'.* Edited by Bustani. 4 vols. Beirut: Dar Beyrouth, n.d.
———, *Risâla* = *Risâla Jami'a.* Edited by M. Ghâlib. Beyrouth: Dar al-Andaloss, 1984.
Skinner, *Beyond* = Skinner, Burrhus Frederick. *Beyond Freedom and Dignity.* New York: Knopf, 1971.
———, *Walden Two* = *Walden Two.* Indianapolis: Hackett, 1948. Reprint, New York: Knopf, 1971.
Soloviev, *Leçons* = Soloviev, V. *Leçons sur la divino-humanité.* Translated by B. Marchadier. Paris: Cerf, 1991.
———, *RO* = Собрание сочинений [Collected Works]. Saint Petersburg: Prosvechenie, 1901. Facsimile reprint. Brussels: Foyer Oriental Chrétien, 1966.
Songe = *Le Songe du Vergier.* Edited by M. Schnerb-Lièvre. Paris: CNRS, 1982.

Spee, *Cautio* = Spee, Friedrich. *Cautio criminalis seu de processibus contra sagas liber*. Rinteln, 1631. Translated into German by J.-F. Ritter. *Cautio criminalis, oder Rechtliches Bedenken wegen der Hexenprozesse*. Munich: dtv, 2000.

Spencer, *Social* = Spencer, H. *Social Statics, or The Conditions Essential to Happiness Specified, and the First of Them Developed*. London, 1851.

Spenser, *Faerie Queene* = Spenser, E. *Faerie Queene*. Edited by J. W. Hales. London: Dent, 1965.

Spinoza, *O* = Spinoza, Benedict de. *Opera quotquot reperta sunt*. Edited by J. Van Vloten and J. P. N. Land. 3rd ed. 4 vols. The Hague: Nijhoff, 1914.

Staël, *Considérations* = Staël, Madame de. *Considérations sur la Révolution française*. Edited by J. Godechot. Paris: Tallandier, 1983.

Strauss, *Glaube* = Strauss, D. F. *Der alte und der neue Glaube: Ein Bekenntnis*. 8th ed. Bonn, 1881. First published in 1872.

Suetonius, *Caesars* = Suetonius. *Lives of the Caesars*. Edited by J. C. Rolfe. Loeb, 1997.

Swift, *Correspondence* = Swift, Jonathan. *The Correspondence of Jonathan Swift, D.D.* Edited by D. Woolley. Frankfurt: Lang, 2001.

———, *Gulliver* = Swift, Jonathan. *Gullivers's Travels*. World's Classics. Oxford: Oxford University Press, 1948.

Tacitus, *Histories* = Tacitus. *Histories*. Edited by K. Halm. Leipzig, 1889.

Taine, *Origines* = Taine, Hippolyte. *Les Origines de la France contemporaine*. Paris: Laffont, 1986.

Tchernychevski [Chernyshevsky], *Antropologičeskij* = Tchernychevski, N. G. *Antropologičeskij prinśip v filosofii, Polnoe sobranie sočinenijj*. Moscow: Éditions d'État de Belles-Lettres, 1950.

———, *Philosophiques* = *Textes philosophiques choisis*. Moscow: Éditions en langues étrangères, 1957.

Telesio, *De natura* = Telesio. *De natura juxta propriis principiis*. Edited by R. Bondi. 2nd ed. Milan: Bompiani, 2009. First published in 1570.

Thomas à Kempis, *Imitation* = Thomas à Kempis. *De imitatione Christi*. Edited by P. E. Puyol. Paris, 1898.

Thomas Aquinas, *Metaphysicorum* = Thomas Aquinas. *In duodecim libros Metaphysicorum Aristotelis expositio*. Edited by M. R. Cathala and R. M. Spiazzi. Turin: Marietti, 1964.

———, *Opera* = *Opera Omnia*. Stuttgart: Frommann-Holzboog, 1980.

———, *Sent* = *Quattuor Libros Sententiarum*. Edited by R. Busa. Vol. 1 of *Opera*.

———, *ST* = *Summa Theologica*. Paris: Lethielleux, 1939.

Thomson, "Heat" = Thomson, W. "On the Age of the Sun's Heat." *Macmillan's Magazine*, 5 March 1862, 288–93.

———, "Tendency" = Thomson, W. "On a Universal Tendency in Nature to the Dissipation of Mechanical Energy." *Philosophical Magazine*, October 1852, 256–60.

Thomson, *Poems* = Thomson, James. *The Poems*. Edited by J. Logie Robertson. London: Oxford University Press, 1908.

Thoreau, *Walden* = Thoreau, H. D. *Walden*. Edited by M. Meyer. London: Penguin, 1983.

Tieck, *Werke* = Tieck, L. *Werke in vier Bänden*. Edited by M. Thalmann. Munich: Winkler, 1963.
Tocqueville, *Démocratie* = Tocqueville, A. de. *De la démocratie en Amérique*. Edited by A. Jardin. Paris, Gallimard, 1992.
———, *Inédites* = *Oeuvres et correspondance inédites*. Edited by G. de Beaumont. Paris, 1861.
Traherne, *Centuries* = Traherne, T. *Centuries*. In *Centuries, Poems and Thanksgivings*, edited by H. M. Margoliouth. Oxford: Clarendon Press, 1958.
Trotski, *Denkzettel* = Trotski, L. *Denkzettel: Politische Erfahrungen im Zeitalter der permanenten Revolution*. Edited by I. Deutscher, G. Novack, and H. Dahmer. Frankfurt: Suhrkamp, 1981.
Turgot, *ODC* = Turgot, Anne-Robert-Jacques. *Oeuvres de Turgot et documents le concernant*. Edited by G. Schelle. 5 vols. Paris: Alcan, 1913–23.
Turmeda, *Ass* = Turmeda, Anselm. *Dispute de l'âne*. Edited by A. Llinares. Paris: Vrin, 1984.
Vair, *Oeuvres* = Vair, G. du. *Oeuvres*. Geneva: Slatkine, 1970. First published in Paris, 1641.
Valéry, *Oeuvres* = Valéry, Paul. *Oeuvres*. Edited by J. Hytier. Paris: Gallimard, 1957–60.
Vega, *Anticristo* = Vega, Lope de. *El Anticristo: Obras de Lope de Vega*. Madrid: Biblioteca de autores españoles, 1963.
Verne, *Île* = Verne, Jules. *L'Île mystérieuse*. 3 vols. Paris: Hachette, 1925.
Verri, *Osservazioni* = Verri, P. *Osservazioni sulla tortura*. Edited by S. Contarini. Milan: Rizzoli, 2006. Written in 1776. First published in 1804.
Vico, *MM* = Vico, Giambattista. *Metafisica e metodo*. Edited by C. Faschilli et al. Milan: Bompiani, 2008.
———, *O* = *Opere*. Edited by A. Battistini. 2 vols. Milan: Mondadori, 1990.
Vigny, *PC* = Vigny, Alfred de. *"Poésies"; "Chatterton."* Paris: Hachette, 1950.
Villeneuve, *Économie* = Villeneuve, Joachim Faiguet de. *L'Économie politique: Projet pour enrichir et perfectionner l'espèce humaine*. Paris: Moreau, 1763.
Villermé, *Tableau* = Villermé, Louis-René. *Tableau de l'état physique et moral des ouvriers employés dans les manufactures de coton, de laine, et de soie*. 2 vols. Paris, 1840. Reprint, Paris: Études et documentations internationales, 1989.
Villers, *Briefe* = Villers, Alexander von. *Briefe eines Unbekannten*. Edited by M. Gideon. Zurich: Manesse, n.d.
Villiers, *Eve* = Villiers de l'Isle-Adam, Auguste. *L'Eve Future*. Edited by N. Satiat. Paris: Garnier-Flammarion, 1992.
Vischer, *Briefwechsel* = Vischer, F. T. *Briefwechsel zwischen Eduard Mörike und Friedrich Theodor Vischer*. Edited by R. Vischer. Munich: Beck, 1926.
Vitruvius, *Architecture* = Vitruvius. *De l'architecture*. Edited by C. Fensterbusch. Darmstadt: Wissenschaftliche Buchgesellschaft, 1964.
Voltaire, *Dictionnaire* = Voltaire. *Dictionnaire philosophique*. Edited by R. Naves. Paris: Garnier.
———, *Essai* = *Essai sur les moeurs et l'esprit des nations et sur les principaux faits de l'histoire depuis Charlemagne jusqu'à Louis XIII*. 2 vols. Edited by R. Pomeau. Paris: Garnier, 1990.

———, *Lettres* = *Lettres philosophiques*. Paris: Flammarion, 2008.
———, *Oeuvres* = *Oeuvres complètes*. Paris, 1879.
———, *Oeuvres/Besterman* = *Oeuvres complètes*. Edited by T. Besterman. Banbury: The Voltaire Foundation, 1973.
———, *Oeuvres h.* = *Oeuvres historiques*. Edited by R. Pomeau. Paris: Gallimard, 1957.
Weber, *Entlastung* = Weber, M. M. von. *Die Entlastung der Culturarbeit durch den Dienst der physikalischen Kräfte*. Berlin, 1880.
Weber, *Folterkammern* = Weber, E. von. *Die Folterkammern der Wissenschaft: Eine Sammlung von Tatsachen für das Laienpublikum*. Berlin, 1879.
Wells, *Men* = Wells, Herbert George. *Men like Gods*. London: Cassell and Co., 1923. Reprint, London: Sphere Books, 1976.
———, *Mind* = *Mind at the End of Its Tether*. London: W. Heinemann, 1945.
Wieland, *Werke* = Wieland, C. M. *Werke*. Edited by F. Martini and H. W. Seiffert. Munich: Hanser, 1985.
Wilde, *Profundis* = Wilde, Oscar. *De profundis, and Other Writings*. Edited by H. Pearson. London: Penguin, 1986.
William of Auvergne, *Universo* = William of Auvergne. *De universo*. Paris, 1674.
Winckelmann, *Schriften* = Winckelmann, J. J. *Kleine Schriften; Vorreden; Entwürfe*. Edited by W. Rehm. Berlin: De Gruyter, 1968.
Wreszinski, *Inschriften* = Wreszinski, W. 1906. *Ägyptische Inschriften aus dem K. K. Hofmuseum in Wien*. Leipzig: Hinrich.
Xunzi = *Xunzi: A Translation and Study of the Complete Works*. Translated by John Knoblock. Vol. 3, *Books 17–32*. Stanford: Stanford University Press, 1994.
Zola, *Lettres* = Zola, Emile. *Lettres de Paris: Nouvelles artistiques et littéraires, Écrits sur l'art*. Edited by J.-P. Leduc-Adine. Paris: Gallimard, 1991.
———, *Pascal* = *Le docteur Pascal*. 1893. Reprint edited by J.-L. Cabanès. Paris: Le livre de poche, 2004.

Secondary Sources
Reference Works

Dizionario = *Dizionario biografico degli italiani*. Edited by P. Viti. Rome: Istituto della Enciclopedia Italiana, 1994.
DW = *Deutsches Wörterbuch*. By Jacob Grimm and Wilhelm Grimm. New edition. Stuttgart: Hirzel, 1983–.
EN = *Enzyklopädie der Neuzeit*. Edited by F. Jaeger. Stuttgart: Metzler, 2005–.
GG = *Geschichtliche Grundbegriffe: Historisches Lexikon zur politisch-sozialen Sprache in Deutschland*. Edited by O. Brunner, W. Conze, and R. Koselleck. 9 vols. Stuttgart: Klett-Cotta, 1972–97.
HDA = *Handwörterbuch des deutschen Aberglaubens*. Edited by Eduard Hoffmann-Krayer and Hanns Bächtold-Stäubli. Berlin: De Gruyter, 1935–36.
HWPh = *Historisches Wörterbuch der Philosophie*. Edited by J. Ritter et al. 12 vols. Basel: Schwabe, 1971–2004.

Littré = Littré, Emile. *Dictionnaire de la Langue Française*. 7 vols. Paris: Pauvert, 1956–.
NDHI = *New Dictionary of the History of Ideas*. Edited by M. C. Horowitz. 6 vols. Detroit: Scribner, 2005.
OED = *Oxford English Dictionary*. Edited by J. A. H. Murray. 13 vols. Oxford: Oxford University Press, 1933.
TLF = *Trésor de la Langue Française: Dictionnaire de la langue du xixe et du xxe siècle (1789–1960)*. Edited by P. Imbs. 16 vols. Vols. 1–10, Paris: Centre National de la Recherche Scientifique, 1971–83; vols. 11–16, Paris: Gallimard, 1971–94.

Monographs and Articles

Adams, Robert P. 1949. "The Social Responsibilities of Science in Utopia, New Atlantis, and After." *Journal of the History of Ideas* 10:374–98.
Allen, Don Cameron. 1938. "The Degeneration of Man and Renaissance Pessimism." *Studies in Philology* 35:202–27.
Althusser, L. 1964. "Marxisme et humanisme." *Cahiers de l'Institut des sciences économiques appliquées* 20:109–34.
———. 1965. *Pour Marx*. Paris: Maspero.
Alvar, C., and J. Talens, eds. 2009. *Locus amoenus: Antología de la lírica medieval de la peninsula ibérica*. Barcelona: Galaxia Gutenberg.
Ammer, Vera. 1988. *Gottmenschentum und Menschgottum: Zur Auseinandersetzung von Christentum und Atheismus im russischen Denken*. Slavistische Beiträge 228. Munich: Sagner, 1988.
Anders, Günther. 2002a. *Die Antiquiertheit des Menschen*. Vol. 1, *Über die Zerstörung der Seele im Zeitalter der zweiten industriellen Revolution*. Munich: Beck. First published in 1956.
———. 2002b. *Die Antiquiertheit des Menschen*. Vol. 2, *Über die Zerstörung des Lebens im Zeitalter der dritten industriellen Revolution*. Munich: Beck. First published in 1980.
Andia, Ysabel de. 1996. *Henosis: L'Union à Dieu chez Denys l'Aréopagite*. Paris: Etudes Augustiniennes.
Arendt, Hannah. 1951. *The Origins of Totalitarianism*. New York: Schocken. Reprint, 2004.
———. 1958. *The Human Condition*. Chicago: University of Chicago Press.
———. 1963. *On Revolution*. London: Faber & Faber.
Armogathe, Jean-Robert. 2001. "Une ancienne querelle." In *QAM*, 801–49.
———. 2005. *L'Antéchrist à l'âge classique: Exégèse et politique*. Paris: Mille et une nuits.
———. 2007. *La Nature du monde: Science nouvelle et exégèse au xviie siècle*. Paris: Presses Universitaires de France.
Assmann, Aleida. 1993. *Arbeit am nationalen Gedächtnis: Eine kurze Geschichte der deutschen Bildungsidee*. Frankfurt: Campus.
Attwood, Lynne, and Catriona Kelly. 1998. "Programmes for Identity: The 'New Man' and the 'New Woman.'" In *Constructing Russian Culture in the Age of*

Revolution: 1881–1940, edited by C. Kelly and D. Shepherd, 256–90, 322–26. Oxford: Oxford University Press.

Baczko, Bronislaw. 1982. *Une éducation pour la démocratie: Textes et projets de l'époque révolutionnaire.* Paris: Garnier.

Baechler, Jean. 2002. *Esquisse d'une histoire universelle.* Paris: Fayard.

Baille, S., et al. 1963. *Le Monde actuel: Histoire et civilisations.* Paris: Belin.

Baker, Herschel Clay. 1961. *The Image of Man: A Study of the Idea of Human Dignity in Classical Antiquity, the Middle Ages and the Renaissance.* New York: Harper. First published in 1947 as *The Dignity of Man: Studies in the Persistence of an Idea.* Cambridge, MA: Harvard University Press.

Balthasar, Hans Urs von. 1998. *Geschichte des apokalyptischen Problems in der deutschen Literatur.* Einsiedeln: Johannes Verlag. First published in 1930.

———. 1956. *Die Gottesfrage des heutigen Menschen.* Vienna: Herold.

Barr, James. 1972. "Man and Nature—The Ecological Controversy and the Old Testament." *Bulletin of the John Rylands Library* 55:9–32.

Batut, Jean-Pierre. 2009. *Pantocrator: "Dieu le Père tout-puissant" dans la théologie prénicéenne.* Paris: Etudes Augustiniennes.

Beaujouan, Guy. 1975. "Réflexions sur les rapports entre théorie et pratique au Moyen Âge." In *The Cultural Context of Medieval Learning*, edited by J. E. Murdoch and D. Sylla, 437–84. Dordrecht: Reidel.

———. 1991. "La prise de conscience de l'aptitude à innover (le tournant du milieu du 13ᵉ siècle)." In *Le Moyen Age et la science*, edited by B. Ribemont, 5–14. Paris: Klincksieck.

Becker, Carl L. 1932. *The Heavenly City of the Eighteenth Century Philosophers.* New Haven: Yale University Press.

Bénichou, Paul. 2003. *Romantismes français.* Vol. 1, *Le Sacre de l'écrivain: Le Temps des prophètes.* Paris: Gallimard.

———. 2004. *Romantismes français.* Vol. 2, *Les Mages romantiques: L'Ecole du désenchantement.* Paris: Gallimard.

Benz, Ernst. 1937. *Der vollkommene Mensch nach Jacob Boehme.* Stuttgart: Kohlhammer.

———. 1961a. "Das Bild des Übermenschen in der europäischen Geistesgeschichte." In *Der Übermensch*, edited by Ernst Benz, 19–161. Zurich: Rhein-Verlag.

———. 1961b. "Der 'Übermensch'-Begriff in der Theologie der Alten Kirche." In *Studien zum Neuen Testament und zur Patristik: Erich Klostermann zum 90. Geburtstag dargebracht*, edited by Kommission für Spätantike Religionsgeschichte, 135–60. Berlin: Akademie-Verlag.

———. 1974. "Der dreifache Aspekt des Übermenschen." In *Urbild und Abbild: Der Mensch und die mythische Welt; Gesammelte Eranos-Beiträge*, 337–420. Leiden: Brill. The essay was first published in 1960.

Berlin, Isaiah. 1990. *The Crooked Timber of Humanity: Chapters in the History of Ideas.* Edited by H. Hardy. Princeton: Princeton University Press.

———. 1999. *The Roots of Romanticism.* Edited by H. Hardy. Princeton: Princeton University Press.

———. 2000. *Three Critics of the Enlightenment: Vico, Hamann and Herder.* Princeton: Princeton University Press.
Besançon, Alain. 1977. *Les Origines intellectuelles du léninisme.* Paris: Calmann-Lévy.
———. 1994. *L'Image interdite: Une histoire intellectuelle de l'iconoclasme.* Paris: Fayard.
Bettetini, Maria. 2004. *Figure di verità: La finzione nel Medioevo occidentale.* Turin: Einaudi.
Bickermann, Elias. 1937. *Der Gott der Makkabäer.* Berlin: Schocken.
Biermann, Kurt R. 1990. *Miscellanea Humboldtiana.* Berlin: Akademie Verlag.
Billington, James H. 1970. *The Icon and the Axe: An Interpretive History of Russian Culture.* New York: Vintage.
Black, John. 1970. *The Dominion of Man: The Search for Ecological Responsibility.* Edinburgh: Edinburgh University Press.
Blumenberg, Hans. 1951. "Das Verhältnis von Natur und Technik als philosophisches Problem." In *Ästhetische und Metaphorologische Schriften*, by Hans Blumenberg, edited by A. Haverkamp, 253–65. Frankfurt: Suhrkamp, 2001.
———. 1957. "'Nachahmung der Natur': Zur Vorgeschichte der Idee des schöpferischen Menschen." In *Ästhetische und Metaphorologische Schriften*, by Hans Blumenberg, edited by A. Haverkamp, 9–46. Frankfurt: Suhrkamp, 2001.
———. 1975. *Die Genesis der kopernikanischen Welt.* 3 vols. Frankfurt: Suhrkamp.
———. 1984. *Arbeit am Mythos.* 3rd ed. Frankfurt: Suhrkamp.
———. 1988. *Die Legitimität der Neuzeit: Erneuerte Ausgabe.* Frankfurt: Suhrkamp. [c.r. "La galaxie Blumenberg," *Le Débat* 83 (1995): 173–86.]
Böckenförde, E. W. 1991. *Recht, Staat, Freiheit: Studien zur Rechtsphilosophie, Staatstheorie und Verfassungsgeschichte.* Frankfurt: Suhrkamp.
Boehme, Hartmut, and Gernot Boehme. 1983. *Das Andere der Vernunft: Zur Entwicklung von Rationalitätsstrukturen am Beispiel Kants.* Frankfurt: Suhrkamp.
Boll, Franz. 1917. "Technische Träume des Mittelalters." *Die Umschau: Wochenschrift über die Fortschritte in Wissenschaft und Technik* 21:678–80.
Bollnow, Otto-Friedrich. 1958. *Wesen und Wandel der Tugenden.* Frankfurt: Ullstein.
Bonnet, Jean-Claude. 1998. *Naissance du Panthéon: Essai sur le culte des grands hommes.* Paris: Fayard.
Bossi, Laura. 2003. *Histoire naturelle de l'âme.* Paris: Presses Universitaires de France.
Bouwsma, William J. 1993. "The Renaissance Discovery of Human Creativity." In *Humanity and Divinity in Renaissance and Reformation: Essays in Honor of Charles Trinkaus*, edited by J. W. O'Malley et al., 17–34. Leiden: Brill.
Brague, Rémi. 1988. *Aristote et la question du monde: Essai sur le contexte cosmologique et anthropologique de l'ontologie.* Paris: Cerf, 2009.
———. 1993. "L'anthropologie de l'humilité." In *Saint Bernard et la Philosophie*, edited by R. Brague, 129–52. Paris: Presses Universitaires de France.
———. 1995. "La galaxie Blumenberg." Review of *Die Legitimität der Neuzeit: Erneuerte Ausgabe*, by Hans Blumenberg. *Le Débat* 83:173–86.
———. 1998. "Le problème de l'homme moderne." In *Charles Taylor et l'interprétation de l'identité moderne*, edited by G. Laforest and P. de Lara, 217–29. Paris: Cerf; Québec: Presses Universitaire de Lyon.

———. 2000. "Schwung oder Schwund? Das alte und das Neue Europa, Kontinuitäten und Brüche." In *Die Furie des Verschwindens: Über das Schicksal des Alten im Zeitalter des Neuen*, edited by K. P. Liessmann, 41–59. (First presented at the third meeting of a philosophical symposium in Lech, Austria.) Vienna: Paul Zsolnay.

———. 2002a. "Le jeu des quatre sagesses." Interview by P.-H. Tavoillot. *Le Point*, no. 1559, 2 August, 73–75.

———. 2002b. *La Sagesse du monde: Histoire de l'expérience humaine de l'univers*. 2nd ed. Paris: Hachette.

———. 2005. "Völkerwanderungen und Überschwemmungen: Die Flut als Metapher des Vergessens." In *Sintflut und Gedächtnis*, edited by M. Mulsow and J. Assmann, 117–27. Paderborn: Fink.

———. 2006a. *Au moyen du Moyen Age: Philosophies médiévales en chrétienté, judaïsme, et islam*. Chatou: Les Éditions de la Transparence.

———. 2006b. "La phénoménologie comme voie d'accès au monde grec: Note sur la critique de la *Vorhandenheit* comme modèle ontologique dans la lecture heideggérienne d'Aristote." In *Heidegger*, edited by M. Caron, 111–46. Paris: Cerf.

———. 2008a. *Du Dieu des chrétiens et d'un ou deux autres*. Paris: Flammarion.

———. 2008b. *Image vagabonde: Essai sur l'imaginaire baudelairien*. Chatou: Les Éditions de la Transparence.

———. 2008c. *La Loi de Dieu: Histoire philosophique d'une alliance*. 2nd ed. Paris: Gallimard.

———. 2011. *Les ancres dans le ciel: L'infrastructure métaphysique*. Paris: Seuil.

———. 2013. *Le Propre de l'homme: Sur une légitimité menacée*. Paris: Flammarion.

———. 2014. *Modérément moderne*. Paris: Flammarion.

Bredekamp, Horst. 1984. "Der Mensch als Mörder der Natur: Das 'Iudicium Iovis' von Paulus Niavis und die Leibmetaphorik." In *All Geschöpf ist Zung' und Mund: Beiträge aus dem Grenzbereich von Naturkunde und Theologie*, edited by Heimo Reinitzer, 261–83. Vestigia Biblica: Jahrbuch des Deutschen Bibel-Archivs Hamburg 6. Hamburg: Wittig.

———. 2008. *Der Künstler als Verbrecher: Ein Element der frühmodernen Rechts und Staatstheorie*. Munich: Siemens-Stiftung.

Bredvold, Louis I. 1961. *The Brave New World of the Enlightenment*. Ann Arbor: University of Michigan Press.

Brown, Harcourt. 1936. "The Utilitarian Motive in the Age of Descartes." *Annals of Science* 1:182–92.

Bruch, Richard. 1981. "Die Würde des Menschen in der patristischen Tradition." In *Wissen-Glaube-Politik: Festschrift für P. Asveld*, edited by W. Gruber et al., 139–54. Graz: Styria.

Buck, August. 1952. *Italienische Dichtungslehren vom Mittelalter bis zum Ausgang der Renaissance*. Tübingen: Niemeyer.

———. 1958. "Über einige Deutungen des Prometheus-Mythos in der Literatur der Renaissance." In *Die humanistische Tradition in der Romania*, 91–101. Berlin: Gehlen, 1968.

———. 1960. "Die Rangstellung des Menschen in der Renaissance: *Dignitas et miseria hominis.*" *Archiv für Kulturgeschichte* 42:61–75.
Burleigh, Michael. 2005. *Earthly Powers: Religion and Politics in Europe from the Enlightenment to the Great War.* London: HarperCollins.
Bury, John B. 1932. *The Idea of Progress: An Inquiry into Its Origin and Growth.* New York: Dover, 1955.
Campana, Augusto. 1946. "The Origin of the Word 'Humanist.'" *Journal of the Warburg and Courtauld Institutes* 9:60–73.
Carroll, John. 2008. *The Wreck of Western Culture: Humanism Revisited.* Wilmington, DE: ISI Books.
Carrouges, Michel. 1948. *La Mystique du surhomme.* Paris: Gallimard.
Cassirer, Ernst. 1927. *Individuum und Kosmos in der Philosophie der Renaissance.* Darmstadt: Wissenschaftliche Buchgesellschaft, 1987.
———. 1946. *The Myth of the State.* New Haven: Yale University Press.
Castoriadis, Cornelius. 1999. "Anthropogonie chez Eschyle et autocréation de l'homme chez Sophocle." In *Figures du pensable*, vol. 6 of *Les Carrefours du labyrinthe*, 13–34. Paris: Seuil.
Céline, Louis-Ferdinand. 1952. *Mort à crédit.* Paris: Gallimard.
Chan, Wing-Tsit. 1963. *A Source Book in Chinese Philosophy.* Princeton: Princeton University Press.
Chenu, Marie-Dominique. 1955. *Pour une théologie du travail.* Paris: Seuil.
———. 1957. *La Théologie au xiie siècle.* Paris: Vrin.
Cheyron, M. du, ed. 1965. *Romanciers du XVIIIe siècle.* Paris: Gallimard.
Christensen, Michael J., and Jeffery A. Wittung, eds. 2007. *Partakers of the Divine Nature: The History and Development of Deification in the Christian Traditions.* Madison, WI: Fairleigh Dickinson University Press.
Christou, Chrysanthos. 1968. *Potnia theron. Eine Untersuchung über Ursprung, Erscheinungsformen und Gestalt einer Gottheit.* Tübingen: Wasmuth.
Clair, Jean. 2003. *Du surréalisme considéré dans ses rapports avec le totalitarisme et les tables tournantes: Contribution à une histoire de l'insensé.* Paris: Mille et une nuits.
Close, Anthony J. 1969. "Commonplace Theories of Art and Nature in Classical Antiquity and the Renaissance." *Journal of the History of Ideas* 30:467–86.
Clynes, Manfred E., and Nathan S. Kline. 1970. "Cyborgs and Space." *Astronautics* (September): 29–33.
Cohen, H. Floris. 1994. *The Scientific Revolution: A Historiographical Inquiry.* Chicago: University of Chicago Press.
Cohen, Jeremy. 1989. *'Be Fertile and Increase, Fill the Earth and Master It': The Ancient and Medieval Career of a Biblical Text.* Ithaca, NY: Cornell University Press.
Compagnon, Antoine. 1990. *Les cinq paradoxes de la modernité.* Paris: Seuil.
Comprendre et maîtriser la nature au Moyen Age: Mélanges d'histoire des sciences offerts à Guy Beaujouan. 1994. Geneva: Droz.
Courtine, Jean-François. 1999. *Nature et empire de la loi: Etudes suaréziennes.* Paris: Vrin.

Couzinet, Marie-Dominique. 2007. Sub specie hominis: *Études sur le savoir humain au xvie siècle*. Paris: Vrin.
Cragg, Kenneth. 1968. *The Privilege of Man: A Theme in Judaism, Islam and Christianity*. London: Athlone Press.
Crocker, Lester G. 1952. "The Discussion of Suicide in the Eighteenth Century." *Journal of the History of Ideas* 13:47–72.
———. 1959. *An Age of Crisis: Man and World in Eighteenth Century French Thought*. Baltimore: Johns Hopkins University Press.
Curtius, Ernst Robert. 1953. *Europäische Literatur und lateinisches Mittelalter*. Bern: Francke, 1973.
Čyževśkyj, D. 1936. "Literarische Lesefrüchte. IV." *Zeitschrift für Slavische Philologie* 13:51–76.
Dales, Richard C. 1977. "A Medieval View of Human Dignity." *Journal of the History of Ideas* 38:557–72.
Debus, Allen G. 1978. *Man and Nature in the Renaissance*. Cambridge: Cambridge University Press.
Dédéyan, Charles. 1955–64. *Le Thème de Faust dans la littérature européenne*. 6 vols. Paris: Lettres Modernes.
De Keyser, Eugénie. 1965. *L'Occident romantique: 1789–1850*. Geneva: Skira.
De Koninck, Thomas. 1995. *De la Dignité humaine*. Paris: Presses Universitaires de France.
Denzinger, H. 1908. *Enchiridion Symbolorum*. 10th ed. Freiburg im Breisgau: Herder.
Derrida, J. 1967. "La structure, le signe et le jeu dans le discours des sciences humaines." In *L'Écriture et la différence*. Paris: Seuil. The essay was first published in 1966.
Deuchler, Florens. 1984. "Warum malte Konrad Witz die 'erste' Landschaft? Hic et nunc im Genfer Altar von 1444." *Medium Aevum Quotidianum Newsletter* 3:39–49.
Dienel, Hans-Liudger. 1992. *Herrschaft über die Natur? Naturvorstellungen deutscher Ingenieure, 1871–1914*. Stuttgart: Verlag für Geschichte der Naturwissenschaften und der Technik.
———. 1995. "Herrschaft über die Natur? Naturvorstellungen deutscher Ingenieure im 19. und frühen 20. Jahrhundert." In *Aufklärung und späte Neuzeit*, edited by L. Schäfer and E. Stöker, 121–48. Vol. 3 of *Naturauffassungen in Philosophie, Wissenschaft, Technik*. Freiburg im Breisgau: Alber, 1995.
Dilthey, Wilhelm. 1914. *Weltanschauung und Analyse des Menschen seit der Renaissance und Reformation: Abhandlungen zur Geschichte der Philosophie und Religion*. Leipzig: Teubner, 1923.
Dodds, Eric R. 1951. *The Greeks and the Irrational*. Berkeley: University of California Press.
———. 1965. *Pagan and Christian in an Age of Anxiety: Some Aspects of Religious Experience from Marcus Aurelius to Constantine*. Cambridge: Cambridge University Press.
———. 1973. *The Ancient Concept of Progress, and Other Essays on Greek Literature and Belief*. Oxford: Clarendon Press.

Duby, Georges. 1966. *Fondements d'un nouvel humanisme: 1280–1440*. Geneva: Skira.
Duchesne, Jean. 2013. *Incurable romantisme? La pandémie culturelle qui défie la nouvelle évangélisation*. Paris: Parole et silence.
Dupré, Louis. 1993. *Passage to Modernity: An Essay in the Hermeneutics of Nature and Culture*. New Haven: Yale University Press.
———. 2004. *The Enlightenment and the Intellectual Foundations of Modern Culture*. New Haven: Yale University Press.
Du Toit, David S. 1997. *Theios Anthropos: Zur Verwendung von theios anthrōpos und sinnverwandten Ausdrücken in der Literatur der Kaiserzeit*. Wissenschaftliche Untersuchungen zum Neuen Testament 2/91. Tübingen: Mohr.
Duviols, J.-P., and C. Minguet. 1994. *Humboldt, savant-citoyen du monde*. Paris: Gallimard.
Dyson, George B. 1998. *Darwin among the Machines: The Evolution of Global Intelligence*. New York: Perseus.
Eamon, William. 1983. "Technology as Magic in the Late Middle Ages and the Renaissance." *Janus* 70:171–212.
———. 1994. *Science and the Secrets of Nature: Books of Secrets in Medieval and Early Modern Culture*. Princeton: Princeton University Press.
Eberle, Mathias. 1980. *Individuum und Landschaft: Zur Entstehung und Entwicklung der Landschaftsmalerei*. Giessen: Anabas.
Ehlen, Peter. 2000. "Der Begriff des 'Gottmenschentums' in der Philosophie V. S. Solov'evs und S. L. Franks." *Forum für osteuropäische Ideen- und Zeitgeschichte* 4:41–74.
Eliade, Mircea. 1956. *Forgerons et alchimistes*. Paris: Flammarion.
Faivre, Antoine. 1988. "La postérité de l'hermétisme alexandrin (repères historiques et bibliographiques)." In *Présence d'Hermès Trismégiste, Cahiers de l'Hermétisme*, edited by Antoine Faivre, 13–23. Paris: Albin Michel.
Farge, A. 1989. *Le Goût de l'archive*. Paris: Seuil.
Faye, Emmanuel. 1998. *Philosophie et perfection de l'homme: De la Renaissance à Descartes*. Paris: Vrin.
Fehrenbach, Frank. 1997. *Licht und Wasser: Zur Dynamik naturphilosophischer Leitbilder im Werk Leonardo da Vincis*. Tübingen: Wasmuth.
Fellmann, Ferdinand. 1976. *Das Vico-Axiom: Der Mensch macht die Geschichte*. Fribourg: Alber.
Ferrarin, Alfredo. 2001. *Artificio, desiderio, considerazione di sé: Hobbes e i fondamenti antropologici della politica*. Pisa: ETS.
Ferrone, Vincenzo. 1989. "Clio e Prometeo: La storia della scienza tra Illuministi e Positivisti." *Studi Storici* 30:339–57.
Ferry, Luc. 1996. *L'Homme Dieu ou le sens de la vie*. Paris: Grasset.
Findlen, Paula. 1994. *Possessing Nature: Museums, Collecting and Scientific Culture in Early Modern Italy*. Berkeley: University of California Press.
Fischer, Hubertus. 1985. "Naturwahrnehmung im Mittelalter und Neuzeit." *Landschaft + Stadt* 17:97–110.
Flasch, Kurt. 2006. *Meister Eckhart: Die Geburt der "Deutschen Mystik" aus dem Geiste der arabischen Philosophie*. Munich: Beck.

Flint, Valerie I. J. 1991. *The Rise of Magic in Early Medieval Europe*. Princeton: Princeton University Press.

Fögen, Marie Theres. 1997. *Die Enteignung der Wahrsager: Studien zum kaiserlichen Wissensmonopol in der Spätantike*. Frankfurt: Suhrkamp.

Forbes, Robert James. 1968. *The Conquest of Nature: Technology and Its Consequences*. New York: Praeger.

Foucault, M. 1966. *Les Mots et les choses: Une archéologie des sciences humaines*. Paris: Gallimard.

———. 1975. *Surveiller et punir: Naissance de la prison*. Paris: Gallimard.

———. 1984. *Histoire de la sexualité*. Vol. 3, *Le Souci de soi*. Paris: Gallimard.

———. 1994. *Dits et écrits*. Paris: Gallimard.

Fowden, Garth. 1986. *The Egyptian Hermes: A Historical Approach to the Late Pagan Mind*. Cambridge: Cambridge University Press.

Freund, Walter. 1957. *Modernus und andere Zeitbegriffe des Mittelalters*. Cologne: Böhlau.

Fried, Johannes. 2001. *Aufstieg aus dem Untergang: Apokalyptisches Denken und die Entstehung der modernen Naturwissenschaft im Mittelalter*. Munich: Beck.

Friedrich, Hugo. 1955. "Abendländischer Humanismus." Reprinted in *Romanische Literaturen: Aufsätze I, Frankreich*, 1–17. Frankfurt: Klostermann, 1972.

———. 1964. *Epochen der italienischen Lyrik*. Frankfurt: Klostermann.

———. 1967. *Die Struktur der modernen Lyrik: Von der Mitte des neunzehnten bis zur Mitte des zwanzigsten Jahrhunderts*. New, enlarged ed. Hamburg: Rowohlt.

Friedrich, Udo. 2003. "*Contra naturam*: Mittelalterliche Automatisierung im Spannungsfeld politischer, theologischer und technologischer Naturkonzepte." In *Automaten in Kunst und Literatur des Mittelalters und der frühen Neuzeit*, edited by K. Grubmüller and M. Stock, 91–114. Wiesbaden: Harrassowitz.

Fromm, Waldemar. 1999. "Spiegelbilder des Ichs: Beobachtungen zum Affenmotiv im literatur- und kunstgeschichtlichen Kontext (E. T. A. Hoffmann, Wilhelm Hauff, Franz Kafka)." *Literatur in Bayern* 57:49–60.

Fukuyama, Francis. 1992. *The End of History and the Last Man: With a New Afterword*. New York: Free Press, 2006.

———. 2002. *Our Posthuman Future: Consequences of the Biotechnology Revolution*. New York: Farrar, Straus & Giroux.

Fumaroli, Marc. 2001. "Les abeilles et les araignées." In *QAM*, 7–218.

Fung Yu-lan. 1983. *A History of Chinese Philosophy*. Translated by D. Bodde. Vol. 1, *The Period of the Philosophers (from the Beginnings to circa 100 B.C.)*. Princeton: Princeton University Press. Translation of vol. 1 first published in 1937.

Gagnebin, B. 1971. "J.-J. Rousseau: Sur le péché d'Adam et le salut universel." *Dix-Huitième Siècle* 3:41–50.

Garin, Eugenio. 1938. "La 'Dignitas Hominis' e la letteratura patristica." *Rinascità* 1:102–46.

———. 1969. "La crise de la pensée médiévale." In *Moyen Age et Renaissance*, by Eugenio Garin, translated by C. Carme, 17–35. Paris: Gallimard.

Garrigues, Jean-Miguel. 1982. *Dieu sans idée du mal: La liberté de l'homme au cœur de Dieu*. Limoges: Criterion.

Gauchet, Marcel, and Gladys Swain. 1980. *La Pratique de l'esprit humain: L'Institution asilaire et la révolution démocratique*. Paris: Gallimard.
———. 1985. *Le Désenchantement du monde: Une histoire politique de la religion*. Paris: Gallimard.
———. 1992. *L'inconscient cérébral*. Paris: Gallimard.
Gay, Peter. 1966. *The Enlightenment: An Interpretation*. Vol. 1, *The Rise of Modern Paganism*. New York: Knopf.
———. 1969. *The Enlightenment: An Interpretation*. Vol. 2, *The Science of Freedom*. New York: Knopf.
Gentile, Emilio. 2002. *Fascismo: Storia e Interpretazione*. Rome: Laterza.
Gentile, Giovanni. 1916. "Il concetto dell'uomo nel Rinascimento." Reprinted in *Giordano Bruno e il pensiero del Rinascimento*, 3–67. Florence: Le Lettere, 1991.
Gérard, Alain. 1999. *"Par principe d'humanité . . ." La Terreur et la Vendée*. Paris: Fayard.
Gilson, Étienne. 1955. "Humanisme médiéval et renaissance." In *Les idées et les lettres*, 171–96. Paris: Vrin. First published in 1930.
Gimpel, Jean. 1975. *La Révolution industrielle du Moyen Age*. Paris: Seuil.
Glacken, Clarence J. 1967. *Traces on the Rhodian Shore: Nature and Culture in Western Thought from Ancient Times to the End of the Eighteenth Century*. Berkeley: University of California Press.
Glad, John. 2003. "Hermann J. Muller's 1936 Letter to Stalin." *Mankind Quarterly* 43:305–19.
Glasenapp, H. von. 1948. *Der Stufenweg zum Göttlichen: Shankaras Philosophie der All-Einheit*. Baden-Baden: Hans Böhler.
Gloy, Karen. 1996. *Das Verständnis der Natur*. Vol. 2, *Die Geschichte des ganzheitlichen Denkens*. Munich: Beck.
Gobineau, A. de. 1987. "L'illustre magicien." In *Nouvelles asiatiques*, in *Oeuvres*, edited by J. Gaulmier, 3:367–73. Paris: Gallimard. First published in 1876.
Godin, Christian. 2003. *La Fin de l'humanité*. Seyssel: Champ Vallon.
———. 2007. *Le Triomphe de la volonté*. Seyssel: Champ Vallon.
Gombrich, Ernst. 1953. "The Renaissance Theory of Art and the Rise of Landscape." *Norm and Form: Studies in the Art of the Renaissance*. London: Phaidon, 1966.
Gouhier, Henri. 1987. *L'anti-humanisme au xviie siècle*. Paris: Vrin.
Granada, Miguel A. 2002. *Giordano Bruno: Universo infinito, unión con Dios, perfección del hombre*. Barcelona: Herder.
Granel, Gérard. 1972. *Traditionis traditio: Essais*. Paris: Gallimard.
Gray, John N. 1995. "Enlightenment's Wake." In *Enlightenment's Wake: Politics and Culture at the Close of the Modern Age*, 144–84, 192–95. London: Routledge.
Gregory, Brad S. 2012. *The Unintended Reformation: How a Religious Revolution Secularized Society*. Cambridge, MA: Harvard University Press.
Groethuysen, Bernhard. 1928. *Philosophische Anthropologie*. Munich: Oldenbourg.
Groh, Dieter. 2003. *Schöpfung im Widerspruch: Deutungen von der Natur des Menschen von der Genesis bis zur Reformation*. Frankfurt: Suhrkamp.

———. 2010. *Göttliche Weltökonomie: Perspektiven der wissenschaftlichen Revolution vom 15. bis zum 17. Jahrhundert*. Frankfurt: Suhrkamp.

Groh, Dieter, and Ruth Groh. 1991. *Zur Kulturgeschichte der Natur*. Vol. 1, *Weltbild und Naturaneignung*. Frankfurt: Suhrkamp.

———. 1996. *Zur Kulturgeschichte der Natur*. Vol. 2, *Die Außenwelt der Innenwelt*. Frankfurt: Suhrkamp.

Grove, Richard H. 1995. *Green Imperialism: Colonial Expansion, Tropical Island Edens and the Origins of Environmentalism, 1600–1860*. Cambridge: Cambridge University Press.

Gruman, Gerald J. 1966. *A History of the Ideas about the Prolongation of Life: The Evolution of Prolongevity Hypotheses to 1800*. Philadelphia: American Philosophical Society.

Guardini, Romano. 1949. *Das Ende der Neuzeit*. Munich: Matthias Grünewald Verlag, 2001.

Guillou, J.-M. Le. 1973. *Le Mystère du Père: Foi des apôtres, gnoses actuelles*. Paris: Fayard.

Günther, Hans. 1993. *Der sozialistische Übermensch: M. Gor'kij und der sowietische Heldenmythos*. Stuttgart: Metzler.

Habermas, Jürgen. 1981. "Die Moderne: Ein unvollendetes Projekt." In *Kleine politische Schriften, I–IV*, 444–64. Frankfurt: Suhrkamp. First published in 1980.

Habicht, Christian. 1970. *Gottmenschentum und griechische Städte*. 2nd ed. Munich: Beck.

Hadjadj, F. 2008. *La Profondeur des sexes: Pour une mystique de la chair*. Paris: Seuil.

Hadot, Pierre. 2004. *Le voile d'Isis: Essai sur l'histoire de l'idée de nature*. Paris: Gallimard.

Hagemeister, Michael. 1983. "Valerian Nikolaevic Murav'ev (1885–1931) und das 'Prometheische Denken' der frühen Sowjetzeit." In Murav'ev, *Domination du Temps*, 1–27.

———. 1989. *Nikolaj Fedorov: Studien zu Leben, Werk und Wirkung*. Munich: Sagner.

———. 2005. "'Unser Körper muss unser Werk sein.' Beherrschung der Natur und Überwindung des Todes in russischen Projekten des frühen 20. Jahrhunderts." In *NM*, 19–67.

Halleux, R. 1981. *Les Alchimistes grecs*. Paris: Les Belles Lettres.

Hansen, Bert. 1978. "Science and Magic." In *Science in the Middle Ages*, edited by David C. Lindberg, 483–506. Chicago: University of Chicago Press.

Hauser, Linus. 2004. *Kritik der neomythischen Vernunft*. Vol. 1, *Menschen als Götter der Erde (1800–1945)*. Paderborn: Schöningh.

Hazard, Paul. 1989. *La Crise de la conscience européenne, 1680–1615*. Paris: Fayard. First published in 1935.

Heller, Leonid, and Michel Niqueux. 1995. *Histoire de l'utopie en Russie*. Paris: Presses Universitaires de France.

Henry, Anne, ed. 1989. *Schopenhauer et la création littéraire en Europe*. Paris: Klincksieck.

Henry, Michel. 1976. *Marx*. Vol. 1, *Une philosophie de la réalité*. Vol. 2, *Une philosophie de l'économie*. Paris: Gallimard.

———. 1985. *Généalogie de la psychanalyse. Le commencement perdu*. Paris: Presses Universitaires de France.

———. 1987. *La Barbarie*. Paris: Grasset.

Hof, Walter. 1970. *Pessimistisch-nihilistische Strömungen in der deutschen Literatur vom Sturm und Drang bis zum Jungen Deutschland*. Tübingen: Niemeyer.

Hofmann, Werner. 2010. *Das Atelier: Courbets Jahrhundertbild*. Munich: Beck.

Horkheimer, M. 1967. *Zur Kritik der instrumentellen Vernunft [. . .]*. Edited by A. Schmidt. Frankfurt: Fischer.

Hornung, Erik. 1967. "Der Mensch als 'Bild Gottes' in Ägypten." In *Die Gottebenbildlichkeit des Menschen*, edited by O. Loretz, 123–56. Munich: Kösel.

———. 1971. *Der Eine und die Vielen: Ägyptische Gottesvorstellungen*. Darmstadt: Wissenschaftliche Buchgesellschaft.

Hübscher, Arthur. 1973. *Denker gegen den Strom: Schopenhauer; Gestern – Heute – Morgen*. Bonn: Bouvier.

Huyn, Hans. 1988. *Ihr werdet sein wie Gott: Der Irrtum des modernen Menschen von der Französischen Revolution bis heute*. Munich: Universitas.

Idel, Moshe. 1992. *Le Golem*. Translated by C. Aslanoff. Paris: Cerf.

Irrgang, Bernhard. 1986. "Zur Problemgeschichte des Topos 'Christliche Anthropozentrik' und seine Bedeutung für die Umweltethik." *Münchener Theologische Zeitschrift* 37:185–203.

Ivanhoe, P. J., and B. W. Van Norden, eds. 2001. *Readings in Classical Chinese Philosophy*. Indianapolis: Hackett.

Jakobson, Roman. 1931. "О поколении, растратившем своих поэтов" [A generation that kills its poets]. In *Selected Writings*. Vol. 5, *On Verse, Its Masters and Explorers*, edited by S. Rudy and M. Taylor, 355–81. The Hague: Mouton, 1979.

Janicaud, Dominique. 1985. *La Puissance du rationnel*. Paris: Gallimard.

Jauss, Hans-Robert. 1970. *Literaturgeschichte als Provokation*. Frankfurt: Suhrkamp.

Johansson, Kurt. 1983. *Aleksej Gastev: Proletarian Bard of the Machine Age*. Stockholm: Almqvist & Wiksell.

Jonas, Hans. 1954. *Gnosis und spätantiker Geist*. Vol. 1, *Die mythologische Gnosis*. Göttingen: Vandenhoeck & Ruprecht.

———. 1979. *Das Prinzip Verantwortung: Versuch einer Ethik für die technologische Zivilisation*. Frankfurt: Insel.

Joravsky, David. 1970. *The Lysenko Affair*. Cambridge, MA: Harvard University Press.

Kamen, Henry. 1997. *The Spanish Inquisition: A Historical Revision*. New Haven: Yale University Press.

Kantorowicz, Ernst H. 1961. "The Sovereignty of the Artist: A Note on Legal Maxims and Renaissance Theories of Art." In *Selected Studies*, 352–65. Locust Valley, NY: J. J. Augustin, 1965.

Kaufmann, Thomas Da Costa. 1993. *The Mastery of Nature: Aspects of Art, Science, and Humanism in the Renaissance*. Princeton: Princeton University Press.

Kennington, Richard. 2004. *On Modern Origins: Essays in Early Modern Philosophy*. Edited by P. Kraus and F. Hunt. Lanham, MD: Lexington Books.

Kinneging, Andreas. 2000. "Het conservatisme: Kritiek van de Verlichting en de moderniteit." *Philosophia reformata* 65(2):126–53.

Kline, George L. 1969. "'Nietzschean Marxism' in Russia." In *Demythologizing Marxism: A Series of Studies in Marxism*, edited by F. J. Adelmann, S.J., 166–83. Chestnut Hill, MA: Boston College; The Hague: Nijhoff.

Kobusch, Theo. 1993. *Die Entdeckung der Person: Metaphysik der Freiheit und modernes Menschenbild*. 2nd ed. Darmstadt: Wissenschaftliche Buchgesellschaft.

Kohn-Waechter, Gudrun. 1995. "Ersatzwelt, totale Herrschaft, Risikolust—Elemente eines modernen Technikdiskurses am Beispiel von John Desmond Bernal." In *Der Technikdiskurs in der Hitler-Stalin-Ära*, edited by W. Emmerich and C. Wege, 47–71. Stuttgart: Metzler.

Kojève, Alexandre. 1947. *Introduction à la lecture de Hegel: Leçons sur la "Phénoménologie de l'Esprit" professées de 1933 a 1939 à l'École des Hautes Études*. Edited by R. Queneau. Paris: Gallimard.

———. 1964. "Les origines chrétiennes de la science moderne." In *L'Aventure de l'esprit*, vol. 2 of *Mélanges Alexandre Koyré*, 295–306. Paris: Hermann.

Kondylis, Panajotis. 1986. *Die Aufklärung im Rahmen des neuzeitlichen Rationalismus*. Munich: dtv; Stuttgart: Klett-Cotta.

Koyré, Alexandre. 1966a. *Études d'histoire de la pensée scientifique*. Paris: Gallimard.

———. 1966b. *Études galiléennes*. Paris: Hermann.

———. 1968. *Études newtoniennes*. Paris: Gallimard.

———. 1971a. *Études d'histoire de la pensée philosophique*. Paris: Colin.

———. 1971b. *Mystiques, spirituels, alchimistes du xvie siècle allemand*. Paris: Gallimard.

Kraus, Paul. 1942. *Jâbir ibn Ḥayyân: Contribution à l'histoire des idées scientifiques dans l'islam; Jâbir et la science grecque*. Paris: Les Belles Lettres, 1986.

Krauss, Ingrid. 1931. *Studien über Schopenhauer und den Pessimismus in der deutschen Literatur des 19. Jahrhunderts*. Bern: Haupt.

Krauss, Werner. 1987. *Zur Anthropologie des 18. Jahrhunderts: Die Frühgeschichte der Menschheit im Blickpunkt der Aufklärung*. Edited by H. Kortum and C. Gohrisch. Frankfurt: Ullstein.

Krickeberg, Walter. 1928. "Mexikanisch-Peruanische Parallelen: Ein Überblick und eine Ergänzung." In *Festschrift/Publication d'hommage offerte au P. W. Schmidt*, edited by W. Koppers, 378–93. Vienna: Mechitaristen-Congregations-Buchdruckerei.

Kristeller, Paul Oskar. 1944–45. "Humanism and Scholasticism in the Italian Renaissance." Reprinted in *Studies in Renaissance Thought and Letters*, 553–83. Rome: Storia e Letteratura, 1956.

———. 1972. *Renaissance Concepts of Man, and Other Essays*. New York: Harper Torchbooks.

Krolzik, Udo. 1988. *Säkularisierung der Natur. Providentia-Dei-Lehre und Naturverständnis der Frühaufklärung*. Neukirchen-Vluyn: Neukirchener Verlag.

Küenzlen, Gottfried. 1994. *Der Neue Mensch: Eine Untersuchung zur säkularen Religionsgeschichte der Moderne*. Munich: Fink.

Kuhn, Thomas S. 1977. *The Essential Tension: Selected Studies in Scientific Tradition and Change*. Chicago: University of Chicago Press.

Küster, Hansjörg. 2009. *Schöne Aussichten: Kleine Geschichte der Landschaft.* Munich: Beck.
Lacan, Jacques. 1970. "Radiophonie." *Scilicet* 2/3:55–99.
Lachterman, David R. 1989. *The Ethics of Geometry: A Genealogy of Modernity.* London: Routledge.
Landes, David S. 1969. *The Unbound Prometheus: Technical Change and Industrial Development in Western Europe from 1750 to the Present.* Cambridge: Cambridge University Press.
Larchet, Jean-Claude. 1996. *La Divinisation de l'homme selon saint Maxime le Confesseur.* Paris: Cerf.
Larmore, Charles. 1999. "The Idea of a Life Plan." *Social Philosophy and Policy* 16 (1): 96–112.
Leiss, William. 1972. *The Domination of Nature.* New York: Braziller.
Leroy, Michel. 1992. *Le mythe jésuite: De Béranger à Michelet.* Paris: Presses Universitaires de France.
Lewis, Clive Staples. 1954. *English Literature in the Sixteenth Century (Excluding Drama).* Oxford: Clarendon Press.
———. 1963. *Studies in Medieval and Renaissance Literature.* Cambridge: Cambridge University Press.
———. 1975. *Fern-Seed and Elephants, and Other Essays on Christianity.* Edited by W. Hooper. Glasgow: Collins.
———. 1985. *First and Second Things: Essays on Theology and Ethics.* Edited by W. Hooper. Glasgow: Collins.
———. 2000. *The Abolition of Man, or Reflections on Education with Reference to the Teaching of the Upper Forms of Schools.* New York: HarperOne. First published in 1943.
Leys, Simon. 1998. *Essais sur la Chine.* Paris: Laffont.
Libera, Alain de. 1991. *Penser au Moyen Age.* Paris: Seuil.
Lilla, Mark. 1993. *Vico: The Making of an Anti-Modern.* Cambridge: Harvard University Press.
———. 2007. *The Stillborn God: Religion, Politics and the Modern West.* New York: Knopf.
Linck, Gudula. 1999. "Naturverständnis im vormodernen China." In *Natur-Bilder: Wahrnehmungen von Natur und Umwelt in der Geschichte,* edited by R. P. Stieferle and H. Breuninger, 73–116. Frankfurt: Campus.
Lippe, Rudolf zur. 1974. *Naturbeherrschung am Menschen.* Vol. 1, *Körpererfahrung als Entfaltung von Sinnen und Beziehungen in der Ära des italienischen Kaufmannskapitals.* Vol. 2, *Geometrisierung des Menschen und Repräsentation des Privaten im französischen Absolutismus.* Frankfurt: Suhrkamp.
Lovejoy, Arthur O., and George Boas. 1935. *Primitivism and Related Ideas in Antiquity.* Baltimore: Johns Hopkins University Press, 1935.
Löwith, Karl. 1986. "Vicos Grundsatz: Verum et factum convertuntur; Seine theologische Prämisse und deren säkulare Konsequenzen." In *Sämtliche Schriften,* vol. 1, *Gott, Mensch und Welt in der Philosophie der Neuzeit—G. B. Vico—Paul Valéry,* 195–227. Stuttgart: Metzler. First published in 1968.
Lubac, Henri de. 1974. *Pic de la Mirandole: Études et discussions.* Paris: Aubier.

———. 1998. *Le Drame de l'humanisme athée*. Paris: Cerf. First published in 1944.
Machle, E. J. 1993. *Nature and Heaven in the Xunzi: A Study of the "Tian Lun."* Albany, NY: SUNY Press.
Maier, Anneliese. 1951. *Zwei Grundprobleme der scholastischen Naturphilosophie: Das Problem der intensiven Grösse; Die Impetustheorie*. 2nd ed. Rome: Edizioni di Storia e Letteratura.
Maier, Hans. 1966. *Die ältere deutsche Staats- und Verfassungslehre (Polizeiwissenschaft)*. Munich: Luchterhand.
———. 1999. *Welt ohne Christentum – Was wäre anders?* Fribourg: Herder.
———. 2001. *Alter Adam-neuer Mensch? Menschenbilder in der Politik des 20. Jahrhunderts*. Gerda Henkel Vorlesung. Münster: Rhema.
Malraux, A. 1996. *Horizons philosophiques à l'origine de l'Unesco*. Paris: UNESCO.
Manent, Pierre. 1994. *La Cité de l'homme*. Paris: Fayard.
———. 2010a. *Les Métamorphoses de la cité: Essai sur la dynamique de l'Occident*. Paris: Flammarion. Translated by Marc LePain as *Metamorphoses of the City*. Cambridge, MA: Harvard University Press, 2013.
———. 2010b. *Le Regard politique: Entretiens avec Bénédicte Delorme-Montini*. Paris: Flammarion.
Manuel, Frank E. 1962. *The Prophets of Paris*. Cambridge, MA: Harvard University Press.
Marcadé, Jean-Claude. 2008. "Nikolaj Berdjaev et Sergej Bulgakov face à Picasso." *Revue des Etudes Slaves* 79:557–67.
Marion, Jean-Luc. 1981. *Sur la théologie blanche de Descartes: Analogie, création des vérités éternelles et fondement*. Paris: Presses Universitaires de France.
Maritain, Jacques. 1984. *Oeuvres complètes*. Fribourg: Éditions universitaires; Paris: Éditions Saint-Paul.
Marquard, Odo. 1973. *Schwierigkeiten mit der Geschichtsphilosophie*. Frankfurt: Suhrkamp.
———. 1981. *Abschied vom Prinzipiellen: Philosophische Studien*. Stuttgart: Reclam.
Marquet, Yves. 1961. "La place du travail dans la hiérarchie ismaélienne d'après l'Encyclopédie des Frères de la Pureté." *Arabica* 8:225–37.
———. 1988. *La philosophie des alchimistes et l'alchimie des philosophes: Jâbir ibn Ḥayyân et les "Frères de la Pureté."* Paris: Maisonneuve et Larose.
Marsh, G. P. 1965. *Man and Nature, or Physical Geography as Modified by Human Action*. Edited by D. Lowenthal. Cambridge, MA: Belknap Press of Harvard University Press.
Martin, Xavier. 1994. *Nature humaine et Révolution française: Du siècle des Lumières au Code Napoléon*. Bouère: Dominique Martin Morin.
———. 2008. *Régénérer l'espèce humaine: Utopie médicale et Lumières (1750–1850)*. Bouère: Dominique Martin Morin.
Massignon, Louis. 1948. "L'homme parfait en Islam et son originalité eschatologique." In *Opera Minora*, with texts collected, ordered, and introduced by Y. Moubarac, 1:107–25. Beirut: Dar al-Maaref, 1963.
Mauss, M. 1962. "Les techniques du corps." In *Sociologie et anthropologie*, 363–86. Paris: Presses Universitaires de France. First published in 1936.

McKnight, Stephen A. 1989. *Sacralizing the Secular: The Renaissance Origins of Modernity.* Baton Rouge: Louisiana State University Press.
Meier, Heinrich. 2003. *Das theologisch-politische Problem: Zum Thema von Leo Strauss.* Stuttgart: Metzler.
Mensching, Günther. 1993. "Metaphysik und Naturbeherrschung im Denken Roger Bacons." In *Naturauffassungen in Philosophie, Wissenschaft, Technik,* vol. 1, *Antike und Mittelalter,* edited by L. Schäfer and E. Stöker, 161–84. Freiburg im Breisgau: Alber.
Merchant, Carolyn. 1980. *The Death of Nature: Women, Ecology and the Scientific Revolution.* San Francisco: Harper and Row.
Mercier, Roger. 1960. *La réhabilitation de la nature humaine (1700–1750).* Villemomble: La Balance.
Metz, Johann Baptist. 1962. *Christliche Anthropozentrik: Über die Denkform des Thomas von Aquin.* Munich: Kösel.
Michot, Jean R. 1986. *La Destinée de l'homme selon Avicenne: Le retour à Dieu (ma'âd) et l'imagination.* Leuven: Peeters.
Migliorino, Francesco. 1981. "Alchimia lecita e illecita nel Trecento: Oldrado da Ponte." *Quaderni medievali* 11:6–41.
Mittelstrass, Jürgen. 1970. *Neuzeit und Aufklärung: Studien zur Entstehung der neuzeitlichen Wissenschaft und Philosophie.* Berlin: De Gruyter.
Moscovici, Serge. 1968. *Essai sur l'histoire humaine de la nature.* Paris: Flammarion.
Muller, H. J. 1935. *Out of the Night: A Biologist's View of the Future.* New York, Vanguard.
Mulsow, Martin, ed. 2002. *Das Ende des Hermetismus: Historische Kritik und neue Naturphilosophie in der Spätrenaissance; Dokumentation und Analyse der Debatte um die Datierung der hermetischen Schriften von Genebrard bis Casaubon (1567–1614).* Tübingen: Mohr.
———. 2003. "Der vollkommene Mensch: Zur Prähistorie des Posthumanen." *Deutsche Zeitschrift für Philosophie* 51:739–60.
Münch, P., ed. 1984. *Ordnung, Fleiß und Sparsamkeit: Texte und Dokumente zur Entstebung der 'bürgerlichen Tugenden.'* Munich: dtv.
Muray, Philippe. 1999. *Le xixe siècle à travers les âges.* New ed. Paris: Denoël.
Needham, Joseph. 1951. "Human Laws and the Laws of Nature in China and the West." *Journal of the History of Ideas* 12:3–32, 194–230.
Negro, Dalmacio. 2009. *El mito del hombre nuevo.* Madrid: Encuentro.
Nelson, Benjamin. 1967. "The Early Modern Revolution in Science and Philosophy." *Boston Studies in the Philosophy of Science* 3:1–40.
Neumann, Alfred. 1938. "Die Problematik des homo-mensura Satzes." *Classical Philology* 33:368–79.
Newman, William Royall. 1989. "Technology and the Alchemical Debate in the Late Middle Ages." *Isis* 80:423–45.
———. 2004. *Promethean Ambitions: Alchemy and the Quest to Perfect Nature.* Chicago: University of Chicago Press.
Nicholson, Reynold Alleyne. 1921. *Studies in Islamic Mysticism.* Cambridge: Cambridge University Press.

Nobis, Heribert M. 1967. "Frühneuzeitliche Verständnisweisen der Natur und ihr Wandel bis zum 18. Jahrhundert." *Archiv für Begriffsgeschichte* 11:37–58.

Nock, A. D. 1930. "Synnaos Theos." *Harvard Studies in Classical Philology* 41 (January):1–62.

Nunn, Astrid. 2012. *Der Alte Orient: Geschichte und Archäologie*. Darmstadt: Wissenschaftliche Buchgesellschaft.

Obrist, Barbara. 1996. "Art et nature dans l'alchimie médiévale." *Revue d'Histoire des Sciences* 49:215–86.

Ockinga, Boyo. 1984. *Die Gottebenbildlichkeit im alten Ägypten und im Alten Testament*. Wiesbaden: Harrasowitz.

Oehler, Klaus. 1963. *Ein Mensch zeugt einen Menschen: Über den Mißbrauch der Sprachanalyse in der Aristotelesforschung*. Frankfurt: Klostermann.

Osterhammel, Jürgen. 2000. *Sklaverei und die Zivilisation des Westens*. Munich: Siemens-Stiftung.

Osterkamp, Ernst. 2010. *Die Pferde des Expressionismus: Triumph und Tod einer Metapher*. Munich: Siemens-Stiftung.

Ozouf, Mona. 1989. "La Révolution française et la formation de l'homme nouveau." In *L'Homme régénéré: Essais sur la Révolution française*, 116–57. Paris: Gallimard.

Panofsky, Erwin. 1922. *Idea: Ein Beitrag zur Begriffsgeschichte der älteren Kunsttheorie*. 3rd ed. Berlin: Bruno Hessling, 1975.

———. 1962. "Artist, Scientist, Genius: Notes on the 'Renaissance-Dämmerung.'" In *The Renaissance: Six Essays*, edited by Wallace K. Ferguson, 123–82. New York: Harper and Row.

Paparelli, Gioacchino. 1983. *Feritas, humanitas, divinitas: L'essenza umanistica del Rinascimento*. Salerne: Edisud. First published in 1973.

Passmore, John. 1965. "The Malleability of Man in Eighteenth-Century Thought." In *Aspects of the Eighteenth Century*, edited by Earl R. Wasserman, 21–46. Baltimore: Johns Hopkins University Press.

———. 1974. *Man's Responsibility towards Nature: Ecological Problems and Western Traditions*. London: Duckworth.

Pauen, Michael. 1994. *Dithyrambiker des Untergangs: Gnostizismus in Ästhetik und Philosophie der Moderne*. Berlin: Akademie Verlag.

Pinès, Shlomo, and Warren Zeev Harvey. 1984. "Voir les étoiles et les constellations" [written in Hebrew; English: Seeing stars and constellations]. *Mehqarey Yerushalaim be-Makhsheveth Israel* 3(4):507–11.

———. 1996a. "Une encyclopédie arabe du 10ᵉ siècle: Les Épîtres des Frères de la pureté, Rasâ'il Ikhwân al-Safâ.'" In *Studies in the History of Arabic Philosophy*, vol. 3 of *The Collected Works of Shlomo Pinès*, 407–12. Jerusalem: Magnes Press. The essay was first published in 1985.

———. 1996b. "The Origin of the Tale of Salâmân and Absal: A Possible Indian Influence." *Studies in the History of Arabic Philosophy*, vol. 3 of *The Collected Works of Shlomo Pinès*, 343–53. Jerusalem: Magnes Press.

Pingree, David. 1993. "Plato's Hermetic 'Book of the Cow.'" In *Il Neoplatonismo nel Rinascimento*, edited by P. Prini, 133–45. Rome: Istituto della Enciclopedia Italiana.

Poliakov, Léon. 1968. *Histoire de l'antisémitisme*. Vol. 3, *De Voltaire à Wagner*. Paris: Calmann-Lévy.
Pritchard, J. B. 1954. *The Ancient Near East in Pictures Relating to the Old Testament*. Princeton: Princeton University Press.
Pütz, Peter. 1978. *Die deutsche Aufklärung*. Darmstadt: Wissenschaftliche Buchgesellschaft.
Raby, F. J. E., ed. 1959. *The Oxford Book of Medieval Latin Verse*. Oxford: Clarendon Press.
Radkau, Joachim. 2011. *Die Ära der Ökologie: Eine Weltgeschichte*. Munich: Beck.
Randles, W. G. L. 1999. *The Unmaking of the Medieval Christian Cosmos, 1500–1760: From Solid Heavens to Boundless Aether*. Aldershot: Ashgate.
Rawls, John. 1971. *A Theory of Justice*. Cambridge, MA: Harvard University Press.
Reckermann, Alfons. 1993. "Das Konzept kreativer imitatio im Kontext der Renaissance-Kunsttheorie." In *Innovation und Originalität*, edited by W. Haug and B. Wachinger, 98–132. Tübingen: Niemeyer.
Rehm, Walther. 1947. Experimentum medietatis: *Studien zur Geistes- und Literaturgeschichte des 19. Jahrhunderts*. Munich: Rinn.
Rey, Olivier. 2003. *Itinéraire de l'égarement: Du rôle de la science dans l'absurdité contemporaine*. Paris: Seuil.
———. 2006. *Une folle solitude: Le Fantasme de l'homme auto-construit*. Paris: Seuil.
Richter, Horst-Eberhard. 1979. *Der Gotteskomplex: Die Geburt und die Krise des Glaubens an die Allmacht des Menschen*. Reinbeck: Rowohlt.
Rifel, Tadej. 2013. "Gottmensch und Gottmenschentum: Versuch einer historischen Betrachtung des Begriffs und einer philosophischen Darlegung der Idee." PhD diss., Munich, Ludwig Maximilian University.
Ritter, Joachim. 1974. *Subjektivität: Sechs Aufsätze*. Frankfurt: Suhrkamp.
Robitaille, Antoine. 2007. *Le nouvel Homme nouveau: Voyage dans les utopies de la posthumanité*. Montréal: Boréal.
Rorty, R. 1981. *Philosophy and the Mirror of Nature*. Princeton: Princeton University Press.
Rosen, Stanley. 1969. *Nihilism: A Philosophical Essay*. New Haven: Yale University Press.
———. 1987. *Hermeneutics as Politics*. Oxford: Oxford University Press.
———. 1999. *Metaphysics in Ordinary Language*. New Haven: Yale University Press.
Rosenthal, Bernice Glatzer. 2002. *New Myth, New World: From Nietzsche to Stalinism*. University Park: Penn State University Press.
Rossi, Paolo. 1979. *Francesco Bacone: Della magia alla scienza*. 2nd ed. Turin: Einaudi. First published in 1957.
———. 2007. *I filosofi e le macchine: 1400–1700*. Milan: Feltrinelli. First published in 1962.
Rostand, Jean. 1978. *Pensées d'un biologiste*. Paris: Stock. First published in 1954.
Rouvillois, Frédéric. 2010. *L'invention du progrès, 1680–1730*. Paris: CNRS Editions.
Rudolph, Kurt. 1978. *Die Gnosis: Wesen und Geschichte einer spätantiken Religion*. 3rd ed. Göttingen: Vandenhoeck & Ruprecht.

Rüegg, Walter. 1973. "Zur Vorgeschichte des marxistischen Humanismusbegriffs." In *Anstöße: Aufsätze und Vorträge zur dialogischen Lebensform*, 181–97, 337–39. Frankfurt: Metzner.
Rüfner, Vincenz. 1955. "Homo secundus Deus: Eine Geistesgeschichtliche Studie zum menschlichen Schöpfertum." *Philosophisches Jahrbuch der Görresgesellschaft* 63:248–91.
Russell, B. 1924. *Icarus, or The Future of Science*. London: Kegan Paul.
———. 1962. *The Scientific Outlook*. New York: Norton. First published in 1931.
———. 1992. "On the Notion of Cause." In *Logical and Philosophical Papers, 1909–13*, edited by J. G. Slater and B. Frohmann, 192–210. London: Routledge. The essay was first published in 1913.
Russell, Gül A. 1993. "The Impact of the *Philosophus Autodidactus*: Pococke, John Locke and the Society of Friends." In *The "Arabick Interest" of the Natural Philosophers in Seventeenth-Century England*, edited by Gül A. Russell, 224–66. Leiden: Brill.
Russell, Norman. 2004. *The Doctrine of Deification in the Greek Patristic Tradition*. Oxford: Oxford University Press.
———. 2009. *Fellow Workers with God: Orthodox Thinking on Theosis*. Crestwood, NY: St. Vladimir's Seminary Press.
Russo, François. 1986. *Introduction à l'histoire des techniques*. Paris: Blanchard.
Saint-Sernin, Bertrand. 2007. *Le Rationalisme qui vient*. Paris: Gallimard.
Salamito, Jean-Marie. 1996. "De l'éloge des mains au respect des travailleurs." In *La Main*, 51–75. Orléans: Institut d'arts visuels.
Sarkisyanz, Emanuel. 1955. *Russland und der Messianismus des Orients: Sendungsbewußtsein und politischer Chiliasmus des Ostens*. Tübingen: Mohr.
Schabert, Tilo. 1969. *Natur und Revolution: Untersuchungen zum politischen Denken im Frankreich des achtzehnten Jahrhunderts*. Munich: List.
———. 1990. *Modernität und Geschichte: Das Experiment der modernen Zivilisation*. Würzburg: Königshausen & Neumann.
Schaeder, Hans Heinrich. 1925. "Die islamische Lehre vom Vollkommenen Menschen: Ihre Herkunft und ihre dichterische Gestaltung." *Zeitschrift der Deutschen Morgenländischen Gesellschaft* 79:192–268.
Schaffer, Simon. 1983. "Natural Philosophy and Public Spectacle in the Eighteenth Century." *History of Science* 21:1–43.
———. 1990. "Genius in Romantic Natural Philosophy." In *Romanticism and the Sciences*, edited by A. Cunningham and N. Jardine, 82–98. Cambridge: Cambridge University Press.
Schalk, Fritz. 1966. "Humanitas im Romanischen." In *Exempla romanischer Wortgeschichte*, 255–94. Frankfurt: Klostermann.
Scheibert, Peter. 1967. "Die Besiegung des Todes—Ein theologisches Programm aus der Sowjetunion (1926)." In *Glaube – Geist – Geschichte: Festschrift für Ernst Benz zum 60. Geburstage am 17. November 1967*, edited by G. Müller and W. Zeller, 431–47. Leiden: Brill.
Schenke, Hans-Martin. 1962. *Der Gott 'Mensch' in der Gnosis: Ein religionsgeschichtlicher Beitrag zur Diskussion über die paulinische Anschauung von der Kirche als Leib Christi*. Göttingen: Vandenhoeck & Ruprecht.

Schimmel, Annemarie. 1989. *Und Muhammad ist sein Prophet: Die Verehrung des Propheten in der islamischen Frömmigkeit*. Munich: Diederichs.

Schlier, Heinrich. 1959. *Mächte und Gewalten im Neuen Testament*. Fribourg: Herder.

Schmidt, Alfred. 1982. "Humanismus und Naturbeherrschung." In *Das Naturbild des Menschen*, edited by J. Zimmermann, 301–6. Munich: Fink.

Scholem, Gershom. 1992. "Die Vorstellung vom Golem in ihren tellurischen und magischen Beziehungen." In *Zur Kabbala und ihrer Symbolik*, 209–59. Frankfurt: Suhrkamp. First published in 1953.

Schuhl, Pierre-Maxime. 1947. *Machinisme et philosophie*. Paris: Presses Universitaires de France.

Schwarz, Gerhard. 2004. *Est Deus in nobis. Die Identität von Gott und reiner praktischer Vernunft in Immanuel Kants. "Kritik der praktischen Vernunft."* Berlin: Verlag TU Berlin.

Schwonke, Martin. 1957. *Vom Staatsroman zur Science Fiction: Eine Untersuchung über Geschichte und Funktion der naturwissenschaftlich-technischen Utopie*. Stuttgart: Ferdinand Enke.

Secord, James A. 1989. "Extraordinary Experiment: Electricity and the Creation of Life in Victorian England." In *The Uses of Experiment: Studies in the Natural Sciences*, edited by D. Gooding et al., 337–83. Cambridge: Cambridge University Press.

Sedlmayr, Hans. 1948. *Verlust der Mitte: Die bildende Kunst des 19. und 20. Jahrhunderts als Symptom und Symbol der Zeit*. Salzburg: Otto Müller.

Séris, Jean-Pierre. 1994. *La Technique*. Paris: Presses Universitaires de France.

Sesterhenn, Raimund. 1982. *Das Bogostroitel'stvo bei Gor'kij und Lunačarskij bis 1909: Zur ideologischen und literarischen Vorgeschichte der Parteischule von Capri*. Munich: Sagner.

Seznec, Jean. 1980. *La Survivance des dieux antiques: Essai sur le rôle de l'imagination mythologique dans l'humanisme et dans l'art de la Renaissance*. Paris: Flammarion.

Shattuck, Roger. 1968. *The Banquet Years: The Origins of the Avant Garde in France, 1885 to World War I*. New York: Vintage Books.

———. 1986. *The Innocent Eye: On Modern Literature and the Arts*. New York: Washington Square Press.

———. 1996. *Forbidden Knowledge: From Prometheus to Pornography*. New York: Saint Martin's Press.

Shea, William R. 2003. *Designing Experiments and Games of Chance: The Unconventional Science of Blaise Pascal*. Canton, MA: Science History Publications.

Sloterdijk, Peter. 1999. *Regeln für den Menschenpark: Ein Antwortschreiben zu Heideggers Brief über den Humanismus*. Frankfurt: Suhrkamp.

Sorabji, Richard. 1993. *Animal Minds and Human Morals: The Origins of the Western Debate*. Ithaca, NY: Cornell University Press.

Spaemann, Robert. 1963. *Reflexion und Spontaneität: Studien über Fénelon*. Stuttgart: Kohlhammer.

———. 1996. *Personen: Versuche über den Unterschied zwischen "etwas" und "jemand."* Stuttgart: Klett-Cotta.

———. 2001. *Grenzen: Zur ethischen Dimension des Handelns*. Stuttgart: Klett-Cotta.

Squier, Susan Merrill. 1994. *Babies in Bottles: Twentieth-Century Visions of Reproductive Technology*. New Brunswick, NJ: Rutgers University Press.

Stafford, Fiona J. 1994. *The Last of the Race: The Growth of a Myth from Milton to Darwin*. Oxford: Clarendon Press.

Starobinski, Jean. 1964. *L'Invention de la liberté, 1700–1789*. Geneva: Skira.

Starr, S. Frederick. 1981. *Melnikov: Solo Architect in a Mass Society*. Princeton: Princeton University Press.

Steinschneider, Moritz. 1956. *Die hebräischen Übersetzungen des Mittelalters und die Juden als Dolmetscher*. Graz: Akademische Verlagsanstalt. First published in Berlin, 1893.

Sternagel, Peter. 1966. *Die* artes mechanicae *im Mittelalter*. Kallmünz: Lassleben.

Sternhell, Zeev. 1985. *Maurice Barrès et le nationalisme français*. Paris: Complexe. First published in 1972.

Stites, Richard. 1989. *Revolutionary Dreams: Utopian Vision and Experimental Life in the Russian Revolution*. New York: Oxford University Press.

Stöcklein, Ansgar. 1969. *Leitbilder der Technik: Biblische Tradition und technischer Fortschritt*. Munich: Moos.

Strauss, Leo. 1953. *Natural Right and History*. Chicago: University of Chicago Press.

———. 1958. *Thoughts on Machiavelli*. Glencoe, IL: Free Press.

———. 1959. *What Is Political Philosophy? and Other Studies*. Glencoe, IL: Free Press.

———. 1964. *The City and Man*. Chicago: Rand McNally.

———. 1975. "The Three Waves of Modernity." In *Political Philosophy: Six Essays by Leo Strauss*, edited by H. Gildin, 81–98. Indianapolis: Bobbs Merrill/Pegasus.

———. 2001. *Hobbes Kritik der Religion: Ein Beitrag zum Verständnis der Aufklärung*. In *Gesammelte Schriften*, by Leo Strauss, edited by H. Meier, 3:263–373. Stuttgart: Metzler. First published in 1933–34.

Stroh, Wilfried. 2008. "De origine vocum humanitatis et humanismi." *Gymnasium* 115:535–71.

Taguieff, Pierre-André. 2000. *L'Effacement de l'avenir*. Paris: Galilée.

Takeshita, Masataka. 1987. *Ibn Arabi's Theory of the Perfect Man and Its Place in the History of Islamic Thought*. Tokyo: Institute for the Study of Languages and Cultures of Asia and Africa.

Taubes, Jacob. 1991. *Abendländische Eschatologie*. Munich: Matthes & Seitz. First published in 1947.

Tayler, E. W. 1964. *Nature and Art in Renaissance Literature*. New York: Columbia University Press.

Taylor, Charles. 1989. *Sources of the Self: The Making of Modern Identity*. Cambridge, MA: Harvard University Press.

———. 2007. *A Secular Age*. Cambridge, MA: Harvard University Press.

Tenbruck, Friedrich H. 1984. *Die unbewältigten Sozialwissenschaften, oder Die Abschaffung des Menschen*. Graz: Styria.

Thomas, Keith. 1971. *Religion and the Decline of Magic: Studies in Popular Beliefs in Sixteenth- and Seventeenth-Century England*. London: Weidenfeld & Nicolson.
———. 1984. *Man and the Natural World: Changing Attitudes in England, 1500–1800*. London: Penguin Books. First published in 1983.
Thompson, Kenneth. 1980. "Forests and Climatic Change in America: Some Early Views." *Climatic Change* 3:47–64.
Thorndike, Lynn. 1923–58. *A History of Magic and Experimental Science during the First Thirteen Centuries of Our Era*. 8 vols. New York: Columbia University Press.
Tigerstedt, E. N. 1968. "The Poet as Creator: Origins of a Metaphor." *Comparative Literature Studies* 5:455–88.
Topitsch, Ernst. 1973. *Gottwerdung und Revolution: Beiträge zur Weltanschauungsanalyse und Ideologiekritik*. Pullach: Dokumentation.
Toulmin, Stephen. 1990. *Cosmopolis: The Hidden Agenda of Modernity*. New York: Free Press.
Trinkaus, Charles Edward. 1970. *In Our Image and Likeness: Humanity and Divinity in Italian Humanist Thought*. 2 vols. Chicago: University of Chicago Press.
Trousson, Raymond. 1964. *Le Thème de Prométhée dans la Littérature européenne*. 2 vols. Geneva: Droz.
Tschižewskij, Dimitri. 1930. "Übermensch, übermenschlich: Zur Geschichte dieser Worte und Begriffe." *Festschrift Th. G. Masaryk zum 80. Geburtstag am 7. März 1930*, part 1, 265–69. Bonn: Cohen.
Tuveson, Ernest Lee. 1972. *Millennium and Utopia: A Study in the Background of the Idea of Progress*. Gloucester, MA: Peter Smith.
Urbach, Ephraim E. 1979. *The Sages: Their Concepts and Beliefs*. Translated by I. Abrahams. 2 vols. Jerusalem: Magnes Press.
Vallat, Philippe. 2005. *Farabi et l'école d'Alexandrie: Des prémisses de la connaissance à la philosophie politique*. Paris: Vrin.
Van Delft, Louis. 1993. *Littérature et anthropologie: Nature humaine et caractère à l'âge classique*. Paris: Presses Universitaires de France.
———. 2008. *Les Moralistes: Une apologie*. Paris: Gallimard.
Van Engen, John. 1980. "Theophilus Presbyter and Rupert of Deutz: The Manual Arts and Benedictine Theology." *Viator* 11:147–63.
Vasoli, Cesare. 1984. "Un scritto inedito di Giulio Camillo 'De l'humana deificatione.'" *Rinascimento* 24:191–227.
Venturelli, Aldo. 2008. "Goethe, Hölderlin, Feuerbach." In *Wagner und Nietzsche: Kultur-Werk-Wirkung*, edited by S. L. Sorgner et al., 344–54. Hamburg: Rowohlt.
Venturi, Franco. 1969–90. *Settecento riformatore*. 7 vols. Turin: Einaudi.
Veyne, Paul. 1983. *Les Grecs ont-ils cru à leurs mythes? Essai sur l'imagination constituante*. Paris: Seuil.
Voegelin, Eric. 1952. *The New Science of Politics: An Introduction*. Chicago: University of Chicago Press.
———. 1975. *From Enlightenment to Revolution*. Edited by J. H. Hallowell. Durham, NC: Duke University Press.

———. 2004. *Science, Politics and Gnosticism: Two Essays*. With an introduction by E. Sandoz. Wilmington, DE: ISI Books. First published in 1968.
Völker, Klaus, ed. 1971. *Künstliche Menschen: Dichtungen und Dokumente über Golems, Homonculi, lebende Statuen und Androiden*. Munich: Hanser.
Volpi, Franco. 1996. *Il nichilismo*. Bari: Laterza.
Weaver, Richard M. 1948. *Ideas Have Consequences*. Chicago: University of Chicago Press.
Webster, Charles. 1975. *The Great Instauration: Science, Medicine and Reform, 1626–1660*. London: Duckworth.
Weidlé, Wladimir. 2002. *Les Abeilles d'Aristée: Essai sur le destin actuel des lettres et des arts*. Geneva: Ad solem. First published in 1954.
Wellbery, D. E. 1998. *Schopenhauers Bedeutung für die moderne Literatur*. Munich: Siemens-Stiftung.
Wentzlaff-Eggebert, Harald, ed. 1999. *Naciendo el hombre nuevo . . . Fundir literatura, arte y vida como práctica de las vanguardias en el mundo ibérico*. Madrid: Iberoamerica; Frankfurt: Vervuert.
Wenzel, Siegfried. 1960. *The Sin of Sloth: Acedia in Medieval Thought and Literature*. Chapel Hill: University of North Carolina Press.
Westermann, C. *Genesis*. 1974. Neukirchen/Vluyn: Neukirchner Verlag.
White, Lynn J., Jr. 1962. *Medieval Technology and Social Change*. Oxford: Clarendon Press.
———. 1968. *Machina ex deo: Essays in the Dynamism of Western Culture*. Cambridge, MA: MIT Press.
———. 1978. *Medieval Religion and Technology: Collected Essays*. Berkeley: University of California Press.
Whitney, Elspeth. 1990. *Paradise Restored: The Mechanical Arts from Antiquity through the Thirteenth Century*. Philadelphia: American Philosophical Society.
Wieland, Georg. 1983. "Zwischen Naturnachahmung und Kreativität: Zum mittelalterlichen Verständnis der Technik." *Philosophisches Jahrbuch der Görres-Gesellschaft* 90:258–76.
Wilks, Michael. 1963. *The Problem of Sovereignty in the Later Middle Ages: The Papal Monarchy with Augustinus Triumphus and the Publicists*. Cambridge: Cambridge University Press.
Winner, Langdon. 1977. *Autonomous Technology: Technics-out-of-Control as a Theme in Political Thought*. Cambridge, MA: MIT Press.
Wolfson, Eliot R. 1990. "God, the Intellect, and the Demiurge: On the Usage of the Word *Kol* in Abraham ibn Ezra." *Revue des études juives* 149:77–111.
Yates, Frances A. 1964. *Giordano Bruno and the Hermetic Tradition*. Chicago: University of Chicago Press.
———. 1972. *The Rosicrucian Enlightenment*. London: Routledge & Kegan.
Zamoyski, Adam. 2000. *Holy Madness: Romantics, Patriots and Revolutionaries, 1776–1871*. London: Weidenfeld and Nicolson.
Zanker, Paul. 2004. *Die Apotheose der römischen Kaiser: Ritual und städtische Bühne*. Munich: Siemens-Stiftung.
Zilsel, Edgar. 1926. *Die Entstehung des Geniebegriffs*. Tübingen: Mohr.
Zlotnik, Dov. 1975. "'Al meqor ha-mašal 'ha-nanos we ha-'anaq' we-gilgulaw." *Sinaï* 77:184–89.

Index

Adams, Henry, 115
Agobard of Lyon, 54
Agrippa of Nettesheim, Heinrich Cornelius, 53, 55
Alberti, Leone Battista, 49, 169
Albert the Great, Saint, 29, 52, 55, 85
alchemy, 56–58
Alexander, Samuel, 190
al-Farabi
   Enumeration of the Sciences, 65
Althusser, Louis, 204
American Republic, as experiment, 195
American Revolution, 134
Anders, Günther, 162, 187
Andreae, Johann Valentin, 78
angels, 24, 25
animals
   defense of the soul of, 154–55
   empires represented by, 26–27
   vs. man, 142, 143, 155, 156
   rationality of, 155
   representations of, 18
   societies for protection of, 143
   valorization of, 156
Anselm, Saint, archbishop of Canterbury, 25
anthropology, 4, 84–86, 85
anthropomorphism, 18, 154
anthropotheism, 123
antihumanism, 201, 202–3, 214
Antipater of Thessalonica, 165

Antonio de Barga, 46
Apollinaire, Guillaume, 202
Aristotle
   on construction, 35
   "man engenders man" formula, 123, 214
   Metaphysics, 65
   on politics, 34
   on productive activity of man, 69
   theory of intellect, 32, 132
   treatise on simple machines, 19
Arndt, Ernst Moritz, 145
Artaud, Antonin, 207
artificial production of the living, idea of, 172–73
artist
   domination of, 39
   as imitator of God, 40
   as "lord and teacher of matter," 48
   originality of, 41
   power of, 41
arts, 41, 51
Asclepius, 15, 16, 45, 52
astrology, 67–68
Athanasius, Saint, Patriarch of Alexandria, 30
atheism, 128–31, 206, 210
atheistic humanism, 136, 157, 205
Augustine, Saint, bishop of Hippo
   on essence of sin, 30
   man as replacing the angels, 190

318 Index

Augustine, Saint, bishop of Hippo (*cont.*)
   on replacement of man, 190
   on superiority of man, 21, 22
   on technological success of man, 20
   treatise on the activity of monks, 44
autonomy, idea of, 4
Averroës (Ibn Rushd), 13, 29, 35, 57
Avicenna, 52, 57, 126

Bacon, Francis
   on cabinet of curiosities, 39
   criticism of, 76
   devalue of contemplation by, 68–69
   on domination of man, 68, 69, 70
   on end of knowledge, 68, 69
   on fall of man, 69
   as father of philosophy, 76
   on *imitabile fulmen*, 66
   influence of, 73
   knowledge as power, 141
   on magic, 55
   The New Atlantis, 69–70, 74, 78
   Novum Organon, 69, 73, 74
   on *praxis*, 69
   on technological orientation of science, 106
   on three states of nature, 70
Bacon, Roger, 52, 55, 64, 78
Baekeland, Leo Hendrik, 114
Bakunin, Mikhail, 87, 124–25
balloons, invention of, 77
Barlach, Ernst, 197
Barruel, Abbé, 90
Basil of Caesarea, Saint, 22, 30
Baudelaire, Charles Pierre, 39, 137, 205
Beaurieu, Gaspard Guillard de, 163
Beccaria, Cesare, 87
Benson, R. H.
   Lord of the World, 210
Bentham, Jeremy, 159
Berdyaev, Nikolai, 202, 206

Bergson, Henri, 127, 176
Bernal, J. D., 111, 163, 180, 188–89
   The World, the Flesh and the Devil, 189
Bernard, Claude, 76, 106, 109, 110, 111
Bessarion, Cardinal, 64
Betzky, Ivan I., 177
Billaud-Varenne, Jacques Nicolas, 135
birth, idea of new, 171
Blake, William, 192
Blok, Aleksandr, 177, 178, 203
Bloy, Leon, 206
Blumenberg, Hans, 129
Blunt, Wilfrid Scawen, 149
Boaistuau, Pierre, 48
Böckenförde, Ernst-Wolfgang, 152
Bodin, Jean, 37, 86, 141
body
   and asceticism, 33
   mastery of, 32–33
   and nature, 32
Boehme, Jacob, 13
Boissy d'Anglas, 135
Bonald, Louis de, 206
Bonneville, Nicolas de, 136
Boratynski, Evgenii
   "The last death," 148
Borchert, Wolfgang, 200
Bovelles, Charles de, 48, 131
Boyle, Robert, 73, 74, 96–97, 143
Bracciolini, Poggio, 47, 67
Brecht, Bertolt, 111
Breton, André, 163
Browne, Thomas, 55
Bruno, Giordano, 49
Büchner, Georg, 208
Büchner, Ludwig, 178
   Force and Matter, 120
Buddhism, 128–29
Buffon, Georges-Louis Leclerc, comte de, 84, 145–46
Bulgakov, Mikhail, 119
Bulwer-Lytton, Edward
   The Coming Race, 183–84
   The Last Days of Pompeii, 148

Burckhardt, Jacob
   History of Greek Civilization, 194
Burke, Edmund, 151, 213
Burnett, James, Lord Monboddo, 155, 181
Butler, Samuel
   "Darwin among the Machines," 166
   Erewhon, 166
Byron, Charles, 93, 147, 211

cabinet of curiosities, 39
calendars, changes in illustration of, 64
Calvin, John, 145
Camillo, Giulio, 31
Campanella, Tommaso, 55, 178
   On the Sense of Things and on Natural Magic, 50
Campbell, Thomas, 148
Camus, Albert, 210
Čapek, Karel
   R.U.R., 167
Cardan, Jerome, 36
Carlowitz, Hans Carl von, 145
Carlyle, Thomas, 93
Carroll, Lewis, 143, 205
Cartesian revolution, 72
Casaubon, Isaac, 45
Cassiodorus, Flavius Magnus Aurelius, 19
Catherine the Great, Empress of Russia, 177
Catholic Church, as object of condemnation, 90–91
Cellini, Benvenuto, 38
Cervantes Saavedra, Miguel de
   Don Quijote, 192
Chastellux, François-Jean, marquis de, 134
Chateaubriand, François-René de, 205
Chekhov, Anton, 171
Chenavard, Paul, 147
Chénier, Marie-Joseph, 135

Chernyshevsky, Nikolay, 124
   What Is to Be Done?, 177
Chesterton, G. K., 152
child labor law enactment, 142
Chopin, Kate, 208
Chrysippus, 10
Cicero, 19, 49, 99, 105
Coleridge, S. T., 100
Colletet, Guillaume, 85
Collins, Anthony, 92
Columbus, Christopher, 145
Comte, Auguste
   on collective organism, 147
   on conquest of nature, 114
   definition of society, 107–8
   dogma of human wisdom, 81
   on domination, 163
   as founder of sociology, 107
   on Francis Bacon, 76
   on future of the planet, 149
   on glorifying fatality, 200
   on human action, 130
   on humanism, 124
   on ideal resurrection, 79
   on idea of new man, 177
   on idea of new philosophy, 176
   on man as "rational animal," 155
   on man *vs.* humanity, 182–83
   pragmatism of, 108–9
   on propagative function, 187
   on religion of humanity, 91
   on replacing the government of human beings, 115
   on superiority of man, 68
   on supreme being, 136, 137, 190
   on value of science, 108
   view of anthropology, 85
Condorcet, Jacques Caritat de, 149, 175–76
Conrad, Joseph
   Nostromo, 208
construction, idea of, 35–37
contraception, practice of, 175–76
Cooper, James Fenimore
   The Last of the Mohicans, 148

Corneille, Pierre
   Cinna, 102
Corpus Hermeticum, 66
Cortés, Donoso, 205
Courbet, Gustave
   Painter's Studio (painting), 125
Cournot, A. A., 146
Cousin de Grainville, Jean-Baptiste François Xavier, 147
Cowley, Abraham, 74
creation, 38, 39–40
Cromwell, Oliver, 102
Crosse, Andrew, 172
Crystal Palace Exhibition, 168
curiosity, criticism of useless, 111
Cuvier, Georges, 75
cyborg, idea of, 187–89

D'Alembert, Jean le Rond, 192
Daniel, prophet, vision of history, 26–27
Dante, Alighieri, 13, 31, 38, 39, 63–64, 151, 215
Darrow, Clarence S., 194
Darwin, Charles, 143, 182, 183
   The Descent of Man, 183
   Origin of Species, 81
Darwin, Erasmus, 155
Darwinism, 81, 166
David, Jacques-Louis, 94
death, 199, 200, 205
Dedekind, Richard, 36
Dee, John, 64
Defoe, Daniel, 2
   Robinson Crusoe, 133
dehumanization, 201–2
Delacroix, Eugène, 39
Deleyre, Alexandre, 76
Derrida, Jacques, 205
Descartes, René
   Bacon's influence on, 70–71
   Discourse on Method, 2, 71
   encounter with Bérulle, 71
   on idea of industry, 72
   on idea of mastery, 72, 102
   on idea of value, 99–100
   on nature, 71
   on speculative *vs.* practical knowledge, 71, 72
   Treatise on Man, 78
D'Holbach, Paul Henri Thiry, baron, 107, 108, 147, 155
Dickens, Charles, 144
Diderot, Denis, 100, 126, 131, 151
dignity of man, idea of
   displacement of, 86
   doctrine of sin and, 88–89
   new concept of, 42–44
   as a reign, 46
   Renaissance and, 43, 46
   roots of, 12, 42
   transformation of, 95, 105
   treatises on, 46–48
dignity of work, idea of, 105–6
Diogenes the Cynic, 23
Dion of Prusa, 39
Dionysius the Areopagite, 30
divinity, 17, 18–19
divinization of man, 28–29, 30–31, 45–46, 89
Diviš, Václav Prokop, 77
Döblin, Alfred, 149
domination *by* nature *over* man, 197
domination of man by man, 162–65
domination of nature by man
   in biblical traditions, 19–22
   Chinese idea of, 17–18
   church fathers on, 21–22
   in classical literature, 19
   consequences of, 141, 201
   and demonstration of miracles, 51
   desire for, 129
   emergence of idea of, 42
   evolution of project of, 113, 119–20
   in Greek philosophy, 18–19
   Jewish exegesis on, 22
   in political though of the Ancient East, 17–18
   as practical realization of anthropology, 95

Qur'an on, 21
Soviet project of, 119
domination of the earth, battle for, 185–86
dominion, idea of, 102
dominion of the king, 20
Dostoyevsky, Fyodor
  The Adolescent, 125
  The Brothers Karamazov, 177
  Demons, 177
  "Dream of a Ridiculous Man," 209–10
  "Legend of the Grand Inquisitor," 164
  on love to humanity, 92
  on man as object of experiment, 196
  Notes from the Underground, 157
  on reproduction of men, 79
  suicide theme in novels of, 137, 209–10
Dubos, Abbé, 150
Dühring, Eugen
  The Worth of Life, 194
Dumont d'Urville, Jules, 144
Dürer, Albrecht, 41
Durkheim, Émile, 206, 207, 210
duty to reign, 101
Dyson, George B., 168

earth, as object of worship, 124–25
Eckhart, Meister, 13, 56
ecological consciousness, 145–46
ecological movement, 143
Eichendorff, Joseph von, 130
Eliot, George, 125
Eliot, John
  The Monarchie of Man, 34
Elyahou of Helm, 172
Encyclopedia, frontispiece of, 191–92
end of the world, fear of, 146–47
Engels, Friedrich, 123, 126, 146
engineer, 142
Enlightenment, 192–93, 201
Epictetus, 29, 111

Epicureanism, 31, 67, 128, 129
Epicurus, 29
Eriugena, John Scotus, 36, 49
error, theory of, 110
Esquiros, Alphonse, 182
Eucken, Rudolf
  The Meaning and Worth of Life, 194
eugenics, 178–79
experimental method, 109–10, 195
experimentation, idea of, 195–97

Fabre, Jean Antoine, 145
Facio, Bartolomeo, 46
Farabi, al-. *See* al-Farabi
Faraday, Michael, 144
Farrère, Claude
  Useless Hands, 168
fascism, 177
Fechner, Gustav Theodor, 124
Fedorov, Nicolai, 79
Ferguson, Adam
  Essay on the History of Civil Society, 213
Feuerbach, Ludwig, 122–23, 125
Fichte, Johann Gottlieb, 3, 91, 104–6, 126, 136–37, 195, 208
Ficino, Marsilio, 40, 44, 53, 65, 114
  Platonic Theology of the Immortality of Souls, 48
fiction, idea of, 38
Firmicus Maternus, Julius, 20
Flammarion, Camille
  The End of the World, 147
Flaubert, Gustave, 117, 149, 157, 191, 205, 214
Fonseca, Pedro, 35
Fontenelle, Bernard Le Bovier de, 75, 146
Forster, E. M., 167
fortuna, idea of, 49
Foucault, Michel, 205
Fourier, Charles, 176
Fourier, Jean Baptiste Joseph, 108
Franklin, Benjamin, 77, 78, 136

Frederick II, Emperor of the Holy Roman Empire, 64
French Revolution, 134, 135
Fried, Johannes, 129
Füssli, Heinrich, 201
future, 83, 149–51

Galilei, Galileo, 65, 154, 171
   Assayer, 2
Galton, Francis, 149, 178, 179
Garin, Eugenio, 43
Genesis, book of
   on creation of Adam, 156
   on domination of man, 20
geographic discoveries, 66
geological time, 146
German idealism, 103–6, 161–62, 195
Gersonides, 22
Gilbert, Claude, 89
Ǧīlī, Abd el-Karīm al-, 16
Gilson, Étienne, 206
Glanvill, Joseph, 82
God
   as Creator of nature, 128, 129
   as foreign power, 136
   imitation of, 30
   relation to man, 130, 189–90
Godwin, William, 79, 173
   Enquiry concerning Political Justice, 78
Goethe, Johann Wolfgang von, 115, 196
   Der Zauberlehrling, 167
   Faust, 142
   Sorrows of Young Werther, 207
Goguet, Antoine Yves, 82
Gorki, Maxim, 119, 190
Gray, John N., 214
Graziosi, Antonio, 82
Great Witch Hunt, 86
Gregory of Nyssa, Saint, 21, 32, 43, 49
Grimm, Melchior, 82
Guépin, Ange, 142
Guibert of Tournai, 80
Guy of Arezzo, 64

Haber, Fritz, 144
Habermas, Jürgen, 2
Haeckel, Ernst, 81, 146
Hakewill, George, 151
Haldane, J. B. S., 119, 131, 188, 189
Hamilton, Alexander, 136
Hartmann, Eduard von
   Philosophy of the Unconscious, 209
Hawthorne, Nathaniel, 144
Hegel, Georg Wilhelm Friedrich, 20, 102, 137
Heidegger, Martin, 3, 162, 176, 203, 204
   Being and Time, 203
   Letter on Humanism, 203–4
Heine, Heinrich, 124, 137
Helvétius, Claude-Adrien, 87
Heracles (divine hero), 131
Herder, Johann Gottfried von, 181, 182
Hermes Trismegistus, 32, 44
Hermetic writings, 14–15, 45
heroes, canonization and condemnation of, 93–94
Hess, Moses, 122
Hippocrates, 29, 70
historiography, 81–82
Hobbes, Thomas, 36, 73, 80
   Leviathan, 176
Hoffmann, E. T. A., 167
Holbein, Hans, the Younger
   The Ambassadors, 200
homo homini deus formula, 122
homunculus, 165, 172, 254n23
Hood, Thomas, 148
Hopkins, Gerard Manley
   "The Wreck of the Deutschland," 143
Hornung, Erik, 18
Hugh of Saint-Victor, 69
human, 86–88, 135, 187–90
human activity, models of, 51
human body, search for perfection of, 144
humanism
   atheistic, 4, 128

birth of concept of, 121–22
critique of, 202
genealogy of, 203–4
Heidegger on, 204
interpretations of, 123–24
and materialism, 123
meaning of, 112
possibility of, 212
rejection of, 204–5
religion and, 206
self-destructive dialectic of, 201–2
humanity
creation of, 98
cult of, 91–94
as experiment of life, 196–97
formulations of principle of, 87–88
happiness and, 207
idea of surpassing, 182
idea of the end of, 147–49, 158
man vs., 182–83
models of, 92
nature and, 5, 6
as opposite to God, 137
origin of word, 87
relationship to the past, 151–52
religion of, 91
as single subject, 27
See also superiority of humanity
humanization, 97–98, 131
"human material," idea of, 170
human nature, 88, 171
Humboldt, Alexander von, 176
Hume, David, 159
Husserl, Edmund Gustav Albrecht, 163
Hutcheson, Francis, 175
Huxley, Aldous, 196
  Brave New World, 188
Huxley, Julian S., 171

Iamblichus, 54
Ibn Arabi, 15, 16
Ibn Ezra, Abraham, 16, 22
Ibn Khaldun, 57, 65
Ibn Naghrela, 16
idolatry, 205

Ignatius of Loyola, Saint
  Exercises, 132
illusion, 193
imagination, 36, 37
Imitation of Christ, The (Thomas à
  Kempis), 102
industry, idea of, 72
inferior beings, liquidation of, 179–80
Innocent III, Pope, 46
Inquisition, 86
intellect, 53
Islam
  on divinization, 29
  idea of perfect man in, 14, 15–16
  miracles in, 51, 52

Jâbir ibn Ḥayyân (Geber), 56
Jacobi, Friedrich Heinrich, 75
Jacobsen, Jens Peter, 125
Jakobson, Roman, 79
James, William, 112, 194
James of Venice, 65
Jarry, Alfred, 184, 207
Jesuits, 91
Jewish people, 90
John II, King of Portugal, 66
John Philoponus, 22
Johnson, Samuel, 88
Jonas, Hans, 196
Jozsef, Attila, 144
Julian the Chaldean, 54
Jünger, Ernst, 162

Kant, Immanuel
  on anthropology, 98
  Critique of Pure Reason, 9, 103
  on definition of man, 9
  on development of reason, 89
  on knowledge, 111
  Lectures on Pedagogy, 161
  on mathematics, 36
  on nature's provision, 146
  pragmatism of, 111
  on subjection of nature by man,
    103–4

Keats, John, 192
Keller, Gottfried, 125
Kepler, Johannes, 36, 68
kingdom of man
    Bacon on entrance into, 69
    divine intervention, 27
    Earth as, 124–26
    idea of, 6, 34, 128, 184, 191
    source of expression, 26
Klein, Fritz, 88
Klinger, F. M., 211
knowledge
    of causes, 106
    consequences of, 192
    danger of, 173
    goal of, 68
    joy of, 72
    of laws, 106
    of man and God, 36
    and power, 110–11
    speculative *vs.* practical, 71–72
    and vanity, 192
Kyeser, Konrad
    Bellifortis, 66

La Beaumelle, Laurent Angliviel de, 178
Lamb, Charles, 192
Lancisi, Giovanni Maria, 73
Landino, Cristoforo, 40
Langenfeld, Friedrich Spee von, 86
"last man," idea of, 147–48
Lavoisier, Antoine Laurent, 77
Lawrence, D. H., 149
Laws of Plato, 172
Le Dantec, Félix, 210
legal fiction, 37
Leibniz, Gottfried Wilhelm, 75, 215
Leiris, Michel, 207
Lenin, Vladimir, 114, 119
Leonardo da Vinci, 40, 77, 144
Leopardi, Giacomo, 38, 193, 213
Leo XIII, Pope, 136
Leroux, Pierre, 124
Letter of the Animals, 15, 23

Lévi-Strauss, Claude, 204
Liebenfels, Jörg Lanz von, 180
Liebig, Justus von, 76
life, 160–61, 193, 194, 198–99
light, image of, 213
Lille, Alain de, 31, 177
    Anticlaudianus, 13
Lipiner, Siegfried, 206
Lipsius, Justus, 96
Lisbon earthquake, 143
Liu An, 18, 145
Locke, John
    on creation, 101
    Essay concerning Human Understanding, 133
    on human beings, 169
    interest in slave trade, 141–42
    on invention of machines, 74
    on origin of value, 100
    Second Treatise of Civil Government, 133
    Some Thoughts concerning Education, 161
    on work, 97
Lord Monboddo. *See* Burnett, James, Lord Monboddo
Lothar of Segni, 46
Lucretius
    De rerum natura, 67
Luddism, 165–66
Lull, Raymond, 65
Lunacharsky, Anatoly, 119
Lyell, Charles, 124
    Principles of Geology, 146
Lysander, 28
Lysenko, T., 119, 188, 189

Maccabees, revolt of, 26
Machiavelli, Niccoló, 49, 149, 156
machines, 165–66, 167, 168
Madden, Samuel
    Memoirs of the Twentieth Century, 83
magic, 53–56
magician in literature, figure of, 58–59
Maimon, Salomon, 36

Maistre, Joseph de, 135
  Examen de la philosophie de Bacon, 76
Mallarmé, Stéphane, 186, 190, 201
Mallock, William Hurrell
  Is Life Worth Living?, 194
Malraux, André, 171
Malthus, Thomas Robert
  Essay on the Principle of Population, 149
man
  among other living things, 9, 10, 11, 67–68
  vs. animals, 23, 28, 105, 142–43
  as "the chimera," 157
  comparison to machine, 186–87
  contempt for, 156–58
  creation of, 25, 47, 169
  danger of overpopulation, 149
  Dasein in, 203
  defined by reason, 108
  definition of, 9–10
  description of good, 131–32
  dialectic of, 158–59
  dignity of, 24, 46–47, 153
  disdain for, 158
  double nature of, 45
  Egyptian texts on, 10
  elimination of useless, 175, 179
  encounter between mineral world and, 168
  end of, 147–49, 205
  essential indeterminacy of, 104–5
  fear of disappearance of, 148–49
  in Hermetic writings, 14–15
  vs. humanity, 182–83
  idea of artificial, 172–74
  idea of new, 135, 177
  idea of self-constitution of, 134
  idea of surpassing of, 181–82, 184
  immortality of, 79
  imperfection of, 186
  initial, 14
  interpretation of the fall of, 171
  judgement of, 216
  as magician, 58–59
  as object of experiment, 195–96
  as object of faith, 91
  as object of science, 84–86, 157
  as political animal, 107, 108
  power of, 48
  primordial, 14–16
  privileged status of, 153
  productive activity of, 69
  project of empowerment of, 131
  "promethean shame" of, 187
  in relation to angel, 24, 25, 68
  in relation to God, 10, 28, 43, 47, 49, 130, 189–90
  remaking of, 169–72, 176–78
  replacement of, 187–90
  responsibilities of, 158–59
  resurrection of, 79
  rights of, 159
  root of, 123
  selection of, 178
  sexual reproduction of, 79
  singularity of, 42
  smallness of, 153–54
  spiritual vs. natural, 13
  status of, 22
  studies of, 85
  as supreme being, 136–37
  technological and artistic successes of, 20
  uniqueness of, 10
  valorization of, 11–12
  will to power, 185
  as workshop, 12
  See also superiority of man
Manetti, Gianozzo, 46, 47
Manzoni, Alessandro, 40, 87
Marc, Franz, 202
Marcus Aurelius, 32
Marinetti, F. T.
  Mafarka the Futurist, 187–88
Maritain, Jacques, 68
Marlowe, Christopher, 58–59
Marsh, George Perkins, 146
Marsilius of Padua, 149

Martin, John, 148
Marx, Karl
  Communist Manifesto, 126
  Darwin's influence on, 81, 123, 166
  formulation of atheistic humanism, 136
  on man, 123, 126, 146, 157
Marxism, 126–27
mastery
  of the body, 32–33
  idea of, 72
  model of, 33–34
  of self, 31, 33, 102
  vs. self-mastery, 33–34
Maupassant, Guy de, 156, 184
Max, Gabriel von, 143
Maximus, the Confessor, 12, 30
Melnikov, Constantin S., 79
Mercier, Louis Sebastien
  Year 2440, or Dream, If Ever There Were One, 83
Méré, Chevalier de, 85
Merezhkovski, Konstantin, 180
messianism, 26–28
metamorphosis, idea of, 215
Mettrie, Julien Offray de la, 155
Meung, Jean de, 57
Meyer, C. F., 200
Michael of Ephesus (Pseudo-Alexander), 35
Michelet, Jules, 92, 143
Middle Ages
  idea of progress in, 64
  practical geometry, 64–65
  scientific knowledge, 65
  technological inventions, 63–64, 66
Mill, John Stuart, 115, 151, 195
Milton, John, 102, 211
Mirabeau, Honoré Gabriel Riqueti, count of, 135
miracles, 51, 52–53
modernity
  biblical origin of, 4
  concept of, 1–2
  dialectic of, 212

and morality, 216
  origins of, 1, 215
  parasitical nature of, 152
  as project, 2–3
modern project, 4, 34, 63, 212, 214
Monboddo. *See* Burnett, James, Lord Monboddo
Montaigne, Michel de, 23, 85, 99
  Essays, 2
Montesquieu, Charles de Secondat, baron de, 87
More, Thomas, 77, 179
Morelly, Etienne-Gabriel, 100, 106
Most, Johann, 179
Muller, Hermann J., 188
Murav'ev, Valerian, 180, 188
Musil, Robert, 157–58

Nachmanides, 22, 85
natural resources, fear of depletion of, 144–46, 150
nature
  ancient philosophy on, 31–32
  art as servant of, 51
  artifice and, 70
  as authority in moral domain, 97
  conquest of, 43–44
  Descartes on, 71
  devalorization of, 114–15
  grace and, 67
  human capacity to change, 49–50
  humanity and, 5, 6
  imitation of, 39
  insufficiency of, 6
  magic as domination over, 53–56
  neutralization of, 95–97
  as object of human action, 144
  in Old Testament, 96–97
  politics and, 214
  project of conquest of, 67, 128–29
  project of mastering, 27–28
  rediscovery of, 66–67
  representations of, 95–97
  as subject of subordination, 16, 65
  three states of, 70
Naudé, Gabriel, 56

nazism, 186
Needham, Joseph, 17
Newton, Isaac, 192
Newton, John F., 143
Nicolas of Cusa, 11, 36, 45, 49, 80
Nietzsche, Friedrich Wilhelm
  on dialectic of value, 100
  on domination, 164
  on eternal return of the same, 179, 185–86
  on failure of experiment, 197
  on fidelity to earth, 125
  "Hellenism and pessimism," 194
  on idea of experimentation, 195
  on idea of superman, 184, 185
  on intellectual probity, 193
  on parasitical nature of modernity, 152
  on replacement of man, 188
  on scientific method, 110
  on surpassing man, 184–85
Nifo, Agostino, 35
nihilism, 191
nobility, idea of, 12–13
nothingness, 191
Novalis, Gerhard Schulz, 115, 208

Olesha, Yuri, 177
Ollé-Laprune, Léon
  Price of Life, 194
order, idea of, 4
Origen, 21
Ortega y Gasset, José, 202
Ovid, 19

Paine, Thomas, 134
  Common Sense, 135
Palissy, Bernard, 58
Paracelsus (Theophrastus von Hohenheim), 36, 55, 172
paradox of the good, 214
Pascal, Blaise, 10, 89, 157
Paul, Jean, 92, 130
Paul the Apostle, Saint, 24, 27
Paul of Taranto
  Theorica et Pratica, 57

pedagogy, 161, 163–64
Péguy, Charles, 137, 152
Pereira, Gómez, 96
Pérez de Oliva, Fernán, 48
Périers, Bonaventure des, 131
Pestalozzi, J. H., 161
Petrarch, Francesco, 111
Picatrix, 54
Pico della Mirandola, Giovanni
  On the Dignity of Man, 43
Pincus, Gregory, 175
Pinthus, Kurt
  The Twilight of Humanity, 202–3
Plantin, Christopher, 75
Plato
  on deforestation, 144
  on imitation, 40
  on the nature of man, 11, 29, 84, 166–67
  on pedagogy, 163
  on soul, 32
Pliny the Elder, 145
Plotinus, 32, 40, 54, 84–85
Plutarch, 23
Polybius, 172
Pope, Alexander, 86
Popper, Karl, 164
Porphyry, 54
positivism, 106–7, 108
posterity, idea of, 151
practical philosophy, 71
pragmatism, 108–9, 111–12
praxis, 69
prejudice, idea of, 132
Price, Richard, 82
Priestley, Joseph, 82
Proclus, 36
prodigies, psychological explanation of, 52
progress
  in antiquity, 80
  evolution of idea of, 64, 79–83
  medieval notion of, 80
  necessity of, 81
  scientific basis of, 81
  unlimited, 82

project, etymology of word, 3
Prometheus, 130–31
Protagoras, 11
Proudhon, Pierre-Joseph, 123, 130
Proust, Marcel, 77
Pseudo-Apollonius
  Secret of Creation, 19
Puruṣa (original man), 14
Pushkin, Alexander, 170–71, 193

Quinet, Edgar, 91, 182
Qur'an, on creation of man, 25

Rabbe, Alphonse, 207
Rauch, François Antoine, 145
Raynal, Guillaume-Thomas, Abbé, 169
"red giants" discovery, 147
Reginald of Prüm, 58
religion, denial of, 205–6
Renan, Ernest, 124, 127, 141, 182, 192
  The Future of Science, 208
Richter, Jean Paul, 167
Rilke, R. M., 190, 196
Robeck, Johann, 207
Robespierre, Maximilien, 136, 171
Robinet, Jean-Baptiste, 196
Rorty, Richard, 112
Rose-Croix, manifestos of, 78
Rosny, J. H., Sr., 147, 168, 210
Rostand, Jean, 158
Rousseau, Jean-Jacques
  Discourse on the Sciences and Arts, 150, 212
  Émile, 98, 161
  First Discourse, 103
  on goodness of man, 88, 91
  on humanity, 87
  on man as author of evil, 90
  on man's self-creation, 98
  "men, be human" tautology, 87
  on pedagogy, 163–64
  on virtue, 102
Rozkov, Nikolai A., 119

Ruge, Arnold, 122
Rupert of Deutz, 43
Russell, Bertrand, 108, 141
  Icarus, 188

Sade, Donatien Alphonse François de, 156, 157, 158
Saint-Étienne, Rabaut, 134
Saint-Exupéry
  Night Flight, 162
Saint-Martin, Louis Claude de, 25
Saint-Pierre, Charles Irénée Castel de, 3
Saint-Simon, Henri de, 115, 147
Salt, Henry, 143
Sartre, Jean-Paul, 3, 206–7, 211, 216
Savérien, Alexander, 82
Scheler, Max, 190
Schiller, Ferdinand Canning Scott, 112
Schiller, Friedrich, 87, 104, 136
Schlegel, Friedrich, 208
Schneevogel, Paul (Niavis)
  Judgment of Jupiter, 145
Schopenhauer, Arthur, 115, 125, 143, 147, 194, 208
Schwenkfeld, Caspar, 89
science
  application to improvement of human life, 76
  development of, 74, 75
  experimental method in, 109–10
  future of, 111
  goal of, 75
  history of, 82
  mastery of nature and, 109
  notion of new, 65, 69
  and production of weapons, 144
  sadistic, 141
  separation of technology and, 113
science is power maxim, 110
scientific knowledge, 65
scientific utopia, 78
Secchi, Angelo, 147
self-destruction, 197–98, 207, 215
self-mastery, 102–3, 160

Seneca, 99
   Apocolocyntosis of the Emperor Claudius, 28
Shelley, Mary, 148
   Frankenstein, or The Modern Prometheus, 3, 173–74
Sibiuda, Ramon, 46
sin, 78, 88
"Sincere Brethren" of Basra, 23, 24
Skinner, B. F., 164
   Beyond Freedom and Dignity, 165
   Walden Two, 164–65
Skovoroda, Gregory, 31
slavery, 33–34, 141
Sloterdijk, Peter, 176
social engineering, 164
society, definition of, 107–8
Soloviev, Vladimir, 31, 209
   Lectures on Theandrism, 159
Sophocles, 11
soul, 32, 48, 54
sovereignty, concept of, 13, 37, 38
Spencer, Herbert, 81
Spenser, Edmund, 97, 145
Spinoza, Benedictus de, 75, 86, 88, 155
Staël, Madame de (Anne-Louise-Germaine), 185
Stalin, Joseph, 177, 188
Statius, P. Papinius, 158
Stirner, Max, 209
Stoicism, 31–32, 34, 96
Strauss, Leo, 19, 129
suicide
   demographics, 216
   end of illusions and, 209
   vs. life, 215
   in literature, 209–10
   as philosophical act, 208
   studies of, 207
   as training for death, 208
   unpleasant nature of, 216
sun, as symbol of domination of nature, 125–26
superhuman, 181

superiority, *vs.* domination, 11
superiority of humanity, 6
superiority of man
   acquisition of, 26
   over animals, 21, 22, 23
   over the angel, 24
   critique of, 23–25
   in literature, depiction of, 11
   vis-à-vis the other beings, 84
   realization of, 26
   Xunzi on, 10
Swift, Jonathan, 3, 92, 156

Tanner, Adam, S.J., 86
task, idea of, 5
Tassoni, Alessandro, 82
Tauler, Jean, 31
Teaching for King Merikare, 10, 18
technological dreams, 76–79
technological innovations, 63–64, 66, 77
technology
   fabrication of new materials, 114
   in historical context, 113–15
   Industrial Revolution and, 116
   separation of science and, 113
   in Soviet Russia, role of, 119
   worker and, 162
Telesio, Bernardino, 96
theandrism, 31, 244n9
Theodorus, of Mopsuestia, 39
theology, 122–23
Theology of Aristotle, 15
Theophilus of Antioch, 21, 43
theurgy, 54
Thomas à Kempis
   The Imitation of Christ, 102
Thomas Aquinas, Saint, 12, 25, 35, 39, 54, 67
Thomson, William, 147
Thoreau, Henry David, 189
Tieck, L., 115
time, limits of, 146–47
Titans, revolt of, 130
Tocqueville, Alexis de, 151

Tolstoy, Leo
   Anna Karenina, 144
Traherne, Thomas, 99
transhumanism, 171
Traversari, Ambrogio, 67
Trotsky, Leon, 188
truth, 191, 192
Turgot, Anne-Robert-Jacques, 82
Turmeda, Anselm
   Dispute of the Ass, 23, 24
Tziolkovsky, Konstantin, 180

utopia, 77–78, 117, 177

Valentine, Saint, 28
Valeriano, Piero
   De infelicitate literatorum, 92
Valéry, Paul, 37
value, 98–99, 100
vanity, 192, 193
Vega, Lope de, 130
vegetarianism, 142–43
Verne, Jules, 115, 116
   The Begum's Fortune, 117
   The Mysterious Island, 116–17, 146
Verri, Pietro, 87
Vespasian, Emperor of Rome, 28
Vico, Giambattista, 36, 65, 98, 149
   Scienza nuova, 212
Vigny, Alfred de, 115
   Chatterton, 207
Villeneuve, Faiguet de, 178
Villeneuve-Bargemont, Alban de, 142
Villermé, Louis-René, 142
Villers, Alexander von, 197
Villiers de l'Isle-Adam, Auguste de
   The Future Eve, 174, 196
virtues, 101–2
Vischer, Friedrich Theodor, 208
Viviani, René, 201
Voegelin, Eric, 129
Voltaire (François Marie Arouet)
   on Bacon, 76
   on century of the English, 75
   concern of population growth, 175
   Essai sur les moeurs, 80
   historiographical method, 80–81
   on human dignity, 89
   on man, 86
   on virtue, 87

Wagner, Richard, 125, 143, 194, 200
Wallace, Alfred Russel, 178, 183
Watson, J. D., 164
Weber, Carl Maria von, 145
Weber, Ernst von
   The Torture Chambers of Science, 143
Weber, Max, 67, 115
Weidle, Vladimir, 202
Wells, H. G., 115, 148–49
   Men like Gods, 117–19
Western culture, sources of, 214–15
White, Lynn, Jr., 19
Wieland, C. M., 193
Wier, Jan, 86
Wilde, Oscar, 38, 170
William of Auvergne, 55
witch trials, 86
Witz, Konrad
   The Miraculous Draught of Fishes, 96
Wöhler, Friedrich, 172
work
   appropriation of nature by, 126–27
   as quality of the human, 97
   valorization of, 44
workers, 142, 162

Xenophon, 28
Xunzi (Hsün Tzu), 10, 17

Zola, Émile, 92
   Doctor Pascal, 198–99
   The Human Beast, 162
zoomorphism, 18
Zosimus of Panopolis, 70

Rémi Brague is emeritus professor of medieval and Arabic philosophy at the University of Paris I and Romano Guardini Chair Emeritus of Philosophy at Ludwig-Maximilians-Universität (Munich). He is a member of the Institut de France and author of many books, including *The Law of God: The Philosophical History of an Idea* and *The Wisdom of the World: The Human Experience of the Universe in Western Thought.*

Paul Seaton is associate professor of philosophy at St. Mary's Seminary.

www.ingramcontent.com/pod-product-compliance
Lightning Source LLC
Chambersburg PA
CBHW030520230426
43665CB00010B/692